Legal Studies in International, European and Comparative Criminal Law

Volume 9

The main purpose of this book series is to provide sound analyses of major developments in national, EU and international law and case law, as well as insights into court practice and legislative proposals in the areas concerned. The analyses address a broad readership, such as lawyers and practitioners, while also providing guidance for courts. In terms of scope, the series encompasses four main areas, the first of which concerns international criminal law and especially international case law in relevant criminal law subjects. The second addresses international human rights law with a particular focus on the impact of international jurisprudences on national criminal law and criminal justice systems, as well as their interrelations. In turn the third area focuses on European criminal law and case law. Here, particular weight will be attached to studies on European criminal law conducted from a comparative perspective. The fourth and final area presents surveys of comparative criminal law inside and outside Europe. By combining these various aspects, the series especially highlights research aimed at proposing new legal solutions, while focusing on the new challenges of a European area based on high standards of human rights protection.

As a rule, book proposals are subject to peer review, which is carried out by two members of the editorial board in anonymous form.

Vincenzo Militello • Alessandro Spena
Editors

The Challenges of Illegal Trafficking in the Mediterranean Area

Springer

With the support of the Erasmus+ Programme of the European Union

Editors
Vincenzo Militello
Department of Law
University of Palermo
Palermo, Italy

Alessandro Spena
Department of Law
University of Palermo
Palermo, Italy

ISSN 2524-8049 ISSN 2524-8057 (electronic)
Legal Studies in International, European and Comparative Criminal Law
ISBN 978-3-031-45398-4 ISBN 978-3-031-45399-1 (eBook)
https://doi.org/10.1007/978-3-031-45399-1

This Springer imprint is published by the registered company Springer Nature Switzerland AG
The registered company address is: Gewerbestrasse 11, 6330 Cham, Switzerland

Paper in this product is recyclable.

Preface

Illicit markets have long been a dark side of world economies. Despite the structural differences between them, there are also remarkable similarities between their operating mechanisms, core components, business sectors and international operational dimensions. The specific characteristics of the territorial context in which the various illegal trades take place contribute to determining such similarities, in terms of the origin and routes of the trades themselves, the type of means used to carry them out, and the social consequences of their execution. The "space-movement" of the Mediterranean Sea is a particularly significant example of this, due to the fact that it is a long-standing trade route, traditionally intertwined with different types of illegal trafficking, and that it lies at the crossroads of different social and legal cultures.

The prominence of international movements of people in the public debate should not lead one to overlook the fact that other types of illicit trafficking also take place in the Mediterranean basin: some more traditionally present, such as cigarette and drug smuggling, and others of more recent emergence and smaller scope, including in terms of profits, but no less important for a wide-ranging fight, such as trafficking in arms, waste and cultural goods. Most of these trades exploit the unstoppable trend toward a borderless world, in connection with the freedom of action made possible by the so-called global economy, in order to conceal ill-gotten goods and make creative use of the possibilities offered by web-based e-commerce.

This is undeniably happening at the EU's southern borders, which have become a dark gateway to the attractive European market, offering criminal organizations the opportunity to accumulate huge illicit proceeds. This book, which constitutes the final synthesis of the research and teaching activities carried out during the three-year Jean Monnet Center of Excellence "Europe Between Mobility and Security: The Challenges of Illicit Trades in the Mediterranean Area" (EuMOSIT), approaches the topic of illicit trafficking in the Mediterranean Sea from two different, albeit intertwined perspectives: on the one hand, it aims to highlight some structural problems common to different types of trafficking, problems that concern both the description of the general phenomenon of "illegal trafficking" as such and the preventive and repressive tools deployed to counter it; on the other hand, it addresses some issues concerning specific illicit traffics in order to show how they differ not only in the goods respectively trafficked, but also in some of the ways in which they are carried out, as well as, consequently, in the type of actions that need to be put in place to combat them.

The book brings together contributions from scholars who, over the years, have animated the life of the Centre, participating in the seminars and discussions promoted within its framework. Since the Center's main topic has been the interdisciplinary study of different types of illicit trafficking in the Mediterranean area, seen as a boundary issue between mobility and security, this is also the main focus of this book, which also takes a strongly interdisciplinary approach to different—criminological, criminal law, criminal procedure, but also international law issues—issues that cut across that general topic.

In the introductory chapter, the analysis of the role of transnational criminal organizations in illicit trafficking in the Mediterranean helps to test the possibilities and limits of a kind of general theory of illicit trafficking, showing its recurring aspects and identifying the legal and politico-criminal issues that could best be addressed by a unified approach to the subject. As for the remaining parts, while the first deals with some controversial issues of jurisdiction over the sea that cut across illegal trafficking in the Mediterranean Sea, the others are devoted to presenting a special-part overview of illegal trafficking. Both the second and third parts revolve, in particular, around illegal trafficking involving human beings: more specifically, the second deals with migrant smuggling, which has a central relevance—criminological and politico-criminal—among the illegal trades taking place in the Mediterranean Sea, while the third part deals with the contiguous topic of human trafficking, seen especially in its connection with the problem of labour exploitation. Finally, the fourth part focuses on trafficking in commodities, with a selected overview of some of the most significant forms such trafficking can take: drug trafficking, trafficking in cultural property and trafficking in human organs.

Palermo, Italy

Vincenzo Militello
Alessandro Spena

Contents

Illicit Trades of Persons and Goods in the Mediterranean and Transnational Criminal Organizations . . . 1
Vincenzo Militello

Part I Jurisdictional Issues

Territorialising the Extraterritorial: The Role of 'Suppression' Conventions . . . 23
Micheál Ó Floinn

Adjudicative Jurisdiction for Crimes at Sea: An International Law Perspective . . . 67
Serena Forlati

Coercive Powers and Jurisdiction on the High Seas to Combat Human Smuggling . . . 81
Tommaso Rafaraci

Part II Migrant Smuggling

Anti-smuggling Penal Policies: A Cross-National Exploration . . . 91
José Ángel Brandariz

The Distinction between Facilitation of Irregular Immigration and Organised Smuggling of Migrants and Its Relevance for the Italian Criminal Law? . . . 117
Alessandro Spena

Challenging the Hostile Environment for Search and Rescue at Sea: Reflections from the Sea Watch Litigation . . . 141
Valsamis Mitsilegas

Part III Human Trafficking and Labour Market

The Problems of Trafficking in Human Beings in Spain. Criminal Regulations and Jurisprudential Treatment 151
Mirentxu Corcoy Bidasolo

Organised Crime, Illicit Manpower Brokerage and Recent Italian Legislation 169
Antonio La Spina

International and Domestic Perspectives to Combat Gangmaster Systems 179
Salvatore Orlando

Part IV Traffickings of Goods and Human Organs

Soft Drugs and Organized Crime: A Problematic Relationship 201
Licia Siracusa

Trafficking in Cultural Property. An Evolving International Legal Framework 227
Arianna Visconti

The Criminal Policy on Trafficking in Cultural Goods 263
Riccardo Ercole Omodei

Trafficking in Human Organs: A Portuguese Perspective 281
Sónia Fidalgo

Illicit Trades of Persons and Goods in the Mediterranean and Transnational Criminal Organizations

Vincenzo Militello

Abstract The long history of the Mediterranean characterizes it as a space-movement, in which also people and goods are moved as object of illicit trades. The paper first points out the differences between the various criminal systems that are crossed by the related illegal routes and examines the degree of presence in them of transnational criminal groups and their respective main organisational forms. In particular, there is highlighted the emergence of organizations, that can be characterized as poly-criminal, because they operate in different illicit markets (for example, people and cigarettes). The multilevel regulatory responses to this relationship between illicit markets and criminal organizations are considered, and the need is indicated to take the reference to this notion in sufficiently determined terms. To verify the degree of harmonization at European level, the focus is on the specific area of the trafficking in human beings in five European justice systems (Italy, Portugal, Greece, Spain, and Germany). Some concluding remarks are then dedicated to the issues of the possibility of formulating a general notion of illicit trades, marking the difference between its fundamental admissibility at a criminological level and the difficulties of its precise legal delimitation. The plurality of national regulations on the level of substantive law dedicated to the various illicit markets does not prevent some procedural instruments from being fungible for many of these areas (e.g. wiretapping or undercover infiltrators), and the problems connected with determining the competent jurisdiction are also common to the various illicit trades.

1 Movements in the Mediterranean: Yesterday and Today

The Mediterranean is an extremely rich *topos* in history. It lacks any definition that is both comprehensive enough in terms of the experiences included and precise enough to avoid indeterminate meanings. Since ancient times it has represented a

V. Militello (✉)
Department of Law, University of Palermo, Palermo, Italy
e-mail: vincenzo.militello@unipa.it

V. Militello, A. Spena (eds.), *The Challenges of Illegal Trafficking in the Mediterranean Area*, Legal Studies in International, European and Comparative Criminal Law 9, https://doi.org/10.1007/978-3-031-45399-1_1

'space-movement' (Braudel), not limited to the so-called marine environment but including the entire area of the countries that look out to it, each with their own culture and historical and social events.

The richness of this space-movement is already evident in the travels of Ulysses or Aeneas, where the sea is a bridge between different lands and not an insurmountable liquid border. Although the modern theory of the State includes territory as one of its essential components, the idea of the border has always had a fundamental duplicity. On the one hand, it is an end, a limit (from Latin *finis*, *limes*), and therefore a line defining a space and thus concluding it, by attributing ownership to its inhabitants (with the right to use it, but also to exclude others). A metaphor is that of a castle surrounded by a fosse, which protects those inside it but also isolates them from the rest of the territory. On the other hand, the border is a frontier, and therefore a hinge or a bridge to another space, one with which you may come into contact to develop new possibilities you did not have in your territory: here the metaphor is personified and becomes that of the pioneer who ventures into new territories to discover their potential.

Both meanings come into play when that ancient crossroads of trade is studied today as an area for illicit trade. In these hidden, but not secondary components of mobility and globalization, transnational criminal organizations play a driving role. The lines of action in the Mediterranean Sea are essentially three: *western trade routes*, from the coasts of Morocco and Algeria to Spain; *central* ones, from Libya, Tunisia, and partly Syria, especially towards Italy, and Sicily in particular; *eastern* ones, from Syria and Egypt to Greece, and partly to Italy. Despite the geographical diversity of these routes, they all allow access to Europe, whose Southern marine border has an overall much wider extension than the land border to the East, referred to as the Balkan route of illicit trade.

The plurality of countries and relevant State systems facing the Mediterranean basin, the specificity of this marine space as the theater of their relationships, the economic and social gap between the northern (Euro-continental) and the southern (African and Middle Eastern) shore, the presence of areas in which the culture of legality is not a widespread value—these are all geopolitical factors that influence the context in which illicit trade arises, but which cannot be further explored below. Rather, we will try to focus on the meaning and contexts of illicit trades, with particular attention to the role that criminal organizations play, especially in the Mediterranean area. In this regard, we will use the results of a line of research developed over several years and whose international dissemination will be fostered by the essays collected in this volume.[1]

[1] The research is part of the activities promoted between 2019 and 2022 by the Jean Monnet Centre of Excellence "Europe Between Mobility and Security: The Challenges of Illicit Trades in the Mediterranean Area" (https://www.unipa.it/dipartimenti/di.gi./progetti/eumosit/). The international research team has developed themes already initiated in the previous projects: "The New Era of Smuggling in the Mediterranean Sea" (NESMeS: 2018–2019) (https://www.pmi-impact.com); "Mobility, Security and New Media" (Jean Monnet Module 2015–2018).

2 The Emergence of Poly-criminal Organizations

Overall, illicit trades represent an "invisible hand" of the markets, albeit a very different one from that which *Adam Smith* conceived when he pointed out that the selfish interests of individual market operators, in any case, contribute to developing the economy.

Although a need for rules in the conduct of multiple economic activities soon arose to counteract possible "market abuse" behaviors, illicit trades are still characterized as "markets necessarily without ethics." These activities, although supported by purposes of enrichment of those who carry them out, are however contrary to the collective interests and thus they are qualified as illegal and also prohibited criminally. The invisibility of this "other market" against the legal one, on the one hand, favors the operation and development of the complex multi-agent systems that operate in it, while, on the other hand, it hinders the investigation regarding the various features of such groups: sectors, dimensions, structures, dynamics, etc.

The financial nature of the driving interests suggest that the choices of action in these trades are nevertheless subject to rationality in assessing the many factors of their respective contexts. Among these elements, a pivotal role is played by public interventions aimed at both sides of the market: consumption (demand), with prevention of recourse to illicitly exchanged goods or use of illicit services, and offer (supply), with the fight against those who make them available despite its prohibition. Preventive actions—which are fundamental, although often insufficiently supported—are conditioned by the specific type of illicit goods or services: *e.g.*, education or treatment against drug addictions are very different from policies to prevent migrations. Instead, law enforcement activities against those who offer illicit goods or services may present needs that are common to the various illicit areas and above all that can benefit from shared tools among the various jurisdictions involved in each market. The transnational dimension of illicit trades in the Mediterranean makes cooperation necessary between the countries bordering it and with those most directly in contact with them. In turn, the effectiveness of the action to combat illicit trades is linked to the degree of harmonization of the various criminal systems involved in the illicit markets. Harmonization of those rules is, moreover, an objective that has been pursued by the European Union for some time to create an area of freedom, security, and justice within itself.[2] The EU must also take a stand, albeit with the necessary adaptations, concerning the external dimension of cooperative relations with the countries of the Southern front of the Mediterranean.

The chances of common action to combat illicit trades must not neglect the features and particular issues of each type of illicit market: in addition to those mentioned above (migrants and narcotics), also firearms, cultural goods, labor market intermediation, waste, human organs, drugs, doping substances, cigarette

---

[2] Although the fight against illegal trades has not become part of the material competence attributed to the European Public Prosecutor's Office, which has finally started its activity concerning crimes against EU Financial Interests: Vilas Àlvarez (2018), pp. 25 ff.; Vervaele (2014), pp. 259 ff.

smuggling. For example, as to the socio-economic factors that fuel it, migrant smuggling is connected to the widespread need for a better existence for the inhabitants of countries devastated by famine or wars. On the other hand, the drug market is supported by a demand often related to the growth of the vital and productive rhythms of Western societies, with the associated states of anxiety, stress, and a sense of inadequacy *vis-à-vis* widespread behavioral models. Furthermore, it is relevant to take into account the condition of the subjects who support the demand for illicit services: the position of the migrants who face the journey towards the desired destination, with its burden of danger for themselves and often for their family members, is very different from the condition of those who will at most risk a financial loss by merely receiving a good (e.g. artworks), although many of the traded goods may impact individual and collective health (drugs, doping substances, cigarettes, waste, firearms).

As to the subjects who operate on the supply side, in the most significant cases, they are not single and isolated players. The organization of the criminal activity requires setting aside time for production, transport, and marketing of the good or service, besides collateral activities (falsification of documents, forms of corruption) or consequent activities (laundering of illicit proceeds). The segmentation of these phases often occurs in territorial contexts that are not limited to a State but often belong to different countries. These are the main factors why today there are organizations made up of a plurality of subjects, often structured in a hierarchical way and with reciprocal relationships between different groups. These relationships can be not only collaborative, to widen the operational network, but also adversarial, aiming to control—without competitors—a certain share of the market in a specific territorial area of operation.

As is known, the forms of criminal organizations are very different, though traditionally traced to two main models, *i.e.,* the ones hierarchically structured and dealing with a particular illicit trade (*e.g.,* narcotics) or operating through a network of connected groups engaged in specific sectors of criminal activity. Indeed, the presence of criminal organizations in illicit markets in a context such as the Mediterranean raises the question of whether a further organizational typology may be emerging. Here the organization, especially if it operates transnationally, acts as a *platform for criminal services*: it deals with illegal trade exchanges of various goods each on their respective markets, to achieve (criminal) scale economies, similar to forms of concentration typical of advanced (lawful) markets.[3]

This trend towards an aggregation of criminal activities by transnational organizations operating in the European Union is more generally reported by *Europol.* They note that about 40% of all transnational criminal networks active in the EU carry out a plurality of criminal activities (*poly-criminal organizations*), and operate

[3]In this regard, see the contribution by La Spina (2019), pp. 67 ff. This perspective was not adequately focused in previous research on organized crime in European illicit markets: e.g., Fijnaut and Paoli (2004).

on different illicit markets (almost 70% of criminal networks are active in more than three countries).[4]

3 Plurality of Organizational Forms of Illicit Trades in the Mediterranean

The issues covered by the research can be traced back to two main areas: one concerning the possible intersections between the different types of illicit markets and the criminal organizations that operate on them; the other referring instead to the related attempts to fight them, at the national and supranational levels.

The first question, aimed at identifying the key features of the players of illicit trades, required an approach integrated with a criminological investigation, focusing on the empirical dimension of the phenomena. The other part, *i.e.* the legal analysis of the responses, was also carried out through a method of comparison, selecting—due to time and energy constraints—the situation of some countries that have direct access to the Mediterranean Sea (specifically, Italy, Spain, and Greece) and European countries which do not directly look out on this basin, but appear to be places of transit or even a destination for the illicit trades (Germany and Portugal).

Furthermore, we focus on those organizations identified for migrant smuggling and then we check whether the related organizations also engage in other types of illicit trades.

a) First, we should not overlook the fact that in migrant smuggling there is no shortage of individual players, who provide specific short-range services, *e.g.,* in areas close to the borders of a State. However, *criminal groups* take center stage, albeit with varying numbers, human resources, and structural organizations. The largest among those have high rates of affiliates and links, even transnational ones. They organize the different phases of a trading transaction, by connecting with other groups, even smaller ones, for specific needs.

More specifically, many of the cases that went to trial in Sicily—a true crossroads in the Mediterranean for illicit trades—have retraced the journey of migrants: first by land to reach the coasts of North Africa and then through the marine strait that separates those coasts from Sicily. Some trials proved that each different moment or phase of the journey is dominated by an organized group. They do not operate within a unitary structure but have reciprocal contacts that can be traced back to a strategy of maximum advantage in actual situations: the relationships between them are

[4] Europol, EU Serious and Organized Crime Threat Assessment (SOCTA 2021) (in www.europol.europa.eu), Luxembourg, 2021, p. 19.

neither necessary nor stable nor involving fixed collaboration, but rather are opportunistic, contingent and variable.[5]

Compartmentalization of groups intervening in the entire cycle of the journey undertaken by irregular migrants not only multiplies the extortion opportunities against them, but also hinders a full tracking of the personal composition of criminal groups by law enforcement authorities. The activities of the latter mostly concern events that take place abroad, often in the North African States, where it can be very difficult to collect evidence, even by means of judicial cooperation, for the related investigations and subsequent trials.

b) However, there are also *criminal organizations on an ethnic basis* that have established themselves in the Italian territory. They exploit irregular immigration as a tool to gain profits from the use of human beings for prostitution or agricultural work. The distinction between "migrant smuggling" and "trafficking of human beings", recognized in international and European standards and implemented in numerous national laws, must not neglect the criminal contexts in which these crimes are at least interrelated.[6]

For example, local branches of a Nigerian criminal organization with international ramifications, called *Black Axe*, have also been active in Italy—as was reconstructed in a trial in Palermo, and previously also in Turin in 2007 and in Brescia. It is "*a highly hierarchical and mixed structure pyramidal organization*", with precise entry rituals and internal rules among the affiliates, who swear obedience to the values of the group after a period of initial indoctrination. In particular, the Palermo group settled there at least as long ago as 2011, "*with aims of territorial dominance and criminal solidarity (...) within the Nigerian community*", operating in the sector of trafficking in human beings for purposes of sexual exploitation, as well as in the sale of narcotics and other related crimes (*e.g.,* robbery, injury, attempted murder). The group contacted some subjects already in their home country; their victims were initially willing to contract a debt with the organization to seek their fortune in Europe, but instead ended up being exploited in illegal activities. To this end, the group managed their journey to Italy, solving the local logistics (from internal transport to accommodation and supply of mobile phones) and subjecting people to strict control until the initial debt was paid, thus creating a tunnel of exploitation in inhumane conditions from which people could only free themselves after many years.

The operational characteristics of the group in the various phases show its high intimidation capacity, which takes the form of forms of violent retaliation "*to obtain debt payment or to impose extortion such as paying a sum of money for the loss of a supply of drugs or to ensure full control over prostitutes.*" This applies both to the

---

[5]In particular, see judgment no. 1412/2018 of the Preliminary Hearing Judge of Palermo, who convicted two migrants, one Ghanaian and one Nigerian, for the crimes of trafficking in human beings, enslavement, and related mafia-type criminal organization aimed at committing such crimes. On this and other cases of transnational criminal organisations operating in the Strait of Sicily see La Chioma (2019), pp. 84 ff.

[6]On this subject, see Militello (2019), pp. 55 ff., 65 ff.

victims of trafficking in human beings and reduction to slavery, as well as to their relatives who remained at home, with the additional psychological bond deriving from magical-religious rituals to which victims were subjected (such as *voodoo*), a *modus operandi* witnessed also in other Mediterranean countries where trafficking in Nigerian women is widespread.[7]

Hence it is a situation that in Italy corresponds to the *mafia* method. In the activities described above, there is the exploitation of the intimidation force of the group and the consequent condition of subjugation and silence. This makes the crime of mafia-type criminal organization applicable under art. 416 bis of the Italian Penal Code.

It should also be noted that in the face of these new "ethnic *mafias*", no involvement of the traditional criminal groups emerged in the migrants' journeys through the central Mediterranean, despite them being rooted in the target regions of migrants (*mafia* in Sicily, *'Ndrangheta* in Calabria, or *Sacra Corona Unita* in Apulia). This contrasts with previous warnings of a potential danger of intermingling between local and ethnic criminal organizations. Rather, Italian criminal groups have started exploiting the management of migrants on the local territory, carrying out various forms of abuse and corruption in the related public-private system.[8]

The attitude of the *mafia* organization traditionally established in Sicily appears significant observing the presence in Palermo of a criminal structure such as *Black Axe*. In general, domination of illicit affairs of a criminal sector in a given territory is an essential component to affirm the force of intimidation typical of the *mafia* organization. This makes it difficult to believe that the latter would tolerate a different criminal organization, also interested in the market of narcotics drugs, as the Sicilian mafia has been for some time. However, the proven coexistence of the two criminal organizations in the Palermo area seems connected to the different subjects involved: *Black Axe* focuses only on Nigerian citizens, regarding both prostitution and drugs. Furthermore, this case also reflects the diminished strength of the *mafia* organization itself, also thanks to the significant results obtained with prolonged action against it. Finally, the transformations resulting from illegal immigration have strongly affected the control of illicit markets such as drugs, prostitution, and exploitation of the workforce, introducing new forces into the scenario that characterizes these illicit markets.

c) The division between criminal groups of different ethnic groups is not absolute, however: a third organizational model has emerged, one in which the transnational criminal organization active in migrant smuggling has a mixed ethnic composition divided by the region concerned. Rather recent investigations have identified some organizations made up of foreign citizens (especially Tunisians) and Italians

---

[7] In particular, in Spain: cf. Tribunal Supremo 1228/2017 of 29 March 2017.

[8] E.g., in the Reception Center for Asylum Seekers (CARA) in Mineo (Catania, Sicily): see the report of the Parliamentary Commission of Inquiry, Chamber of Deputies, XVII legislature, Boll. Giunte e Commissioni Parlamentari of 21.6.2017.

operating together between the coasts of Tunisia and those of western Sicily aimed at aiding illegal immigration but also smuggling foreign manufactured tobacco.

The operational characteristics of these *poly-criminal groups* are very different from the traditional ones that intervene in controlling the migrants' path, fragmenting it into various phases, with ever-changing and contingent contacts. These types of criminal organizations with a high level of integration between the various traffics have a stable composition in terms of members, even if numerically rather limited (up to 15 members), in which pivotal roles go to foreign subjects, while the participation of Italian subjects is only subordinate.

Moreover, the general context of the phenomenon is changing, being increasingly characterized by significant operational differences compared to the traditional and more widespread forms in which migrant smuggling may take place. In the latter, the crossing is entrusted at least in its final stretch to small vessels, crammed with migrants to the point of risking a shipwreck, so that there is no space to transport goods (such as tobacco or narcotics). Their destiny is to sink or be seized as soon as they are intercepted by the naval forces of the destination countries, resulting in the loss of any illicit goods transported. The Central-Mediterranean route in recent years has also found new starting bases on the Tunisian coasts with the growing use of smaller and more agile means of transport than the old wooden boats: the preference goes to powerfully motorized inflatable boats that take a few hours for the entire journey to Sicily. This option has much higher individual costs (2000–7000 EUR per person), which are imposed by traffickers to ensure an adequate profit in the face of the limited number of persons transported for each trip (about 15); it is aimed at those migrants who are willing to pay more to face lesser safety risks and to have a better chance of arriving at their destination without being intercepted (so-called ghost landings).

In light of the characteristics of poly-criminality and transnationality thus highlighted, we shall verify whether the relevant legislation is sufficient to allow adequate counteraction, regarding the role played by criminal groups, their division into different types, and the connections existing among the various illegal activities—concerning not only the individual national responses but also the European Union's intervention to harmonize them.

4 Normative Paths to Counter Illicit Trades: The European standards of penal protection

An analysis of the regulations to combat these illegal trades, even if only in EU countries, reveals a non-homogeneous framework of the legal bases legitimizing the intervention of the European Union in terms of harmonization of national legislative responses: the list of the various forms of "serious crime" pursuant to art. 83 TFEU contains, for example, trafficking in illicit drugs, illicit firearms and human beings, but not other types of illicit trades, such as that of cigarettes or even artworks.

One could think of overcoming, or at least circumventing this disparity through a common action to combat the various types of trades, *i.e.* by rooting the legal basis for all interventions to counter the various types of illicit trades starting in the common presence in each of them of criminal organizations. This reference is placed at the end of the list of crimes in art 83 TFEU that legitimize european harmonization of the criminal law provisions of the Member States. However, the notion of organized crime in the context of this provision must not be understood in general and criminological terms; instead, it must be inferred from the international covenants that define its main features. In particular, the 2000 UN Palermo Convention (UNTOC) not only provides the global reference framework for combating criminal organizations operating throughout different States but also deals with their connection with illicit trades, devoting to it its protocols relating to smuggling and trafficking, in addition to the firearms trade.

At the European level too, there are several supranational legislative instruments of harmonization, which date back to different times; they are linked to distinct normative basis in the path that the European Union has taken toward the construction of a common area of freedom, security, and justice. Overall, however, the framework for combating the various forms of illicit trades reflects a specific and differentiated approach to each of them, although the respective regulations have a largely similar structure. This is precisely the case, for example, in terms of carrying out unlawful conducts by criminal organizations, envisioning as many hypotheses of liability of legal persons as the corresponding offenses, extending the punishment for instigating acts, and introducing rules in favor of people cooperating with the police. This form of harmonization of contents in the various European interventions on the subject of combating illicit trades, which can be said to be horizontal, must however be completed by further verification, this time relating to the degree of implementation of the individual European legislative instruments in the systems of the Member States, and therefore considering the respective degree of a further type of harmonization, which, to distinguish it from the other aforementioned one, could be called vertical. In this regard, European regulations of different illicit trades must be considered separately.

As to the rules to combat trafficking of human beings, it has long been a topic drawing particular attention and therefore greater consensus between States: for this reason, it is a leading sector of harmonization, at least at the European level. The 1997 "Joint Action concerning action to combat trafficking in human beings and sexual exploitation of children" (*1997/154/GAI*) was the first EU action in which standards of indictment were imposed on Member States, albeit still in the limited framework offered by the Maastricht version of the Treaty. Following the evolution of the European institutional framework about cooperation in the field of criminal justice, the new instrument of Framework Decisions replaced, in the Amsterdam version of the EU Treaty, Joint Actions for matters falling within the third pillar of the Union and was very soon employed on the subject (*Framework Decision of 19 July 2002 on combating trafficking in human beings - 2002/629/JHA*). In turn, the

2011 directive (*2011/36/EU on preventing and combating trafficking in human beings and protecting its victims*) was the first adopted in criminal matters, which, according to the most recent and current Lisbon version of the treaties, are part of the unified competences of the Union. Besides these repeated EU interventions, there were also the protocol on human trafficking of the UN Convention of Palermo of 2000 and the Council of Europe Convention of 2005. This multilevel synergy on the matter has led to significant harmonization of national regulations: an example is the EU Directive that provides a list of illegal conducts that are all punishable in the European countries specifically considered by the research (Italy, Spain Greece, Portugal, and Germany). The structure of the attempted crime is common to all aforementioned legal systems, which define the various conducts through reference to the particular purpose of exploitation (sexual, work, organ transplantation, etc.). The sanction levels are also congruent with the Directive, while there is an extensive, albeit not absolute, correspondence between the circumstances that aggravate responsibility.

On the subject of migrant smuggling, however, there is still today a European legislative framework that reflects the situation before the turning point in Lisbon: the "*Facilitators Package*" dates back to 2002, and consists of two different tools, in line with the distinct attribution of competences on the subject in the EU institutional architecture of the time. There is a directive (2002/90/EC) relating to conducts to facilitate illegal immigration that States must consider illegal, accompanied by a framework decision (2002/946/JHA) for the related criminal sanctions. The European Commission has verified that already in 2015 both regulations were implemented in all Member States, albeit with some differences in the description of the offending conduct.[9] However, a result of greater convergenze between the criminal systems of the Member States in the repression of illegal conduct defined at the European level cannot be denied: this is a significant result in a matter such as irregular immigration, which has been long subject to local pressures in the various countries and to the difficulty of arriving at a common vision of the underlying problems. One may think of the reluctance, and indeed of the open hostility in some cases, regarding a serious policy of relocation between the individual Member States of migrants irregularly landing on the southern coasts of Europe, albeit aiming to reach countries in central and northern Europe.

Narcotics drug trafficking is also one of the first types of crime for the European Union—together with terrorism and organized crime—subject to EU-standards of incrimination that are binding for Member States: already based on the previous Amsterdam version of the Treaty in 2004, a Framework Decision (2004/757/JHA) was adopted, establishing minimum standards relating to the key elements of the offenses and the penalties applicable to illicit drug trafficking. Although here, too,

---

[9] See, Spena, in this volume, chapter 'Facilitation of Irregular Immigration vs. Organised Smuggling of Migrants: Is This Dichotomy Relevant to the Interpretation of Italian Criminal Law?'.

Moreover, the Commission document on the evaluation of the "Facilitators Package": COM SWD (2017) 117 (22.3.2017), p. 13 s. The text summarizes two additional external studies carried out between 2014 and 2016.

specific points have been identified in which Member States have not transposed the EU indications in the same way,[10] the tendency to harmonize a series of aspects of national legal systems is embedded onto a terrain that was already familiar with previous international instruments (in particular the 1988 UN Convention), and it is found in the framework decision concerning e.g. indictment of the basic conduct of illicit trafficking (described in Article 2), the provision of a more serious liability when the actions are committed by a criminal organization (Article 4 paragraph 3) and the liability of legal persons for related offenses (Article 6).

Finally, cigarette smuggling, although it has long been a widespread form of illicit trafficking, is often considered to present limited criminal dangerousness and is not considered among the types of serious crime that the current EU Treaties recognize as possible fields of criminal harmonization. Hence the current absence in this matter of a specific common European standard of penal protection: the directive on the subject (2014/40/EU) only deals with the administrative discipline of production and marketing of cigarettes, to guarantee a traceability system for tackling the illicit tobacco market. The counteracting legislative responses in the various member countries are differentiated: the Italian regime, the Consolidated Customs Law (Article 291 bis and following of Presidential Decree no. 43 of 1973) identifies severe penalties for tobacco smuggling; however, it is flanked by other countries not foreseeing any specific criminal norm on tobacco products, but rather link the related illicit trade (above a certain value threshold) to the general offenseA of smuggling as a customs-related crime.[11]

5 The Importance of the Relationship Between Illicit Trafficking and Criminal Organizations in Supranational Sources

The organized structure of players managing the most significant part of illicit trafficking, despite the variety of group compositions and their reciprocal connections, is significantly considered in both European and national legislative instruments. This is one of the aspects on which, as already mentioned, there is an important convergence of the various legislative interventions that, at the different levels, are distinguished in terms of the type of traffic considered.

[10] Here the delay in consideration is also noted in the fact that the evaluation report on the implementation of the Framework Decision is now out of date: see Commission report COM (2009) 669 and related working document SEC(2009)1661. For a more recent assessment, see Siracusa, in this volume, chapter 'Soft Drugs and Organized Crime: A Problematic Relationship', para 6.

[11] On this topic, see Omodei (2020), pp. 98 ff.

Legislative consideration of the relationship between criminal organizations and illicit trades is supported by judicial findings on the main features of these phenomena. For this reason, the traditional vagueness of the notion of organized crime does not apply to the regulations on illicit trades referring to criminal organizations operating in these various markets. However, we should underline the relationship between these rules and those incriminating the criminal organization as such, to avoid any overlapping of rules and criminal sanctions.

If the issues indicated in relation to trafficking in human beings arise, it is firstly noted that not only Directive 2011/36/EU highlights the connection between this crime and organized crime at the start of its criminal policy groundings (recital 1), but its articles also deem it of specific importance: for the case in which trafficking is committed in the context of a criminal organization, a more serious maximum penalty is contemplated, amounting to at least 10 years' imprisonment (art. 4 para. 2 letter b), i.e. double the basic provision, which is at least 5 years' imprisonment (art. 4 para. 1). The notion of organized crime relevant for the purposes of the aggravated penalty for trafficking thus receives a definition that is not direct, but *per relationem*, as the Directive recalls the corresponding text contained in the 2008 Framework Decision on the fight against organized crime (2008/841/GAI: Art. 1). This is a frequent pattern in the European legislative interventions on other types of illicit trafficking: among those already considered, entirely similar rules—albeit referring to the antecedent Joint Action 98/733/JHA—can be found in Framework Decision 2004/757/JHA on the subject of illicit drug trafficking (art. 4 para. 3), as well as in Framework Decision 2002/946/JHA on criminal sanctions against "facilitating entry, illegal transit and stay" (art.1 para. 3-1).

This internal reference within the European legislation in criminal matters avoids relying on a vague criminological notion of organized crime. Nevertheless, it fails to make a connection with the transnational nature of the activity carried out by the group, as usually happens in the case of illicit trafficking and in particular of groups that manage the international trafficking of persons. This aspect is instead expressly considered in the UN Convention of Palermo on transnational organized crime (UNTOC): in this respect too, the harmonizing legislation of European sources in criminal matters requires broader consideration of the international legislative instruments on the subject. This also allows for an important connection to the definition of criminal organizations, which would otherwise be excessively vague. Moreover, the definition of a criminal organization derived from international sources does not solve every problem of the precision of this notion. In the Palermo Convention, as in the EU sources setting a similar standard of offense, two different constructions of the criminal group coexist without any possibility of *reductio ad unitatem*, one of Euro-continental origin (attributable to the French charge of *association de malfaiteurs*) and one of Anglo-Saxon origin (linked to the conspiracy model).[12]

[12]On this dual model, see Militello (2017), pp. 191 ff.

Hence it becomes pivotal to verify not only whether the relevance of the organizations operating in illicit trafficking has been recognized in the transposition of European standards in the national criminal law systems, but also how this internal implementation defined the notion of criminal organization or group.

6 *Focus*: Trafficking in Human Beings and Criminal Organizations in Five European Justice Systems (Italy, Portugal, Greece, Spain, and Germany)

In particular, when considering trafficking in human beings, the five examined countries have expressly recognized the role of criminal organizations in this specific sector among illicit trades, albeit through non-identical solutions in recognizing greater criminal responsibility upon organizations operating in their respective illicit contexts.

In *Italy,* the basic crime of trafficking in human beings (Art. 601 Penal Code) involves an increase in the prison sentence, like other crimes against individual freedom (such as reduction to or maintenance in slavery: Article 600 Penal Code) and the crime of aiding and abetting illegal immigration (art. 12 para. 3-*bis* Consolidated Immigration Act), when they fall within the agenda of a criminal organization: the sanctions range rises from imprisonment between 3 and 7 years for leaders and organizers and between 1 and 5 years for those associated with the organization to imprisonment between 5 and 15 years for the former and between 4 and 9 years for the latter, if trafficking is involved (Art. 416 para.6 Penal Code).

In Italian criminal law, the offense of criminal organization requires that at least three people are associated with a criminal program aimed at any crime; in the most serious form mentioned above, the group's program of activities is instead aimed at specific offenses—justified by the fact that these are criminal typologies that typically manifest themselves in an organized form. These special cases of crimes committed by criminal organizations are distinct, however, from the other special model of criminal organization introduced in Italy decades ago, specifically to combat the criminal organizations traditionally present in its territory: mafia-type criminal organizations (Art. 416*bis* Penal Code). Here the special feature of the general associative rule consists in the particular method used (called, in fact, "mafia-type method") and not in a defined typology of the organization's criminal purposes (so much so that some of these purposes may even be lawful, but are carried out through illicit means). As to transnationality, although not expressly referred to as a qualifying factor in the specific context of organizations aimed at illicit trafficking, it was generally included in the Italian legal system in the transposition of the UN Palermo Convention of 2000, which took place with law 146 no. 2006. In particular, this provided for a particular aggravating circumstance valid for all crimes that are committed "with the contribution of an organized criminal group engaged in criminal activities in more than one state" (Art. 61*bis* Penal Code).[13]

In *Portugal*, too, enactment of the slave trade by a criminal organization is expressly considered, in line with the EU directive of 2011 and the specific Protocol of the UN Palermo Convention (ratified by Portugal in 2004).[14] Art. 160 Penal Code contains the basic hypothesis of trafficking in human beings and punishes it with a prison sentence of 3 to 10 years, but if the offense is committed in the context of a criminal organization, the penalty is aggravated using a specific sentencing increase by one third (provided for in paragraph 4). In turn, the notion of criminal organization is established by the same code: art. 299 incriminates the conduct of those who promote, establish, take part in a criminal organization or support a 'group, organization or association' whose purpose is the commission of one or more crimes in one of several expressly listed ways (providing weapons, ammunition, crime tools, meeting rooms, or helping to recruit new members). The custodial sentence is from 1 to 5 years, increased from 2 to 8 years for leaders or organizers (art. 299 paras. 1–3). Since 2007, the aforementioned notion of "group, organization or association" has been explicitly defined in line with the wording of the 1998 EU joint action: the "existence of a union of at least three persons, operating in an agreed manner for a certain period of time" is considered.[15] If the crime of trafficking is committed by participants in an organization, only the crime of trafficking will be applicable, with the aforementioned increase in the penalty, which includes all the elements of the action, and also the plurality of subjects participating in the relevant organization. However, there is no specific provision in the Portuguese code for criminal groups that use the mafia method. Neither the transnationality profile of the crime is given specific importance, as it is not considered in the specific context of art. 160, although it is an element connected to many situations of trafficking in human beings, nor there is a hint to it in the general provision that punishes the criminal organization.

Greece has recently amended its law on trafficking in human beings (Article 323a Penal Code, as reformulated by Law No. 4219 of 2019, which issued the new Penal Code) in terms that comply with the corresponding provision of the 2011 EU Directive. It also foresees an aggravated responsibility for some of the aggravating circumstances provided for by the Directive (with a prison sentence of up to 20 years, much higher than that required by the European standard, which requires at least a ten-year prison sentence). However, the provision of the aggravating circumstance for the commission of a crime in the context of a criminal group is missing from the law on trafficking; instead, they refer to the different situations of

[13]On the circumstance in question and its relations with the other aggravating circumstance of the mafia method in situations of illicit trafficking, cf. e.g. Apollonio (2018), pp. 10 ff.

[14]This supranational legislative base is expressly referred to by Rodrigues (2009), pp. 577 ff.

[15]Art. 1 Lei n. 59/2007, de 04/09 (23ª Alteração ao Código Penal) adds to art. 299 of the Penal Code (Associação criminosa) para. 5: "Para os efeitos do presente artigo, considera-se que existe grupo, organização ou associação quando esteja em causa um conjunto de, pelo menos, três pessoas, actuando concertadamente durante um certo período de tempo".

the crimes committed on a "professional basis", not envisaged by the European standards. In Greece, however, the concept of criminal organization specifies the relevant crimes as possible purposes of the group, defined as a structure of at least three people who carry out continuous activities: the long list of individual crimes that art. 187 Penal Code indicates as possible purposes of the criminal organization also includes the trafficking of persons referred to in art. 323a. In this case, the penalty is up to ten years of imprisonment, and therefore within the limits provided for by art. 4 para. 2 letter b of the 2011 EU Directive. The latter can be said to be implemented in the Greek system, both for trafficking by criminal organizations and for their penalties.

The transnational dimension, frequent in trafficking, is also linked with the fight against the facilitation of illegal immigration: the law on trafficking has an aggravating circumstance for the performance of the related conduct in connection with "entry to, stay in or exit from the country of the victim" when such acts are illegal (art. 323a para. 3 letter c). This solution, therefore, links the transnational nature of the crime to the nationality of the victim and not to the objective enactment in different States of the illegal conduct, according to the model defined in the UNTOC Palermo Convention. This leads to a delicate coordination problem when the actions are committed by criminal organizations: in fact, the facilitation of irregular immigration is structurally connected with the transnational dimension but if it is a criminal organization that acts pursuant to art. 187 (which also contemplates this crime among those specifically indicated as possible purposes of the organization), a multi-layered classification of the action is reached when the organization aims both at aiding immigration and at the trafficking of persons. What at an individual level is considered a unitary action, albeit aggravated (trafficking is aggravated by the connection with facilitation of irregular immigration, but at the same time incorporates it), instead becomes a duplication of crimes by a criminal organization, albeit according to a regime of the concurrence of crimes regulated by a particular legal system of accumulation (Art. 94 Greek Penal Code).

Then, in *Spain,* concerning the consideration of criminal organizations operating in the trafficking of human beings, the system envisaged by the 2011 EU Directive is faithfully reproduced in the responsibility for the basic crime (imprisonment between 5 and 8 years). Furthermore, the related conduct is more harshly punished when it is performed by an "organization or association of more than two people, even if of a transitory nature", to which "the guilty person belongs" (art. 177 bis para. 6 Spanish Penal Code). Further increases in punishment are envisaged when the criminal organization includes among its activities other situations considered as aggravating liability for the basic act (and described in paragraphs 4 and 5 of the same art. 177bis).[16]

---

[16] See Corcoy, in this volume, chapter 'The Problems of Trafficking in Human Beings in Spain. Criminal Regulations and Jurisprudential Treatment'.

However, the problem posed by the Spanish wording concerns the use of a notion that does not refer to the criminal organization specifically defined in the Penal Code (Article 570 *bis*, in the formulation most recently amended by Organic Law 1/2015, implementing the 2008 Framework Decision on organized crime). Instead, the organization is described by replacing the requirement of *stability* (or at least of being "formed for an indefinite time") with the possibility of its "transitory" activity. This seems to allow a significant expansion of the notion of "organization or association" dedicated to trafficking. Considering that in the Spanish code there are already other provisions referring to aggregations of subjects who commit crimes (illegal organization: art. 515; criminal group: art. 570 *ter* no. 1), the overall picture of the relevance of criminal organizations is particularly crowded.[17] In this situation, the work of the courts becomes very relevant: they have interpreted the provision of the aggravating circumstance of trafficking in the sense that the reference to a transitory activity does not eliminate the need for a network which, although elementary, must be, in any case, stable and hierarchically ordered. Instead, an occasional agreement between several people, which would be a simple conspiracy, is not considered sufficient.[18] Furthermore, to be "dedicated" to trafficking activities, the group must have committed a plurality of trafficking actions: it is therefore neither enough that they are the object of a mere idea of a criminal plan to be carried out in the future, nor that only a single trafficking action has been committed. At the same time, the group's criminal activity needs not ne be limited to this activity, as it may also include other crimes. Finally, case law stated that the aggravating circumstance require also the fact that the organization can rely on coordinated material and human means for the transport of foreign citizens to Spain:[19] an element indeed that is only possible, although ordinarily present in these crimes.

When the trafficking is carried out by a person who participates in an organization dedicated to this activity, the qualification of the fact (pursuant to the aforementioned art. 177 bis para. 6) prevails as a special rule over the general rule on criminal organization referred to in art. 570*bis* CP (art. 8.1a Spanish Penal Code).[20]

Finally, *Germany* also attributes aggravating importance to trafficking in human beings by a member of an organization committed to the continuous commission of such crimes (sect. 232, para. 3, no. 3 German Penal Code). From this point of view, Germany also complies with the corresponding provision of the 2011 EU Directive; moreover, it also respects the sanction profile (imprisonment for a maximum of 10 years). As in Spain, however, in this matter there is no reference to the general notion of "criminal organization", which is defined in Germany as a structure of at

[17] On the related problems of concurrence of rules and/or offenses, cf. Faraldo Cabana (2012), pp. 357 ff.

[18] See Corcoy, in this volume, in relation to Tribunal Supremo 6.10.2003. Recently the Tribunal Supremo (no. 167 of 15.3.2017), in relation to four people who between China and Spain handled the arrival of several people in Spain, acknowledged the aggravating circumstance in terms of trafficking.

[19] Tribunal Supremo 1595/2005, 30-12.

[20] Santana Vega (2011), pp. 79 ff., 104. Cf. also Faraldo Cabana (2012), p. 367.

least three people, having distinct roles and continuously belonging to the organization, who pursue in a prolonged manner a common illegal interest over time (art. 129 para. 2 German Penal Code). On the other hand, to be seen as a criminal organization involved in trafficking in human beings in Germany, it is sufficient for the group to operate continuously in this illegal activity. There is therefore a difference with the EU-directive that recalls the notion of "criminal organization" referred to in the 2008 Framework Decision, which instead defines it as a structured organization of at least three people who act in a concerted way to commit several crimes punishable with imprisonment sentences of at least four years. The difference should not be sought in the possibility that the members of the organization are only two people, as this traditional requirement is now opposed by case law, which has raised the minimum number of participants in the organization to three; rather, the lack of distribution of roles and a plurality of purpose-based crimes committed by these subjects does not allow the two German notions of "gang" and of "criminal organization" to overlap.[21] Moreover, there is no particular reference in Germany to the transnational nature of the crime and its possible connection both with the facilitation of illegal immigration and with other types of illicit trafficking.

7 Summary Remarks

In light of the considerations made starting from the research on illicit trades in the Mediterranean and on the counteraction responses on the subject, some brief points for a summary can be identified, especially concerning the relationship with transnational criminal organizations. These reflections do not aim at concluding the debate on such a widespread and complex phenomenon; instead, they grow from the path of research undertaken to stimulate further theoretical insights and more extensive empirical verifications.

- The establishment of a notion of illicit trades which does not consider separately the various types of exchanges and therefore aspires to act as a general collector of the related analyzes is only possible at an empirical-criminological level but is still far from being matched in the context of supranational legislative instruments.
- The plurality of supranational legislative sources on illicit trades only allows separate analyses of individual and respective types. The corresponding levels of harmonization of national implementation choices must therefore be verified in the different areas of illegal activity specifically considered.
- A common element is instead the notion of "criminal organization", which represents a qualifying trait of the most widespread cases of illicit trades, at least the transnational ones. If we then consider a single type of illicit trade,

[21] On the traditional notion of "gang" see Küper (2008)[7], p. 46. The difference between the aggravating circumstance of the gang (sec. 232 para. 3 no. 3) and the crime of criminal organization (sec. 129) is emphasized in Bürger (2017), p. 177.

such as that related to the trafficking of human beings and migrant smuggling, various commonalities can be found between the individual national responses, thanks also to the harmonization process fostered by the international instruments on the subject.
- There is no single organizational model in the groups controlling the illicit markets, but different operational and collaborative organizations coexist, in some cases not even excluding the presence of individual operators for single activities and with limited scope. The variety of possible actual configurations of the plurality of active subjects does not remove the need for rationalization of the relationships between the current legislative responses, which sometimes deem it a mere aggravating factor of the basic crime and sometimes as a separate crime, in some cases even indicating specifically the crimes that are part of the group's activity.
- To implement forms of rationalization of the rules to combat transnational criminal organizations operating in these illicit trades, it would be useful to envisage legislative solutions that consider poly-criminality in at least some of these sectors. If, on the one hand, this factor increases the criminal dangerousness of the groups in question, on the other hand, it must not lead to artificial duplications of the sanctions, when the facts of the crime are substantially connected with the reality of the action committed.
- The differences between legislative responses to individual types of illicit trades impacts the substantial framing of the phenomena, while on the procedural side there is greater fungibility of the tools that can be used (*e.g.*, wiretapping or undercover infiltrators). The key here is the reference to criminal organizations granting access to the procedural subsystem connected to special investigation and trial rules, with the associated risks of making it a *passe-partout* formula that neglects the differentiated subjective composition of the criminal organizations.
- However, there are still many issues to be faced, on both substantial and procedural profiles: one may think, for example, of the determination of the competent jurisdiction and the validity of criminal law rules in space. These too could benefit from common solutions for the various types of illicit trades, even if drafting a higher unitary notion of the category could not probably understand the distinguishing features of each specific area of unlawful trades.

References

Apollonio A (2018) Il metodo mafioso nello spazio transfrontaliero. Diritto Penale Contemporaneo Rivista Trimestrale 1:10

Bürger S (2017) Die Neuregelung des Menschenhandels. ZIS: 17

Faraldo Cabana P (2012) Asociaciones ilícitas y organizaciones criminales en el código penal español. Tirant Lo Blach Madrid

Fijnaut C., Paoli L (2004), Organised Crime in Europe. Concepts, Patterns and Control Policies in the European Union and Beyond. Springer Dordrecht

Küper W (2008) Strafrecht. Besonderer Teil, Müller Heidelberg

La Chioma F (2019) Organizzazioni criminali transnazionali e traffico di migranti. L'esperienza nel Canale di Sicilia. In: Militello V, Spena A, Mangiaracina A, Siracusa L (eds) I traffici illeciti nel Mediterraneo. Persone, stupefacenti, tabacco. Giappichelli Torino, pp 81–113

La Spina A (2019) The role of organized crime in illicit trades: drug trafficking, migrant smuggling, arms trafficking and cigarette smuggling. In: Militello V, Spena A, Mangiaracina A, Siracusa L (eds) I traffici illeciti nel Mediterraneo. Persone, stupefacenti, tabacco. Giappichelli Torino, pp 67–79

Militello V (2017) The notion of organised crime in EU law. In: Carnevale S, Giolo O, Forlati S (eds) Redefining organised crime. A challenge for the European Union? Hart, Oxford, pp 191–223

Militello V (2019) In: Militello V, Spena A (eds) Between criminalization and protection. The Italian way of dealing with migrant smuggling and trafficking within the European and international context. Brill, pp 55–78

Omodei RE (2020) Il ruolo dell'organizzazione criminale nel contrasto al traffico di tabacchi lavorati esteri. Rivista Trimestrale Diritto Penale dell'Economia. 1:91–127

Rodrigues AM (2009) A incriminação do tráfico de pessoas no contexto da política criminal contemporânea. In: da Costa Andrade M, Aires de Sousa S, João Antunes M (eds) Estudos em Homenagem Figueiredo Dias, vol III. Coimbra, pp 577–585

Santana Vega DM (2011) El nuevo delito de trata de seres humanos (LO 5/2010, 22-6). Quadernos De Politica Criminal 2:79–104

Vervaele JA (2014) The material scope of competence of the European Public Prosecutor's Office: a harmonised national patchwork? In: Fornasari G, Sartori D (eds) Id. European criminal justice in the post-Lisbon area of freedom, security and justice. Editoriale Scientifica, Trento, pp 259–277

Vilas Àlvarez D (2018) The material competence of the European Public Prosecutor's Office. In: Bachmaier Winter L (ed) The European Public Prosecutor's Office. The challenge ahead. Springer, Cham, p 25

Part I
Jurisdictional Issues

Territorialising the Extraterritorial: The Role of 'Suppression' Conventions

Micheál Ó Floinn

Abstract This chapter traces two jurisdictional developments in 'suppression' conventions. The first considers how these instruments grew to require states to implement a complex web of jurisdictional bases for transnational offences, and I analyse the role of the territoriality principle as part of this process. Through a range of devices and territorial fictions, the conventions have incentivised a 'territorialisation' of the extraterritorial. The second jurisdictional trajectory is of more recent vintage. Enforcement jurisdiction has always been understood as strictly territorial, so while states may prescribe extraterritorial reach in their criminal offences on the basis of permissive principles, the enforcement of these laws are in practice usually territorially bounded and constrained. But taking the example of the Cybercrime Convention, I demonstrate how a 'territorialisation of the extraterritorial' is also being incentivised in the realm of enforcement jurisdiction.

Given the capaciousness and malleability of the territoriality principle, and law enforcement needs in an increasingly globalised and interpenetrable world, these trends are not unexpected. However, when taken together, I claim that these jurisdictional trajectories are 'uneasy bedfellows' in suppression conventions. Ultimately, I argue that the jurisdictional assumptions and law enforcement priorities which drive the suppression process need to be reappraised and recalibrated in light of these jurisdictional trajectories, and I highlight the *ne bis in idem* principle as an area requiring urgent attention within this process.

M. Ó Floinn (✉)
School of Law, University of Glasgow, Glasgow, Scotland
e-mail: Micheal.OFlynn@glasgow.ac.uk

V. Militello, A. Spena (eds.), *The Challenges of Illegal Trafficking in the Mediterranean Area*, Legal Studies in International, European and Comparative Criminal Law 9, https://doi.org/10.1007/978-3-031-45399-1_2

1 Introduction

This chapter traces a particular jurisdictional phenomenon in 'suppression conventions'[1]—what has been referred to as a '*territorialization* of the *extraterritorial*'.[2] This phenomenon is shaping and influencing state interpretations of all of the traditional heads of jurisdiction in international law,[3] and when these jurisdictional trajectories are understood together, and promulgated through instruments that can have global reach, I argue that the problem of jurisdictional concurrency over transnational crime becomes an ever greater concern.

In the realm of 'prescriptive' jurisdiction—which in the criminal law sphere refers to questions about the scope or ambit of the criminal law of a state and the authority of states to assert its criminal law outside its territorial borders—there has been some recent scholarly treatment of criminal jurisdiction which has traced how these suppression instruments have developed an increasingly expansive and complex web of jurisdictional bases for addressing transnational crime.[4] However, critique and concern of such developments are usually reserved for 'extraterritorial' bases of jurisdiction,[5] with the attendant jurisdictional concurrency they create for territorial states and the questionable normative status of some of the extraterritorial bases that are being advanced through suppression conventions.[6] On one account, a crucial cog in the entire 'turn' to suppression was the "de-territorialization of jurisdiction and the enforcement of that jurisdiction".[7] While this has undoubtedly played a part, it is an incomplete characterisation of what the suppression conventions have done, as they have promoted a process of both *de-territorialisation* (through e.g. provisions on mandatory or discretionary bases of extraterritorial jurisdiction) and expansive *territorialisation* of criminal jurisdiction, through a range of devices and territorial fictions, and I argue here that the latter is an under-studied but potentially insidious

---

[1] For the purposes of this chapter, I will adopt the understandings of 'transnational criminal law' and 'suppression conventions' as described in Boister et al. (2021), p. 3. Transnational criminal law is defined there to mean "the suppression by international law through domestic penal law of criminal activities that have (i) actual or (ii) potential transboundary effects or (iii) transboundary moral impact" (quoting Boister 2015), with suppression conventions being the usual international law instrument utilised by states for this purpose. The trafficking conventions addressed in the present volume form a substantial core of the 'suppression conventions.'

[2] See Ryngaert (2020), p. 140.

[3] Principally, in the criminal sphere, prescriptive and enforcement jurisdiction. For classical treatments of these categorisations of jurisdiction see Mann (1985) and Akehurst (1972). For more recently scholarly accounts see Ryngaert (2015) and Mills (2014).

[4] See e.g. Garrod (2023a), Jeßberger (2021), Clarke (2014), and Clarke (1988).

[5] Szigeti (2019), p. 44, for example, notes how some "commentators have argued that widespread extraterritorial jurisdiction results in over-regulation, but widespread territorial jurisdiction results in under-regulation."

[6] For a critique of e.g. active and passive personality principles of jurisdiction, see Chehtman (2010). It has long been recognised that tenuous assertions of extraterritorial jurisdiction can hamper international relations and co-operation. See e.g. Gibney (1996).

[7] Boister et al. (2021), p. 12.

development. The malleability of the territoriality principle, and the ease with which states can characterise transnational events as 'territorial', means that states can claim jurisdiction over offences where there may only be a tenuous nexus with the events in question, but the identification of a territorial connection—as the core and most widely accepted basis for criminal jurisdiction in international law—provides a jurisdictional claim with an air of legitimacy, particularly as compared to some of the more controversial principles of extraterritorial jurisdiction. However, exercises of jurisdiction based on the outer edges of what can be understood as a 'territorial' offence, can raise the same, or even greater, concerns for international co-operation and the rights of the accused.

A more striking and recent development is that a territorialisation of the extra-territorial is also now being incentivised by suppression conventions in the realm of enforcement jurisdiction. While with respect to the jurisdiction to prescribe, states have long sought to implement extraterritorial jurisdiction based on general principles (active or passive personality, protection, and universality),[8] enforcement jurisdiction has, on the other hand, traditionally been understood as strictly territorial.[9] In the infamous and seminal *Lotus* case,[10] a majority of the Permanent Court of International Justice (PCIJ) found that enforcement jurisdiction is 'certainly' territorial: "it cannot be exercised by a state outside its territory except by virtue of a permissive rule derived from international custom or from a convention."[11] In some contexts, recent state practice appears to be challenging this bright-line separation between enforcement jurisdiction and other jurisdictional heads,[12] even if the extent to which international customary law has crystallised with respect to extraterritorial enforcement jurisdiction is unclear. But taking the example of the Cybercrime Convention,[13] what I will highlight is the role that a suppression convention is playing to facilitate extraterritorial enforcement by incentivising expansive interpretations of territoriality with respect to domestic procedural powers. While this may not be clear from the text of the Convention, broad readings of this instrument are now being advocated by certain factions within the Council of Europe through authoritative guidance notes on key provisions. Moreover, the recent Second Additional Protocol to the Cybercrime Convention[14] has now rendered some of these practices explicit by allowing for the direct extraterritorial enforcement of procedural

---

[8] See e.g. Chehtman (2014).

[9] Lombois once succinctly captured the traditional limitations of enforcement jurisdiction: "[t]he law may very well decide to cast its shadow beyond its borders; the judge may well have a voice so loud that, speaking in his house, his condemnations are heard outside; the reach of the police officer is only as long as his arm . . . he is constable only at home." See Lombois (1979) cited and translated in Trudel (1998).

[10] *S.S. Lotus (France v. Turkey)*, (1927), P.C.I.J. (ser. A) No. 10 (the *Lotus* case).

[11] Ibid, 18–19.

[12] See Ryngaert (2023) and Lubin (2023).

[13] Budapest Convention on Cybercrime (European Treaty Series No 185, 23.XI.2001).

[14] Second Additional Protocol to the Convention on Cybercrime on Enhanced Co-Operation and Disclosure of Electronic Evidence (Strasbourg, 12 May 2022) CETS 224.

powers on entities in other State Parties, with implications for third parties and other indirect effects a significant likelihood in practice.

Given the capaciousness and malleability of the concept of territoriality, the highly fluid and spectral nature of internet data, and law enforcement needs in an increasingly globalised and interpenetrable world, these trends are not unexpected. However, when taken together, I argue that these jurisdictional trajectories in suppression conventions are a cause for concern, particularly with respect to the rights of the accused. Jurisdictional concurrency over crime may no longer be a phenomenon of 'paper' offences which are jurisdictionally expansive in theory, but with little bite in practice. The international law machinery is in place, or is being put in place, to pull foreign data, dinghies and defendants from abroad, making conflicts in *exercise* a more tangible and real problem for many countries. Ultimately, I argue that the jurisdictional assumptions and law enforcement priorities that have driven the suppression process to date need to be reappraised and recalibrated, and I highlight the risk of double jeopardy as an area in need of urgent attention within the suppression process.

Before proceeding further some preliminary remarks are needed to clarify some of the terminology that will be used. First, the term 'territory' requires some elaboration. This can of course refer to rocks, mountains and patches of the earth, and as Szigeti notes, lawyers have a tendency of thinking about territory in this way—as a geographical, physical fact.[15] On the basis of such a narrow understanding, it would be difficult to imagine how a drug trafficking offence that is committed on the high seas on an unregistered vessel could be prosecuted on a 'territorial' basis in Italy. In traditional jurisdictional analysis, territory serves as the factual input to determine where events can be said to have occurred and which country, if any, has a territorial connection with those events.[16] However, territoriality is a legal construct that can easily capture transnational and/or extraterritorial conduct, whether on the basis of its actual or potential impact on state 'territory'. This is because while the territoriality principle, as a source of authority under international law, refers to the regulation of conduct that occurs in the territory (including territorial airspace and seas) of a state, this can occur there in whole or *in part*. Moreover, state 'territory' itself has an inherent elasticity and is an abstraction to which the territoriality principle applies. As Elden notes "territory is not simply an object: the outcome of actions conducted toward it or some previously supposedly neutral area. Territory is itself a process, made and remade, shaped and shaping, active and reactive."[17] Therefore, contrary to the narratives of this being constraining for regulating transnational harms, I will argue that this is rather an incredibly enabling basis of jurisdiction, easily accommodating expansive (extra)territorial claims of authority. When we view legal 'territory' in this way, we see how the concept

---

[15] Szigeti (2019), p. 32.

[16] Buxbaum (2009), p. 634.

[17] Elden (2013), p. 17. See further Kohl's discussion of the distinction between physical territory and 'territory-as-control.' Kohl (2023), p. 198.

extends as "far as the reach of power"[18] and this demands attention to be placed on the sources of power, and how territoriality is being instrumentalised to extend this power. This contribution focuses on the role of suppression conventions in this process.

Second, the 'extraterritorial' also requires some further elucidation. Obviously, it implies something existing or taking place beyond particular territorial limits (or any territory at all), and lawyers often speak generally of domestic laws applying 'extraterritorially' when "a court applies domestic laws to [...] conduct occurring beyond a country's borders."[19] Confusion arises, however, as the line between the territorial and the extraterritorial becomes increasingly blurred, and where elements of extraterritoriality in a case are conflated with extraterritorial jurisdiction in a formal international law sense. As Ryngaert notes "[e]xtraterritorial jurisdiction" ought to imply that a State exercises its jurisdiction without any territorial link ("*extra*-territorial"), although the expression is typically used in a context of States asserting jurisdiction on the basis of some, admittedly non-exclusive, territorial link."[20] This suggests that further analytical precision is required, separating extraterritoriality and extraterritorial jurisdiction as a matter of international law. In the words of Buxbaum territoriality and extraterritoriality "are claims of authority or of resistance to authority, that are made by particular actors with particular substantive interests to promote."[21] A person prosecuted in Italy for trafficking activities that took place in France, may challenge the prosecution on the basis of an inexistent or insufficient territorial connection, thus relying on an extraterritorial framing of events. The Italian prosecutors, on the other hand, may seek to substantiate a territorial offence by focusing on e.g. the domestic territorial effects of the 'extraterritorial' conduct.[22] Territoriality and extraterritoriality, in this example, can thus work as a jurisdictional sword and shield. Where, on the other hand, the claim of authority rests on a ground of *extraterritorial jurisdiction* such as the active personality principle, territoriality may play no role at all in terms of the jurisdictional nexus in the case. While some of these international law bases of jurisdiction may be better described as *non-territorial*, in the sense that there is no territorial claim grounding the assertion of jurisdiction, it may still be claimed that others are 'extraterritorial' precisely because they were developed to supplement jurisdictional powers and escape the perceived limitations of territorial jurisdiction.

---

[18] Chimni (2022), p. 36.

[19] Parrish (2009), p. 818 (footnote 15).

[20] Ryngaert (2015), p. 7.

[21] Buxbaum (2009), p. 634.

[22] As Colangelo notes, "[m]any activities or events we might think of as outside a territory can be recharacterized as inside a territory." See Colangelo (2014), p. 1313. Some contend that the 'effects' doctrine is a separate ground of extraterritorial jurisdiction in international law, and that it should not be considered an extension of the territoriality principle (see e.g. O'Keefe (2022), p. 520, footnote 23) but this is quite a narrow interpretation of territoriality and there does not appear to be consensus on this in international law scholarship.

Therefore, a case could present elements of extraterritoriality whether or not it is prosecuted on the basis of territorial or extraterritorial principles but there is an important analytical distinction to be drawn between the two. The distinction can be of legal significance by, for example, determining the preconditions required to be satisfied in order to bring a prosecution in a particular country, or in the context of extradition law where states may determine that they will not extradite an accused person if the requesting state is relying on an extraterritorial base of jurisdiction, and the requested state has a territorial nexus with the offence. More generally, I argue that jurisdictional and analytical precision is required because, as Szigeti notes, "the problem of ambiguous territoriality has hardly been realised"[23] and this is particularly true in the context of suppression conventions.

The discussion will proceed as follows. In Sect. 2, I first consider some general jurisdictional trends in suppression conventions, before focusing on how certain provisions are incentivising a territorialisation of the extraterritorial in the realm of prescriptive jurisdiction over criminal offences. In Sect. 3, I turn to the Cybercrime Convention to analyse how this document is instrumentalising territoriality in order to facilitate the same in the realm of enforcement jurisdiction, and more recent international instruments which continue, in different and more explicit ways, to attempt to overcome traditional territorial constraints in enforcement jurisdiction. In Sect. 4, I bring these jurisdictional trajectories together to consider some of the resultant problems stemming from jurisdictional concurrency over transnational crime, and the role that suppression conventions can and should play in addressing these consequences. Section 5 concludes.

2 Expanding the Territoriality of Offences in Suppression Conventions

2.1 Jurisdictional Trends in the Suppression Conventions

For a long time, jurisdiction in suppression conventions was a relatively neglected area in transnational criminal law and international law literature, but recent work has begun to trace the development of the jurisdictional provisions in these instruments, identifying patterns, common elements and general trends. Jeßberger notes how jurisdictional provisions in suppression conventions in the early twentieth century were "rather conservative"[24] with state practice in treaty-making suggesting a reluctance to bind states or to demand departure from their domestic rules of jurisdiction. General saving clauses were included in instruments like the Counterfeiting Currency Convention 1929, assuring states in Article 17 that the "Convention shall not be interpreted as affecting that Party's attitude on the general

[23] Szigeti (2019), p. 31.

[24] *See* Jeßberger (2021), p. 266.

question of criminal jurisdiction as a question of international law",[25] while other provisions ensured prioritisation of domestic and constitutional limitations in the definition, prosecution and punishment of convention offences.[26] Where traditional grounds of extraterritorial jurisdiction were included, based on, for example, the nationality principle, they were not mandatory; they only recognised that if the laws of a contracting party permitted nationality jurisdiction, this could be relied upon to make the offences in the instrument amenable to the jurisdiction of domestic courts.[27]

However, in the century that followed, this jurisdictional conservativism is said to have fallen away and a distinct pattern emerged, particularly since the 1970s. Jurisdiction became a central component of the "triadic structure of conventional duties"[28] whereby states agreed to criminalise the 'suppressed' activities, enact jurisdictional provisions to ensure those activities could be prosecuted domestically, and create a range of international co-operation mechanisms to assist with transnational enforcement. In terms of structure, a common language and format took shape. One or more jurisdictional provisions required states to ensure certain bases of jurisdiction were available domestically (mandatory jurisdiction)—most commonly, this took the form of a requirement to provide for territorial jurisdiction over offences. A multitude of permissive or optional grounds of jurisdiction also became commonplace allowing states to pick and choose other jurisdictional bases as they thought necessary. The conventions thus operated to extend the jurisdictional bases utilised by states in relation to the suppressed activities, or at least demanded their recognition vis-à-vis other State Parties to the convention.[29] A standard jurisdictional 'toolbox' emerged, allowing drafters to follow a tried-and-tested structure, often copying verbatim the provisions from one convention to the next.[30] This borrowing and building from earlier models is partly explained by continuity in some of the personnel involved in the drafting of some conventions[31] and the use of

[25] International Convention for the Suppression of Counterfeiting Currency (adopted 20 April 1929) 112 LNTS 371 ('Counterfeiting Currency Convention'). This provision was replicated in later conventions such as in Article 14 of the Convention for the Suppression of the Illicit Traffic in Dangerous Drugs, (adopted 26 June 1936) 198 LNTS 301 ('Dangerous Drugs Convention 1936').

[26] See e.g. Article 15 of the Dangerous Drugs Convention 1936 (n 25). Garrod traces this jurisdictional hesitance in treaty-making during the period of the League of Nations to a clash of views between states that adhered to a strict approach to territorial jurisdiction (in particular, in common law countries), and those that more readily utilised various bases of extraterritorial jurisdiction. See for discussion Garrod (2023a).

[27] See e.g. Article 2 of the International Convention for the Suppression of the Circulation of and Traffic in Obscene Publications (adopted 12 September 1923) 27 LNTS 214.

[28] Jeßberger (2021), p. 265.

[29] As Boister notes, "[b]y adopting a particular convention the parties make reciprocal grants of special competence on the jurisdictional principles listed in the conventions and in doing so waive their rights to object to the establishment of extraterritorial jurisdiction on the basis of these principles." See Boister (2018), p. 250.

[30] Jeßberger (2021), p. 272.

[31] See Clarke (1988), p. 86.

models during negotiations.[32] But more obviously, it is a consequence of widespread agreement with respect to the jurisdictional provisions in earlier conventions; the job of the drafter is simplified if they can point to provisions which previously garnered state support, as this can serve to placate concerns about the interpretation and implications of provisions in subsequent instruments.

One clear consequence of this has been a growth in the grounds of extraterritorial jurisdiction in suppression instruments. In an empirical investigation of 78 international and regional treaties covering transnational crimes between 1937–2017, Garrod finds that the conventions are recognising, with increasing frequency, a range of bases of extraterritorial jurisdiction.[33] Moreover, he finds that states have increasingly accepted mandatory jurisdictional bases, thus constraining domestic discretion on the establishment of jurisdiction.[34] This is consistent with Jeßberger's assessment of jurisdictional rules in suppression conventions since the late nineteenth century, where he argues that there has been a "continuous extension" of jurisdictional reach through mandatory and optional clauses.[35]

My immediate concern, however, is with respect to the use of the territoriality principle in these instruments, and the broader reliance on state 'territory' for criminalisation purposes. Here, a more muddled picture emerges because while the general trends identified above also hold true, it may be misleading to regard even the early twentieth century instruments as jurisdictionally conservative in this area. I will draw on three examples of jurisdictional provisions below to illustrate how these instruments have incentivised broad interpretations of territoriality, in order to criminalise foreign (suppressed) activities, before turning to other convention devices related to the obligation to extradite or prosecute (*aut dedere aut judicare*) which have also, in different ways, promoted a 'territorialisation' of the extraterritorial.

2.2 *Expanding the Territorial Ambit of Offences*

The first example may appear uncontroversial. The establishment of territorial jurisdiction over suppressed offences is by now a standard provision in suppression

[32] Nadelmann (1993), p. 346.

[33] See Garrod (2023a).

[34] For mandatory nationality jurisdiction see, for example, art. 5(1)(b) International Convention Against the Taking of Hostages (Adopted 17 December 1979) 1316 UNTS 205 ('Hostages Convention'); art. 3(1)(a) Convention on the Prevention and Punishment of Crimes Against Internationally Protected Persons, Including Diplomatic Agents (Adopted 14 December 1973) 1035 UNTS 167 ('Protected Persons Convention'); art. 6(1)(c) International Convention for the Suppression of Terrorist Bombings (Adopted 15 December 1997) 2149 UNTS 256 ('Terrorist Bombings Convention'); art. 6(1)(c) Convention for the Suppression of Unlawful Acts Against the Safety of Maritime Navigation (Adopted 10 March 1988) 1678 UNTS 222 ('SUA Convention').

[35] Jeßberger (2021), p. 273.

conventions, but some explicitly specify that this must include any offence that is committed 'in part' in a state's territory, or requires states to consider any of the criminal acts covered by the convention to be treated as distinct offences where committed in different countries.[36] As some of these instruments, such as the Dangerous Drugs Convention 1936, cover a wide range of primary and secondary modes of liability—from principal acts with narcotic drugs (such as their offering for sale) to secondary liability (e.g. participation in the principal offences) and inchoate offences (such as conspiracy and attempts)—these provisions could potentially greatly expand the territorial ambit of offences where ratified, particularly in common law jurisdictions like England and Wales where a rather conservative approach to territorial jurisdiction traditionally applied.[37] In transnational drugs trafficking cases it could, for example, mean that separate offences are committed in every country where drugs are imported and exported, which may appear uncontentious as a matter of stating sovereign territorial rights of punishment, but raises questions as to whether each of these countries could separately and consecutively prosecute the same individual for the 'distinct' offences, which will be discussed below.[38] This issue is particularly acute with respect to some types of transnational crime, such as cybercrime. We live, after all, in a world where someone could, at the click of a button, cause computer infections globally through the release of malware, and if the territoriality principle permits regulation by any state where the offence has been

---

[36]The OECD Convention on Combatting Bribery of Foreign Public Official in International Business Transactions, art 4(1) is an example of where a suppression instrument required states to establish jurisdiction over bribery offences that occur 'in part' in the territory of a state, while the Dangerous Drugs Convention 1936, art. 4 (n 25) is an example of where the conventions required states to consider offences that were committed in different countries as distinct offences. The latter repeated almost verbatim a similar provision in Article 4 of the Counterfeiting Currency Convention, but is more wide-reaching as it covers a broader range of principal and inchoate (e.g. conspiracy) offences. Similar provisions are to be found in e.g. art. 36(2)(a)(i) of the Single Convention on Narcotic Drugs 1961, (adopted 30 March 1961) 520 UNTS 151 (as amended by the Protocol Amending the Single Convention on Narcotic Drugs (adopted 25 March 1972) 976 UNTS 3) and art. 22(2)(a)(i) Convention on Psychotropic Substances (Adopted 21 February 1971) 1019 UNTS 175.

[37]On the terminatory theory in English law see generally Hirst (2003). Some literature continues to state that English (common) law demands that the 'last act' to have been committed in England or Wales in order for domestic courts to assume territorial jurisdiction over an offence: see e.g. Boister (2018), p. 253 and Szigeti (2019), p. 35. However, this no longer holds true following the decision in *Smith (Wallace Duncan) (No. 4)* [2004] QB 1418, which has been followed in cases such as *R v Sheppard and Whittle* [2010] EWCA Crim 65 and most recently in *Laskowski v R* [2023] EWCA Crim 493. Courts will now entertain (territorial) jurisdiction where a 'substantial measure' of the criminality has occurred within England or Wales. For academic discussion of this development see e.g. Hirst (2013), pp. 31–33, and Hörnle (2021), p. 139. See further *R v Pogmore* [2017] EWCA Crim 925 for judicial discussion of the territorial ambit of criminal jurisdiction in England and Wales, and how statutory provisions have also embraced an expansive approach to territorial jurisdiction.

[38]See *infra* Sect. 4.3. A case which directly considered this point in the context of art. 54 of the Convention Implementing the Schengen Agreement 2000 O.J. (L 239) 19 ('CISA'), is Case C-436/04 *Van Esbroeck* [2006] ECR I-2333.

committed 'in part' in its territory—and state practice clearly suggests that this is undisputed—then 'territorial' offences can be committed the world over in one fell swoop.

A second example of how these conventions have incentivised wide territorial ambits amongst State Parties are provisions providing that states may establish jurisdiction where certain inchoate and secondary participation offences were "committed outside its territory with a view to the commission, within its territory..."[39] This essentially comprises *mens rea* determining jurisdictional ambit; even if all conduct is 'extraterritorial', where relevant offences were intended[40] to occur within a particular territory, that state could establish criminal jurisdiction. Other instruments similarly incentivise criminal jurisdiction where offences are 'directed towards' the carrying out of offences in state territory,[41] which is potentially an even more enabling basis for claiming territorial jurisdiction.

The Italian case of *Hassen* illustrates how these provisions can operate in practice in domestic implementation.[42] There the question arose as to whether foreign people smugglers, who abandoned migrants on the High Seas, could be prosecuted for smuggling offences where the migrants were brought to Italy through the actions of rescuers. Though the Italian Supreme Court ultimately found that the actions of the smugglers did entail territorial offences[43]—attributing the acts of the rescuers in bringing the migrants to Italy to the people smugglers[44]—there was also reliance on Article 15(2)(c)(i) of the Convention Against Transnational Organized Crime. This is a permissive jurisdictional provision which provides that a state can establish jurisdiction over particular offences where they are "committed outside its territory with a view to the commission of a serious crime within its territory". The organised criminal group in the case was set up and operating from Libya but, it was found, *intended* serious offences on Italian territory, therefore the Court also found that the requirements of Article 15(2)(c)(i) would be met which could operate as a separate

[39] See art. 4(1)(b)(iii) United Nations Convention Against Illicit Traffic in Narcotic Drugs and Psychotropic Substances (Adopted 20 December 1988) 1582 UNTS 95 ('Narcotic Drugs Convention 1988'). Similar provisions are to be found in art. 15(2)(c) United Nations Convention Against Transnational Organized Crime (Adopted 15 November 2000) 2225 UNTS 209 ('UNCTOC') and Article 42(2)(c) United Nations Convention against Corruption (Adopted 31 October 2003) 2349 UNTS 41 ('UNCAC'). See further art. 3 of the Convention for the Prevention and Punishment of Terrorism (adopted 16 November 1937) 19 League of Nations O.J. 23 (1938), League of Nations Doc C.546(I).M.383(I).1937.V (1938) ('Terrorism Convention 1937').

[40] Depending on how the words 'with a view' are interpreted in a domestic context, even a lesser *mens rea* such as knowledge or subjective recklessness could suffice. For discussion of even negligence standards driving jurisdictional ambit in the context of US drugs trafficking laws, see Brown (2023), p. 66.

[41] See e.g. art. 7(2) Convention for the Suppression of the Financing of Terrorism (adopted 9 December 1999) 2178 UNTS 197.

[42] *Haji Hassan*, Final appeal judgment, No 14510/2014, ILDC 2876 (IT 2014), 27th March 2014.

[43] Ibid, at para A2.

[44] In common law jurisprudence, a similar result might be achieved through the doctrine of innocent agency and the continuing act theory.

jurisdictional basis for prosecution via Article 7(5) of the Italian Criminal Code.[45] Although some countries have long embraced wide interpretations of territoriality to address e.g. inchoate offences with transnational dimensions,[46] others may have traditionally been more jurisdictionally conservative but the suppression conventions can work to 'globalise' such interpretations of the territoriality principle.[47] This is of particular concern given the imprecision in drafting of elements of culpability in relation to inchoate and participatory offences in the conventions.[48]

A third example of how these instruments have expanded territorial ambits is so-called 'landing state'[49] jurisdiction.[50] In suppression instruments, this first appeared in the 1970 Convention on the Suppression of Unlawful Seizure of Aircraft (the 'Hague Convention').[51] Article 4(1)(b) obliged parties to establish jurisdiction "when the aircraft on board which the offence is committed lands in its territory with the alleged offender still on board." In terms of closing potential jurisdictional gaps, preventing impunity, and simplifying jurisdictional determinations[52] there is much to be said for 'landing state' jurisdiction. However, what it does in practice is make a criminal hotspot of the territory of every state that has ratified the instrument. The criminal act may have been committed extraterritorially, but it becomes a domestic offence, determined simply by where in the world the aircraft lands, even if that state

---

[45] *Hassan* (n 42), A4.

[46] Even English law has adopted a wide jurisdictional ambit here. As Hirst notes, English law developed special rules in cases of attempt and conspiracy "according to which jurisdiction can be asserted over any such inchoate offence that *was intended to take effect* through the commission of a substantive offence in England or Wales." See Hirst (2013), p. 34 (emphasis added). For discussion of similar approaches in the US, see Boister (2018), p. 256.

[47] Jeßberger (2021), p. 273.

[48] Clarke has long ago expressed concern about the elements of culpability in relation to offences such as conspiracy, which have "shown remarkable resiliency in finding [their] ... way into many of the treaty formulations", calling for more thought to be given to such definitional issues in the criminalisation provisions. See Clarke (1988), p. 86. Petzsche also points to the need for more doctrinal coherency in the drafting of provisions on modes of liability in suppression conventions. See Petzsche (2021).

[49] See Clarke (2014), p. 96.

[50] Some commentators have also treated 'flag state' jurisdiction over vessels, and the jurisdiction of the State of registration of aircrafts (see e.g. art. 15(1)(b) UNCTOC (n 39)) as extensions of territorial jurisdiction. See e.g. Clarke (2014), p. 96. This matter has been long debated. See, for instance, the commentaries to Article 4 of the Harvard Draft Convention on Jurisdiction with Respect to Crime, noting uncertainty and confusion on the theoretical basis for such jurisdiction, and differing views of members of the Permanent Court of International Justice in the *Lotus* case (n 10) on this point. See 'Jurisdiction with Respect to Crime' (1935) 29 AJIL Supp 435, 510. More recently, Boister refers to these bases of jurisdiction as 'quasi-territoriality' but thinks they are "actually species of nationality [jurisdiction]." Boister (2018), p. 252.

[51] Convention for the Suppression of Unlawful Seizure of Aircraft (Adopted 16 December 1970) 860 UNTS 105 (the 'Hague Convention').

[52] In other words, potentially avoiding complex decisions on when and where offences committed on board aircrafts occurred, if other bases of jurisdiction (like jurisdiction based on the state of registration) are unavailable.

has no other territorial connection with the aircraft (e.g. the aircraft was neither originally destined for or originated in that state) or the offence(s). Questions remain as to how it should apply when other states have a stronger nexus with the offence, and with respect to nationals of non-state parties to the convention.[53]

2.3 *Expanding Territorial Jurisdiction Through Aut Dedere Aut Judicare Obligations*

The final examples that I will refer to on substantive criminal jurisdiction relate to various convention provisions concerning extradition, and the obligation to extradite or prosecute. As with the jurisdictional provisions in these instruments, provisions regulating extradition were absent from the earlier suppression conventions, but soon became a regular stablemate in all of them. Typically the conventions will deem the suppressed offences to be extraditable under extradition treaties existing between Parties,[54] and will enable the suppression convention itself to serve as an extradition treaty if one party requires such for extraditions to proceed.[55] Therefore, extradition provisions in conventions normally focus only on ways to facilitate the process, rarely considering safeguards for the accused,[56] or if they do, try to prompt states into interpreting these safeguards broadly.[57] Provisions have become common which ask parties to simplify and expedite extradition procedures, lower evidential thresholds,[58] and remove barriers to extradition.[59]

However, when it comes to *jurisdiction* and extradition, even the early twentieth century suppression conventions were innovative in the way they utilised territoriality to criminalise extraterritorial conduct. Articles 8 and 9 of the Counterfeiting Currency Convention 1929, for example, employed territorial fictions in order to

[53] Clarke (2014), pp. 96–97.

[54] See art. 10 Counterfeiting Currency Convention (n 25), art. 10(1) Hostages Convention (n 34), art. 8(1) Protected Persons Convention (n 34), art. 8(1) Hague Convention (n 51), art. 11(1) SUA Convention (n 34), art. 6(2) Narcotic Drugs Convention 1988 (n 39), art. 16(3) UNCTOC (n 39) and art. 44(4) UNCAC (n 39).

[55] See e.g. art. 8(2) Hague Convention (n 51), art. 8(2), Protected Persons Convention (n 34), art. 10(2) Hostages Convention (n 34), art. 11(2) SUA Convention (n 34), art. 16(4) UNCTOC (n 39) and art. 44(5) UNCAC (n 39).

[56] One exception here is e.g. the non-discrimination clause, found in art. 9(1) Hostages Convention (n 33), Article 6(6) Narcotic Drugs Convention 1988 (n 39) and Article 44(15) UNCAC (n 39).

[57] See e.g. art. 43(2) UNCAC (n 39) which deems dual criminality requirements as being fulfilled, irrespective of legal classification, provided the underlying conduct constitutes an offence in both countries.

[58] See art. 6(7) Narcotic Drugs Convention 1988 (n 39), art. 16(8) UNCTOC (n 39) and art. 44(9) UNCAC (n 39).

[59] See e.g. art. 16(15) UNCTOC (n 39) and art. 44(16) UNCAC (n 39), which prevent parties from refusing extradition on the ground that the offence involves fiscal matters.

address situations where individuals could not be extradited to countries where the offences were committed. Article 8 addressed the situation where a State Party's domestic rules prohibited the extradition of nationals. It demanded that if a national of that state returned 'to the territory of their own country after the commission abroad of an offence ... [it] should be punishable in the same manner *as if the offence had been committed in their own territory*...'. In short, State Parties were obliged to 'territorialise' extraterritorial criminal acts, if they could not extradite their nationals to the state(s) where those acts were committed. Article 9 created the same territorial 'fiction'[60] in situations where a) a foreigner is in a State Party to the convention, having committed a relevant offence abroad b) extradition has been requested but cannot occur 'for some reason which has no connection with the offence' and c) the State Party 'recognises as a general rule the principle of the prosecution of offences committed abroad.'[61] If these threefold conditions were met, the state was obliged to take proceedings against the accused, and treat the extraterritorial offence(s) by way of this territorial fiction, even if there was no other jurisdictional nexus with the offence other than this treaty obligation. These provisions were substantially replicated in subsequent instruments like the 1936 Convention for the Suppression of the Illicit Traffic in Dangerous Drugs,[62] with others adding to[63] or tweaking the conditions required for the obligation(s) to apply. A number of other treaties continue to employ similar territorial fictions in their general extradition provisions.[64]

The conventions now also invariably contain explicit obligations to extradite or prosecute *(aut dedere aut judicare)*[65] with a variety of formulations emerging[66] but

[60] Clarke (1988), p. 59.

[61] It is unclear how this could, or should, be interpreted. For example, if a country recognised certain grounds of extraterritorial jurisdiction (like nationality) over particularly serious offences, but not counterfeiting offences, could that country be said to recognise '*as a general rule* the principle of the prosecution of offences committed abroad'?

[62] See arts. 7 and 8 of the Dangerous Drugs Convention 1936 (n 25).

[63] See e.g. art. 10(c) of the Terrorism Convention 1937 (n 39).

[64] For the purposes of extradition, offences are treated 'as if' they had been committed in the territories of states required to establish their jurisdiction due to convention obligations. The need for this fiction arose because many bilateral extradition treaties allowed extradition to proceed only if the requesting state could point to offences committed within its 'territory' or 'jurisdiction.' In order to overcome such a restriction and facilitate extradition on extraterritorial grounds, some conventions created a fiction that treated acts committed outside of the territories of the requested or requesting Parties as having been committed within them. See e.g. art. 16(1) Convention on Offences and Certain Other Acts Committed on Board Aircraft (Adopted 14 September 1963) 704 UNTS 219 ('Tokyo Convention'), art. 8(4) Convention against Torture and Other Cruel, Inhuman or Degrading Treatment or Punishment (Adopted 10 December 1984) 1465 UNTS 85 ('Torture Convention'); art. 10(4) Hostages Convention (n 34), art. 8(4) Protected Persons Convention (n 34), art. 9(4) Terrorist Bombings Convention (n 34).

[65] The Latin term is usually traced to Grotius's phrase '*aut dedere aut punire*' (extradite or punish), the modern equivalent being less presumptive of guilt.

[66] See International Law Commission Final Report, 'The Obligation to Extradite or Prosecute (aut dedere aut judicare)', in International Law Commission Report on the Work of its Sixty-Sixth

most commonly based on Article 7 of the 1970 Convention on the Suppression of Unlawful Seizure of Aircraft (known as the 'Hague formula').[67] This states that "[t]he Contracting State in the territory of which the alleged offender is found shall, if it does not extradite him, be obliged without exception whatsoever and whether or not the offence was committed in its territory, to submit the case to its competent authorities for the purpose of prosecution." This provision clearly envisages prosecutions even where the prosecuting state cannot point to jurisdiction under any of the traditional jurisdictional heads. The 'formula' therefore supplemented the general extradite or prosecute obligation with a requirement to establish a ground of jurisdiction to cater for such prosecutions. Article 4(2) obligates State Parties to "likewise take such measures as may be necessary to establish its jurisdiction over the offence in the case where the alleged offender is present in its territory and it does not extradite him pursuant to article 8 to any of the states mentioned in paragraph 1." This is, thus, a jurisdictional basis for prosecution which is distinct from the other mandatory bases mentioned in Article 4(1). The preparatory works show that this was a late amendment which was thought necessary to implement the corresponding obligation to extradite or prosecute in Article 7. The Spanish delegate who proposed the provision explained the rationale as follows:

> The reason behind [this] proposal was that Article 7, which obliged States that did not concede extradition to submit the case to their competent authorities for their decision whether to prosecute, would be a dead letter provision if the States did not have jurisdiction under Article 4, paragraphs 1 or 2. Since no mandatory extradition existed under the Convention, it was essential in its absence for the offender to be punished by the courts of the State in which he was held.[68]

The difficulty lies in trying to conceptualise what sort of jurisdiction this is where it is implemented and relied upon by a State Party for the prosecution of the suppressed activities. This question is complicated by the different forms of the *aut dedere aut judicare* (ADAJ) obligation with which the jurisdictional provision is associated. The International Law Commission (ILC) has identified two broad categories from the treaties containing such an obligation. The first category contains an obligation to prosecute only when extradition has been requested and not granted. Here, there is no *ipso facto* obligation to prosecute an alleged offender that is present in a State Party's territory, as these "conventions are structured in such a way that gives priority to extradition to the State in whose territory the crime is committed."[69] In the second category, the obligation is said to "impose an obligation to prosecute *ipso*

Session (UN Doc A/69/10), chapter VI, available at https://legal.un.org/ilc/texts/instruments/english/reports/7_6_2014.pdf (the 'ILC Report').

[67] Ibid, para 13.

[68] International Civil Aviation Organization, *International Conference of Air Law,* (The Hague, vol 1, December 1970), Doc. 8979-LC/165-1, p. 75, para 17.

[69] ILC Report (n 66), para. 12. See further ibid, para 39.

facto in that it arises as soon as the presence of the alleged offender in the territory of the State concerned is ascertained."[70]

Remarkably, given the extent to which the 'Hague formula' has served as a model for other suppression instruments,[71] the ILC note that the precise wording of the obligation in the 1970 Convention "does not unequivocally resolve the question of whether the obligation to prosecute arises *ipso facto* or only once a request for extradition is submitted and not granted."[72] This uncertainty has resulted in a large body of literature trying to understand how to frame any state implementations (and prosecutions thereunder) of the jurisdictional provision tied to the extradite or prosecute obligation in many of these conventions. Most commonly, it is treated as an instance of universal jurisdiction,[73] particularly with respect to the conventions that clearly follow the model in the second category mentioned above, or some of the jurisdictional provisions of more recent suppression conventions which incentivise the creation of jurisdiction without any express tie to a convention ADAJ obligation.[74] This framing can be defended in that it can, de-facto, operate *like* universal jurisdiction to close all jurisdictional gaps where the convention is widely ratified and where there is a primary obligation to prosecute. However, as these instruments relate to an array of crimes that are not typically associated with universal jurisdiction in standard accounts of the doctrine, some distinguish between universal jurisdiction *stricto sensu* and the jurisdictional provisions associated with the extradite or prosecute obligation.[75] Others frame the jurisdictional basis as a 'subsidiary'[76] or 'representative'[77] form of jurisdiction. This may more accurately capture

[70] Ibid, para 40.

[71] The ILC note that '[o]f the conventions drafted on or after 1970, approximately three-quarters follow the "Hague formula".' Ibid, para 13.

[72] Ibid, para 40.

[73] See e.g. Caligiuri (2018), p. 250 and d'Aspremont (2010).

[74] See e.g. art. 15(4) UNCTOC (n 39) which incentivises, but does not mandate, wider jurisdictional measures in any case where an individual is present in the territory of a State Party, alleged to have committed offences covered by the Convention, and the state does not extradite the individual. There is no corresponding extradite or prosecute obligation expressly tied to this jurisdictional provision (unlike art 15(3)). For a recent state interpretation of these provisions see: *In the Matter of Criminal Proceedings against Youssef Tartoussi*, Final appeal judgment, No 19672/2020, ILDC 3171 (IT 2020), 17th June 2020, where the Italian Supreme Court found that art 15(4) was not self-executing.

[75] See e.g. Boister (2018), p. 266. Garrod (2018) refers to these jurisdictional provisions as simply a form of 'treaty-based jurisdiction.'

[76] This treats it as subsidiary or secondary to another state's jurisdictional claim. It is noteworthy that some delegates, in the drafting of the 1970 Unlawful Seizure of Aircraft Convention (n 48), referred to art. 4(2) as a form of 'subsidiary criminal jurisdiction', suggesting that the Hague 'formula' was envisaged to accord jurisdictional priority to a forum State that requested extradition. See International Conference on Air Law, vol. I, (n 68) at 74. Garrod, however, notes that there were mixed interventions from delegates on this point, with some referring to art. 4(2) as creating 'universal jurisdiction.' See Garrod (2023b), p. 130.

[77] Kreß (2006), p. 567 argues that the distinct nature and purpose of this jurisdiction should be separated from 'true' universal jurisdiction by recognising a sub-category comprising a

the first category of jurisdictional provision noted above, which operates where the obligation to prosecute applies following a request for extradition by another state that was not granted.[78]

An alternative way of framing these provisions, however, is to simply treat them as instances of 'territorial jurisdiction over persons for extraterritorial events.'[79] This was how Judges Higgins, Kooijmans and Buergenthal, in the International Court of Justice, understood the extradite or prosecute provisions in a number of conventions following the Hague formula.[80] This view highlights the crucial role that the location of the accused plays in determining whether a state has jurisdiction over the offence (s). Like 'landing state' jurisdiction, it creates a criminal hotspot of the territory of every state that has ratified the instrument, with varying conditions across the different suppression instruments determining when this becomes a domestic offence. Criminality is determined by where in the world a suspect is *found*, regardless of where in the world the crime was *committed.* While this is thus distinguishable from convention provisions that incentivise states to expand framings of territoriality in domestic criminal offences,[81] 'territory' is still playing a crucial role.

Regardless of how particular ADAJ jurisdictional provisions are conceptualised, what is clear is that they can serve to expand jurisdictional ambits over transnational offences,[82] and increase instances of jurisdictional concurrency. What is also clear is

'representative universal jurisdiction principle.' Boister (2018), p. 266, on the other hand, refers to it as a form of "'representative or vicarious administration of justice' based on territorial jurisdiction over the presence of the alleged offender".

[78] Provisions such as art. 16(10) UNCTOC (n 39) and art. 44(11) UNCAC (n 39) are clearly in this mould. The obligation to submit the case for the purpose of prosecution arises there only "at the request of the State Party seeking extradition." Prosecution via any domestic implementations of the associated jurisdictional provisions of art. 15(3) UNCTOC and art 42(3) UNCAC, could thus be interpreted as a form 'representation' of the requesting state.

[79] *Arrest Warrant of 11 April 2000 (Democratic Republic of the Congo* v. *Belgium)*, Judgment (2002) ICJ Rep 3; para. 42 (Joint Separate Opinion of Judges Higgins, Kooijmans and Buergenthal).

[80] The judges critiqued the "loose use of language" whereby the jurisdictional provisions associated with the extradite or prosecute obligation became referred to as 'universal jurisdiction.' Ibid.

[81] In other words, the territoriality of the criminal acts or omissions is not the animating force behind the ADAJ jurisdictional provisions and states are not e.g. being asked to treat or deem the 'extraterritorial' events as having been committed in the territory of the state that is seeking to comply with the prosecute or extradite obligation.

[82] An example of an incredibly expansive jurisdictional approach to a convention provision like this is s. 35(2) of the South Africa Prevention and Combatting of Corrupt Activities Act 2004. This section criminalises extraterritorial acts, even if they were not criminal offences where they were committed (rejecting dual criminality), and 'deems' them to have been committed domestically where a. the act 'affects or is intended to affect' a person or entity in South Africa b. the suspect is found in South Africa and c. the person isn't extradited, or no application to extradite the person is received in South Africa. This combines the jurisdictional devices discussed above concerning *mens rea,* territorial fictions, and the ADAJ principle, and illustrates how provisions like art. 42(4) UNCAC (n 39) can incentivise expansive jurisdictional interpretations in domestic

that the provisions in the second category identified by the ILC above, in particular, have significant potential for generating jurisdictional conflict between countries that have ratified these instruments. This is for a couple of reasons. First, uncertainty prevails over how some of these provisions can be interpreted by states. One State (A) may have ratified a suppression convention and applied the ADAJ jurisdictional provision on the (reasonable) assumption that it fell within the first category. On this basis, it may expect that another State (B) would not prosecute an offence that occurred in the territory of State A, unless State A has requested extradition, this has been refused, and there was a subsequent request by State A for prosecution in State B. Such uncertainty has already generated litigation between countries before the International Court of Justice.[83] The second related reason is that in this example, State A may clearly have a stronger jurisdictional claim over the wrongdoing as the harm may all have been sustained within that country. Where the only jurisdictional nexus that State B can point to is a vague and (often) contestable ADAJ jurisdictional provision in a treaty, and the presence of the accused in its territory, State A may well view State B as having a weaker jurisdictional claim over the case, or even a legally impermissible claim if it disagrees over the interpretation of whether the relevant treaty provision fell within the first or second of the general categories outlined above.

This suggests that many of these treaty provisions are in need of quite urgent rationalisation. It also suggests that the conclusion by the ILC that "when drafting treaties, States can decide for themselves which conventional formula on the obligation to extradite or prosecute best suits their objective in a particular circumstances",[84] was cursory, uncritical, and did not do not enough to spell out the jurisdictional risks for states in choosing one over another formula.

3 Expanding the (Extra)territoriality of Enforcement Jurisdiction

Beyond requiring the criminalisation of the 'suppressed' activities, one of the main mechanisms for achieving the aims of a suppression convention is to require states to implement procedural powers which are deemed necessary for the investigation and prosecution of the offences contained in the convention. Domestic use of these powers to suppress local criminal activities indirectly assists foreign states, and it also facilitates international co-operation in the form of, for example, mutual legal assistance (MLA) measures. However, for some, these procedures move too slowly

---

implementation. As the preamble to the 2004 Act makes clear, South Africa enacted the statute desiring 'to be in compliance' with the UNCAC.

[83] *Questions Relating to the Obligation to Prosecute or Extradite (Belgium* v. *Senegal)*, Judgment (2012) ICJ Rep 422.

[84] ILC Report (n 66), para 12.

for policing many types of transnational crime, and the suppression process has been alive to this, charting paths for law enforcement to navigate around traditional territorial (enforcement) limitations, and with this, the safeguards that usually inhere in MLA procedures.

In this section I will focus on certain procedural powers contained in the Cybercrime Convention to demonstrate that in the realm of enforcement jurisdiction, an expansive approach to the (extra)territoriality of investigative powers is also being incentivised there. The procedural provisions of this instrument are significant because State Parties to the Convention agree to apply the powers and procedures not only to the cybercrimes that are enumerated for in the Convention, but also to "any other criminal offences committed by means of a computer system" and "the collection of evidence in electronic form of a criminal offence."[85] Given that in almost every transnational crime and trafficking investigation, 'evidence in electronic form' will play a part in one way or another,[86] powers enacted pursuant to the Convention may apply far beyond the context of cybercrime enforcement.

What is particularly striking about the expansive jurisdictional approach in the Cybercrime Convention is how it cuts against the traditionally (territorially) circumscribed approach to enforcement jurisdiction in international law, as noted in the introduction, but also in other suppression instruments. Provisions like Art 2(3) of the 1988 Narcotic Drugs Convention state that "[a] Party shall not undertake in the territory of another Party the exercise of jurisdiction and performance of functions which are exclusively reserved for the authorities of that other Party by its domestic law."[87] In the context of extraterritorial data requests and data interventions (like hacking), when and how jurisdiction can be said to be 'exercised' in another state territory, or a function 'performed' there, are questions of the utmost contemporary significance. Kohl, against the current of much of the literature on this topic, contends that the law of enforcement jurisdiction will rarely be engaged by data requests, as it is an area of law concerned with prohibiting 'physical displays' of state functions in the territory of another state.[88] Others attempt to distinguish enforcement jurisdiction from 'investigative jurisdiction' which could apply to extraterritorial data requests and other forms of data interventions,[89] but there is hitherto insufficient evidence of this latter category as a matter of customary international law, or a clear understanding of its parameters or the principles that could guide its

[85] See art. 14(2)(b)&(c).

[86] In one EU study it was estimated that electronic evidence is relevant in "around 85% of total (criminal) investigations." See Commission Staff Working Document: Impact Assessment accompanying the document Proposal for a Regulation of the European Parliament and of the Council on European Production and Preservation Orders for electronic evidence in criminal matters and Proposal for a Directive of the European Parliament and of the Council laying down harmonised rules on the appointment of legal representatives for the purpose of gathering evidence in criminal proceedings (17 April 2018, SWD (2018) 119), p. 14.

[87] See also e.g. art. 4(2) in both the UNCAC (n 39) and UNCTOC (n 39).

[88] Kohl (2023), p. 210.

[89] See Hörnle (2021), p. 7.

exercise. While space does not permit for further analysis of this debate, what can be assumed for the purposes of this chapter is that the legality of extraterritorial data interventions and requests can be uncertain and difficult to determine as a matter of international law, with customary international law in a state of flux, and in such an environment states may be expected to exercise particular care in crafting provisions in international agreements that may engage the law of extraterritorial enforcement jurisdiction. It is against this backdrop that I will consider two provisions in the Cybercrime Convention—Articles 18 and 32—to illustrate how they are, rather, promoting an expansive interpretation of territoriality in domestic procedural powers and facilitating a policing of the extraterritorial in implementation, by purporting to allow states to directly apply their domestic powers of production to data and legal entities outside of the requesting state.

3.1 Article 18

Article 18 of the Convention requires Parties to implement a production order, of which there are two forms mentioned: the first requires "a person in its territory to submit specified computer data in that person's *possession or control*..."[90] (the 'person-in-territory' production order); the second requires "a service provider *offering its services in the territory* of the Party to submit subscriber information relating to such services in that service provider's possession or control"[91] (the service-in-territory production order).

The potential scope of the person-in-territory production order is illustrated by the US *Microsoft Warrant* case.[92] Here US authorities served an order on Microsoft in the US to obtain data, including the contents of emails, relating to one of its customers. The contents of the emails were stored on a server located in Dublin. Microsoft argued, *inter alia,* that the particular procedural power at play in the case (a warrant under section 2703(a) of the Stored Communications Act ('SCA'))[93] could not be used to compel data held extraterritorially[94] and would require mutual legal assistance. The case was proceeding to the US Supreme Court[95] before

---

[90] Art. 18(1)(a).

[91] Art. 18(1)(b).

[92] See *Warrant to Search a Certain E-Mail Account Controlled and Maintained by Microsoft Corp*, 829 F3d 197 (2d Cir 2016) ('Microsoft Warrant Case').

[93] 18 USC §§ 2701–2713 (as amended by the Clarifying Lawful Overseas use of Data (CLOUD) Act, Pub L No 115-141, 132 Stat 1213 (2018).

[94] On this argument, it was seeking to distinguish the warrant from the operation of subpoenas which, in the US, have long been used to compel the production of business records and documents stored extraterritorially. In *Tiffany v Andrew* 276 FRD 143, 147-8 (SDNY 2011), for example, it was said "[i]f the party subpoenaed has the practical ability to obtain the documents, the actual physical location of the documents – even if overseas – is immaterial."

[95] *United States v Microsoft Corp*, 138 S Ct 356 (2017), vacated as moot, 138 S Ct 1186 (2018).

Congress intervened through the Clarifying Lawful Overseas Use of Data Act ('CLOUD Act').[96] The SCA's new § 2713, now requires service providers that are subject to US jurisdiction to disclose data pursuant to SCA requests "within such provider's possession, custody, or control, regardless of" the location of the data.[97] The similarities in language with Article 18(1)(a) are striking,[98] and two issues are worth highlighting that are of relevance to both the Convention provision, and the newly enacted US provision (§ 2713). First, these provisions fixate on a territorial or other jurisdictional connection (a person 'in its territory'[99] or service providers that are regulated in the US and subject to US jurisdiction[100]), to justify a wider extraterritorial reach in enforcement power in relation to foreign data. In US law, this is now explicit in the provision.[101] In the Convention, a guidance note on Article 18 has similarly suggested that the provision should be interpreted to apply to extraterritorial data.[102] This clearly risks generating international (jurisdictional) conflicts, when the state(s) where the data is located (when identifiable) takes issue with the enforcement action or where the data sought raises other sovereignty concerns for foreign states.[103] Second, as alluded to above, it is fair to say that the international law of jurisdiction is not settled with respect to such extraterritorial production orders, making it even more remarkable that a general provision of this nature has made its way into an international agreement. While US courts have long ordered domestic entities to produce documents and business records held extraterritorially under threat of subpoena,[104] thus essentially treating them as territorial exercises of jurisdiction, the courts of other countries have framed such

---

[96] CLOUD Act § 103(a)(1).

[97] 18 USC § 2713.

[98] It is beyond the scope of the current piece to consider US influence on the drafting of the Cybercrime Convention, or the extent to which the Convention has influenced US domestic law, but it is known that the US and other non-Council of Europe countries (e.g. Canada, Japan, and South Africa) were involved in drafting the Convention and the text of the Convention suggests that the US had a powerful role in shaping the normative content of many provisions of this instrument.

[99] This term is not defined in the Convention or the Explanatory Report to the Convention, though in the Guidance note on Article 18, there is mention of legal or physical presence, which could be interpreted broadly even if e.g. a company is not headquartered in a particular country but still 'in its territory.' See Cybercrime Convention Committee, 'T-CY Guidance Note #10: Production orders for subscriber information (Article 18 Budapest Convention) (Council of Europe, 2017), para 3.2 ('Article 18 Guidance Note').

[100] For discussion of when the US will consider that it has 'personal jurisdiction' over a service provider in the context of the SCA, see Cochrane (2021), pp. 166–169.

[101] 'Located within or outside the United States.' See 18 USC § 2713.

[102] See 'Article 18 Guidance Note' (n 97), para 3.5: 'The storage of subscriber information in another jurisdiction does not prevent the application of Article 18 Budapest Convention as long as such data is in the possession or control of the service provider.'

[103] As Cochrane (2021), p. 170 has noted, the US purportedly sought to reduce jurisdictional conflict through the CLOUD Act, but "18 USC § 2713, risks precisely the opposite, i.e. intensifying conflicts."

[104] See e.g. *United States v Bank of Nova Scotia I*, 619 F.2d 1384 (11th Cir 1982).

orders as 'extraterritorial' and thus as impermissible.[105] The latter may be consistent with FA Mann's characterisation of (domestically served) discovery orders as indirect extraterritorial enforcement jurisdiction.[106] None of this is to say that there are not compelling arguments for focusing on the location of a provider, and its control or possession of data, rather than the location at any moment of highly fluid data, for determining jurisdictional competence. But the guidance note clearly belies the complexity of the jurisdictional reach of the power, where it advocates this expansive extraterritorial interpretation, without clearly articulating and acknowledging how other sovereign interests can be engaged in such enforcement practices.

Article 18(1)(b) is also capable of interpretation to permit of wide extraterritoriality in enforcement, albeit only with respect to "subscriber data". Walden long ago observed that a possible interpretation of the provision was that it may "mean that an order may be served where both entity and data reside in a foreign jurisdiction."[107] On both fronts, the guidance note to Article 18 has advocated the widest possible (extraterritorial) interpretation. A service provider is said to be 'offering its services in the territory' of the Party ordering production, simply by enabling persons in the territory to subscribe to its services,[108] and the guidance note specifically suggests that parties could apply the provision even where the provider "is neither legally nor physically present in the territory."[109] On the relevance of the location of data, the guidance note again suggests that this is not determinative as to the jurisdictional ambit of any production powers enacted pursuant to the convention obligations in Article 18: "[r]egarding Article 18.1.b, a situation may include a service provider that has its headquarters in one jurisdiction, but stores the data in another jurisdiction."[110]

This further illustrates the protean nature of territoriality, and how it is being instrumentalised in the suppression process to expand investigative powers extraterritorially. Article 18 demands the creation of production powers with certain territorial anchors (e.g. persons 'in territory', or where services are offered 'in the territory'), but which are then being relied upon to justify expansive jurisdictional reach. The guidance note suggests that location of data is not determinative for jurisdictional purposes,[111] but this must be a context-dependent question and the location of data *can* be an important jurisdictional consideration for many states,[112]

---

[105] See e.g. the UK case of *R (KBR Inc) v Director of the Serious Fraud Office* [2021] UKSC 2. The Supreme Court ruled that even a domestically served notice could not compel a non-UK company to produce documents held outside the UK, relying on the presumption against extraterritoriality. For analysis see Cochrane (2022).

[106] See Mann (1985), p. 49.

[107] Walden (2013), p. 50.

[108] See 'Article 18 Guidance Note' (n 99), para 3.6.

[109] Ibid, para 3.2.

[110] Ibid, para 3.5.

[111] Ibid, para 3.5.

[112] In the *Microsoft Warrant* case (n 92), for example, there were some suggestions from some prominent Irish lawyers and commentators that directly accessing the (Irish-stored) data via a US

and sometimes determinative. While the guidance note does include some 'savers' suggesting that it is not binding,[113] and that "[a]greement to this Guidance Note does not entail consent to the extraterritorial service or enforcement of a domestic production order issued by another State nor creates new obligations or relationships between the Parties",[114] this is incongruous with other parts of the document, and might be said to be a case of the Cybercrime Convention Committee seeking to have their cake, and eating it. The guidance note is said to "represent the common understanding of the Parties to this treaty regarding the use of the Convention."[115] Even if one line carves out the possibility of states refusing to consent to the extraterritorial service and enforcement of production orders in individual cases, thus hoping to placate those with concerns about the implications for state sovereignty, the general thrust of the document is to suggest that State Parties ought to prepare for data stored 'in' their territory being directly accessed via a production order served in another country, and for service providers 'in' their territory to be served directly with production orders from foreign governments. The carrot is that states can in turn expect to exercise such powers in specified circumstances, at least in the territories of other State Parties to the Convention.[116]

3.2 *Article 32*

Another provision in the Cybercrime Convention that seeks to (at least partially) address the problem of "un-territoriality of data"[117] in cybercrime investigations is Article 32. Article 32(a) is (relatively) uncontroversial, and must now represent customary international law on the matter addressed therein; it states that a Party may, without the authorisation of another Party 'access publicly available (open source) stored computer data, regardless of where the data is located geographically.' Article 32(b), however, is more controversial, and is potentially an alternative source of authority for seeking data from foreign, globally operating, service providers. This

order, may be a breach of Irish sovereignty. See O'Connor (2014). See also 'Brief of *Amicus Curiae* Anthony J. Colangelo, International Law Scholar, in Support of Appellant', *Microsoft Warrant Case* (15 December 2014). Having said that, the Irish government did not directly claim in its amicus curiae brief that Ireland's territorial sovereignty would be engaged in the case (23 December 2014). See https://blogs.microsoft.com/wp-content/uploads/sites/149/2014/09/Ireland-AmicusBrief.pdf. While Ireland signed the Cybercrime Convention in 2002, it is yet to ratify it. The international legality of any enforcement in Ireland could therefore not be determined on the basis of Article 18(1)(a) of the Convention.

[113] See 'Article 18 Guidance Note' (n 99), para 1.

[114] Ibid, para 3.3.

[115] Ibid, para 1.

[116] A treaty cannot create rights or obligations for third states. See Article 34 of the 1969 Vienna Convention on the Law of Treaties (1155 UNTS 331) ('the Vienna Convention').

[117] See on the un-territoriality of data: Daskal (2015).

allows a Party, without the authorisation of another Party, "to access or receive, through a computer system *in its territory*, stored computer data located in another Party, if the Party obtains the *lawful and voluntary consent of the person who has the lawful authority to disclose the data to the Party*."[118]

This provision has its roots in the G8 Principles on "transborder access to stored data",[119] which is in substantially similar terms.[120] Article 32(b) is a rather innocuous provision on first glance, but is the most controversial in the entire Convention, and widely known to be one of the main reasons for some countries, like Russia, refusing to sign or ratify the Convention. It has been described as the "most important provision on transborder access foreseen in the Convention",[121] was the result of protracted negotiations, but remains "often misunderstood."[122] This is not helped by the lack of publication of the *travaux préparatoires* for the convention, although the drafters apparently left "'constructive ambiguity' so that it could address different situations."[123]

While it is commonly assumed that Article 32(b) is authority for the law enforcement agencies of states to send requests for data extraterritorially,[124] there are numerous points of contention concerning this interpretation of Article 32(b), such as the meaning of "lawful and voluntary consent" and "lawful authority to disclose."[125] A guidance note[126] was again published to assist State Parties on these, and many other, interpretative points, and the key issues for present purposes, are i) whether a "person" can include a legal entity, such as a cloud service provider, and ii) whether the provision permits directly contacting a (legal) person when they are located or otherwise established in a foreign territory.

The guidance note again gives a wide interpretation of these issues. On the "person" that can consent to disclosure of data, the note suggests it can be a physical person, but also a legal person.[127] But in departing somewhat from its first draft

---

[118] Emphasis added.

[119] Released at the Ministerial Conference of the G8 Countries on Combatting Transnational Organized Crime, (Moscow, October 19–20, 1999).

[120] Unlike Article 32, however, the principles required searching states to "consider notifying the searched State, if such notification is permitted by national law and the data reveals a violation of criminal law or otherwise appears to be of interest to the searched State." Ibid.

[121] T-CY, 'Transborder Access and Jurisdiction: What are the Options?' (Council of Europe, 2012), para. 89.

[122] Ibid, para. 295.

[123] Ibid, para. 95.

[124] See e.g. the UNODC 'Comprehensive Study on Cybercrime' (February 2013), 219.

[125] The Explanatory Report to the Convention provides little explanation or assistance on any of these issues, stating vaguely that "[w]ho is a person that is "lawfully authorised" to disclose data may vary depending on the circumstances, the nature of the person and the applicable law concerned." See Explanatory Report to the Cybercrime Convention, para. 294.

[126] Cybercrime Convention Committee, 'T-CY Guidance Note # 3: Transborder access to data (Article 32)' (Council of Europe, 2014) ('Article 32 Guidance Note').

[127] Ibid, para. 3.6.

guidance note on the provision,[128] it currently states that "[s]ervice providers are highly unlikely to be able to consent validly and voluntarily to disclosure of their users' data."[129] The only reason provided for this is because "they will not control or own the data."[130] This seems to conflate the authority to disclose with the issue of whether a service provider can voluntarily consent. It also implies that if the law applicable to the services *was* such that the service providers did 'control' or 'own' the data, the data could be provided transnationally to foreign law enforcement agencies.

On whether that 'person' can be in a foreign territory, the guidance note admits that "[t]he standard hypothesis is that the person providing access is physically located in the territory of the requesting Party. However, multiple situations are possible."[131] The note specifically suggests that a legal person could be located in a third country when co-operating.[132] This contradicts the views of Henrik Kaspersen, the "father"[133] of the Convention who chaired the Committee of Experts on Crime in Cyber-space responsible for drafting the Convention.[134] Kaspersen previously stated that

> [t]he person who co-operates with law enforcement authorities in the case of art. 32(b) is present in the territory of [the] investigating Party ... and cannot be used to obtain co-operation of a person that does not fall under the jurisdiction of the investigating State.[135]

Therefore, the guidance note on Article 32 again illustrates an effort to 'territorialise the extraterritorial' through the suppression process, by regularising direct interaction between law enforcement authorities of one country, and individuals or legal entities in another, and by providing a guise of (international) legality for them. Through a tenuous territorial hook (the data being accessible through a computer system *in its territory*) states can access extraterritorial data located in another State Party, where it secures the co-operation of a person or legal entity, even if they are also located outside of the requesting state. The (supposedly) deliberate 'constructive ambiguity' in relation to Article 32(b) was moulded to suit the interests of law

---

[128] The February 2013 Draft of the Guidance Note, para. 3.5, stated "the person providing access may be an Internet or cloud service provider ... if the terms of service or contract permit this."

[129] Article 32 Guidance Note (n 126), para. 3.6.

[130] Ibid.

[131] Ibid, para 3.8.

[132] Ibid.

[133] S Schjolberg 'The History of Global Harmonization on Cybercrime Legislation: The Road to Geneva' (2014), p. 2. Available at: http://www.cybercrimelaw.net/documents/cybercrime_history.pdf.

[134] Kaspersen (2006), p. 9.

[135] H Kaspersen 'Cybercrime and Jurisdiction' (2009) Council of Europe Discussion Paper, para 81. This aspect of the Guidance note neither sits well with provisions of previous Council of Europe guidelines which suggest that "domestic law enforcement authorities should be encouraged not to direct requests directly to non-domestic Internet Service Providers." Council of Europe, 'Guidelines for the cooperation between law enforcement and internet service providers against cybercrime' (2008), para. 36.

enforcement, which is very much in keeping with the general trend of suppression conventions. But it is concerning because it incentivises a form of transnational (voluntary) co-operation that is poorly regulated either as a matter of domestic or international law, with significant risks for the security of data transmission procedures,[136] and the fundamental rights of those implicated in the requests.[137] It has, nevertheless, been influential even amongst states that are not party to the Cybercrime Convention.[138]

3.3 *The Future of 'Direct Access'*

From the perspective of suppressing crime, it may of course be a laudable and necessary aim to seek to regulate foreign service providers—and the liquid data that they hold—when they are implicated in criminal activities through the activities of their users. But these 'direct access' mechanisms can clearly generate concerns for international co-operation, where other states may also have legitimate sovereignty claims over the data or service providers implicated in the case.[139] Even where there is bilateral consent for co-operation between law enforcement in one country, and a service provider in another, this may not be sufficient to determine international legality which may be a "multifactorial rather than binary question."[140]

Nevertheless, the trajectory at both the bilateral and multilateral level is for increasing mechanisms for 'direct access', whereby law enforcement in one country can serve legal orders directly on entities in other countries. At the bilateral level, US CLOUD Act agreements are the platform for this new generation of direct access

[136] While some of the major service providers provide relatively secure communication channels for 'voluntary co-operation', others reportedly respond to police requests originating from generic email accounts with no secure mechanisms for verifying the authenticity of the request, or the transmission of data. See generally the 'Practical Guide for Requesting Electronic Evidence Across Borders' (UNODC, 2021).

[137] The EU's Article 29 Data Protection Working Party, for example, raised issues with how service providers could provide data 'voluntarily' whilst remaining in compliance with data protection law, but this was given short shrift by the Cybercrime Transborder Group. See Transborder Group Report 'Transborder Access to Data and Jurisdiction: Options for Further Action by the T-CY' (T-CY 2014 16, 3rd December, 2014), para. 2.2.4.

[138] See e.g. section 39(2B) of the Singapore Criminal Procedure Code, which was reportedly 'inspired' by art. 32(b) and has greatly expanded remote access powers over extraterritorial data.

[139] It is not difficult to imagine how this could generate international conflict. In the *Microsoft Warrant* case, for example, it was argued that the exercise of jurisdiction in relation to foreign data would set a precedent which would outrage the "American people" if the converse occurred, whereby a foreign government compelled a local service provider to produce information about a "New York Times reporter, a Member of Congress, or a federal judge." See *re Warrant to Search a Certain E-mail Account Controlled and Maintained by Microsoft Corp*, Microsoft Reply Brief (July 24 2014), 1.

[140] Cochrane (2021), p. 187.

mechanisms, and the first agreements have been signed with the UK[141] and Australia.[142] At the multilateral level, the EU's e-Evidence Regulation has recently been adopted,[143] and within the Council of Europe, an important development is the Second Additional Protocol to the Budapest Convention on Cybercrime on enhanced co-operation and disclosure of electronic evidence.[144] The most significant aspect of the latter, for present purposes, is that it allows State Parties to directly order the production of subscriber and domain name registration information—but not traffic or content data—from foreign service providers.[145] It thus renders explicit some of what was (argued to be) implicit in Article 18 of the Convention, and expressly addresses the privacy and data protection implications of these orders.[146] It also moves away from requiring *any* territorial 'hook' with respect to the information, service, or service providers implicated in the orders. The domain name registration services can be provided entirely 'in the territory of another Party' and still subject to domestic legal process.[147] Likewise, subscriber information can be requested from service providers that are 'in the territory of another Party'.[148] At the multilateral level then, this new generation of direct access mechanisms are an even wider jurisdictional approach, but with third country and other indirect effects in practice still a significant likelihood.[149]

It may be argued that this 'direct access' trend in the Second Additional Protocol is tempered and limited by the possibility of reservations and additional conditions for direct service provider compliance, as catered for within the terms of the instrument.[150] The argument here could be that ratification of these instruments

[141] Agreement between the Government of the United Kingdom of Great Britain and Northern Ireland and the Government of the United States of America on Access to Electronic Data for the Purpose of Countering Serious Crime (Washington DC, October 3, 2019).

[142] Agreement between the Government of the United States of America and the Government of Australia on Access to Electronic Data for the Purpose of Countering Serious Crime (15 December 2021).

[143] See EU Regulation 2023/1543 of the European Parliament and of the Council of 12 July 2023 on European Production Orders and European Preservation Orders for electronic evidence in criminal proceedings and for the execution of custodial sentences following criminal proceedings [2023] OJ L191/118.

[144] Second Additional Protocol (n 14). As of the end of August 2023, the Protocol has 42 signatories, with two ratifications. It will enter into force after five ratifications.

[145] Second Additional Protocol (n 14), arts 6(1)–7(1).

[146] Second Additional Protocol (n 14), art 14.

[147] Second Additional Protocol (n 14), art 6(1).

[148] Second Additional Protocol (n 14), art 7(1).

[149] For example, the provisions continue to employ the concepts of 'possession and control.' See Second Additional Protocol (n 14), arts 6(1)–7(1).

[150] See e.g. Second Additional Protocol (n 14), art. 7(9)(a) and art. 7(5). This clearly evidences efforts to compromise and satisfy diverse state and law enforcement interests, and a hesitancy in ceding territorial sovereignty.

will be low, due to the potential risks for state sovereignty domestically, or that these 'direct access' risks will be toothless in practice, as states will avail widely of the reservation provisions. It is too early to assess how the Second Additional Protocol will be taken up by states, although some have already indicated that they will indeed be entering reservations concerning the direct access provision for subscriber information.[151] However, the counterargument here is to focus on the macro trends as revealed by these provisions in the Second Additional Protocol, and the wider significance of some of the provisions in the Second Additional Protocol. Article 6, concerning direct access to domain name registration information, is illustrative here. The UK, for example, has already indicated that it is 'compliant' with this provision, pointing to the terms and conditions of one domain name registry (Nominet, the registry for .uk domain names) located in Oxford. This suggests express consent to direct foreign service of orders within the UK, and consent to extraterritorial data requests being mediated through the terms and conditions of a private company.[152]

Moreover, concerning direct access to subscriber information, the UK has indicated that it will keep any reservation under review and "may later seek to lift or address the reservation if an evidence base can be developed to suggest that it is worthwhile doing so."[153] The compelling law enforcement narratives that will inform these assessments, both before and after ratification, should not be underestimated here. States require timely access to data held by globally operating service providers for even routine criminal investigations into domestic assaults or other such crimes. For those states that are unable to secure this via voluntary co-operation or other formal interstate processes, they may well view these direct access mechanisms in instruments like the Second Additional Protocol as attractive. This will require weighing up the potential law enforcement gains for domestic investigations, as against any risks to sovereignty and other rights which can be engaged in direct access requests, appreciating that the former can only be realised through reciprocal grants of competence to other states in the 'club' of suppression conventions. When understood as part of the wider trends, where direct access has been developing first informally between globally operating service providers and foreign law enforcement,[154] and now more formally through bilateral and multilateral instruments (implied, but now express), we appear to be at the precipice of a new phenomenon in the 'suppression process' that is only likely to gain further traction moving forwards. Interstate processes like MLA will either be undergirded, or circumvented

---

[151] See e.g. the UK's 'Explanatory Memorandum on the Second Additional Protocol to the Council of Europe Convention on Cybercrime on enhanced co-operation and disclosure of electronic evidence' (2022, CP 734), para. 5.

[152] This consent would also presumably extend to other domain name service providers (e.g. domain name registrars) operating from the UK, where their terms and conditions and internal policies also anticipate cooperation with foreign law enforcement.

[153] UK's Explanatory Memorandum (n 151), para 5.

[154] See e.g. 'Practical Guide for Requesting Electronic Evidence Across Borders' (UNODC, 2021), Sect. 2.3.

altogether, by the direct movement of investigative and evidential material from private entities in one country, and law enforcement in another. The result could be transformative for the investigative capabilities of domestic law enforcement agencies. 'Extraterritorial' evidence may no longer be off-limits or too cumbersome or costly to acquire through interstate co-operation mechanisms; it may instead be accessible to any law enforcement agent with access to a computer and an internet connection. It will also mean that service providers will likely take on an even greater role in this process moving forwards, essentially supplanting the *interstate* co-operation frameworks that determined when material could move from one state to another, and with it the safeguards that inhered in that system. This is not a role that service providers want or one that many will feel equipped to take on, and few will have a meaningful incentive to fulfil the role whilst respecting the fundamental rights of the affected person(s) in these requests.

In the next section I situate these 'direct access' jurisdictional trajectories alongside the wider jurisdictional trends that were identified in Sect. 2, to argue that they are uneasy (jurisdictional) bedfellows in suppression instruments and that there has been insufficient attention given to the consequences of these trajectories colliding in the suppression process.

4 Uneasy Bedfellows

4.1 (Not) Addressing Jurisdictional Concurrency in Suppression Conventions

The widespread agreement to an ever expanding range of jurisdictional bases in suppression instruments shows an enduring commitment to preventing impunity to secure transnational public goods, like protecting from the harms of trafficking offences. Such is the commitment to these global prohibition regimes that states are willing to forgo aspects of their territorial sovereignty via multilateralism; historically, this occurred by accepting that, for example, foreign states could exercise extraterritorial prescriptive jurisdiction over what may be entirely domestic affairs, but more recently there is growing evidence that states are even willing to create in-roads in the realms of enforcement jurisdiction by allowing foreign states to directly exercise certain powers in domestic territory. States clearly recognise the potential for jurisdictional overlap over data and defendants, but this is accepted and, in some quarters, not treated as something that is of any practical concern. For example, concerning substantive criminal jurisdiction Scassa and Currie observe that "[s]imply because a state notionally has jurisdiction does not necessarily mean that it will have any interest in exercising it,"[155] while Schultz contends that "[t]he submission of Internet actors to a worldwide range of paper rules may be true, but their

[155] Scassa and Currie (2011), p. 1026.

submission to effective rules is far more limited."[156] Indeed, Ram, a lawyer for the Canadian Department of Justice, delivered a paper in 2011 with one section titled "the non-problem of concurrent or overlapping jurisdiction",[157] a perspective which has also undoubtedly been behind some of the jurisdictional provisions in suppression conventions. For example, in the preparatory works for the Convention against Transnational Organized Crime (UNCTOC) it was said that

> [c]oncurrent jurisdiction might not be a negative development, as it would indicate the interest of numerous States to deal with specific problems. In addition, conflicts of jurisdiction were rather rare and were invariably resolved at the practical level by an eventual determination of which jurisdiction would be ultimately exercised on the basis of the chances for successful prosecution and adjudication of the particular case.[158]

Ram elaborates on why, even in an era of cybercrime, jurisdictional concurrency can be regarded as a 'non-problem':

> [i]n general, and increasingly in the era of globalization, scenarios such as mass-frauds and cybercrime do raise competing jurisdictional interests, but the understandable desire of States where victims reside and serious effects are felt to take a leading role in prosecution and punishment is often tempered by the costs and complexities of conducting a multinational prosecution and of incarcerating the offender, especially over long periods, if he or she is convicted.[159]

These are undoubtedly practical realities and help explain how jurisdictional concurrency was posited—albeit hesitantly—as potentially even a positive development in the UNCTOC drafting discussions. This view can be said to prioritise the eradication of jurisdictional lacunae, focusing efforts on addressing negative, rather than positive, conflicts of jurisdiction in the investigation and prosecution of transnational crime. Positive conflicts, or "conflicts of exercise of jurisdiction",[160] are said to be rare, and can be addressed through law enforcement consultation and co-ordination. Negative conflicts, on the other hand, are 'statutory' conflicts of jurisdiction,[161] which arise whenever there is concurrent criminal jurisdiction over acts, with none of the relevant countries exercising their potential enforcement power. The latter are clearly treated as the greater concern in the suppression process. The fear is that transnational criminals will operate in a place where no state can exercise criminal jurisdiction. The expansion of jurisdictional grounds in suppression conventions, and placing obligations on states to investigate and/or prosecute in different scenarios,[162] mitigates this threat, as it provides more states with the capability and (legal) incentive to seize the initiative.

Within the suppression process, the problem of jurisdictional concurrency is therefore recognised, but deliberately excluded as something that can, or should, be directly

[156] Schultz (2008), p. 813.

[157] C Ram, 'The Globalisation of Crime as a Jurisdictional Challenge' ICCLR/ISRCL (Ottawa, 2011).

[158] Report of the meeting of the Inter-Sessional Open-Ended Intergovernmental Group of Experts on the Elaboration of a Possible Comprehensive International Convention against Transnational Organized Crime (Warsaw, 2–6 February 1998), UN Doc. C/CN.15/1998/5.

[159] Ram (n 157), p. 27.

[160] See e.g. Herrnfeld (2013).

[161] Ibid, 185.

[162] See e.g. art. 16(10) UNCTOC (n 39).

addressed in the context of a suppression instrument.[163] Although core elements of the suppressed crimes are defined in these instruments, when it comes to how these should be interpreted and applied when they assume a transnational character, states are often left to their own devices—the issue is for the domestic laws of the implementing party.[164] States are either encouraged to adopt broad interpretations of territoriality, as discussed in Sect 2., or the variety in approaches to the territoriality principle in criminal jurisdiction[165] are effectively rubberstamped as it is domestic law, not international law, which defines how the constituent elements are to be understood.[166] Moreover, there is little interest in any attempt to prioritise or order jurisdictional bases,[167] a task which is certainly fraught with normative and practical challenges.

---

[163] See e.g. the commentary on the United Nations Convention Against Illicit Traffic in Narcotic Drugs and Psychotropic Substances (Vienna, 20 December 1988) 1998 E/CN,7/590, para. 4.4: "The recognition of the validity of multiple grounds for the establishment of jurisdiction raises the possibility of the conduct in question being subject to the criminal law of two or more States. This is particularly likely in the area of drug trafficking, which is inherently transnational in nature. While concurrent claims to jurisdiction will inevitably arise within the context of the 1988 Convention, the text does not seek to solve the problem of what priority to give to such competing assertions. Similarly, there is no adequate solution to this matter in the corpus of existing norms of customary international law."

[164] See ibid at para. 4.4: "[t]he text does not attempt to deal with the well-known problem of deciding in which State an offence, elements of which are located in more than one State, should be deemed to have been committed. It will be for each national legal system to determine whether what occurred on its territory satisfies the definition of the relevant offence created by its own law."

[165] It has long been recognised that a state can exercise jurisdiction over acts which constitute domestic crimes and have been committed "in whole or in part" within its territory. See Harvard Research in International Law, 'Draft Convention on Jurisdiction with Respect to Crime: Article 3. Territorial Jurisdiction' (1935) 29 AJIL Supp 435, 480. In the Harvard research, two separate territorial principles were identified within national legislation and jurisprudence. The first was the subjective principle, which provides jurisdiction when a crime was "commenced within the State but completed or consummated abroad." Ibid, 484. The second was the objective principle, which provides a power to prosecute and punish when a crime was "commenced without the State but consummated within its territory." Ibid, 488. Although the issue of which of these states, if any, should enjoy priority was a topic debated in the literature on jurisdiction at the turn of the last century, by the time of the drafting of the Harvard Convention it was realised that the arguments were so evenly matched that neither, taken alone, could explain contemporary practice, and there was no reason for prioritising one over the other. See further Akehurst (1972), p. 152.

[166] As Ryngaert (2015), p. 78 notes, international law seems "to have satisfied itself with requiring that either the criminal act or its effects have taken place within a State's territory for the State to legitimately exercise territorial jurisdiction." See further Ryngaert (2009) and Crawford (2019), p. 442.

[167] Jeßberger (2021), p. 264 does note efforts to provide for hierarchies between jurisdictional principles in some regional nineteenth century treaties, while Clarke (2014), p. 104 highlights how some Consular conventions and Status of Forces Agreements do provide priority systems. However, he notes that "[n]o such rules have found their way into the multilateral suppression conventions." This is not entirely accurate as the League of Arab States Convention on Combating Information Technology Offences (Cairo, 21 December 2010) provides a priority system. Article 30(3) states "[i]f more than one State Party claims to have jurisdiction over an offence set forth in this Convention, priority shall be accorded to the request of the State whose *security or interests* were disrupted by the offence, followed by the State in whose territory the offence was committed, and then by the State of which the wanted person is a national." This places something resembling the protective principle above the territorial principle, which does not appear to be a generally accepted or recognised hierarchy in customary international law. Moreover, given how malleable and uncertain this jurisdictional criteria is (e.g. determining when a State 'interest' is engaged by a transnational offence), it is unlikely to be very helpful in resolving cases of jurisdictional concurrency.

The most that any of modern suppression conventions do to address jurisdictional concurrency is to nudge states towards consultation or transfers of proceedings. Article 22(5) of the Cybercrime Convention, for example, states that "[w]hen more than one Party claims jurisdiction over an alleged offence established in accordance with this Convention, the Parties shall, where appropriate, consult with a view to determining the most appropriate jurisdiction for prosecution."[168] Use of the word 'shall' is suggestive of this being a binding requirement, but the subsequent words make clear that this is not the case: consultation must only take place 'where appropriate.' The Explanatory Report to the Convention gives examples of when this might not be necessary, such as where "a Party is of the view that the consultation may impair its investigation or proceeding, it may delay or decline consultation."[169] This effectively renders the provision redundant: a Party that knows another country is interested in its case will already consult of its own initiative, if it wishes to do so, or will not if it envisages domestic complications.

Provisions on the topic of transfers of proceedings have also made their way into some suppression conventions, but as with provisions concerning jurisdictional consultation, transfers are incentivised at most, but not mandated in any circumstances.[170] Experience from within the European Union (EU) and the Council of Europe suggest that there would be formidable challenges in any attempt to further institutionalise formal transfers of proceedings, whether within or outside the suppression frameworks. While there is a Council of Europe Convention on the Transfer of Proceedings in Criminal Matters,[171] it is rarely used, not widely ratified,[172] and it has been described as a result to being "close to useless."[173] Even within the EU, where EU law has regulated almost all significant forms of international co-operation between Member States in criminal matters, proposals to formalise transfers of

[168] A similar provision can be found in art. 15(5) of the UNCTOC (n 39).

[169] Explanatory Report to the Cybercrime Convention, para. 239.

[170] See e.g. art. 21 UNCTOC (n 39) which encourages, but does not mandate, transfers of criminal proceedings: the 'possibility' of transfers must only be 'considered'.

[171] European Convention on the Transfer of Criminal Proceedings (CETS No. 073, 15 May 1972).

[172] Only 25 states have ratified the Convention.

[173] See Hörnle (2021), p. 106, quoting Patrone.

proceedings have so far failed to materialise.[174] Interestingly, it was a provision which required the *extension* of Member State jurisdiction, in order to cater for situations where the requested state cannot prosecute under any traditional jurisdictional principles,[175] that turned out to be the primary stumbling block in previous negotiations.[176] Evidence from the wider international suppression process would suggest that such expansive jurisdictional approaches may not engender similar levels of dissent in this context.

4.2 Problematising Jurisdictional Concurrency Over Offences

State practice, as evidenced by ratification of suppression conventions, suggests a clear prioritisation of the eradication of jurisdictional lacunae over any attempt to avoid overlapping jurisdictional competence. The problem with the current paradigm, however, is that when the problems of impunity and negative conflicts of jurisdiction are placed on a pedestal, it paves the way for unprincipled extensions of jurisdiction,[177] in the name of efficiency and enforcement, which in turn augments the risk of jurisdictional concurrency becoming an issue for states and individuals in practice. While jurisdictional concurrency causes difficulties on various fronts, such as negative externalities and inefficiencies for national investigations, I will highlight two particular concerns.

First, it can, quite obviously, generate interstate conflict. Despite some narratives to the contrary, the risks of positive conflicts here are not illusory. One only needs to consider the recent history of the extradition relationship between the United Kingdom and the United States to see how jurisdictional concurrency over transnational crime, and aggressive enforcement from one state, can prompt the introduction of

---

[174] See e.g. 'Proposal for a Council Framework Decision on the Transfer of Proceedings in Criminal Matters' (Council Doc. 16437/09, 23 November 2009). The European Commission has, however, recently proposed a regulation on the matter. See 'Proposal for a Regulation of the European Parliament and of the Council on the Transfer of Proceedings in Criminal Matters' (Com (2023) 185 final, 5th April 2023).

[175] See Art. 5 Proposal for a Council Framework Decision on the Transfer of Proceedings in Criminal Matters. (Council Doc. 4934/09, 28 October 2009) and the proposed introduction of "subsidiary jurisdiction" (for discussion, see 'Proposal' (n 174) para. 5). The Presidency suggested that "[a]ll Member States should, for the purpose of applying an instrument on transfer of proceedings, to some extent *be obliged to extend their national rules on jurisdiction* to include other offences committed outside the territory of their Member State. This would contribute to the fight against cross border crime." Presidency Note, 'Draft [. . .] on Transfer of Proceedings in Criminal Matters' (Council Doc. 16437/09, 24 November 2009), para. 13. Emphasis added.

[176] For discussion see de Jonge (2020), p. 454.

[177] The provisions associated with the *aud dedere aut judicare* obligation which incentivise the creation of criminal jurisdiction, without an extradition request or any required consultation with the state(s) where the crime was committed, are particularly vulnerable to this critique.

barriers to co-operation (in this case, extradition) even between states that are historically close law enforcement co-operation partners.[178] Backlash against extradition requests concerning individuals like Gary McKinnon, where both the US and the UK could have prosecuted on the basis of a territorial nexus with the events,[179] prompted the UK to amend its extradition legislation to introduce a 'forum bar' to extradition, which allows courts to block extraditions on the basis of a multi-factor 'interests of justice' analysis.[180] The lesson here is that some of the enforcement gains that may be made via the suppression instruments, may begin to be undone in practice where the implications of jurisdictional concurrency are not taken seriously at the negotiating table.

Second, there is significant potential for unfairness for the accused: they may be prosecuted in a foreign justice system without the resources they may have had to defend themselves in their home country,[181] subject to the criminal laws of countries which could not have been foreseen at the time of acting,[182] and even reprosecuted repeatedly by different countries for the same acts. Here the '*ne bis in idem*' principle may be assumed to play a role where there is concurrent jurisdiction between different states, and a risk of individuals being tried, convicted and punished in each state. However, as a matter of international law, this principle is not recognised interstate[183] and the double jeopardy risks here are illustrated by the ongoing litigation in *Trabelsi.* In 2001, Trabelsi was convicted of various terrorist offences in Belgium, for attempting to destroy the Kleine-Brogel military base in Belgium that has both Belgian and US Air Force units based there. While serving a ten-year sentence, he was then indicted in the US for various offences relating to this incident. His extradition was sought, and ultimately granted, despite a provision of the Extradition Treaty between the two countries prohibiting extradition where a person has previously been convicted or acquitted for the same "offense".[184] In the Ministerial Decision to grant extradition, the Belgian Minister of Justice found that it is not the "acts but the legal classification of the acts, namely the offenses, which must be

[178] For discussion see Efrat (2018) and Mann et al. (2018).

[179] See e.g. *Gary McKinnon v Government of the USA and Secretary of State for the Home Department* [2007] EWHC 762, [36]-[37].

[180] See Extradition Act 2003 ss 19B-F, 83A-E. For critique see Arnell and Davies (2020).

[181] For an argument about fair trial deficiencies in US 'extraterritorial' prosecutions, see Farbiarz (2016).

[182] For discussion of the implications of jurisdictional concurrency with respect to the principle of legality see Hildebrandt (2023) and Luchtman (2012).

[183] Stessens and Van den Wyngaert (1999), pp. 803–804 long ago argued that that "[a]n international non bis in idem principle constitutes an essential guarantee for an individual facing criminal charges in a world which is increasingly internationalised" and that the time was ripe for the international community to adopt a more comprehensive and detailed concept of same. However, this is yet to materialise.

[184] See Extradition Treaty between the United States of America and the Kingdom of Belgium, (Brussels, April 27, 1987), art 5.

identical."[185] A similar 'offense-based' analysis to the Extradition Treaty was adopted by a US court when the legality of the extradition was challenged after it had occurred.[186] Following legal challenges in Belgium, however, the Brussels Court of Appeal ordered that Trabelsi could not be prosecuted for four of the 'Overt Acts' contained in the US indictment, as they had already been addressed in the Belgian prosecution and conviction. This set off a series of confrontations between the Belgian executive and courts,[187] but the US Court of Appeals (D.C Circuit), in the meantime, has ordered that the US prosecution can proceed on all charges. The Court restated the now infamous 'dual sovereignty' doctrine in the US, noting that the "Double Jeopardy Clause does not bar successive prosecutions by separate sovereigns."[188]

Cases like this highlight the risk of unfairness to the accused where there is concurrent jurisdiction over transnational offences. Examples exist of others being prosecuted consecutively in this way, including where all prosecuting states were relying on territorial claims over transnational criminal activities.[189] These risks are ever more present in an era of jurisdictional expansion, as spurred on by the suppression conventions. As states avail of the malleability of territoriality so as to criminalise foreign and transnational activities, expand extraterritorial bases of criminal jurisdiction, and extend the reach of their investigative powers abroad, states not only have the 'paper rules' to prosecute foreign actors, but also the

---

[185] Quoted in the European Court of Human Rights Decision in *Trabelsi v Belgium* (App no. 140/10, 16th Feb 2015), para. 31.

[186] *US v Trabelsi* 28 F.4th 1291 (D.C. Cir. 2022), at 1295-6.

[187] Ibid, 1296-7.

[188] Ibid, 1303, citing the recent US Supreme Court case in *Gamble v US* 139 S. Ct. 1964 (2019). See further on the dual sovereignty doctrine Colangelo (2009). For critique see Hörnle (2021), pp. 111–113 and on the historical foundations of the doctrine in English law, see Mumford and Alldridge (2023).

[189] See e.g. the case of Marcel Lehel Lazar (a.k.a. Guccifer), a Romanian hacker who used quite basic password guessing techniques to gain access to information from a large number of public figures in Romania and the United States of America. He was first prosecuted and convicted in Romania for illegally gaining access to the email accounts of public figures and later charged with similar crimes from the same period (October 2012–January 2014) in relation to American victims. See Radu-Sorin Marinas, 'Romania Approves Extradition of Convicted Hacker "Guccifer" to U.S.', REUTERS (Mar 4, 2016), https://www.reuters.com/article/uk-usa-cyber-guccifer-idAFKCN0W61UR; Press Release, Dep't of Justice, U.S. Attorney's Office, E. Dist. of Va., 'Romanian Hacker "Guccifer" Pleads Guilty to Computer Hacking Crimes' (May 25, 2016) https://www.justice.gov/opa/pr/romanian-hacker-guccifer-pleads-guilty-computer-hacking-crimes. He was sentenced to 52 months imprisonment in the US. See Press Release, Dep't of Justice, U.S. Attorney's Office, E. Dist. of Va., 'Romanian Hacker "Guccifer" Sentenced to 52 Months in Prison for Computer Hacking Crimes' (Sept 1, 2016) https://www.justice.gov/opa/pr/romanian-hacker-guccifer-sentenced-52-months-prison-computer-hacking-crimes. The court ordered that he was first to be sent to Romania to serve a prison sentence there, before being then returned to the US to serve out the prison term relating to the US prosecutions. See Hacker "Guccifer" who revealed Clinton's private email server gets 4+ years in jail, RT (Sept. 1, 2016) https://www.rt.com/usa/357918-guccifer-jail-clinton-email/.

enforcement capacity to seize foreign evidence and have suspects surrendered or extradited through a web of bilateral and multilateral enforcement machinery. Viewed only from the perspective of criminal law enforcement this may appear to be quite a 'positive' development: what matters from this point of view is that criminals are prosecuted, not where it is done, or maybe even how often it is done. However, this clearly cannot be the only lens through which the phenomenon is viewed.

4.3 Re-orientating Suppression Instruments

The above analysis has charted some of the ways that a 'territorialisation of the extraterritorial' has been effected in the drafting of suppression treaties, and flagged the potentially serious consequences for individuals and other transnational entities who may get caught up in networks of overlapping jurisdictional competence and prosecution. In this final subsection I will elaborate further on these concerns, and the role of these instruments in addressing such consequences, which will demand a change of perspective within the suppression process.

The first concern relates to drafting practices, and the call here is for greater clarity in expression. While we cannot always expect that the obligations created by multilateral treaties will be, or can be, expressed with the precision that may be expected in domestic legal instruments[190]—they are, after all, the product of diplomatic negotiations and political compromise between states that often have very different legal systems, agendas, and priorities—drafters should be particularly attuned to the dangers of vagueness where interpretations of provisions in a treaty could generate obligations that are normatively questionable and likely to generate interstate conflict as a result. Some iterations of the 'Hague formula' for the ADAJ obligation, and the procedural powers required by Articles 18 and 32 of the Cybercrime Convention are cases in point here. The general rule of interpretation of treaties in Article 31(1) of the Vienna Convention on the Law of Treaties[191] is that a treaty "shall be interpreted in good faith in accordance with the ordinary meaning to be given to the terms of the treaty in their context and in light of its object and purpose." However, the express language of some versions of the Hague formula does not make clear if the obligation to submit the case to domestic authorities for the purpose of prosecution arises only after an extradition request is received and a decision taken to refuse extradition, or if it arises regardless of the existence of a prior request. In some treaties, one reading creates a form of de-facto universal jurisdiction. Another reasonable reading of the same instrument could accord

[190] As noted by one Australian judge in *The Commonwealth v Tasmania* [1983] HCA 21, [261] (*per* Deane J): 'International agreements are commonly "not expressed with the precision of formal domestic documents as in English law"'.

[191] Vienna Convention (n 116).

priority to the territorial state (where one is identifiable), with any competence to exercise jurisdiction in the state where the accused is found emanating from a request from the territorial state (and thus, interpreted to be a form of representative jurisdiction).

Similarly, if Articles 18 and 32 covered foreign service providers, or were ever intended to do so by the drafters, this was implicit, rather than clear and explicit in the text of the document. Extraterritoriality was essentially 'read in' via guidance notes. One problem with this is that it can generate jurisdictional conflict and confusion, rather than the clarity and consensus which should be sought in an international instrument addressing transnational investigative powers. On the one hand, State Parties are told that in the domestic implementation of these procedural powers, they can legislate for various forms of extraterritorial jurisdiction. On the other hand, states are told that agreement to the guidance note, "does not entail consent to the extraterritorial service or enforcement of a domestic production order..."[192] What this does is it pushes the international law question(s) to be resolved between states through enforcement practices and on a case-by-case basis. One state may seek to serve a production order in another State Party, relying on Article 18. The other state, if it becomes aware of this, may then determine if this is permissible in the circumstances. But neither may know beforehand how the other views the legality of the enforcement as a matter of international law. This is a recipe for a cocktail of dysfunctional flexibility and jurisdictional conflict.

While some of the jurisdictional ambiguities may be clarified by consulting the *travaux préparatoires* of these instruments, as suggested by Article 32 of the VCLT, or associated explanatory notes or related documents, these may not always be available or determinative. The drafting of the Cybercrime Convention is particularly egregious in this regard. The work on drafting the Cybercrime Convention began in 1997 when the 'Committee of Experts on Crime in Cyber-space' began its work on the instrument,[193] but from the outset its work was shrouded in controversy with little publicly known even about the make-up of the drafting committee. Banisar and Hosein observed how the "process has been exceedingly secretive and has not benefited from any input except from selected law enforcement officials for several years."[194] Official records were never published and the Explanatory Notes and Guidance Notes raised more questions than answers in terms of many of the jurisdictional ramifications of the Convention.

The Second Additional Protocol can be praised for more explicitly stating the extraterritorial scope of the procedural powers contained therein, but it moves too

---

[192] 'Article 18 Guidance Note' (n 99), para 3.3.

[193] Committee of Ministers, Decision no. CM/Del/Dec(97) 583 (February 4th 1997). The European Committee on Crime Problems had also, the previous year, set up a committee of experts tasked with examining a range of cybercrime issues, the work of which fed into the Committee of Experts on Crime in Cyber-Space (PC-CY). A more detailed account of the background to these groups is contained in the Explanatory Report to the Cybercrime Convention, paras. 7–15.

[194] D Banisar and G Hosein, 'A Draft Commentary on the Council of Europe Cybercrime Convention' (2000), 5, available at: http://privacy.openflows.org/pdf/coe_analysis.pdf.

quickly in attempting to cast off the territorial restrictions that have traditionally limited extraterritorial enforcement activities. The attitude here is to again embrace overlapping jurisdictional competence over the data and service providers implicated in transnational criminal investigations,[195] however, with the powers cast in such general and all-encompassing terms, conflicts in exercise are inevitable, even with states that are not party to the Protocol. The paradox is that while data may be said to be 'un-territorial'[196] in many respects, its territoriality will continue to be a sticking point until clearer jurisdictional principles are developed for governing enforcement jurisdiction with respect to this data. Such principles will need time to crystallise and find their way into multilateral suppression instruments, and experience with bilateral instruments will likely serve as a springboard here. In the short term, therefore, states will continue to be drawn to direct access mechanisms in the multilateral context, but their ultimate success will turn on whether further jurisdictional principles can be identified and expressed with sufficient precision and granularity in a treaty, such that a state can anticipate with some certainty how the procedures will operate in practice.

The second area of concern which I have highlighted relates to human rights law, and in particular, the *ne bis in idem* principle. Clarke has previously observed that suppression conventions are "for the most part 'law and order' rather than 'human rights' documents and concern for the rights of the accused is not in the forefront of any of them."[197] This remark still holds true today.[198] As noted above, one potential consequence of states embracing expansive conceptions of territorial and extraterritorial jurisdiction over transnational crime is the risk of double jeopardy. It is sometimes assumed that these risks are overstated and addressed in practice (through non-enforcement) or through implementations of the *ne bis in idem* principle in international human rights law. This view tends to overstate the actual protection that is afforded to the *ne bis in idem* principle in international law in transnational criminal cases, and may also underestimate the capacity or willingness of certain states to exercise jurisdictional restraint in enforcement practices. This is primarily because, as noted, an international *ne bis in idem* principle has yet to crystallise as a norm of customary international law, such that one state's prosecution would bar another state from prosecuting the same conduct. While there are certain regional *ne bis in idem* protections which apply *interstate*, such as within the EU,[199] it is an *intrastate* protection in international human rights treaties, and thus only applies to

[195] For a broader argument as to how some states are pushing for a relaxation of the traditional limitations of extraterritorial enforcement jurisdiction, and collapsing distinctions between prescriptive and enforcement jurisdiction, see Ryngaert (2023).

[196] See Daskal (2015).

[197] Clarke (1988), p. 86.

[198] For analysis of suppression instruments on this point see Currie (2014).

[199] See art. 54 CISA (n 38) and Charter of Fundamental Rights of the European Union, art. 50, Oct. 26, 2012 O.J. (C 326) 391.

sequential prosecutions and punishments in a single legal system.[200] This challenges assumptions that the suppression conventions can cater for double jeopardy risks indirectly. For example, the Drafting Committee for the Cybercrime Convention was asked to examine the principle of *ne bis in idem*,[201] but nothing made its way into the final text of the instrument on the topic. While the Convention contains provisions on conditions and safeguards which require that State Parties ensure 'adequate protection of human rights',[202] in practice this does not ensure or require that states respect the outcomes of criminal proceedings in other countries in any circumstances.

Alternatively, it is sometimes assumed that *ne bis in idem* protections will be available via extradition arrangements and bilateral extradition treaties.[203] But this argument is clearly contingent. First, suppression conventions can regulate extradition between countries which do not have any bilateral extradition agreements. Second, extradition is not the only means of securing the presence of a transnational criminal for enforcement.[204] Third, no international cooperation machinery at all will be required when the suspect unwittingly travels to a state voluntarily, where they are then arrested and subject to a second prosecution regarding an incident for which they have already been prosecuted in a different state. Fourth, as the *Trabelsi* case illustrates, even where bilateral treaties *do* make provision for the *ne bis in idem* principle, this may not ensure effective protection, particularly where these treaties adopt *idem crimen* formulations.[205] This was the key issue which generated so much confusion and disagreement between the different branches of government in Belgium in *Trabelsi.* In previous work, I have analysed the limitations of various

[200] See Council of Europe, Protocol No. 7 to the Convention for the Protection of Human Rights and Fundamental Freedoms art. 4, Nov. 22, 1984, ETS. 117; United Nations, International Covenant on Civil and Political Rights art. 14(7), (adopted December 16, 1966), 999 UNTS 17.

[201] Explanatory Report, Cybercrime Convention, para. 11.

[202] See art. 15 Cybercrime Convention (n 13), and the Explanatory Report, paras 145–48, referring to Protocol 7 ECHR.

[203] See e.g. ILC Report (n 66), para 22.

[204] For example, there are many reports of extraordinary rendition being used in terrorism cases (see e.g. the ECtHRs' decision in *Al Nashiri v Poland* (2015) 60 EHRR 16. For discussion see Blackbourn (2019). Less known is that there are also reports of such practices in organised crime and trafficking cases. See e.g. reports concerning Roman Seleznev (*US v Zolotarev and others* Criminal Indictment 2:12-CR-604 (Nevada, December 10 2012)) who was convicted of various offences, in a number of separate prosecutions across US states for his involvement in the Carder.su forum. Seleznev was seized by US authorities in the Maldives, and then transferred to the US. The US and the Maldives did not have an extradition treaty, and the incident predated the enactment of the Maldives Extradition Act 2015. For further see Shaun Walker, 'Russia hits out at 'kidnapping' of MP's son by US secret service', The Guardian (July 8, 2014), http://www.theguardian.com/world/2014/jul/08/russia-mps-son-seleznev-arrest-us-secret-service.

[205] Generally speaking, there are two formulations of *idem*: an *idem crimen* approach relates to the *offence* (no one should be prosecuted or punished for the same *offence* twice); an *idem factum* approach relates to the facts of the case (no one should be prosecuted or punished for the same facts twice). For criticism of 'fact-based tests' in the context of US extradition requests in German caselaw, see Gallagher (2021), pp. 248–251.

approaches to 'idem' in the transnational crime context.[206] While an *idem factum* approach is more suitable in this area, current expositions of this in the jurisprudence of the European Court of Human Rights and the Court of Justice of the European Union, remain vague, and can be underprotective in some cases, while overprotective and overinclusive in others. The *ne bis is idem* principle, I argue, needs to be reconceptualised as a component of the right to a fair trial,[207] which would facilitate a fairer and more comprehensive resolution of the issues and interests implicated, and this could also assist in finding ways to build *ne bis in idem* protections into the suppression instruments.

Clarke notes that *ne bis in idem* is "best regarded as a work in progress in transnational criminal law."[208] This may even overstate the situation, at least with respect to the texts of the suppression treaties, as there is almost nothing being done to even consider the principle in this context. While there are some rare examples where the *ne bis in idem* principle is mentioned in some of the suppression conventions, it is conceived of there as a right of the *state*, rather than the individual, which is in keeping with the general trend of suppression conventions being 'law and order' rather than human rights focused. Article 2 of the Traffic in Obscene Publications Convention, for example, envisages potential jurisdictional concurrency by recognising nationality jurisdiction, and states that each "Contracting Party shall, however, have the right to apply the maxim *non bis in idem* in accordance with the rules laid down in its legislation."[209] The corollary is that states have the right not to apply the 'maxim' if it so chooses, even if there has already been a foreign prosecution for the same acts.

Clearly, this is a complex and contentious issue for states. As Hörnle points out, fairness to the accused demands further protection for the principle transnationally, yet there are also strong countervailing interests where states seek to enforce criminal laws that have had harmful domestic effects, and may take very different views on appropriate offences and sanctions and the procedural rules which ought to determine when a re-prosecution is permissible.[210] While considering how transnational *ne bis in idem* protections operate within the EU may be instructive, this is a context of mutual trust and with social, legal, and political ties and shared values, even if the extent of this is contested. Trying to generate consensus on the topic amongst the nearly 200 countries that may be party to a suppression convention presents a challenge of a different order of magnitude.

Hörnle argues that the "way forward should be the development of principles, which reflect the underlying interests more clearly with less emphasis on sovereignty

---

[206] See Ó Floinn (2017).

[207] Ibid 103–108. The CJEU has also described the protection afforded by art. 54 CISA (n 37) as intended to ensure the "right to freedom of movement, the aim being to ensure legal certainty." See *WS Bundesrepublik Deutschland*, Case C-505/19, EU:C:2021:376, [79]. See further Lelieur (2013).

[208] Clarke (2014), p. 106.

[209] Traffic in Obscene Publications Convention (n 27).

[210] Hörnle (2021), p. 112.

and more emphasis on coordination between different legal orders."[211] This is a challenging but laudable path to begin to chart. While it is beyond the scope of this contribution to consider the prospects of this, and the conditions under which it could be achieved, my argument here is simply that the suppression process is one of the key multilateral forums where this coordination and development of principles could be realised, and that it is incumbent on the drafters of suppression conventions to do so given the role that these instruments play in increasing the risk of double jeopardy arising through state enforcement practices. Addressing the *ne bis in idem* principle in the extradition provisions of these instruments could be a starting point but would require a change of mindset from drafters, with less prioritisation on the removal of barriers to extradition, and more emphasis on safeguards for the accused.

5 Conclusion

In an increasingly globalised and inter-connected world, jurisdictional concurrency over trafficking and other transnational offences is inevitable, and as the evidence necessary for the investigation and prosecution of these offences can span multiple states, it is to be expected that some will test the international law limits of their investigative and enforcement powers. For some this sounds the death knell for territorial jurisdiction.[212] Szigeti, for example, is "tempted to draw the conclusion that territorial jurisdiction is broken".[213] But this is certainly not the view of states, even if, as Krisch has recently nicely captured, territoriality has become "'unbound' . . . from its constraining aspects, opening the door to an exercise of jurisdiction on the basis of thin connections with the issue at hand".[214] Krisch notes how social and political changes, technological advancements, and globalised economic and communicative relations, have challenged the legal frameworks which largely allocate jurisdiction along territorial lines. The result, he argues, is a jurisdictional "assemblage"[215] where states have wide and overlapping jurisdictional claims, and few jurisdictional limits "other than those of factual control".[216] This favours enforcement by powerful countries who have the capacity to exercise this jurisdiction,[217] and while Krisch is sensitive to the dangers of this and the normative challenges it

[211] Ibid, p. 113.

[212] See e.g. Svantesson (2015), p. 70. See further Svantesson (2017).

[213] Szigeti (2019), p. 44.

[214] Krisch (2022), p. 482.

[215] Krisch (2022), p. 502.

[216] Krisch (2022), p. 498.

[217] For analysis of how the US utilises concepts of territoriality in transnational criminal law enforcement, see Brown (2023).

raises, he views this as a form of 'unilateral global governance' which is only likely to grow further in importance moving forwards.[218]

This clearly raises fundamental questions for a territorially focused law of criminal jurisdiction. Territoriality, at least in certain spheres of transnational regulation, is clearly struggling to fulfil any form of limiting function to reduce conflicts between states, and there is reason to doubt the potential efficacy of any techniques of jurisdictional restraint.[219] Krisch's solution is to focus attention on accountability mechanisms, but others have already questioned whether he is too accepting of the current paradigm, and too quick to give up on the international law of jurisdiction and multilateralism in the (jurisdictional) regulation of transnational activities. For Chehtman, collective action problems require agreed solutions by all states and multilateral agreement, and he maintains that jurisdictional devices and principles, like the presumption against extraterritorial jurisdiction, must continue to play a role in articulating jurisdictional competence.[220] O'Keefe in similar vein, argues that what is needed today is the "political will and diplomatic agreement to use even further the existing law, especially the treaty-based possibilities that it offers..."[221]

This chapter does not present a particularly encouraging picture for this alternative, showing that "unbound territoriality",[222] if anything, is also being incentivised through these multilateral instruments with little attention to consequences, or the tools that may be necessary to limit the risks of jurisdictional overreach. And as the territorialisation of the extraterritorial moves also into the realm of investigative powers, we enter a new era for criminal law enforcement. As a matter of substantive criminal jurisdiction, expansive territoriality may not have been of much consequence where states did not also have the enforcement machinery to investigate and prosecute foreign offending. However, these instruments are now also being utilised to facilitate expansive extraterritorial enforcement jurisdiction, and when coupled with their extradition procedures, and other bilateral and regional law enforcement co-operation arrangements, the consequence is that more states may gain the ability to exercise 'factual control' over transnational criminal actors to actually enforce the expansive jurisdictional ambit of transnational offences. While this may, to some extent, level the playing field between powerful and weaker states in transnational criminal enforcement, and contribute to the realisation of global justice as part of a cosmopolitan agenda,[223] it may also serve to make jurisdictional conflicts in exercise, and double jeopardy risks, a much more real prospect for states and individuals moving forwards. This demands that states need to reflect carefully on the enforcement assumptions that are currently driving the suppression process, the

[218] Krisch (2022), p. 513.

[219] Krisch (2022), p. 502. For a more hopeful perspective, see Ryngaert (2020).

[220] See Chehtman (2023).

[221] See O'Keefe (2022), p. 526.

[222] Krisch (2022), p. 501.

[223] Ryngaert (2020).

consequences of this 'territorialisation of the extraterritorial' in practice, and whether suppression instruments can and should be doing more to address this.

References

Akehurst M (1972–73) Jurisdiction in international law. Br Yearb Int Law 46:145

Arnell P, Davies G (2020) The forum bar in UK extradition law: an unnecessary failure. J Crim Law 84:142

Blackbourn J (2019) The European Court of Human Rights and counter-terrorism initiatives. In: Shor E, Hoadley S (eds) International human rights and counter-terrorism. Springer, Singapore

Boister N (2015) Further reflections on the concept of transnational criminal law. Transnatl Leg Theory 6(1):9

Boister N (2018) An introduction to transnational criminal law, 2nd edn. Oxford University Press, Oxford

Boister N, Gless S, Jeßberger F (eds) (2021) Histories of transnational criminal law. Oxford University Press, Oxford

Brown D (2023) Extraterritorial ambit through offence definitions, technology and economic power. In: Ó Floinn M, Farmer L, Hörnle J, Ormerod D (eds) Transformations in criminal jurisdiction: extraterritoriality and enforcement. Hart Publishing, Oxford

Buxbaum H (2009) Territory, territoriality, and the resolution of jurisdictional conflict. Am J Comp Law 57(3):631

Caligiuri A (2018) Governing international cooperation in criminal matters: the role of the *aut dedere aut judicare* principle. Int Crim Law Rev 18:244

Chehtman A (2010) The philosophical foundations of extraterritorial punishment. Oxford University Press, Oxford

Chehtman A (2014) Jurisdiction. In: Dubber M, Hörnle T (eds) The Oxford handbook of criminal law. Oxford University Press, Oxford

Chehtman A (2023) The presumption against extraterritorial criminal jurisdiction. In: Ó Floinn M, Farmer L, Hörnle J, Ormerod D (eds) Transformations in criminal jurisdiction: extraterritoriality and enforcement. Hart Publishing, Oxford

Chimni B (2022) The international law of jurisdiction: a TWAIL perspective. Leiden J Int Law 35: 29

Clarke R (1988) Offences of international concern: multilateral treaty practice in the forty years since Nuremberg. Nord J Int Law 57:49

Clarke R (2014) Jurisdiction over transnational crime. In: Boister N, Currie R (eds) Routledge handbook of transnational criminal law, 1st edn. Routledge, London

Cochrane T (2021) Hiding in the eye of the storm cloud: how CLOUD act agreements expand US extraterritorial investigatory powers. Duke J Comp Int Law 32:153

Cochrane T (2022) The presumption against extraterritoriality, mutual legal assistance, and the future of law enforcement cross-border evidence collection. Mod Law Rev 85:526

Colangelo AJ (2009) Double jeopardy and multiple sovereigns: a jurisdictional theory. Wash Univ Law Rev 86(4):769

Colangelo AJ (2014) What is extraterritorial jurisdiction? Cornell Law Rev 99(6):1303

Crawford J (2019) Brownlie's principles of public international law, 9th edn. Oxford University Press, Oxford

Currie R (2014) The protection of human rights in the suppression of transnational crime. In: Boister N, Currie R (eds) Routledge handbook of transnational criminal law, 1st edn. Routledge, Abingdon

d'Aspremont J (2010) Multilateral versus unilateral exercises of universal criminal jurisdiction. Israel Law Rev 43(2):301

Daskal J (2015) The un-territoriality of data. Yale Law J 125(2):326
de Jonge B (2020) Transfer of criminal proceedings: from stumbling block to cornerstone of cooperation in criminal matters in the EU. ERA Forum 21:449
Efrat A (2018) Resisting cooperation against crime: Britain's extradition controversy 2003-2015. Int J Law Crime Justice 52:118
Elden S (2013) The birth of territory. University of Chicago Press, Chicago
Farbiarz M (2016) Accuracy and adjudication: the promise of extraterritorial due process. Columbia Law Rev 116(3):625
Gallagher C (2021) Know before you go: navigating double jeopardy issues when your investigation heads to Europe. Dep Justice J Fed Law Pract 69(3):237
Garrod M (2018) Unraveling the confused relationship between treaty obligations to extradite or prosecute and 'universal jurisdiction' in the light of the *Habré Case*. Harv Int Law J 59(1):125
Garrod M (2023a) The expansion of treaty-based extraterritorial criminal jurisdiction. In: Parrish A, Ryngaert C (eds) Research handbook on extraterritoriality in international law. Edward Elgar Publishing, Cheltenham
Garrod M (2023b) Extraterritorial criminal jurisdiction in international law: time for an empirical examination. In: Ó Floinn M, Farmer L, Hörnle J, Ormerod D (eds) Transformations in criminal jurisdiction: extraterritoriality and enforcement. Hart Publishing, Oxford
Gibney M (1996) The extraterritorial application of US law: perversion of democratic governance, the reversal of institutional roles, and the imperative of establishing normative principles. Boston Coll Int Comp Law Rev 19(2):297
Herrnfeld H (2013) Mechanisms for settling conflicts of jurisdiction. In: Luchtman M (ed) Choice of forum in cooperation against EU financial crime. Eleven International Publishing, The Hague
Hildebrandt M (2023) Text-driven jurisdiction in cyberspace. In: Ó Floinn M, Farmer L, Hörnle J, Ormerod D (eds) Transformations in criminal jurisdiction: extraterritoriality and enforcement. Hart Publishing, Oxford
Hirst M (2003) Jurisdiction and the ambit of the criminal law. Oxford University Press, Oxford
Hirst M (2013) Country Report 'England and Wales'. In: Böse M, Meyer F, Schneider A (eds) Conflicts of jurisdiction in criminal matters in the European Union: vol 1 national reports and comparative analysis. Nomos, Baden-Baden
Hörnle J (2021) Internet jurisdiction: law and practice. Oxford University Press, Oxford
Jeßberger F (2021) A short history of jurisdiction in transnational criminal law. In: Boister N, Gless S, Jeßberger F (eds) Histories of transnational criminal law. Oxford University Press, Oxford
Kaspersen H (2006) Jurisdiction in the cybercrime convention. In: Koops B-J, Brenner SW (eds) Cybercrime and jurisdiction – a global survey. Springer, The Hague
Kohl U (2023) Fitbit health data, Apple's geodata and Google searches: cross-border law enforcement and the territoriality principle. In: Ó Floinn M, Farmer L, Hörnle J, Ormerod D (eds) Transformations in criminal jurisdiction: extraterritoriality and enforcement. Hart Publishing, Oxford
Kreß C (2006) Universal jurisdiction over international crimes and the Institut de Droit international. J Int Crim Justice 4:561
Krisch N (2022) Jurisdiction unbound: (extra)territorial regulation as global governance'. Eur J Int Law 33(2):481
Lelieur J (2013) 'Transnationalising' Ne bis in Idem: how the rule of Ne Bis in Idem reveals the principle of personal legal certainty. Utrecht Law Rev 9(4):198
Lombois C (1979) Droit Penal International. Dalloz, Paris
Lubin A (2023) The prohibition of extraterritorial enforcement jurisdiction in the datasphere. In: Parrish A, Ryngaert C (eds) Research handbook on extraterritoriality in international law. Edward Elgar Publishing, Cheltenham
Luchtman M (2012) Principles of European criminal law: jurisdiction, choice of forum and the legality principle in the area of freedom, security and justice. Eur Rev Priv Law 20(2):347

Mann FA (1985) The doctrine of international jurisdiction revisited after twenty years. Martinus Nijhoff, The Hague
Mann M, Warren I, Kennedy S (2018) The legal geographies of transnational cyber-prosecutions: extradition, human rights and forum shifting. Global Crime 19(2):107
Mills A (2014) Rethinking jurisdiction in international law. Br Yearb Int Law 84(1):187
Mumford A, Alldridge P (2023) The history of double jeopardy and criminal jurisdiction: US v Gamble (2019) and R. v Hutchinson (1677). Law Q Rev 139:390
Nadelmann E (1993) Cops across borders: the internationalization of US criminal law enforcement. The Pennsylvania State University Press, Pennsylvania
Ó Floinn M (2017) The concept of idem in the European courts: extricating the inextricable link in European double jeopardy law. Columbia J Eur Law 24:75
O'Connor J (2014) The Microsoft warrant case: not just an Irish issue. Comput Law 25(4):10
O'Keefe R (2022) Cooperative national regulation to secure transnational public goods: a reply to Nico Krisch. Eur J Int Law 33(2):515
Parrish A (2009) Reclaiming international law from extraterritoriality. Minn Law Rev 83:815
Petzsche A (2021) A historical perspective on modes of liability in transnational criminal law. In: Boister N, Gless S, Jeßberger F (eds) Histories of transnational criminal law. Oxford University Press, Oxford
Ryngaert C (2009) Territorial jurisdiction over cross-frontier offenses: revisiting a classic problem of international criminal law. Int Crim Law Rev 9(1):187
Ryngaert C (2015) Jurisdiction in international law, 2nd edn. Oxford University Press, Oxford
Ryngaert C (2020) Selfless intervention: the exercise of jurisdiction in the common interest. Oxford University Press, Oxford
Ryngaert C (2023) Enforcement jurisdiction in a-territorial spaces: addressing crime on the high seas and in cyberspace. In: Ó Floinn M, Farmer L, Hörnle J, Ormerod D (eds) Transformations in criminal jurisdiction: extraterritoriality and enforcement. Hart Publishing, Oxford
Scassa T, Currie R (2011) New first principles? Assessing the Internet's challenges to jurisdiction. Georgetown J Int Law 42:1017
Schultz T (2008) Carving up the Internet: jurisdiction, legal orders and the private/public international law interface. Eur J Int Law 19(4):799
Stessens G, Van den Wyngaert C (1999) The international non bis in idem principle: resolving some of the unanswered questions. Int Comp Law Q 48(4):779
Svantesson D (2015) A new jurisprudential framework for jurisdiction: beyond the Harvard draft. AJIL Unbound 109:69
Svantesson D (2017) Solving the internet jurisdiction puzzle. Oxford University Press, Oxford
Szigeti P (2019) In the middle of nowhere: the futile quest to distinguish territoriality from extraterritoriality. In: Margolies D, Özsu U, Pal M, Tzouvala N (eds) The extraterritoriality of law: history, theory, politics. Routledge, London
Trudel P (1998) Jurisdiction over the internet: a Canadian perspective. Int Lawyer 32:1027
Walden I (2013) Accessing data in the cloud: the long arm of the law enforcement agent. In: Pearson S, Yee G (eds) Privacy and security for cloud computing. Springer, London

Adjudicative Jurisdiction for Crimes at Sea: An International Law Perspective

Serena Forlati

Abstract This chapter discusses international rules on the exercise of adjudicatory jurisdiction for crimes at sea and their implementation in Italy. It addresses recent domestic case law which, while purporting to comply with international obligations, is not always fully convincing in this regard; it further questions the adequacy of the domestic legal framework to effectively combating illicit trafficking in the Mediterranean Sea, considering the possible role of the Legislature and the Government in developing a more coherent and effective approach to the fight against impunity in that specific context.

1 Introduction

The traditional international law perspective on the exercise of domestic criminal jurisdiction is anchored to the stance taken by the Permanent Court of International Justice (PCIJ) in the *Lotus* case. The PCIJ posited in general terms that international law leaves states 'a wide measure of discretion which is only limited in certain cases by prohibitive rules; as regards other cases, every State remains free to adopt the principles which it regards as best and most suitable'.[1]

International law rules out any form of jurisdiction in the territory of other states unless a permissive rule to that effect exists; this stance, however, targets only the so-called "enforcement jurisdiction", that is, the actual exercise of coercive powers by the territorial state.[2] Differently, States may exercise "adjudicative jurisdiction" within their territory also as regards situations located abroad. Already in the context

[1] PCIJ, *The Case of the S.S. Lotus, Series A*, No. 10, September 7th, 1927, p. 19.

[2] On the distinction between jurisdiction to prescribe, jurisdiction to enforce and jurisdiction to adjudicate see Ryngaert (2015); see also American Law Institute, Restatement of the Law – Fourth, §§ 401 ff.

S. Forlati (✉)
Department of Law, University of Ferrara, Ferrara, Italy
e-mail: serena.forlati@unife.it

V. Militello, A. Spena (eds.), *The Challenges of Illegal Trafficking in the Mediterranean Area*, Legal Studies in International, European and Comparative Criminal Law 9, https://doi.org/10.1007/978-3-031-45399-1_3

of "classic" international law "[i]n practice, the principle of territorial sovereignty did not permit of any exception in respect of coercive action, but it was not the case in regard to legislative and judicial jurisdiction".[3]

Specifically as regards jurisdiction in criminal matters, the *Lotus* judgment is to the effect that although

> in all systems of law the principle of the territorial character of criminal law is fundamental, it is equally true that all or nearly all these systems of law extend their action to offences committed outside the territory of the State which adopts them, and they do so in ways which vary from State to State. The territoriality of criminal law, therefore, is not an absolute principle of international law and by no means coincides with territorial sovereignty (. . .).[4]

Crime at sea is regulated in a similar way, but poses some specific problems.

In order to appraise them properly, one should keep in mind that the freedom of States to define their own spheres of jurisdiction entails a few risks: as Cedric Ryngaert contends, jurisdiction "becomes a concern of international law when a State, in its eagerness to promote its sovereign interests abroad, adopts laws that govern matters of not purely domestic concern".[5] In this perspective, "positive conflicts" of jurisdiction are perceived as problematic especially in the area of criminal law, which is a particularly sensitive expression of State sovereignty, shaping the identity of any State. In more than one instance States have disputed the lawfulness of other States' shaping of their domestic criminal jurisdiction so as to apply to events occurred outside their own territory; recent, prominent instances include *Arrest Warrant* and *Enrica Lexie*, as well as the *Belgium v. Senegal*[6] and *Immunities and Criminal Proceedings* case.[7]

---

[3] International Court of Justice, *Arrest Warrant of 11 April 2000 (Democratic Republic of the Congo v. Belgium), Judgment*, Separate opinion of President Guillaume, *I.C.J. Reports 2002*, p. 37, para. 4. See already PCIJ, *Lotus*, pp. 18–19:

> [T]he first and foremost restriction imposed by international law upon a State is that – failing the existence of a permissive rule to the contrary – it may not exercise its power in any form in the territory of another State. In this sense jurisdiction is certainly territorial; it cannot be exercised by a State outside its territory except by virtue of a permissive rule derived from international custom or from a convention. It does not, however, follow that international law prohibits a State from exercising jurisdiction in its own territory, in respect of any case which relates to acts which have taken place abroad, and in which it cannot rely on some permissive rule of international law. Such a view would only be tenable if international law contained a general prohibition to States to extend the application of their laws and the jurisdiction of their courts to persons, property and acts 'outside their territory, and if, as an exception to this general prohibition, it allowed States to do so in certain specific cases. But this is certainly not the case under international law as it stands at present.

[4] Ibid., p. 20.

[5] Cedric Ryngaert (2015), p. 6.

[6] *Questions relating to the Obligation to Prosecute or Extradite (Belgium v. Senegal)*, I.C.J. Reports 2012, p. 422.

[7] ICJ, *Immunities and Criminal Proceedings (Equatorial Guinea v. France), Preliminary Objections, Judgment*, I.C.J. Reports 2018, p. 292 at 324, para 104 ff.

However, international instruments dealing with penal matters aim at addressing not only "positive", but also "negative" conflicts of jurisdiction: as the Legislative guide to the United Nations Convention against Corruption points out,

> The international community wishes to ensure that no serious crime goes unpunished and that all parts of the crime are punished wherever they took place. Jurisdictional gaps that enable fugitives to find safe havens need to be reduced or eliminated.[8]

Regrettably, recent experience as regards the fight against illicit trafficking in the Mediterranean Sea points to a legal framework that does not necessarily ensure an effective exercise by *any State* of jurisdiction over very serious crimes committed at sea. Particularly human trafficking and migrant smuggling have caused countless maritime tragedies, for which avoiding impunity is all the more important. In the face of this, even the Security Council decided to take action, notably through the adoption of resolution 2240(2015).[9]

After a brief analysis of the applicable international legal regime, this contribution purports to discuss the problem by addressing, specifically, the Italian experience in countering such forms of trafficking. While some of the hurdles that Italian courts face in tackling such cases may be caused by peculiarities of the domestic legal and political system, there is arguably a more general difficulty arising in this respect in the interaction between international and national legal regimes regulating adjudicative jurisdiction over crime at sea.

2 The Applicable International Legal Framework

The international customary regime regulating the exercise of adjudicative criminal jurisdiction over crimes committed at sea is still largely similar to the one applicable at the time of *Lotus*. On that occasion the PCIJ extended by analogy the general rule on territorial criminal jurisdiction quoted above to crime at sea, confirming that

> vessels on the high seas are subject to no authority except that of the State whose flag they fly' [but] there is no rule of international law prohibiting the State to which the ship on which the effects of the offence have taken place belongs, from regarding the offence as having been committed in its territory and prosecuting, accordingly, the delinquent.[10]

Although the idea that a ship is a "floating territory" is now perceived as old fashioned, the "flag state principle" is still a key component of customary international law and is reflected in Article 92(1) of the United Nations Convention on the Law of the Sea (UNCLOS): "Ships shall sail under the flag of one State only and, save in exceptional cases expressly provided for in international treaties or in this

[8] Para. 492. Cf. UNTOC Legislative guide, p. 75, para. 244.

[9] The resolution has been renewed on a yearly basis thereafter.

[10] , *Lotus*, p. 25.

Convention, shall be subject to its exclusive jurisdiction on the high sea".[11] As the Arbitral Tribunal maintained in *Enrica Lexie*, "such an extended territoriality principle is well established, and the domestic criminal legislation of a large number of States confers jurisdiction over offences committed on board national ships or aircraft".[12] This corollary of the territoriality principle is thus still the relevant rule, except to the limited extent where specific exceptions apply. This is the case of situations falling under the scope of Security Council resolution 2240(2015) and its successors: although these resolutions emphasize the existence of a "general principle of exclusive jurisdiction of a flag State over its vessels on the high seas",[13] they also authorize States other than the flag State to inspect and seize "vessels that they have reasonable grounds to suspect are being used for migrant smuggling or human trafficking from Libya, provided that such Member States and regional organisations make good faith efforts to obtain the consent of the vessel's flag State".[14] This authorization applies only to enforcement jurisdiction, not to adjudicative jurisdiction. The Resolution addresses the latter issue in para. 15: albeit without any mandatory prescription in this respect, it does call upon

> all States, with relevant jurisdiction under international law and national legislation, to investigate and prosecute persons responsible for acts of migrant smuggling and human trafficking at sea, consistent with States' obligations under international law, including international human rights law and international refugee law, as applicable (. . .).[15]

Customary and treaty law usually revolve around the flag state principle also as regards adjudicative jurisdiction. In this respect, Article 92 UNCLOS served as a model for the rules on the exercise of jurisdiction at sea enshrined in many relevant suppression conventions. Thus, the United Nations Convention against Transnational Organized Crime (Palermo Convention) engages States Parties to prosecute the relevant offences when, among other conditions, they are committed in their territory or "on board a vessel that is flying [their] flag . . . at the time that the offence is committed";[16] similar provisions are included in other conventions tackling transnational crime, including Article 42 of the United Nations Convention against

[11] Montego Bay, 10 December 1982.

[12] PCA Case No. 2015-28, *In the Matter of an Arbitration before an Arbitral Tribunal Constituted under Annex VII to the 1982 United Nations Convention on the Law of the Sea, The Italian Republic v. The Republic of India Concerning the "Enrica Lexie" Incident*, Award of 21 May 2020, para. 365. The Tribunal went on to note that "In this regard, the Arbitral Tribunal does not consider that this principle amounts to assimilating a vessel with national territory 'for all purposes' as if "a ship is a floating part of state territory" (ibid., footnotes omitted).

[13] Resolution 2240(2015), para. 11. The stance concerns enforcement jurisdiction but can be applied also to adjudicative jurisdiction.

[14] See Security Council Resolution 2240(2015), paras. 7 and 8.

[15] Ibid., para. 15.

[16] United Nations General Assembly, A/RES/55/25 of 15 November 2000, *United Nations Treaty Series*, vol. 2225, p. 209.

Corruption[17] and Article 4 of the Convention on the Illicit Trafficking of Narcotic Drugs.[18]

The flag state principle is however of little use in curbing impunity whenever crimes are committed at least in part on flagless ships (as is often the case with human trafficking and migrant smuggling in the Mediterranean) or the flag State is not keen on exercising adjudicative jurisdiction. In light of this, modern suppression conventions set out not only compulsory grounds of jurisdiction but also a series of optional grounds going beyond territoriality, that states are encouraged to consider or that, at least, cannot be deemed incompatible with international law by the contracting parties. Those grounds are usually linked to the active and passive personality principle—which "today meets with relatively little opposition, at least so far as a particular category of offences is concerned"[19]—, the protective principle and the presence of the accused person on the State's territory.

Thus, for instance, Article 15 (2) of the Palermo Convention sets forth that

> . . . a State Party may also establish its jurisdiction over any [. . .] offence [covered by the Convention] when: *(a)* The offence is committed against a national of that State Party; *(b)* The offence is committed by a national of that State Party or a stateless person who has his or her habitual residence in its territory; or *(c)* The offence is: (i) One of those established in accordance with article 5, paragraph 1, of this Convention and is committed outside its territory with a view to the commission of a serious crime within its territory; (ii) One of those established in accordance with article 6, paragraph 1 *(b)* (ii), of this Convention and is committed outside its territory with a view to the commission of an offence established in accordance with article 6, paragraph 1 *(a)* (i) or (ii) or *(b)* (i), of this Convention within its territory. (. . .)

According to paragraph 4, "Each State Party may also adopt such measures as may be necessary to establish its jurisdiction over the offences covered by this Convention when the alleged offender is present in its territory and it does not extradite him or her".[20] Furthermore, pa follows the example of other suppression conventions when it specifies that the exercise of criminal jurisdiction on the relevant offences by

[17] United Nations General Assembly, A/RES/58/422, *United Nations Treaty Series*, vol. 2349, p. 41.

[18] Vienna, 25 November 1988, *United Nations Treaty Series*, vol. 1582, p. 95. See moreover, among other examples, IMO Convention for the Suppression of Unlawful Acts of Violence against the Safety of Maritime Navigation (SUA Convention), 10 March 1988, Article 6; at the regional level, Council of Europe Convention against Trafficking in Human Organs Santiago de Compostela, 25 March 2015, CETS 216, Article 10; Article Council of Europe Convention on Offences relating to Cultural Property, Nicosia, 19 May 2017, CETS 221, in force for Italy since 1 July 2022, Article 12.

[19] ICJ, *Arrest Warrant*, Joint Separate Opinion of Judges Higgins, Koojimans, and Buergenthal, I.C.J. Reports 2002, p. 77, para. 47; see further Separate Opinion of President Guillaume, ibid., pp. 35 ff. Neither the ICJ on that occasion nor the Arbitral Tribunal in the Enrica Lexie (n 10) ruled upon the issue.

[20] Article 15(3), on the other hand, envisages a compulsory ground of jurisdiction for cases where the accused person is not extradited 'solely on the ground' that he or she is a national of the requested State.

on purely domestic grounds is permissible[21] (arguably covering also domestic rules envisaging universal criminal jurisdiction[22]). Notwithstanding these provisions and the encouragement of the Security Council, human trafficking and attempts to exploitation of migrants by criminal networks and casualties in the Mediterranean Sea continue, together with other serious forms of illicit trafficking.

An effective fight against impunity requires, on the one hand, enhancing international cooperation also in the form of support to flag States and to States from whose territory the illicit activities originate. Arguably such effort would also benefit from exercise of adjudicative jurisdiction by States of destination of those activities even beyond what is the object of strictly binding international obligations, provided that fundamental human rights guarantees set out at the international and at the domestic level are respected. The Italian example is illustrative of a situation that is not always smooth in this respect, also due to the lack of an appropriate synergy between the Legislature, the Government and the Judiciary in this specific regard.

3 The Italian Approach

Italian courts have been at the forefront of the effort to prosecute human traffickers and migrant smugglers, as well as other forms of illicit trafficking, in the Mediterranean route. The legal framework in which those courts operate is not, however, particularly satisfactory.

Indeed, Italy's legislation is in line with its obligations under international law, and therefore complies with the invitation that the Security Council included in resolution 2240 to exercise adjudicative jurisdiction consistently therewith. For instance, the implementing orders of UNTOC and of the UN Convention against Illicit Traffic in Narcotic Drugs and Psychotropic Substances[23] incorporate into domestic law the compulsory grounds of jurisdiction these treaties envisage.

However, Italy has not incorporated any of the optional grounds of criminal jurisdiction these conventions set forth. In a context where illicit trafficking towards Italy in the Mediterranean takes place, more often than not, through ships whose flag states are not particularly keen on prosecuting the authors, or on flagless States, the

[21] See Article 42(6) UNCAC; Article 4 (3) of the United Nations Convention against Illicit Traffic in Narcotic Drugs and Psychotropic Substances; Article 6(5) SUA Convention; compare Article 36 (3) of the Single Convention on Narcotic Drugs and Article 22(4) of the Convention on Psychotropic Substances of 1971.

[22] See e.g., for developments in Spain, Ministry of Foreign affairs, 'Contribution of Spain on the topic "The scope and application of the principle of universal jurisdiction"', 22 February 2016, available https://www.un.org/en/ga/sixth/71/universal_jurisdiction/spain_e.pdf (Accessed 10 August 2023).

[23] Vienna, 20 December 1988. See the implementing order in Law no. 328 of 5 November 1990 in Gazzetta Ufficiale della Repubblica Italiana, General Series, no 267 of 15 November 1990, Suppl. Ord. no. 71, 5.

task of identifying grounds of jurisdiction suitable to prosecution of illicit trafficking somehow affecting Italy, and more generally to crime at sea committed in the framework of such trafficking, has thus been shouldered by Courts. Their interpretative efforts have been aimed at narrowing the impunity gap especially in the face of particularly heinous crimes against human beings. While these efforts are certainly commendable, the lines of reasoning followed in the case law display some inconsistencies in the application of the relevant international legal standards and/or are at times not fully convincing. Three stances by the Court of Cassation—two concerning UNTOC and one involving UNCLOS—stand to particular attention in this regard.

3.1 *Italian Adjudicative Jurisdiction and Article 15(2) and (4) UNTOC*

The first relevant pronouncement, *Haij*,[24] concerned migrant smuggling at sea, and more specifically a situation where a criminal organization operating from Libya had led a group of migrants on a so-called "mother-ship" to the high seas—towards, but not entering into, Italian territorial waters. The group had then been moved to a flagless, unseaworthy smaller vessel (which the accused person conducted) until a Liberian cargo rescued them and led them into Italian territorial waters. This is an unfortunately well-known pattern of irregular migration towards Italy and other Southern European States, whereby the actual crossing of the sea borders that is an element of the crime as described in the UNTOC Smuggling Protocol (and in the Italian implementing legislation) is not put in place by the criminal organization itself, nor by the persons they employ—or force—to conduct the vessels carrying migrants. On the other hand, the ships that rescue the migrants in the high seas are not normally held responsible for smuggling since they performed an international obligation stemming from customary law as well as from international treaty rules such as Article 98 UNCLOS and SOLAS; attempts to criminalize NGOs responsible for rescue operations have so far led to acquittals of the accused persons.[25] In *Haij*, the Court framed a reasoning that was subsequently followed by other Italian courts, leading to the exercise of Italian criminal jurisdiction as against the conductors and the members of the criminal organization as such although they did not directly let the migrants cross its borders.

The judgment posited that the Liberian ship's crew had acted under distress when they took the group of migrants into the Italian territorial waters, being forced to act as mere instrumentalities for the commission of the crime of migrant smuggling by the members of the organized criminal group. This convoluted interpretative approach, which resumed old theoretical approaches to attribution, is certainly

[24] First Criminal Chamber, No. 14510 of 28 February–27 March 2014.

[25] See Salvadego (2021), p. 98; Ruggiero (2020), pp. 203 ff.

expedient insofar as it enables Italian courts to affirm adjudicative jurisdiction over the crime of migrant smuggling,[26] and has been upheld without much discussion in later case law.[27]

Perhaps more significantly for the purposes of this paper, the Court of cassation also upheld jurisdiction over the accused persons also as regards the crime of participation in an organized criminal group (a crime which is covered by Article 5 of the UNTOC). The Court acknowledged that the organized criminal group was set up and active in North Africa, but upheld jurisdiction since that organized criminal group was set up with a view to the commission of human trafficking migrant smuggling in Italy. The Judgment expressly relied on Article 15(2)(c)(i) UNTOC and on Law No. 146/2006 which transposes UNTOC into domestic law. However, as recalled above, Article 15(2)(c)(i) UNTOC simply sets forth an optional ground of jurisdiction and is thus not self-executing: this option must be expressly exercised by the Italian legislature in order to become operational whereas, as discussed above, no provision to this effect is included in law No. 146.

It is noteworthy, in this regard, that the First Criminal Chamber of the Court of cassation read Article 15(4) UNTOC, whose formulation closely follows that of para. (2)(c)(i), as being non-self-executing in *Tartoussi*.

The case concerns allegations of illicit trafficking in firearms as against the captain of a Turkish ship that had brought arms from Turkey to Libya in breach of the Security Council's embargo; immediately thereafter the ship arrived in Genoa and another member of the crew brought notice of these events to the Italian authorities. The Court of cassation eventually upheld jurisdiction under Article 10, paragraph 2, of the Italian Penal Code, which regulates the prosecution of foreign nationals for crimes committed abroad under certain conditions (inter alia, a request by the Minister of Justice, which was submitted in the instant case).[28] However, the Court ruled out that Article 15(4) UNTOC, as transposed by law No. 146/2006, could establish an appropriate ground of jurisdiction under also interpreted Article 15(4) in light of its ordinary meaning, with express reference to Article 31(1) of the Vienna Convention on the Law of Treaties, and positing (correctly, in this author's view) that it only *entitles* Italy to establish a corresponding ground of jurisdiction. Furthermore, the Court considered that the implementing order enshrined in Law No. 146/2006 could not per se establish jurisdiction under this optional ground since "an implementing order implicitly sets forth all domestic norms that enable the State to comply with the treaty obligations it accepted under international law, *but only the domestic*

[26] *Haij* (n. 24), reasoning in points of law. See, however, the criticism in Orlando (2018), p. 145; Annoni (2015), p. 420.

[27] See only Court of cassation, First Criminal Chamber, no. n.31652 of 2 July 2021. Cf. Mandrioli (2022).

[28] It should be noted that this ground of jurisdiction was not available in *Haij*, since the Minister of Justice had not submitted any request: see the criticism in Annoni (2015).

norms that are strictly necessary for this purpose".[29] This stance seems unobjectionable as a matter of domestic constitutional law; and as the wording of Article 15(4) UNTOC closely reflects the one of Article 15(2), it is frankly difficult to understand why the latter would establish a ground of jurisdiction whereas paragraph 4 would only offer UNTOC States Parties an option to do so.[30]

It should be stressed that this inconsistent interpretation of two treaty provisions which, under international law, are both interpreted as providing only for an *optional* ground of jurisdiction is not problematic in the perspective of the Palermo Convention. As stated above, its Article 15(6) does allow for jurisdiction to be exercised on purely domestic grounds. At least in principle, moreover, grounds of jurisdiction established through case law, rather than on the basis of a written law, could be in keeping with international human rights law, most notably with the requirements set forth by Article 6(1) of the European Convention on Human Rights (ECHR) as interpreted by the European Court of Human Rights (ECtHR). According to this provision,

> In the determination of his civil rights and obligations or of any criminal charge against him, everyone is entitled to a fair and public hearing within a reasonable time by an independent and impartial tribunal established by law.

In the framework of the ECHR, the notion of "law" is usually not understood in a formal sense. Thus, notably, in the Convention's perspective the requirement that criminal offences and penalties be established by law, under Article 7, is satisfied if "the individual can know from the wording of the relevant provision, if need be with the assistance of the courts' interpretation of it and after taking appropriate legal advice, what acts and omissions will make him criminally liable and what penalty he faces on that account"[31] and this does not require a written law. Indeed, the Court made clear that, when "speaking of 'law' Article 7 alludes to the very same concept as that to which the Convention refers elsewhere when using that term, a concept which comprises statutory law as well as case-law and implies qualitative requirements, notably those of accessibility and foreseeability".[32] However, specifically as regards Article 6(1), the relevant case law reads this requirement in connection with domestic safeguards: The expression "a tribunal established by law" reflects the

---

[29] Reasoning on points of law, para. 4.3 ("Un ordine di esecuzione produce tutte le norme interne necessarie perché lo Stato possa adempiere, sul piano internazionale, agli obblighi convenzionalmente assunti, ma anche le sole norme strettamente necessarie a tale scopo": translation from the original Italian by the autor).

[30] Court of Cassation, First Criminal Chamber, judgment no. 19762 of 17 June 2020. See for a critical appraisal Gavrysh (2021), p. 717.

[31] Article 25 of the Italian Constitution sets forth: "No one may be removed from the jurisdiction of the natural judge pre-established by law. . . .". English unofficial translation available at https://www.cortecostituzionale.it/documenti/download/pdf/The_Constitution_of_the_Italian_Republic.pdf.

[32] See again Judgment no. 19762/2020; cf. Court of Cassation, 12 September–27 November 2019 no. 48250.

principle of the rule of law, which is inherent in the system of protection established by the Convention and its Protocols. "Law", within the meaning of Article 6 § 1, comprises in particular the legislation on the establishment and competence of judicial organs (. . .). Accordingly, if a tribunal does not have jurisdiction to try a defendant in accordance with the provisions applicable under domestic law, it is not "established by law" within the meaning of Article 6 § 1. . ."[33]. In the context of our discussion, therefore, respect of Article 6(1) ECtHR depends on full compliance with the safeguards enshrined in the domestic legal system, notably with Italian constitutional guarantees. In particular, Article 25 of the Constitution, enshrining the principle of legality, also covers the "right to a natural judge" and prescribes that such judge should be established by the law.[34]

The term "law" must be understood here in the formal sense of written law adopted by Parliament (or other equivalent act); the requirement cannot be fulfilled by developments in the case law or by administrative acts, regardless of their foreseeability. Relying on a non-self-executing provision, without any specific implementing provision beyond the implementing order, arguably does not comply with this requirement.[35]

3.2 *Italian Adjudicative Jurisdiction, the UNTOC Smuggling Protocol and UNCLOS*

Judgment no. 31652/2021, *Jomaa and others*, poses a similar difficulty with regard to the Court of cassation's interpretation of the UNCLOS. Once again, the case concerned human trafficking and migrant smuggling at sea; three young men stood accused of smuggling migrants into the Italian territorial waters through the usual

[33] Ibid, paragraph 2.2 of the reasoning in point of law.

[34] It should be noted that the Court of cassation had previously declined to hear charges concerning murders and torture committed in Libya as against migrants wishing to reach the Italian coasts (see again Judgment no. 48250/2019, above n 36), whereas other cases relating to torture in Libya were heard on the merits on the basis of Article 10(2) of ICC.

[35] See *Jomaa*, paragraph 2.2.1 of the reasoning in point of law.: 'Le disposizioni prima richiamate espressamente riconoscono, dunque, un diritto d'intervento alle forze militari e di polizia e, conseguentemente, dell'autorità giudiziaria di uno Stato Parte, che s'imbattano, anche in «alto mare», in una nave priva di bandiera e che abbiano ragionevoli motivi per sospettare che la stessa sia coinvolta nel traffico di migranti . . . il legittimo (rectius: doveroso) esercizio dei poteri di polizia «in alto mare» da parte della nave militare o di polizia dello Stato Parte della Convenzione comporta, come logica e necessaria conseguenza, la soggezione dei prevenuti alla giurisdizione dello Stato perché i poteri autoritativi esercitati nell'occasione discendono dell'autorità statuale che, ove esercitata alle condizioni previste dalle convenzioni internazionali, racchiude in sé l'esercizio della giurisdizione, quale principale e più evidente estrinsecazione del potere autoritativo dello Stato, non venendo in gioco, in difetto di uno «Stato della bandiera», l'autorità di un altro Stato e trattandosi di una condotta compiuta in «alto mare», cioè al di fuori del territorio di altro Stato' (translation from the original Italian by the author).

"mother ship-unseaworthy vessel" pattern. The conditions of navigation in the latter vessel were appalling especially for those (exclusively black) migrants that were amassed below deck, forty-nine of whom died of asphyxiation while still in the high seas. Lower courts had upheld jurisdiction as regards migrant smuggling on the basis of the *Haij* case law; the Court of cassation confirmed their findings, although the problem had not even been raised by the applicants, since Italian Courts must rule ex officio in this regard. It further posited that the Palermo Convention and the Smuggling protocols would trigger the application of Article 7, no. 5, of the Criminal Code as regards organized criminal activities directed at smuggling of migrants towards Italy.

In the instance under discussion, Italian criminal adjudicative jurisdiction was upheld also as regards the 49 deaths of prospective migrants in the high seas, which were deemed to amount to serious crimes falling under the scope of Articles 2(b) and 3(1)(b) UNTOC. The reasoning in this specific regard is quite complex and is anchored to the idea that the reach of Italian criminal law has a "trend towards universality".[36] Once again, the Court relied on Article 7, no. 5, of the Italian Criminal Code, this time read together with Article 110 (1)(b) and (d) UNCLOS, which regulate the right to board flagless ships and ships suspected of slave trade, and the UNTOC Smuggling of Migrants Protocol, whose Article 8(7) sets forth:

> A State Party that has reasonable grounds to suspect that a vessel is engaged in the smuggling of migrants by sea and is without nationality or may be assimilated to a vessel without nationality may board and search the vessel. If evidence confirming the suspicion is found, that State Party shall take appropriate measures in accordance with relevant domestic and international law.

The Court of cassation thus acknowledged that these provisions only entitle states to use their enforcement jurisdiction (essentially through police activities),[37] without any reference to adjudicative jurisdiction. However, the fact these law-enforcement competences are regulated by Italian law is enough, according to the judgment, in order to conclude that any crimes committed on board are to be judged according to Italian Law[38] thus triggering the application of Article 7, para. 5, of the Criminal Code.

> In the Court's words, 'The above-mentioned provisions expressly acknowledge a right to take action for military and police forces and, consequently, for judicial authorities of a State Party who meet a flagless ship, even in the high seas, and have reasonable grounds to suspect that it is engaging in migrant trafficking . . . the lawful (better, the due) exercise of police powers in the high seas by a military or police ship of the State Party to the Convention entails, as a logical consequence, the subjection of the apprehended persons to the State's [enforcement] jurisdiction which, if it is exercised according with the conditions envisaged

[36] *Jomaa*, para. 2.4.

[37] Para. 2.1 of the reasoning on points of law. See already Court of cassation, First Criminal Section, no. 36052 of 23 May 2014. Cf. G. Di Chiara, "Traffico di migranti via mare, poteri di polizia nelle azioni di contrasto e tutela della dignità della persona", in Diritto Penale e Processo, 2016, 5.

[38] See e.g. Articles 8 and 9 of the International Convention on the Suppression of Counterfeiting of Currency, Geneva, 20 April 1929, League of Nations Treaty Series, vol. 112 no. 2623, and other examples quoted by Treves (1973), p. 178.

> by international treaties, entails the exercise of [adjudicative] jurisdiction, that is, the main and clearest expression of a State's public authority; absent a "flag State", this does not interfere with the authority of any other State, and moreover, since the conduct took place in the high seas, that is, outside the territory of another State'[39]

While the appropriate reading of Article 7, para. 5, is for Italian domestic authorities to assess, the automatic equation between enforcement and adjudicative jurisdiction is arguably not straightforward: on the one hand, the equation between enforcement and adjudicative jurisdiction is not as clear under international law as the Court of Cassation seems to posit.[40] On the other hand, traditional examples of conventions falling under the scope of Article 7, para. 5, clearly and explicitly address prosecution and the exercise of criminal adjudicative jurisdiction, which is not covered by Article 101 UNCLOS nor by Article 8 of the Smuggling Protocol. Specifically, Article 8(7) entitles states to take 'appropriate measures in accordance with relevant domestic and international law'. Such measures could include the exercise of adjudicative jurisdiction, but only insofar as this is actually envisaged by either domestic or international law – while the difficulty lies precisely in identifying an adequate legal basis for such exercise. Once again, any breach of the Italian constitutional principles concerning the exercise of criminal adjudicative jurisdiction would bring about also a breach of international human rights standards; thus, the central role of the principle of legality as enshrined in the Italian Constitution would seem to call for a clear stance by the legislature in order to clarify the issue once and for all. Alternatively, or additionally, the Minister of Justice could make a broader and more consistent use of its prerogatives under Article 10(2) of the criminal code whenever such crimes are committed off the Italian coasts and/or the accused persons are present on the Italian territory. However, the conditions attached to that provision imply that rather serious situations, for instance those relating to deaths that occur as a consequence of other crimes under Article 575 of the Italian Criminal Code, fall outside its scope.[41]

4 Concluding Remarks

One of the key components of any strategy in the fight against transnational crime is the legal framework regulating criminal adjudicative jurisdiction. The current international and domestic (Italian) legal framework concerning adjudicative jurisdiction over crime at sea is not entirely satisfactory in this respect. Although this framework is perfectly in keeping with the mandatory provisions included in the relevant

[39] Cfr. the analysis of Curi (2022), pp. 197 ff.

[40] Compare however Leanza, Graziani (2014) p. 163 ff.

[41] See Court of cassation, First criminal chamber, 21 December 2021-21 April 2022 n. 15556. The minimum penalty for this crime is lower than the threshold set by Article 10, para 2, Italian Criminal Code.

suppression conventions, Italian judges are often faced with very serious crimes committed in the Mediterranean Sea which do not fall squarely under those provisions. While not necessarily striving towards a "universal" application of Italian criminal law and jurisdiction, Italian courts have been clearly inspired by a commendable commitment to curb impunity, often adopting innovative interpretative approaches so as to identify grounds of jurisdiction going beyond territoriality, that would enable them to prosecute those suspected of serious crimes that had a significant connection with the Italian territorial community. However, these developments are not consistent nor fully convincing, arguably raising problems in respect of the right to a "natural judge" as protected by the Italian Constitution, and thus indirectly also by the ECHR, vis-à-vis a group of people who are often themselves vulnerable despite taking up the task of driving unseaworthy ships across the Mediterranean.[42] A better course would be for other State branches, notably Parliament and the Government, to seriously engage in closing the impunity gap as regards illicit trafficking in the Mediterranean: at the very least, the legislature could implement optional grounds of jurisdiction envisaged by Article 15 UNTOC and similar provisions included in other suppression conventions. Beyond this, it could also consider to further expand the extraterritorial reach of Italian Criminal law in respect of extremely serious crimes that are committed at sea off the Italian coasts; alternatively, the Government should exercise its prerogatives under Article 10, para. 2, of the Italian Criminal Code more broadly and consistently.

References

Annoni A (2015) Traffico di migranti via mare: l'ambito di applicazione della legge penale italiana. Rivista di Diritto della Navigazione 44:420–432

Associazione Nazionale Magistrati (2017) La rilevanza penale del fenomeno migratorio tra prassi operative e indirizzi interpretativi. La Magistratura, 29 May 2017. https://www.associazionemagistrati.it/print/2636/la-rilevanza-penale-del-fenomeno-migratorio-tra-prassi-operative-e-indirizzi-interpretativi.htm

Curi F (2022) La giurisdizione in alto mare: tra universalità tentata e territorialità consumata. Diritto, Immigrazione, Cittadinanza 1:197–210

Di Chiara G (2016) Traffico di migranti via mare, poteri di polizia nelle azioni di contrasto e tutela della dignità della persona. Diritto Penale e Processo 1:5–9

Gavrysh K (2021) La natura obbligatoria del criterio di giurisdizione previsto dall'art. 15, par. 2, della Convenzione di Palermo: commento alla sentenza n. 19762 del 17 giugno 2020 della Corte di cassazione. Diritti Umani e Diritto Internazionale 3:717

Leanza U, Graziani F (2014) Poteri di *enforcement* e di *jurisdiction* in materia di traffico di migranti via mare: aspetti operative nell'attività di contrasto. La Comunità Internazionale:163–209

Mandrioli D (2022) La giurisdizione penale extraterritoriale e la Convenzione di Palermo: nuove (o antiche?) riflessioni ispirate dalla Corte di cassazione. SIDIBlog, 31 gennaio 2022

Orlando S (2018) Problemi di giurisdizione nel contrasto al traffico di migranti via mare. Diritto Penale Contemporaneo Rivista Trimestrale 1:145–158

[42] See Associazione nazionale magistrati (2017).

Ruggiero C (2020) Dalla criminalizzazione alla giustificazione delle attività di ricerca e soccorso in mare. Le tendenze interpretative più recenti alla luce dei casi Vos Thalassa e Rackete. Diritto, Immigrazione, Cittadinanza:184–214
Ryngaert C (2015) Jurisdiction in international law, 2nd edn. Oxford University Press, Oxford
Salvadego S (2021) The Smuggling Protocol and the criminalization of humanitarian activities at sea. Brill Research Perspectives in Transnational Crime:98–108
Tullio Treves, La giurisdizione nel diritto penale internazionale (Padova, CEDAM, 1973)

Coercive Powers and Jurisdiction on the High Seas to Combat Human Smuggling

Tommaso Rafaraci

Abstract The paper addresses the main issues arising from the basic distinction between coercive powers and adjudicative jurisdiction, concerning action against migrant smuggling in the High Seas. The paper focusses in particular on the controversial praxis in the fight against the crime of aiding and abetting irregular immigration as provided for by the Italian law.

1 The Prevalence of Praxis in the Context of the Emergency

When the discussion on action against migrant smuggling in the Mediterranean Sea through criminal instruments touches on the crucial aspects of the legitimacy of procedural powers (intervention, investigation, precautionary interdiction) and the existence of jurisdiction on the related crimes, it must be recognized that we are entering a field in which praxis often prevails over rules.

To confirm this, it is sufficient to refer to the overall experience of the various naval missions undertaken, above all within the European Union, to safeguard the life and safety of migrants and at the same time, precisely, to intercept the flows of irregular immigration.[1] Regarding the latter aspect (the strictly repressive one) the use of executive-coercive powers by the authorities responsible for controlling the external borders of the EU (from seizure of ships to arrest of suspected traffickers and their surrender to the national authorities) has mostly taken place outside protocols that comply with clear and accepted regulatory parameters of legitimacy and without adequate consideration of the actual existence of the jurisdiction of the coastal State.

[1] On the subject, for more information see Annoni (2021), pp. 833 ff.

T. Rafaraci (✉)
Law Department, University of Catania, Catania, Italy
e-mail: trafaraci@lex.unict.it

V. Militello, A. Spena (eds.), *The Challenges of Illegal Trafficking in the Mediterranean Area*, Legal Studies in International, European and Comparative Criminal Law 9, https://doi.org/10.1007/978-3-031-45399-1_4

Yet it is evident that the illicit conducts that are of interest here often show, also in light of the peculiarities of their usual forms of manifestation,[2] objective elements of "extraneousness" that characterize them as cross-border crimes. In other words, they are conducts with respect to which the problem of "jurisdiction" inevitably arises in a major way, from the point of view of both jurisdiction to enforce (executive-coercive power) and jurisdiction to adjudicate (jurisdictional power over unlawful conduct).[3]

But the emergency-based approach according to which attempts have been made to tackle migrant smuggling along the routes of the Mediterranean Sea has not favored preparation and sharing of "handbooks" adequate to the issues that it was absolutely foreseeable would arise on the legal-interpretative level as well as on the operational one. In particular, under the pressure of the emergency, if on the one hand there has been a strong trend towards expansion of executive-coercive powers (jurisdiction to enforce), not always modulated proportionately and on a solid basis of legitimacy, on the other hand this has consequently prompted jurisdiction, meaning jurisdictional power (jurisdiction to adjudicate), to force its traditional limits, for the primary aim of avoiding any intermittence or stagnation in the fight against criminal trafficking.

2 The Different Aspects of "Jurisdiction" and the Problem of Their Misalignment

The objective trend towards *de facto* alignment between executive-coercive powers and the margins of jurisdiction on the High Seas is however a phenomenon that risks obscuring the essential distinctive features between the two different aspects of the "jurisdiction" mentioned above. This distinction must instead be firmly maintained in all its scope precisely when, as it has to be established which State powers are legitimately conferred and exercisable in international waters, it is not possible to count on the "coverage" of the principle of territoriality to affirm jurisdiction or to allow exercise of executive-coercive powers. With regard to the latter in particular, it must indeed be remembered that the spatial limits to the powers of coercive action of the State do not only concern the acts of the organs of the executive power but also those adopted by the organs of the judiciary, including those aimed at ascertaining crimes and prosecuting their perpetrators. In this case too it is in fact a material and concrete activity, certainly "territorial", which cannot be carried out outside the territory, except when, extraordinarily, this is provided for by international,

[2]In this regard, reference should be made to the well-known system tested by criminal organizations, based on operating a main ship located on the High Seas, which makes use of smaller boats for embarking migrants on the coasts of their country of origin for the purpose of disembarking them on the coasts of the country they are heading for. For an overview see Punzo (2019), pp. 38 ff.

[3]These are two of the three expressions (upstream there is in fact the jurisdiction to prescribe, i.e. the power to establish rules of conduct) with which, as is well known, especially in the Anglo-Saxon context, as many different meanings are distinguished in the use of the term 'jurisdiction'.

customary or treaty law.[4] Hence it is certainly to be expected that in the face of particularly alarming criminal phenomena with a transnational dimension an international source will authorize exercise of executive-coercive powers in international waters for more effective prevention and repression of illicit conducts not effectively linked to the territory of the State where the crimes are committed. But in this case, of course, exercise of State coercive powers authorized each time is consistent with the overall crime-fighting purpose, as in the same context one can also distinctly rely on certain criteria established by the law of the intervening State to entrench its jurisdiction.

With respect to the requirements posed by these basic principles, experience, in particular Italian experience, denotes often elusive practices, substantially guided by a logic of the result that is as understandable as legally questionable; practices that could have been prevented at least in part by a legislator who had intervened to untie, without even too much effort, the most intricate knots.

3 Executive-Coercive Powers in International Waters: A Basic Framework

Starting from the issue of executive-coercive powers over ships and crew members, the most controversial issues to be mentioned arise precisely with regard to the international maritime space: it is in this context that, based on the relevant international law of the sea—despite the fact that in State praxis we sometimes tend to forget it[5]—the sovereignty/territory binomial does not, in principle, have any effect. It is worth remembering that, conversely, inland waters and the territorial sea are subject to full State sovereignty, and that rather broad powers are authorized in the "contiguous area" to the territorial sea, defined by art. 33 of the Montego Bay Convention as an area in which the coastal State can exercise direct control to prevent and punish infringements regarding customs, fiscal, immigration or sanitary law.[6] The very right of innocent passage, referred to in art. 17 of the Montego Bay Convention, is in fact lost in the presence of some conducts, described in art. 19, para 2, including "loading or unloading of any commodity, currency or person contrary to the customs, fiscal, immigration or sanitary laws and regulations of the coastal State"

[4]On this generally accepted principle, see Amalfitano (2006), p. 3.

[5]A sort of 'creeping jurisdiction' resulting from the attempt by some States to configure "security zones" that go far beyond the marine spaces subject to their sovereignty is referred to, for example, by Leandro (2018), p. 882.

[6]In accordance with para. 2 of art. 33 Montego Bay Convention "The contiguous zone may not extend beyond 24 nautical miles from the baseline from which the breadth of the territorial sea is measured." On the subject of the powers exercisable in the contiguous area and the related controversial points (also with specific reference to the Italian context) see Leanza and Graziani (2014), pp. 167 ff.; Maneggia (2017), pp. 23 ff.

(art. 19 para 2 letter G Montego Bay Convention).[7] In this case, according to Italian law, the ship on police service that encounters a ship which there is reason to believe is used or involved in illicit migrant trafficking can stop it, subject to inspection and, if evidence is found, seize it by taking it to a port of the State (art. 12 c. 9-bis Consolidated Text on Immigration; see also art. 12 c. 7 Consolidated Text on Immigration).[8]

Another projection of territoriality is the right of hot pursuit and so-called 'constructive presence', provided for by art. 111 of the Montego Bay Convention. In these cases, indeed, the power to stop and reroute the boat is also permitted in international waters but as a continuation and development of the reaction (hot pursuit, precisely) that the coastal State has undertaken against a foreign ship that has entered (directly or indirectly[9]) internal waters, as well as the contiguous area, when "the competent authorities of the coastal State have good reason to believe that the ship has violated the laws and regulations of that State" (art. 111 Montego Bay Convention).

These are provisions of considerable importance also in our field. They however, from the point of view of the international source, are still clearly meant as a supplement to the protection of the coastal State in the waters subject to its sovereignty or in any case to its control, so that they say nothing about possible executive-coercive powers on the High Seas, in situations that do not present the prerequisite of a penetration of the foreign ship into the waters subject to State control.

Indeed, in these problematic situations, which are also very frequent in practice, art. 110 of the Montego Bay Convention provides, on the High Seas, for the right of visit (i.e. legitimate boarding for investigations) for ships without a flag (or with a flag of convenience). However, nothing is said about further executive powers which, in fact, would seem excluded, if we consider that the Montego Bay Convention itself, in art. 105, expressly confers them only in relation to piracy.[10] At this point, as regards our topic, one almost immediately thinks of art. 8, para 7 Additional Protocol against the smuggling of migrants to the UN Palermo Convention on transnational organized crime, according to which, a State that has reasonable grounds to suspect that a vessel is engaged in the smuggling of migrants by sea

[7] In other words, para. 2 of art. 19 of the Montego Bay Convention establishes the prohibited activities in relation to which passage can no longer be considered harmless, but "prejudicial to the peace, good order or security of the coastal State".

[8] Likewise, at least in territorial waters, according to the Italian Code of criminal procedure, personal or local searches can also be ordered, while art. 12 para. 4 Consolidated Text on Immigration provides for compulsory arrest *in flagrante delicto* for the crime of aiding and abetting irregular immigration.

[9] It can be an entry that took place—as in the case of the constructive presence—only in an intermediate way, that is, through the use of vessels operating in agreement with a "main" ship that operates as a centre of illegal activity.

[10] Indeed, in this case, art. 105 of the Montego Bay Convention provides for the power to seize the ship, arrest the people on board and seize their property, also establishing the jurisdiction of the State that carried out the seizure.

and is without nationality or may be assimilated to a vessel without nationality may board and search the vessel. If evidence confirming the suspicion is found, that State shall take appropriate measures in accordance with relevant domestic and international law".

However, in this regulatory context, to the ambiguous vagueness of the reference to "appropriate measures"[11] there is added the paucity of effects, at present, of the reference to international law, where only the aforementioned provision of art. 110 of the Montego Bay Convention exists. As for domestic law, however, in Italy art. 12 c. 9-quater of the Consolidated Law on Immigration authorizes also in international waters powers of arrest, inspection and, if appropriate, seizure and escort to a State port (which art. 12 c. 9-bis provides for in territorial waters for ships without a flag).[12] But, if, in the same context, a normative basis is sought for personal coercive measures, in particular those limiting freedom, it appears worrying, in the face of evident requirements of legality and certainty, to observe, on the one hand, that no international source establishes a framework, albeit minimal, of *ad hoc* procedural guarantees, and, on the other hand, that at least in the Italian case, the jurisprudence is oriented towards believing that the generic reference of art. 8 para 7 of the UN Convention Additional Protocol to "appropriate measures in accordance with relevant domestic law..." is a sufficient basis to legitimise adoption of precautionary measures ordinarily provided for by national criminal procedure in interventions in international waters.[13]

4 Uncertainty About Jurisdictional Powers and the Expedient of Territoriality

An evolved framework, although, as we have seen, far from fully adequate, of State executive-coercive powers to combat the smuggling of migrants on the High Seas, certainly does not exempt one from verification of jurisdiction, seen as judicial power, in relation to conducts—such as that of aiding and abetting irregular immigration—which, in light of the methods mainly used by criminal organizations, are interrupted, due to the urgency of carrying out rescue operations, precisely in international waters. In this perspective, it must be ascertained that the State, possibly in line with a generally universalistic approach to its own criminal law, establishes jurisdiction for conducts envisaged as crimes but carried out in marine areas outside its sovereignty. And it is evident that only the existence of such a jurisdiction is able to remove precariousness from legitimate exercise of police executive-coercive powers on the High Seas as mentioned above. But in this regard,

[11] The point is widely shared in the case-law: see, for example, Palazzo (2011), p. 461.

[12] On the subject see, among others, Tondi (2018), p. 69.

[13] In this sense, see e.g. Cass., section I, 23 May 2014 no. 36052. For a critical point of view see Pressacco (2021), pp. 98 ff.

delicate questions of interpretation often arise, whenever there are no clear rules attributing extraterritorial jurisdiction.

The theme cannot be dealt with here. In any case, it will suffice to mention the Italian experience, which in fact denotes—exemplarily in relation to the crime of aiding and abetting irregular immigration—the effort of jurisprudence to overcome an inadequate regulatory framework, in order to avoid weakening the repressive action against migrant trafficking. We refer to the thesis according to which landing of irregular migrants on the Italian coasts, even following their rescue in international waters, would still constitute (as it was artfully provoked by traffickers) an "event" or "result" of the crime of aiding and abetting irregular immigration, with respect to which the traffickers would take on the role of mediated perpetrators, while the rescuers would not be punishable, as mere material executors (all according to the model of art. 54 para 3 of the Criminal Code).[14]

This reconstruction, still mainly followed by jurisprudence, has aroused various major criticisms, proving to be unsuitable both with respect to the structure of the crimes in question ('reati di pericolo' and 'reati di mera condotta') and for what it postulates as for the role that is attributed to the rescuers in order to affirm that they are not punishable: in the latter respect it is in fact more correct to believe that their conduct, rather than—as some would like—determined by others, i.e. by traffickers according to the scheme of art. 54 c. 3 of the Criminal Code, should be set, if anything, within the scope of art. 51 of the Criminal Code, as the fulfillment of a (rescue) duty, already imposed in the first place by international law, suited to interrupting the criminal activity. Not to mention that, according to another thesis, the same conduct, based on the requirement of "double illegality" required by art. 12 of the Consolidate Text on Immigration,[15] should even be considered extraneous to the type of offence in question.[16]

[14]See for example, among the many rulings, Cass., section I, 16 March 2018, no. 29832; Cass., section I, 28 February 2014, no. 14510.

[15]Art. 12 para. 1 Consolidated Text on Immigration: "Unless the action constitutes a more serious crime, whoever, in violation of the provisions of this consolidated text, promotes, directs, organises, finances or carries out transport of foreigners into the territory of the State or performs other acts aimed at illegally procuring their entry into the territory of the State, or of another State of which the person is not a citizen or is not entitled to permanent residence, is punished with imprisonment from one to five years and a fine of 15,000 euros for each person".

[16]On these points see Manacorda (2018), pp. 33 ff. See also Orlando (2018), pp. 145 ff., as well as—also for references to Italian cases arising from the search and rescue activity of non-governmental organisation—Zirulia (2020), pp. 147 ff.

5 Critical Remarks and Prospects

The seriousness of these and similar criticisms juridically undermines the correctness of the thesis followed by jurisprudence and the sustainability of its corollary, i.e., the affirmation of Italian jurisdiction on the basis of art. 6 para 2 of the Criminal Code: that is, through the principle of territoriality, applied according to the criterion of "ubiquity".[17] As is well known, this is a broad criterion, which is, moreover, interpreted extensively; however, calling into question the analysis of the various structural elements of the type of offence, it exposes itself both to the objective uncertainties that can physiologically arise in this regard, and to the frequent risk of forced interpretative operations, suggested precisely by the purpose of confirming jurisdiction in cases that would not allow it.

This is how the ubiquity paradigm, through over-broad readings of art. 6 para 2 of the Criminal Code, brings into play all the evocative power of "sovereignty" that the principle of territoriality in itself is capable of displaying in support of protection needs that involve the State not so much as a *locus commissi delicti*, but more as a point of coagulation and reverberation of the harmful effects and results produced by the criminal conduct.

Faced with the confirmation of this hermeneutical approach also in relation to the resolution of jurisdictional issues concerning the crime of aiding and abetting illegal immigration, two critical observations remain topical, albeit perhaps taken for granted. The first, of a more general nature, is that the expansion of "territorial" jurisdiction once again ends up marginalising—neglecting the underlying balances—the limits and conditions dictated by Articles 7–10 of the Criminal Code to Italian jurisdiction for "external" crimes (crimes committed abroad).[18] The second is that the observed repressive instances of international migrant smuggling could well be supported by a more active legislator, by reducing these limits—as has happened, even recently, albeit in another sector of law[19]—or by expressly

[17] According to art. 6 para. 2 of the Criminal Code "The offense is considered to have been committed in the territory of the State, when the action or omission that constitutes it has occurred there in whole or in part, or the event that is the consequence of the action or omission has occurred there".

[18] On the remaining margins of jurisdiction, according to a non-forced interpretation of these provisions, for combating migrants smuggling in international waters, see the analysis of "alternative" criteria by Pressacco (2021), pp. 89 ff. (in particular, with reference to the crime of conspiracy without connection with the State territory, which jurisprudence links to Italian jurisdiction by resorting to art. 15 para. 2 letter c of the UN Convention on Transnational Organized Crime, combined with art. 7 no. 5 of the Criminal Code).

[19] See articles 9 para. 4, and 10 para. 3 of the Criminal Code, introduced by art. 1 para. 1 letters a and b, law no. 9 January 2019 no. 3, where it is established that some of the traditional conditions provided for therein are not necessary for the exercise of jurisdiction (request of the Minister of Justice, application or complaint of the victim), with regard to a series of crimes against the public administration committed by a citizen or by a foreigner abroad.

providing for jurisdiction in relation to the most important and most frequently encountered criminal offenses in international waters.[20]

References

Amalfitano C (2006) Conflitti di giurisdizione e riconoscimento delle decisioni penali nell'Unione europea. Giuffrè, Milan

Annoni A (2021) Il ruolo delle operazioni Triton e Sophia nella repressione della tratta di esseri umani e del traffico di migranti nel Mediterraneo centrale. Il Diritto dell'Unione Europea 4:829–860

Leandro A (2018) Diritto del mare e sicurezza degli spazi marini: flessioni e adeguamenti nel contrasto ai traffici illeciti. Il Diritto Marittimo 4:877–898

Leanza U, Graziani F (2014) Poteri di *enforcement* e di *jurisdiction* in materia di traffico di migranti via mare: aspetti operativi nell'attività di contrasto. La Comunità Internazionale 2:163–209

Manacorda S (2018) Tratta e traffico di migranti: il nodo della giurisdizione tra territorialità ed extraterritorialità. Diritto Penale Contemporaneo Rivista Trimestrale 3:33–44

Maneggia A (2017) Il "controllo preventivo" nella zona contigua. Rivista di Diritto Internazionale 1:23–67

Orlando S (2018) Problemi di giurisdizione nel contrasto al traffico di migranti via mare. Diritto Penale Contemporaneo 1:145–158

Palazzo F (2011) Scriminanti ed immigrazione clandestina (a proposito dei c.d. "respingimenti" in alto mare). Rivista Italiana di Diritto e Procedura Penale 2:458–473

Pressacco L (2021) Immigrazione irregolare via mare e limiti della giurisdizione penale italiana. Jus Online 2:78–103

Punzo V (2019) I traffici illeciti nel Mediterraneo. Aspetti criminologici e tendenze evolutive. In: Militello V, Spena A, Mangiaracina A, Siracusa L (eds) I traffici illeciti nel Mediterraneo, persone, stupefacenti, tabacco. Giappichelli, Turin, pp 31–66

Tondi V (2018) Sequestro preventivo e confisca quali strumenti di contrasto al traffico di migranti in ambito europeo e internazionale. Diritto Penale Contemporaneo 1:67–77

Zirulia S (2020) Non c'è *smuggling* senza ingiusto profitto. Profili di illegittimità della normativa italiana ed europea in materia di favoreggiamento dell'immigrazione irregolare. Diritto Penale Contemporaneo Rivista Trimestrale 3:143–177

[20] This is the line followed for piracy, in relation to which, on the occasion of the Atlanta and Ocean Shield missions, the legislator expressly established the Italian jurisdiction: see art. 5 decree-law of December 30, 2008 no. 209, converted into law on 24 February, 2009 no. 12; art. 7 decree-law of 12 July 2011 no. 107, converted into law on 2 August 2011 no. 130. On the subject see Pressacco (2021), p. 101.

Part II
Migrant Smuggling

Anti-smuggling Penal Policies: A Cross-National Exploration

José Ángel Brandariz

Abstract Human smuggling crimes and facilitation criminal offences have been widely explored by legal scholars. The legal literature has insightfully pointed out the various shortcomings of the legal provisions criminalising facilitation activities, contrasting them with the principles of a rights-based model of criminal justice. Much less research has been conducted on the actual enforcement of these criminal law provisions on the ground. This research gap is especially noteworthy with regard to comparative studies. This chapter contributes to bridge that gap by considering the various pitfalls stemming from the implementation of anti-smuggling penal policies in a number of western European countries. In so doing, the chapter explores the relative insignificance of smuggling and facilitation crimes in various jurisdictions, as well as their uneasy coexistence with irregular migration criminal offences. In addition, the chapter spotlights the effectiveness dimension of these penal policies, scrutinising what the rare enforcement of smuggling and facilitation crimes tells us about the role played by the criminal justice system in the coercive management of irregular migration.

1 Introduction

EU jurisdictions have long been engaged in countering irregular immigration, and more precisely human smuggling. They have mobilised a variety of legal and policy instruments for these purposes, penal measures among them. EU institutions and

I very much thank Alessandro Spena (University of Palermo) for his insightful comments on a previous version of this chapter.

J. Á. Brandariz (✉)
Public Law Department, University of A Coruna, A Coruna, Spain
e-mail: jose.angel.brandariz@udc.es

V. Militello, A. Spena (eds.), *The Challenges of Illegal Trafficking in the Mediterranean Area*, Legal Studies in International, European and Comparative Criminal Law 9, https://doi.org/10.1007/978-3-031-45399-1_5

other supranational forums have been pivotal in fostering and cementing anti-smuggling penal policies across Europe. In fact, their impulse has decisively contributed to the consolidation of a wide ranging legal and policy package, which features stringent penal measures in order to curb human smuggling.

Despite this resolute supranational agenda, the actual scope and impact of anti-smuggling policies markedly varies across jurisdictions. This is not a minor point. There is a consistent body of literature exploring the anti-smuggling agenda from a legal viewpoint, at both the national and supranational level. By contrast, explorations on the implementation of policies and legal measures on the ground are much scanter. This is especially the case with regard to comparative studies. In short, very little is known about the actual, empirical significance of anti-smuggling penal policies.

This chapter contributes to bridge this research gap by comparatively examining criminal justice data showing the actual relevance of anti-smuggling measures in five European countries. For these purposes, the chapter begins by presenting the main characteristics of the EU anti-smuggling agenda, including its penal components. Subsequently, it explores the main shortcomings—of both a theoretical and empirical nature—affecting the penal policies aimed at curbing human smuggling. In order to dig deeply into those problems, the chapter comparatively examines a range of secondary data on the real scope of criminalisation efforts in various European jurisdictions. Finally, the chapter draws on this comparative analysis to reach a number of conclusions and to propose a research agenda on the current anti-smuggling landscape in Europe.

2 Anti-smuggling Penal Policies: Criminalisation Models

Both in Europe and elsewhere, penal policies against irregular migration are essentially based upon two pillars. Within the first pillar, criminalisation policies crucially target human smuggling and the facilitation of irregular migration as a way to penalise individuals and groups who enable irregular border crossings and allegedly profit from them. In line with liberal criminal justice tenets, this legal model avoids directly penalising undocumented immigrants themselves,[1] who are frequently portrayed as victims of the greedy and inhumane plans of criminal organisations.[2] However, anti-smuggling policies also rely on a second legal pillar, that is, the direct criminalisation of irregular border-crossing activities. In contrast to human smuggling crimes, this second model implies straightforwardly criminalising undocumented immigrants. Some additional remarks are in order to characterise these two-faced penal policies.

[1] See e.g. Article 5 of the UN Protocol Against the Smuggling of Migrants.

[2] See e.g. the 2nd EU Action Plan Against Migrant Smuggling; European Commission (2021).

Criminal law measures outlawing human smuggling and the facilitation of irregular migration, i.e. unauthorised entry and unauthorised residence, are well-established.[3] In international law, these measures are prescribed by Article 6 of the Protocol against the Smuggling of Migrants by Land, Sea and Air supplementing the Convention against Transnational Organized Crime—Palermo Convention—, which was passed by the General Assembly of the UN on 15 November 2000. In EU law, EU institutions have put significant effort in developing penal measures to curb human smuggling since the early 2000s, mainly by shaping the so-called Facilitators Package. A critical component of this legal strategy is the Council Framework Decision 2002/946/JHA of 28 November 2002 on the strengthening of the penal framework to prevent the facilitation of unauthorised entry, transit and residence. Article 1 of this legislative act penalises the facilitation of unauthorised entry, transit and residence as defined by Article 1 of the Council Directive 2002/90/EC of 28 November 2002. This legal provision describes facilitators as '(a) any person who intentionally assists a person who is not a national of a Member State to enter, or transit across, the territory of a Member State in breach of the laws of the State concerned on the entry or transit of aliens', and as '(b) any person who, for financial gain, intentionally assists a person who is not a national of a Member State to reside within the territory of a Member State in breach of the laws of the State concerned on the residence of aliens.'

It has long been stressed that the range of conducts criminalised by the EU Facilitators Package is questionably broad.[4] As the transcribed Article 1 of Directive 2002/90/EC illustrates, this legal regulation does not include the requirement of obtaining financial or other material benefits to punish the facilitation of irregular entry. In addition, this criminalisation package stands out for its noteworthy severity.[5] In fact, pursuant to Articles 1(3) and 1(4) of the FD 2002/946/JHA EU jurisdictions must punish smuggling activities with a maximum imprisonment sentence of not less than eight years (or, exceptionally six years) when such activities are lucrative and either are perpetrated in the framework of a criminal organisation or endanger the lives of noncitizens. In fact, a FRA report released in 2014 reported that a number of EU countries such as Bulgaria, Cyprus, Greece, Ireland, Latvia, Lithuania, Poland, Slovakia, Spain (and the UK) prescribed maximum sentences of not less than 5 years of imprisonment in cases of facilitation of unauthorised entry and unauthorised stay.[6]

This law enforcement policy focusing on facilitation and smuggling activities was boosted in recent years by the passage of two comprehensive EU Action Plans

---

[3] Gallagher and David (2014), Mitsilegas (2015) and Ventrella (2010).

[4] Mitsilegas (2015, 2019) and van Liempt (2022).

[5] See on this the decision No. 63/2022 of the Italian Constitutional Court of 8 February 2022, which overturned Article 12(3)(d) of the 1998 Consolidating Act on Migration. Before being deemed unconstitutional, this legal provision prescribed various aggravated facilitation offences. I thank Alessandro Spena for having brought to my attention this recent Italian Constitutional Court ruling.

[6] FRA (2014b); see also Karamanidou et al. (2020).

against migrant smuggling. The first EU Action Plan was enacted in May 2015, and remained in force until 2020.[7] It was specifically aimed at enhancing the police and judicial response to smuggling activities, mainly by identifying, capturing and disposing of vessels used by smugglers, depriving smugglers of their profits, and enhancing operational cooperation against migrant smuggling. Much more recently, a second EU Action Plan against migrant smuggling was passed in September 2021.[8] This policy plan is grim in portraying the smuggling scenario in Europe and much more optimistic in presenting the achievements of prior anti-smuggling policies. This new Action Plan aims to renew the 'European fight against migrant smuggling' mainly by reinforcing cooperation with partner countries and international organisations, sanctioning smugglers and preventing the exploitation of migrants, and strengthening cooperation and supporting the work of law enforcement and judicial agencies.[9]

Beyond this criminalisation model, which aims to prevent undocumented mobility by penalising facilitation and smuggling acts, there is an additional model, which is focused on criminalising unauthorised migration itself. Certainly, this penal policy is less widespread than the model focusing on human smuggling, which currently has a continent-wide scale.[10] This is unsurprising, since in stark contrast to the consolidated facilitators package, no EU legislative act encourages—let alone obliges—national authorities to criminalise undocumented mobility. In addition, the penalisation of irregular border-crossers themselves stands at odds with the 2000 UN Protocol Against the Smuggling of Migrants, which prevents undocumented immigrants from being criminally prosecuted (Art. 5).

Having said that, the FRA[11] concluded that 21 EU jurisdictions criminalised irregular entry and 14 EU jurisdictions criminalised irregular stay in 2014.[12] To be sure, these are minor offences—largely regulated as misdemeanours—that receive sentences much more lenient than those of facilitation crimes.[13] The many European jurisdictions following this criminalisation path are not alone in embracing this penal model. A detailed report recently released by the US Library of Congress estimated that 123 jurisdictions worldwide (out of 161 analysed countries) criminalised irregular entry in 2019.[14] Therefore, the few EU countries which are reluctant to

[7] European Commission (2015a).

[8] European Commission (2021).

[9] Arrouche et al. (2021).

[10] FRA (2014a).

[11] FRA (2014b).

[12] In 2014, only the Czech Republic, Malta, Portugal, Slovenia, Slovakia, and Spain criminalised neither unauthorised entry nor unauthorised stay. In addition, Bulgaria, Finland, France, Greece, Latvia, Lithuania, and Romania did not criminalise unauthorised stay. See also Karamanidou et al. (2020), who provide updated and slightly different information.

[13] FRA (2014b); see also Karamanidou et al. (2020).

[14] US Library of Congress (2019).

criminalise undocumented mobility are part of a short list also including mainly Latin American and Eastern European jurisdictions.

3 Anti-smuggling Penal Policies: Normative and Factual Pitfalls

Despite being widely consolidated, this two-pillar model that uses criminal law and criminal justice instruments in curbing human smuggling and the facilitation of irregular migration has many problems. As will be seen next, some of these shortcomings are widely acknowledged and debated. By contrast, some others are almost completely absent from academic, legal, and policy conversations.

This gap mirrors a classical law in the books vs law in action gap—at least, to a certain extent. Some widely discussed problems affecting criminalisation efforts against human smuggling have a largely—albeit not exclusively—legal nature and are considered mainly from a law in the books viewpoint. By contrast, some other issues that have hardly called the attention of academic and institutional actors are of factual nature. This differential impact of normative and factual shortcomings is apparently related to data collection and research lacunae. In fact, the second EU Action Plan stresses that the effects of the Facilitators Package 'on the actual level of prosecution and conviction could not be evaluated, due to a lack of robust, comprehensive and comparable data'.[15] This prominent gap explains why enhancing research and data collection in the field of human smuggling is one of the key objectives to be pursued in the framework of the current 5-year Action Plan.[16]

One normative problem of the current anti-smuggling policies pertains to the criminalisation of unauthorised mobility.[17] Although irregular entry and irregular stay are treated as low-level criminal offences, their criminalisation is notably troubling from a legal perspective. In short, it is debatable whether those criminal offences are aligned with the principles setting constitutional and legal boundaries to penal power. More precisely, basic tenets of a rights-based criminal legal system such as the principle of harm and the principle of proportionality recommend regulating those behaviours as non-criminal offences rather than proper—albeit mitigated—crimes.[18]

Despite having a largely normative nature, this issue has evident factual implications. This is a trait shared with another normative debate that has gained significant momentum recently—the questionable scope of the legal provisions criminalising facilitation activities. The EU Facilitators Package goes far beyond

[15] European Commission (2021), pp. 17–18.

[16] See also McAuliffe and Laczko (2016) and Triandafyllidou and McAuliffe (2018).

[17] The criminalisation of facilitation acts has proven to be no less controversial. See Minetti (2020) and Mitsilegas (2019).

[18] Spena (2017); see also Spena (2016).

the 2000 UN Protocol against Smuggling, because Art. 1 of the Directive 2002/90/EC does not oblige EU member States to exclude non-lucrative activities and cases of humanitarian assistance from facilitation crimes. Consequently, the Facilitators Package may lead EU criminal justice systems to severely sentence individuals assisting undocumented newcomers for humanitarian reasons and without obtaining any material or financial benefit. This regulation is untenable from legal and human rights perspectives. However, it is widespread across EU jurisdictions. Back in 2014, the FRA report[19] informed that six EU jurisdictions—Croatia, Denmark, Estonia, Latvia, Romania, and Slovenia—did not require financial and material benefits and did not exclude humanitarian cases from facilitation crimes. Eventually, the European Commission's REFIT evaluation of the Facilitators Package listed only eight EU countries that did not criminalise humanitarian activities as facilitation crimes in 2017.[20]

In contrast to the aforementioned, deeply theoretical debate on the criminalisation of irregular mobility, the humanitarian assistance dilemma has widely called the attention of academic and political actors.[21] On the institutional side, the impact of this debate is noteworthy. This issue was already mentioned by the first EU Action Plan against Smuggling in 2015 and eventually took centre stage in the new 2021 EU Action Plan. In addition, the REFIT evaluation of the Facilitators Package released in 2017 explored at length this shortcoming and advocated the non-criminalisation of cases of humanitarian assistance.[22] This proposal was seconded by a resolution of the European Parliament issued in July 2018.[23] The FRA, in turn, has been spotlighting one concerning dimension of this legal conundrum, that is, the prosecution of activists and NGOs involved in search and rescue operations carried out in the Mediterranean.[24]

The 2020 EU Pact on Migration and Asylum (COM(2020) 609 final) did not overlook this dilemma, either. In fact, the Pact presents the precise definition of the scope of legal rules criminalising facilitation activities as a key action for both the European approach to search and rescue and anti-smuggling policies. Pursuing this goal, the European Commission presented an official Guidance on the implementation of EU rules on definition and prevention of the facilitation of unauthorised entry, transit and residence in September 2020.[25] Although this official Communication acknowledges that the number of criminalised cases of humanitarian assistance has been increasing in recent years,[26] it adopts an intriguingly conservative stance with

---

[19] FRA (2014a).

[20] European Commission (2017); see also European Commission (2020a).

[21] Carrera and Guild (2016a) and Carrera et al. (2018, 2019).

[22] European Commission (2017).

[23] See https://www.europarl.europa.eu/doceo/document/TA-8-2018-0314_EN.html. Accessed 10 August 2023.

[24] FRA (2020).

[25] European Commission (2020a).

[26] See López-Sala and Barbero (2021) and Fernández-Bessa (2019).

regard to the penalisation of those cases. The Communication reaches the relatively banal and taken for granted conclusion that search and rescue operations at sea cannot be criminalised because they are mandated by international law. Beyond these legally uncontroversial cases, the European Commission only invites EU member states to exclude humanitarian assistance activities from the scope of facilitation crimes, without proposing a much-needed reform of current EU law provisions.

Whilst the criminalisation of solidarity actions as facilitation crimes has long called the attention of institutions and stakeholders, there are other, largely overlooked shortcomings of current anti-smuggling penal policies. One of them relates to the biased nature of anti-smuggling penal practices. In fact, facilitation crimes have three distinct traits that pave the way for the consolidation of discriminatory law enforcement arrangements: they deal with borders and noncitizen *others*; they are poorly regulated in terms of criminal wrongdoing and the scope of criminalised conducts; and they prescribe harsh sentences. The combination of these characteristics encourage criminal justice agencies to selectively enforce facilitation crimes. That selectiveness is gradually cementing nationally and ultimately racially biased practices in the field of anti-smuggling policies.[27] Biased practices are particularly prominent in cases of so-called solidarity crimes and assistance provided by fellow national groups already settled in the country of destination.[28] Although incidental evidence abounds,[29] official databases largely disregard the citizenship of individuals prosecuted and sentenced for facilitation crimes. There is a significant and telling exception, though. The German Federal Statistical Office delivers detailed data on various socio-demographic characteristics—including citizenship—of individuals sentenced for human smuggling in Germany. These data expose the bias inherent to anti-smuggling penal practices. Whereas noncitizens accounted for 28.2 per cent of the individuals sentenced by the German criminal justice system from 2010 to 2020, they accounted for 90.6 per cent of the individuals sentenced for smuggling crimes[30] over the same period.[31]

An additional problem of factual nature affecting anti-smuggling penal policies in Europe is the actual effectiveness of law enforcement practices. Although the significance of effectiveness considerations in this field is contested,[32] this shortcoming deserves to be thoroughly scrutinised, not least because it is largely overlooked in both academic and political conversations.

---

[27] See also Hänsel et al. (2020).

[28] Fernández-Bessa (2019).

[29] See e.g. Gennari and Rigo (2021).

[30] Paras 96-97 of the 2004 German Residence Act.

[31] See https://www.statistischebibliothek.de/mir/receive/DESerie_mods_00000107. Accessed 10 August 2023.

[32] Carrera and Allsopp (2018).

4 Anti-smuggling Penal Policies: The Effectiveness Conundrum

The 2nd EU Action Plan against Migrant Smuggling boldly praises the achievements of its predecessor, the EU Action Plan 2015–2020. This is surprising, since the recently enacted 2nd EU Action Plan depicts the current human smuggling scenario in concerning tones.[33] It stresses e.g. that 'more than 90% of the irregular migrants that reach the EU make use of smugglers', and that 'approximately 50% of the networks involved in migrant smuggling are poly-criminal'.[34]

In stark contrast to this ominous criminal landscape, law enforcement outcomes do not seem particularly impressive. The 2nd Action Plan reports that the actions carried out in 2020 in the framework of the European Multidisciplinary Platform Against Criminal Threats (EMPACT) and supported by the European Migrant Smuggling Centre resulted in '2280 arrests, . . . the identification of 27 and dismantling of 14 criminal networks, 2350 document fraud cases, and the seizure of EUR 0.7 million in cash.' The official communication adds that 'in the framework of these actions, 26175 irregular migrants were detected'.[35]

The relative quantitative insignificance of these data raises a question as to what extent the questionable penal policies implemented in European countries to counter facilitation activities are actually effective. This query resonates with a point raised by the socio-legal scholar Ana Aliverti. In exploring immigration crimes in Britain, Aliverti[36] claims that they are rarely applied. Evidently, this is not a minor point. EU institutions are promoting anti-smuggling penal policies, which on top of being questionable on various fronts are apparently having little impact on the ground. This narrow range of anti-smuggling efforts stands in stark contrast to the actual significance of irregular migration in Europe. Irregular mobility peaked in the EU in 2015—when 2.155 million irregular newcomers were detected—and to a far lesser extent in 2016—when national immigration enforcement systems detected almost 0.984 million irregular noncitizens.[37] These peak years aside, the number of detected undocumented noncitizens has rarely fallen below half a million per year since the late 2000s. In fact, on average 606,596 unauthorised migrants were annually detected in the EU from 2017 to 2020.

These data recommend considering whether penal policies criminalising either irregular entry and irregular stay or facilitation activities are largely useless in managing irregular mobility flows. This point has been underexplored as no comparative study has been carried out to check whether Aliverti's findings resonate with what is happening outside Britain, in other EU jurisdictions. In order to bridge

[33] Arrouche et al. (2021).

[34] European Commission (2021), pp. 2, 4.

[35] European Commission (2021), p. 6.

[36] Aliverti (2012a, b, 2013).

[37] Source: Eurostat; https://ec.europa.eu/eurostat/web/migration-asylum/managed-migration/database. Accessed 10 August 2023.

this research gap, this chapter examines official criminal justice data from the five most populated western European jurisdictions: France, Germany, Italy, Spain and the UK, which are also among the top deporting countries in the continent.[38] This analysis may allow one to confirm whether the actual enforcement of immigration crimes in Britain has significantly changed since the early 2010s, when Aliverti published her conclusions, and whether criminalisation policies are also ineffective in other EU jurisdictions.

The official data presented in Table 1 show that Aliverti's conclusions are still valid today. Both facilitation crimes and irregular migration crimes are playing an insignificant role in the UK criminal justice system. On average, 309 facilitation crimes (sections 25-25B Immigration Act 1971) were annually sentenced from 2010 to 2020, accounting for 0.026 per cent of all convictions imposed over that period. This irrelevance is no less striking in the case of irregular migration crimes (section 24 Immigration Act 1971). The UK criminal justice system has only sentenced 38 irregular migration offences per year from 2010 to 2020, which account for 0.0032 per cent of all convictions. In addition, these sentences have had a negligible impact on irregular mobility flows. The number of sentences imposed for irregular migration crimes account for only 0.07 per cent of the undocumented immigrants detected in Britain from 2010 to 2020.

National criminal justice databases show that the British case is somehow extreme, but it is far from exceptional. There are other European jurisdictions not regularly enforcing migration crimes (Table 2).

Spain is one of these cases. Also in Spain the relevance of long enacted immigration crimes is relatively marginal. Spain is one of the countries in which irregular entry and irregular stay are not criminalised.[39] Facilitation crimes (Article 318bis of the 1995 Spanish Penal Code), in turn, averaged only 277 convictions per year from 2010 to 2020. These convictions accounted for 0.086 per cent of all crimes sentenced over the analysed time lapse. Like in Britain, these criminalisation efforts also have a minor impact on irregular mobility in Spain. In fact, on average 56,695 undocumented noncitizens were detected in Spain from 2010 to 2020. Official data show as well that irregular mobility flows seem to be on the rise in the last years.

The French criminal justice system is much more active than those of Spain and the UK in prosecuting immigration crimes. However, those law enforcement practices are far from being a pivotal component of the criminal justice system in France. The declining number of irregular immigration crimes accounted for 0.45 per cent of the criminal offences sentenced in France from 2010 to 2020. These criminalisation efforts are also relatively insignificant with regard to the scale of irregular immigration flows. On average, 2561 immigration crimes were annually sentenced in France

---

[38] Taking into account deportation practices, these European countries rank first (UK, 22.2 per cent of the total number of deportations), second (Germany, 13.3 per cent), fourth (France, 8.5 per cent), fifth (Spain, 8.2 per cent), and ninth (Italy, 2.7 per cent) of all EU member states in terms of the number of deportations enforced from 2008 to 2019 (source: Eurostat; appsso.eurostat.ec.europa.eu/nui/show.do?dataset=migr_eirtn&lang=en. Accessed 10 August 2023).

[39] FRA (2014b).

Table 1 Immigration crimes sentenced in the UK, 2010–2020 (Source: UK Ministry of Justice (https://www.gov.uk/government/statistics/criminal-justice-system-statistics-quarterly-december-2020. Accessed 10 August 2023); Eurostat)

	2010	2011	2012	2013	2014	2015	2016	2017	2018	2019	2020
Convictions (Total)	1.367M	1.314M	1.232M	1.179M	1.218M	1.249M	1.243M	1.213M	1.207M	1.191M	0.818M
Facilitation crimes	398	447	348	334	333	328	341	279	263	208	117
Irregular migration crimes	49	31	33	30	17	20	31	23	33	46	101
Detected irregular migrants	53,700	54,150	49,365	57,415	65,365	70,020	59,895	54,910	27,830	22,275	–

Table 2 Immigration crimes sentenced in Spain, 2010–2020 (Source: National Statistics Office (https://ine.es/dyngs/INEbase/es/operacion.htm?c=Estadistica_C&cid=1254736176793&menu=resultados&idp=1254735573206. Accessed 10 August 2023); Eurostat)

	2010	2011	2012	2013	2014	2015	2016	2017	2018	2019	2020
Sentenced crimes (Total)	266.5K	274K	275.1K	275.2K	278K	288.8K	365.2K	394.3K	406.3K	412.6K	311.3K
Facilitation crimes	312	177	152	206	171	315	279	424	433	387	195
Detected irregular migrants	70,315	68,825	52,485	46,195	47,885	42,605	37,295	44,625	78,280	62,865	72,265

over this eleven-year period; however, during this same period an average of 78,758 irregular noncitizens were detected per year. Interestingly, the official data contained in Table 3 lay bare the gradually shrinking reach of the French criminal justice system over irregular migration.

Unlike the British and Spanish criminal justice systems, law enforcement practices in France are not focused on facilitation crimes[40] but on irregular migration offences (Articles L821-1 to L821-5 of the 2004 Code on the Entry and Stay of Noncitizens and the Right of Asylum), especially irregular entry. In this respect, France is not an exceptional case. In fact, this pattern can be witnessed as well in e.g. Germany (Table 4).

These official data show that the German criminal justice system shares a number of traits with other national systems when it comes to prosecuting and sentencing irregular migration-related offences. Like the other penal systems scrutinised here, facilitation crimes are playing a very minor part in the German criminal justice system, since they account for 0.11 per cent of the criminal offences sentenced from 2010 to 2020. Like the French system, though, irregular migration crimes—i.e. mainly irregular entry, irregular stay, and irregular residence (§ 95 of the 2004 Residence Act)—have a much wider impact, which has slightly increased in recent years. On average, the German criminal justice system sentenced 6847 irregular migration crimes per year from 2010 to 2020, which account for 0.91 per cent of the criminal offences sentenced over this period. The scale of these criminalisation practices, though, is still far narrower than that of irregular migration phenomena. The number of sentenced migration crimes only account from 4.5 per cent of the irregular noncitizens detected in Germany from 2010 to 2020.

In spite of this caveat, the German criminal justice system is apparently more effective than those of France, Spain and the UK in countering facilitation and irregular migration offences. However, Germany cannot be described as an outlier in this regard. This qualification is more appropriate in the Italian case (Table 5).[41]

Italian judicial data are intriguingly poor. The Italian Statistical Office (ISTAT, for its initials in Italian) discontinued their publication in 2017. In addition, it is not completely clear whether the ISTAT database only includes immigration felonies or both felonies and misdemeanours.[42] Yet, even with all these uncertainties official data show that the Italian criminal justice system has been putting significant effort in prosecuting and punishing immigration criminal offences. These crimes have accounted for 4.46 per cent of the individuals sentenced in Italy from 2008 to 2017.

ISTAT data do not allow one to ascertain what specific offences are included within the general label of 'immigration crimes'. ISTAT data show that a small

[40] On the decision of the French Constitutional Council of 6 July 2018 decriminalising the so-called 'solidarity crimes', that is, the cases of assistance to undocumented noncitizens for humanitarian reasons, see https://www.conseil-constitutionnel.fr/decision/2018/2018717_718QPC.htm. Accessed 10 August 2023.

[41] Militello and Spena (2019).

[42] See ISTAT (2020).

Table 3 Immigration crimes sentenced in France, 2010–2020 (Source: Ministry of Justice (www.justice.gouv.fr/statistiques-10054/les-condamnations-32584.html. Accessed 10 August 2023); Eurostat)

	2010	2011	2012	2013	2014	2015	2016	2017	2018	2019	2020
Convictions (Total)	610K	593.1K	610.5K	599.1K	578.5K	574.5K	557.1K	555.2K	550K	562.7K	469.6K
Irregular migration crimes	4016	3435	3071	2323	2195	1965	2068	2290	2418	2414	1972
Detected irregular migrants	56,220	57,975	49,760	48,965	96,375	109,720	91,985	115,085	105,880	120,455	103,915

Table 4 Immigration crimes sentenced in Germany, 2010–2020 (Source: German Federal Statistical Office; Eurostat)

	2010	2011	2012	2013	2014	2015	2016	2017	2018	2019	2020
Convictions (Total)	813.3K	807.8K	773.9K	755.9K	748.8K	739.5K	737.9K	716K	712.3K	728.9K	699.3K
Facilitation crimes	527	548	470	652	1027	1720	1730	623	458	490	485
Irregular migration crimes	6679	6998	6941	6765	6037	5255	5038	6106	7097	8978	9424
Detected irregular migrants	50,250	56,345	64,815	86,305	128,290	376,435	370,555	156,710	134,125	133,525	117,930

Table 5 Number of individuals sentenced for immigration crimes in Italy, 2008–2017 (Source: Italian Statistical Office (dati.istat.it/Index.aspx?lang=it&SubSessionId=708e3729-7cf8-4083-bdde-7c668627f704. Accessed 10 August 2023); Eurostat)

	2008	2009	2010	2011	2012	2013	2014	2015	2016	2017
Convictions (Crimes. Total)	292.2K	292.8K	254.4K	266K	259.9K	247K	226.9K	220.9K	209.9K	207.8K
Migration crimes	23,886	21,987	17,362	14,388	8589	5024	4036	4197	4755	6429
Detected irregular migrants	68,175	53,440	46,955	29,505	29,345	23,945	25,300	27,305	32,365	36,230

percentage of the individuals sentenced for immigration crimes—10.5 per cent from 2015 to 2017—were Italian nationals.[43] Consequently, the data analysed here do not include only irregular migration crimes. Still, irregular migration offences (Art. 10-bis of the 1998 Consolidating Act on Immigration) are surely the lion's share of this indicator. In this respect, the potential impact of these law enforcement practices on irregular migration in Italy is noteworthy. The total number of individuals sentenced for immigration crimes accounts for 29.7 per cent of all irregular noncitizens detected in Italy from 2008 to 2017.

In short, the Italian criminal justice system has proven to be an outlier in terms of the scale and scope of its penal policies aimed at curbing smuggling activities and irregular migration. If there is a national case in western Europe that apparently challenges Ana Aliverti's conclusions on the actual significance and effectiveness of immigration crimes, then it is Italy. One of the dimensions to be taken into account in exploring this peculiar national case has to do with the pivotal role played by gate-keeping tasks[44] in Italy, that is, by border control activities aimed at sealing EU external borders. Indeed, the protection of external borders takes centre stage in the immigration enforcement systems of certain EU jurisdictions, in particular Mediterranean countries.[45] The vital part played by these specific gate-keeping activities in those peripheral EU jurisdictions actually conditions the way in which they react to irregular border crossings. In fact, in the Italian case irregular migration has essentially to do with irregular entry, in contrast to what happens in many other central and northern EU countries. In this regard it is noteworthy that Eurostat reports 172,350 undocumented noncitizens detected in Italy from 2015 to 2020, whilst Frontex counted 527,445 irregular border crossers in the so-called Central Mediterranean route over the same period.[46]

These specific characteristics of irregular mobility and border control practices in Italy help explain the significant part played by the criminal justice system in coercively handling undocumented migration in this specific case. In this regard, it should be noted that irregular entry is treated more severely than irregular stay by EU law provisions and national legal orders.[47] However, this is only part of the story. Additional aspects should be examined to grasp why the Italian case stands in contrast to the relative irrelevance of immigration crimes across Europe. These aspects are explored in the last, closing section, which also outlines a research agenda to develop comparative, cross-national explorations on anti-smuggling penal policies in Europe.

[43] Ibid.

[44] Triandafyllidou and Ambrosini (2011).

[45] Fernández-Bessa (2021).

[46] See https://frontex.europa.eu/we-know/migratory-routes/central-mediterranean-route/. Accessed 10 August 2023.

[47] See Article 1 of the Directive 2002/90/EC; see also FRA (2014b).

5 Conclusions: Towards a Comparative Research Agenda on Anti-smuggling Penal Policies

This study shows that many questions remain to be addressed in the field of anti-smuggling penal policies. For clarification purposes, in this concluding section those queries are going to be grouped in two different clusters.

The first cluster of pending research questions has to do with the biased, unbalanced nature of the criminalisation practices aimed at preventing irregular migration phenomena. It was already pointed out that there is certain evidence that citizenship criteria are deeply conditioning the type and intensity of legal reaction to undocumented migration cases.[48] These biased penal practices require further scrutiny, which should aim to collect and analyse data on the differential impact of law enforcement strategies.

An additional, critical point to be examined in the framework of this first cluster of research questions concerns the relative part played by facilitation criminal offences and irregular migration crimes in countering undocumented mobility. The national cases dissected in this paper, especially those of France, Germany and—arguably—Italy lay bare that the latter category of offences account for the bulk of migration crimes in Europe. In other words, despite the widespread rhetoric presenting undocumented noncitizens as victims of smuggling activities and portraying criminalisation efforts in this field as a way of protecting vulnerable immigrants,[49] it is actually irregular noncitizens themselves who are most frequently criminalised by immigration offences.[50]

This is unsurprising, at least to a certain extent. The US criminal justice system has also developed wide-ranging penal policies aimed at punitively managing undocumented mobility. The scope of these law enforcement arrangements is arguably wider than that of similar policies in the EU. Scale issues aside, though, US penal strategies share a common feature with those of many EU jurisdictions, that is, they prevailingly focus on the criminalisation of irregular border crossings (Table 6).

Official data suggest that US criminalisation efforts in the field of migration control have been largely centred on what Daniel Kanstroom[51] calls extended border control—as opposed to post-entry social control—, that is, on punishing irregular entry activities rather than irregular stay cases. In addition, these US Department of Justice data illustrate that smuggling offences (8 U.S.C. Sections 1323, 1324 and 1327) are far from being the engine of that penalisation agenda. Whereas they accounted for 20 per cent of all immigration crime cases in the late 1990s, their percentage decreased over time to 4–6 per cent in the 2010s.

---

[48] See Fernández-Bessa (2019).

[49] See e.g. European Commission (2021).

[50] See also Spena (2016).

[51] Kanstroom (2012).

Table 6 Number of individuals prosecuted for immigration crimes in the US, 1998–2018 (Source: US Department of Justice (Motivans 2021))

Year	Illegal entry (%)	Illegal re-entry (%)	Smuggling (%)	Other offences (%)	Offences (Total)
1998	3039 (22.9%)	6440 (48.6%)	2711 (20.5%)	1059 (8%)	13,249
1999	4449 (29.3%)	6811 (44.8%)	3200 (21.1%)	727 (4.8%)	15,187
2000	3964 (24.7%)	8081 (50.3%)	3251 (20.3%)	757 (4.7%)	16,053
2001	3281 (21.4%)	8545 (55.8%)	2766 (18.1%)	717 (4.7%)	15,309
2002	3206 (19.8%)	9361 (57.9%)	2948 (18.2%)	656 (4.1%)	16,171
2003	4629 (22.8%)	11,479 (56.4%)	3286 (16.1%)	953 (4.7%)	20,347
2004	18,337 (49.1%)	13,458 (36.1%)	4498 (12.1%)	1033 (2.8%)	37,326
2005	15,456 (42.3%)	14,809 (40.5%)	5051 (13.8%)	1243 (3.4%)	36,559
2006	13,970 (38.6%)	15,735 (43.4%)	5297 (14.6%)	1224 (3.4%)	36,226
2007	14,790 (38%)	17,830 (45.8%)	5045 (13%)	1261 (3.2%)	38,926
2008	52,087 (64.6%)	21,348 (26.5%)	5112 (6.3%)	2068 (2.6%)	80,615
2009	51,864 (58.7%)	30,223 (34.2%)	4251 (4.8%)	1975 (2.2%)	88,313
2010	43,546 (50.9%)	35,899 (42%)	4010 (4.7%)	2090 (2.4%)	85,545
2011	41,017 (49.2%)	36,952 (44.3%)	3596 (4.3%)	1759 (2.1%)	83,324
2012	50,311 (54.5%)	36,857 (39.9%)	3684 (4%)	1493 (1.6%)	92,345
2013	51,378 (54.5%)	37,517 (39.8%)	3996 (4.2%)	1382 (1.5%)	94,273
2014	39,269 (48.3%)	37,166 (45.7%)	3731 (4.6%)	1139 (1.4%)	81,305
2015	35,100 (48.1%)	33,370 (45.7%)	3758 (5.1%)	800 (1.1%)	73,028
2016	35,546 (50.6%)	29,755 (42.4%)	4176 (5.9%)	760 (1.1%)	70,237
2017	27,657 (46.3%)	27,218 (45.5%)	4190 (7%)	732 (1.2%)	59,797
2018	67,603 (62.7%)	34,351 (31.9%)	4851 (4.5%)	989 (0.9%)	107,794

The main driver of this criminal justice sub-system, which has been amplifying its scope over the last fifteen years, are two criminal offences targeting irregular entry conducts, i.e. the misdemeanour of improper entry (8 U.S.C. Section 1325, I.N.A. Section 275) and the felony of re-entry of removed alien (8 U.S.C. Section 1326, I.N.A. Section 276). Official data show that these two offences combined have accounted for more than 90 per cent of immigration crime cases in the US since 2008 (e.g. 94.6 per cent in 2018).

The US case clearly illustrates that it is not legal reforms that alter the course of penal policies in the field of irregular migration. The criminal offences of illegal entry and illegal re-entry have long been part of the US legal order, since they were enacted in 1929.[52] However, they were rarely enforced until the turn of the century.[53] Until then, irregular border crossing cases had been largely treated as non-criminal cases, resulting in undocumented noncitizens being 'pushed back' to Mexico rather than jailed and criminally prosecuted.[54] A number of non-legal factors completely changed the penal landscape in the US borderlands. Burgeoning anti-immigration sentiments led border control concerns to take centre stage in political and public debates.[55] The new crimmigration policies were consolidated via financial[56] and logistical measures—e.g. the remarkable expansion of the immigration detention estate.[57] As it has been the case elsewhere,[58] managerial measures were also pivotal to expand the gamut of the US crimmigration system. So-called 'assembly line justice' arrangements, in which scores of noncitizen defendants are expeditiously tried for irregular re-entry and—especially—irregular entry offences gave a vital boost to criminalisation efforts in the US.[59] Managerial criminal justice schemes such as 'Operation Streamline' are the best evidence of this penal policy turn.

The US case demonstrates that the European countries in which penal policies are actually focused on penalising undocumented immigrants rather than smugglers are no exception. Regardless of whether this penal model is widespread or not, it raises many legal and constitutional questions. Severe criminal law provisions are not the best legal instrument to tackle a phenomenon such as undocumented mobility, whose significance in terms of harm and wrongdoing is relatively negligible.[60] Therefore, penal strategies in the field of irregular migration should not be based on these questionable criminal offences.

The second cluster of research questions to be addressed in the sphere of anti-smuggling penal policies pertain to effectiveness concerns. Efficacy considerations have long had a noticeable impact in the field of EU policies of migration control. They have ranked high in conversations on deportation practices,[61] especially in the political and institutional sphere.[62] They have had certain—albeit much lesser—

[52] Eagly (2010) and García Hernández (2019).

[53] García Hernández (2018).

[54] Abrego et al. (2017), Chazaro (2016) and Vázquez (2017).

[55] Armenta (2017), Kanstroom (2012) and Wadhia (2015).

[56] Golash-Boza (2015) and Kanstroom (2012).

[57] Macías-Rojas (2016) and Koulish (2010).

[58] Brandariz and Fernández-Bessa (2017) and Moffette (2018).

[59] Kubal and Olayo-Méndez (2020) and Martínez et al. (2018).

[60] See also FRA (2014a).

[61] Brandariz (2021a); Gibney (2008); Leerkes and van Houte (2020); see also Carrera and Allsopp (2018).

[62] See e.g. European Commission (2015b) and European Parliament (2020).

influence on human trafficking debates, be they academic[63] or institutional.[64] Surely, these effectiveness tropes cannot be disassociated from the wide availability of data on the performance of criminal justice systems in prosecuting trafficking cases. In fact, these official data show that EU countries are failing to implement wide encompassing policies aimed at preventing human trafficking, with very few exceptions.[65]

By contrast, anti-smuggling penal policies have been largely overlooked by effectiveness debates.[66] It is time to overcome this shortcoming, in order to comparatively explore whether law enforcement arrangements that are debatable from a human rights perspective can also be challenged from an effectiveness viewpoint.

This paper has confirmed that the conclusions on the effectiveness of immigration crimes in the UK elaborated by Ana Aliverti one decade ago are still valid today, and that they can be applied as well to other western EU jurisdictions. In addition, it has verified that Italy is not one of these cases. The analysis presented in the previous section shows that the Italian criminal justice system uses immigration crimes widely to curb irregular immigration flows.

This phenomenon may be examined from a wider perspective. Over-representation rates measure the over-incarceration of noncitizens by comparing the percentage of noncitizen prisoners and that of noncitizen residents.[67] This indicator shows that Italy stands out for the over-representation of noncitizens in their national systems. In 2019, two EU countries had over-incarceration rates higher than 7, i.e. Croatia and Greece.[68] Those exceptional cases aside, the majority of EU jurisdictions had over-incarceration rates between 2 and 4. Certain EU countries had rates below 2 (e.g. Czech Republic, Poland, Romania, Slovakia), and in some others such as Ireland and the UK over-representation is virtually non-existent.[69]

The British over-representation rate was 1.19 in 2019. This intriguingly low rate implies that UK's particular features in terms of the role played by the criminal justice system in coercively managing irregular mobility go far beyond its poor performance in enforcing immigration crimes. In fact, that indicator shows that the UK criminal justice system is not over-policing[70] over-prosecuting and over-incarcerating noncitizens at particularly high rates. Italy stands on the opposite side of the spectrum. Its over-incarceration rate was 4.05 in 2019, ranking third in

[63] Skilbrei (2017); see also Farrel et al. (2014).

[64] European Commission (2020b).

[65] See European Commission (2020b).

[66] See though Carrera and Guild (2016b).

[67] See e.g. Melossi (2015).

[68] Sources: Aebi and Tiago (2020); Eurostat; https://ec.europa.eu/eurostat/web/population-demography/demography-population-stock-balance/database. Accessed 10 August 2023.

[69] See Kaufman and Bosworth (2013) and Melossi (2015).

[70] It should be understood that noncitizens are not being intensively over-policed in Britain for crime control purposes. By contrast, there is no doubt that they are being dramatically over-policed for immigration enforcement purposes (Aliverti 2020; Parmar 2020).

the EU, only below those of Croatia and Greece. In stark contrast to the UK scenario, Italy stands out not only for its frequent utilisation of immigration crimes, but also for its extensive use of the criminal justice system to coercively manage unwanted noncitizen populations.

This marked divergence in terms of penal policies can be further explored by recalling a critical point raised by Aliverti.[71] In examining the rare enforcement of immigration crimes in Britain, she points out that 'prosecution generally follows when a foreigner is not 'readily removable''; in other words, 'the actual enforcement of these offences is bound by practical considerations, mainly the impossibility of immediate removal'.[72] These insightful comments show that the Italian and UK cases have much more in common than what a superficial gaze may lead one to conclude. In fact, the Italian case with its intensive utilisation of criminal justice resources in managing unwanted newcomers is no different from Britain when it comes to adopting an instrumental logic to govern immigration enforcement.[73] The UK has a particularly wide ranging and effective immigration enforcement system that is almost unparalleled across Europe.[74] This consolidated law enforcement apparatus makes criminal justice resources dispensable in handling potentially troubling noncitizen groups. The opposite is true in the case of Italy. The Mediterranean country ranks very low in terms of scope and especially effectiveness of its detention and deportation system.[75] Those shortcomings make the concurrence of the criminal justice system—in managing both noncitizen offenders and irregular immigrants—particularly needed and perfectly reasonable from an instrumental perspective.

This last point suggests that the comparative examination of anti-smuggling penal policies reveals certain dimensions of the interrelation between the immigration enforcement system and the penal system that have been underexplored so far. One of the reasons why smuggling crimes, and migration criminal offences more generally are being more or less enforced has to do with the respective roles played by penal policies and immigration enforcement policies in the coercive governance of migration phenomena at the national level. Therefore, together with the biased and unbalanced nature of criminalisation efforts in this field, a research agenda on

[71] Aliverti (2012a, b, 2013).

[72] Aliverti (2012b), pp. 423–424.

[73] Brandariz (2021b) and Sklansky (2012).

[74] Eurostat data show that the UK ranked first of all EU countries in terms of the number of deportations enforced from 2008 to 2019. It carried out 581,705 deportations over this period, accounting for 22.2 per cent of all deportation orders enforced in the EU. In addition, it ranked second in terms of deportation enforcement rates, having enforced 89.7 per cent of the removal orders issued from 2008 to 2019.

[75] Campesi and Fabini (2020). Italy ranks ninth of all EU countries with regard to the number of deportations carried out from 2008 to 2019. In this period, Italy enforced 71,575 deportations (2.7 per cent of all deportation orders carried out in the EU). In addition, Italy ranks twenty-sixth in the enforcement rate list (16.8 per cent of deportation orders enforced from 2008 to 2019) (source: Eurostat).

anti-smuggling penal policies should take into account the varied combinations of criminal justice instruments and immigration enforcement instruments being used across Europe. In other words, it ought to consider if and to what extent effective deportation systems are superseding criminal law arrangements like the prosecution and sentencing of smuggling, facilitation and irregular migration crimes. This analysis will also shed much needed light on the changing and varied relations between (ordered) penality and bordered penality[76] in European jurisdictions.

References

Aas KF (2013) The ordered and the bordered society: migration control, citizenship, and the northern penal state. In: Aas KF, Bosworth M (eds) The borders of punishment: migration, citizenship, and social exclusion. Oxford University Press, Oxford, pp 21–39

Abrego L, Coleman M, Martínez DE, Menjívar C, Slack J (2017) Making immigrants into criminals: legal processes of criminalization in the post-IIRIRA era. J Migr Hum Secur 5(3): 694–715

Aebi MF, Tiago MM (2020) SPACE I - 2019 – Council of Europe Annual Penal Statistics: prison populations. Council of Europe, Strasbourg. https://wp.unil.ch/space/space-i/annual-reports/. Accessed 10 Aug 2023

Aliverti A (2012a) Exploring the function of criminal law in the policing of foreigners: the decision to prosecute immigration-related offences. Soc Leg Stud 21(4):511–527

Aliverti A (2012b) Making people criminal: the role of the criminal law in immigration enforcement. Theor Criminol 16(4):417–434

Aliverti A (2013) Crimes of mobility: criminal law and the regulation of immigration. Routledge, London

Aliverti A (2020) Patrolling the 'thin blue line' in a world in motion: an exploration of the crime-migration nexus in UK policing. Theor Criminol 24(1):8–27

Armenta A (2017) Serve, protect and deport: the rise of policing as immigration enforcement. University of California Press, Oakland

Arrouche K, Fallone A, Vosyliūtė L (2021) Between politics and inconvenient evidence: assessing the renewed EU Action Plan against migrant smuggling. CEPS Policy Brief 2021-1. https://www.ceps.eu/ceps-publications/between-politics-and-inconvenient-evidence/

Brandariz JA (2021a) An expanded analytical gaze on penal power: border criminology and punitiveness. Int J Crime Justice Soc Democr 10(2):99–112

Brandariz JA (2021b) Criminalization or instrumentalism? New trends in the field of border criminology. Theor Criminol. Epub Ahead of Print 16 April 2021

Brandariz JA, Fernández-Bessa C (2017) The managerial turn: the transformation of Spanish migration control policies since the onset of the economic crisis. Howard J Crime Justice 56(2):198–219

Campesi G, Fabini G (2020) Immigration detention as social defence: policing 'dangerous mobility' in Italy. Theor Criminol 24(1):50–70

Carrera S, Allsopp J (2018) The irregular immigration policy conundrum: problematizing 'effectiveness' as a frame for EU criminalization and expulsion policies. In: Ripoll Servent A, Trauner F (eds) The Routledge handbook of justice and home affairs research. Routledge, London, pp 70–82

[76] Aas (2013).

Carrera S, Guild E (eds) (2016a) Irregular migration, trafficking and smuggling of human beings: policy dilemmas in the EU. CEPS, Brussels
Carrera S, Guild E (2016b) Migrant smuggling in the EU: what do the facts tell us? In: Carrera S, Guild E (eds) Irregular migration, trafficking and smuggling of human beings: policy dilemmas in the EU. CEPS, Brussels, pp 11–16
Carrera S, Vosyliūtė L, Smialowski S, Allsopp J, Sanchez G (2018) Fit for purpose? The Facilitation Directive and the criminalisation of humanitarian assistance to irregular migrants: 2018 Update European Parliament. www.europarl.europa.eu/RegData/etudes/STUD/2018/608838/IPOL_STU(2018)608838_EN.pdf
Carrera S, Mitsilegas V, Allsopp J, Vosyliūtė L (2019) Policing humanitarianism: EU policies against human smuggling and their impact on civil society. Hart, Portland
Chazaro A (2016) Challenging the "Criminal Alien" paradigm. UCLA Law Rev 63(3):594–664
Eagly IV (2010) Prosecuting immigration. Northwest Univ Law Rev 104(4):1281–1359
European Commission (2015a) Communication from the Commission to the European Parliament, the Council, the European Economic and Social Committee and the Committee of the Regions: EU Action Plan against Migrant Smuggling (2015 - 2020). COM/2015/0285 final. eur-lex.europa.eu/legal-content/EN/TXT/PDF/?uri=CELEX:52015DC0285&from=EN
European Commission (2015b) Communication from the Commission to the European Parliament, the Council, the European Economic and Social Committee and the Committee of the Regions: A European Agenda on Migration. COM/2015/0240 final. https://eur-lex.europa.eu/legal-content/EN/TXT/?uri=celex%3A52015DC0240
European Commission (2017) Refit evaluation of the EU legal framework against facilitation of unauthorised entry, transit and residence: The Facilitators Package (Directive 2002/90/EC and Framework Decision 2002/946/JHA). SWD(2017) 117 final. https://ec.europa.eu/transparency/documents-register/detail?ref=SWD(2017)117&lang=en
European Commission (2020a) Commission Guidance on the implementation of EU rules on definition and prevention of the facilitation of unauthorised entry, transit and residence. 2020/C 323/01. https://eur-lex.europa.eu/legal-content/en/TXT/?uri=CELEX%3A52020XC1001%2801%29
European Commission (2020b) Data collection on trafficking in human beings in the EU. https://op.europa.eu/en/publication-detail/-/publication/5b93c49f-12a0-11eb-9a54-01aa75ed71a1
European Commission (2021) Communication from the Commission to the European Parliament, the Council, the European Economic and Social Committee and the Committee of the Regions: A renewed EU action plan against migrant smuggling (2021-2025). COM(2021) 591 final. eur-lex.europa.eu/legal-content/EN/TXT/PDF/?uri=CELEX:52021DC0591&from=EN
European Parliament (2020) European Parliament resolution of 17 December 2020 on the implementation of the Return Directive (2019/2208(INI)). Available from https://eur-lex.europa.eu/legal-content/EN/TXT/?uri=CELEX:52020IP0362. Accessed 10 Aug 2023
Farrel A, Owens C, McDevitt J (2014) New laws but few cases: understanding the challenges to the investigation and prosecution of human trafficking cases. Crime Law Soc Change 61(2):139–168
Fernández-Bessa C (2019) A theoretical typology of border activism: from the streets to the Council. Theor Criminol 23(2):156–174
Fernández-Bessa C (2021) Los Centros de Internamiento de Extranjeros (CIE): Una introducción desde las Ciencias Penales. Iustel, Madrid
FRA (2014a) Criminalisation of irregular migrants and of persons engaging with them. fra.europa.eu/sites/default/files/fra_uploads/fra-2014-criminalisation-of-migrants-1_en.pdf
FRA (2014b) Annex: EU member states' legislation on irregular entry and stay, as well as facilitation of irregular entry and stay. fra.europa.eu/sites/default/files/fra_uploads/fra-2014-criminalisation-of-migrants-annex-0_en.pdf
FRA (2020) Fundamental rights considerations: NGO ships involved in search and rescue in the Mediterranean and legal proceedings against them. https://fra.europa.eu/en/publication/2020/2020-update-ngos-sar-activities#publication-tab-0

Gallagher AT, David F (2014) The international law of migrant smuggling. Cambridge University Press, Cambridge
García Hernández CC (2018) Deconstructing crimmigration. Univ Calif Davis Law Rev 52:197–253
García Hernández CC (2019) Migrating to prison: America's obsession with locking up immigrants. The New Press, New York
Gennari L, Rigo E (2021) Processo alla solidarietà. Il Manifesto, 23 February. https://ilmanifesto.it/processo-alla-solidarieta
Gibney MJ (2008) Asylum and the expansion of deportation in the United Kingdom. Gov Oppos 43(2):146–167
Golash-Boza T (2015) Deported: immigrant policing, disposable labour and global capitalism. New York University Press, New York
Hänsel V, Moloney R, Firla D, Serkepkanî R (2020) Incarcerating the marginalized: the fight against alleged 'smugglers' on the Greek Hotspot Islands. Bordermonitoring.eu, München. https://www.borderline-europe.de/eigene-publikationen/stigmatisiert-inhaftiert-kriminalisiert-der-kampf-gegen-vermeintliche-schleuser?l=en
ISTAT (2020) Delitti, imputati e vittime dei reati. https://www.istat.it/it/archivio/252815
Kanstroom D (2012) Aftermath: deportation law and the new American diaspora. Oxford University Press, New York
Karamanidou L, Kasparek B, Hess S (2020) Border management and migration control: comparative report. Respond Working Papers. Paper 2020/46. https://respondmigration.com/wp-blog/border-management-migration-control-comparative-report
Kaufman E, Bosworth M (2013) The prison and national identity: citizenship, punishment and the sovereign state. In: Scott D (ed) Why prison? Cambridge University Press, Cambridge, pp 170–188
Koulish R (2010) Immigration and American democracy: subverting the rule of law. Routledge, New York
Kubal A, Olayo-Méndez A (2020) Mirrors of justice? Undocumented immigrants in courts in the United States and Russia. In: Koulish R, van der Woude M (eds) Crimmigrant nations: resurgent nationalism and the closing of borders. Fordham University Press, New York, pp 198–224
Leerkes A, van Houte M (2020) Beyond the deportation regime: differential state interests and capacities in dealing with (non-) deportability in Europe. Citizenship Stud 24(3):319–338
López-Sala A, Barbero I (2021) Solidarity under siege: the crimmigration of activism(s) and protest against border control in Spain. Eur J Criminol 18(5):678–694
Macías-Rojas P (2016) From deportation to prison: the politics of immigration enforcement in post-civil rights America. New York University Press, New York
Martínez DE, Slack J, Martínez-Schuldt R (2018) The rise of mass deportation in the United States. In: Martínez R Jr, Hollis ME, Stowell JI (eds) The handbook of race, ethnicity, crime, and justice. Willey Blackwell, Hoboken, pp 173–201
McAuliffe ML, Laczko F (eds) (2016) Migrant smuggling data and research: a global review of the emerging evidence base. IOM, Genève
Melossi D (2015) Crime, punishment and migration. Sage, London
Militello V, Spena A (2019) Between criminalization and protection: the Italian way of dealing with migrant smuggling and trafficking within the European and international context. Brill, Leiden
Minetti M (2020) The facilitators package, penal populism and the rule of law: lessons from Italy. New J Eur Crim Law 11(3):335–350
Mitsilegas V (2015) The criminalisation of migration in Europe: challenges for human rights and the rule of law. Springer, New York
Mitsilegas V (2019) The normative foundations of the criminalization of human smuggling: exploring the fault lines between European and international law. New J Eur Crim Law 10(1): 68–85
Moffette D (2018) Governing irregular migration: bordering culture, labour, and security in Spain. University of British Columbia Press, Vancouver

Motivans M (2021) Immigration, Citizenship, and the Criminal Justice System, 1998-2018. https://bjs.ojp.gov/library/publications/immigration-citizenship-and-federal-justice-system-1998-2018
Parmar A (2020) Arresting (non)citizenship: the policing migration nexus of nationality, race and criminalization. Theor Criminol 24(1):28–49
Skilbrei M (2017) Barriers to prosecution of human trafficking: identifying general challenges from a specific case. In: Rodrigues AM, Guia MJ (eds) Livro de Atas. Conferência Internacional 18 de Outubro Dia Europeu contra o Tráfico de Seres Humanos. Instituto Jurídico Faculdade de Direito, Coimbra
Sklansky DA (2012) Crime, immigration, and ad hoc instrumentalism. New Crim Law Rev 15(2): 157–223
Spena A (2016) Human smuggling and irregular immigration in the EU: from complicity to exploitation? In: Carrera S, Guild E (eds) Irregular migration, trafficking and smuggling of human beings: policy dilemmas in the EU. CEPS, Brussels, pp 33–40
Spena A (2017) A just criminalization of irregular immigration: is it possible? Crim Law Philos 11(2):351–373
Triandafyllidou A, Ambrosini M (2011) Irregular immigration control in Italy and Greece: strong fencing and weak gate-keeping serving the labour market. Eur J Migr Law 13(3):251–273
Triandafyllidou A, McAuliffe ML (eds) (2018) Migrant smuggling data and research: a global review of the emerging evidence base, vol 2. IOM, Genève
US Library of Congress (2019) Criminalization of illegal entry around the world. Law Library, Library of Congress, Washington. www.hsdl.org/?view&did=829757. Accessed 10 Aug 2023
van Liempt I (2022) Humanitarian smuggling in a time of restricting and criminalizing mobility. In: Gallien M, Weigand F (eds) The Routledge handbook of smuggling. Routledge, London
Vázquez Y (2017) Crimmigration: the missing piece of criminal justice reform. Univ Richmond Law Rev 51:1093–1147
Ventrella M (2010) The control of people smuggling and trafficking in the EU: experiences from the UK and Italy. Routledge, London
Wadhia SS (2015) Beyond deportation: the role of prosecutorial discretion in immigration cases. New York University Press, New York

The Distinction between Facilitation of Irregular Immigration and Organised Smuggling of Migrants and Its Relevance for the Italian Criminal Law?

Alessandro Spena

Abstract In its judgement No. 63/2022, the Italian constitutional court advances a reading of Art. 12 of Legislative decree No. 286/1998 (Tuimm) according to which a distinction should be made between mere facilitation, punished in par. 1 and seen as revolving around the "altruistic" conduct of an "individual" author, and smuggling of migrants, which the Court argues to be specifically criminalized instead in paragraphs 3, 3 bis and 3 ter, and to be evoking "scenarios of involvement of criminal organizations." This paper raises some criticisms of this reading, showing how it, in addition to not being necessary for the Court's purpose of showing the unconstitutionality of the two aggravating factors under censure (use of international transportation services and use of counterfeit documents), does not fit to explain the actual contents of Art. 12 Tuimm.

1 Introduction

In its judgement No. 63 of 8.2.2022,[1] the Italian constitutional court (henceforth: the Court) declared illegitimate Art. 12 par. 3, subparagraph d, of d.lgs. 25.7.1998, No. 286 (*Testo unico delle disposizioni concernenti la disciplina dell'immigrazione e norme sulla condizione dello straniero*, henceforth: Tuimm) insofar as it established that a much more severe sentence range ("imprisonment from five to

A previous Italian version of this chapter has been published in Diritto, immigrazione e cittadinanza, 3/2022.

[1] On which see, e.g., Zirulia (2022); Ciervo (2022).

A. Spena (✉)
Department of Law, University of Palermo, Palermo, Italy
e-mail: alessandro.spena@unipa.it

V. Militello, A. Spena (eds.), *The Challenges of Illegal Trafficking in the Mediterranean Area*, Legal Studies in International, European and Comparative Criminal Law 9, https://doi.org/10.1007/978-3-031-45399-1_6

fifteen years and [...] fine of 15. 000 euros for each person") than that provided for the corresponding basic form (which par. 1 punishes "with imprisonment from one to five years and a fine of 15,000 euros for each person") should be applied in those cases in which the crime of facilitation of the irregular entrance of foreigners was carried out "using international transportation services or counterfeit or altered documents or documents obtained in other illegal ways". The particular severity of the punishment aggravation provided was deemed excessive compared to the relevance of the factors on which it was dependent (use of international transportation services or forged documents, etc.), which put it in conflict with the principle of proportionality of the criminal sanction, such as, according to the now established position of the same Court, should be derived from the combined provisions of the re-educative aim, which under Art. 27 par. 3 of the Italian constitution (henceforth: const.) must necessarily characterize the punishment, and the principle of equality, *sub specie* of reasonableness, referred to in Art. 3 const.

The substance of the decision, in addition to being agreeable on its merits, is also to be welcomed from a criminal policy perspective, since it contributes to bringing back some good sense in a matter, that of the (direct and indirect) criminalisation of irregular immigration, in which instead lawmaking has been mostly driven, over the years, by an emotional-populist attitude, which too often has led it to indulge in indiscriminate and overflowing forms of punitivism.

In order to draw this conclusion, however, the Court does not limit itself to a straight application of the criteria on the proportionality of punishment that it has been elaborating for some years now; an application that, in the case at hand, was particularly easy, since the two norms censured represented fairly clear cases of disproportionate punishment. Instead, it adopts a more articulated path, in which that decisional content is dropped into a broader argumentative context, both dogmatic-interpretive and criminological in nature, which ends up assuming a critical role in the development of the reasoning: on the one hand, as I will try to show, such a context appears to be rather redundant in the perspective of the decision taken, and indeed it risks proving partially misleading, or at any rate dysfunctional; on the other hand, however, it provides undoubted stimuli for a wide-ranging reflection on Art. 12 Tuimm, ending up representing the main reason for the judgment's interest, at least for those who set out to analyse it from the perspective of a study of the criminalisation of irregular immigration.

2 A First Reconstruction of the Court's Reasoning

The Court's reasoning starts from the circumstance that the criminalisation of so-called migrant smuggling constitutes part of the more general strategy the state adopts to counter, including through criminal repression, the phenomenon of irregular immigration.[2] From a general teleological point of view, that criminalisation choice thus stands in continuity with the criminalisation of the illegal entry or stay of a foreigner in Art. 10 *bis* Tuimm:

> the entire range of criminal hypotheses described by Art. 12 Tuimm has as its common object of protection the orderly management of migration flows: an interest that this Court has long defined [- *in a well-known decision that declined a question of constitutionality concerning art. 10* bis *Tuimm criminalising the irregular entrance or stay of the foreigner* -] as "an 'instrumental' legal good, through the safeguarding of which the law implements the early protection of 'final' public goods, of obvious constitutional importance, susceptible to being put at risk by uncontrolled immigration" (Judgement No. 250/2010), such as, for instance, the equilibria of the labour market, the (limited) resources of social security, public order and security.

This teleological background, however, finds a peculiarly articulated declination in Art. 12. While indeed in par. 1 (that punishes the mere performance of "acts aiming at procuring" the irregular entrance of the foreigner in the territory of the state) that instrumental good is protected in its pure form, against a conduct—the basic form of cross-border facilitation of irregular immigration—that harms only it, paragraphs 3,[3] 3 *bis*[4] and 3 *ter*[5] are characterized, instead, by the multiharmful dimension of the hypotheses that are regulated therein, which scope of protection is far broader than that of the orderly management of migratory flows. To the point that this Court has argued, in relation the norms in paragraphs 3 and 3 *ter* of Art. 12 Tuimm, that they "are aimed at protecting first and foremost, though not exclusively, the transported

[2]On this topic, see, in general: Caputo (2012); di Martino et al. (2013); Militello and Spena (2015). It is, by the way, a strategy that not only Italy adopts and which, at least in the European context, has been emerging since the late 1990s of the last century, and then exacerbated, especially, in the last two decades or so. See, e.g., Guild and Minderhoud (2006); Guild (2010); Provera (2015); Mitsilegas (2015); Spena and Marin (2016), pp. 147 ff.; Gatta et al. (2021). For an analysis of this politico-criminal trend from the point of view of its theoretical implications, see: Spena (2014), pp. 635 ff.; Id. (2017a), pp. 351 ff.; Id. (2017b), pp. 495 ff.; Id. (2019a), pp. 449 ff.; Id. (2019b), pp. 301 ff.

[3]Where the same conduct referred to in par. 1 is made punishable «by imprisonment for a term of five to fifteen years and a fine of 15,000 euros for each person in the event that: a) the act relates to the illegal entry or stay in the territory of the State of five or more persons; b) the person transported has been exposed to danger to his/her life or safety in order to procure his/her illegal entry or stay; c) the person transported has been subjected to inhumane or degrading treatment to procure his/her illegal entry or stay; d) the act is committed by three or more persons in complicity with each other or by using international transportation services or documents that are forged or altered or otherwise illegally obtained; e) the perpetrators have the availability of weapons or explosive materials.»

[4]"If the acts referred to in par. 3 are committed by recurrence of two or more of the hypotheses referred to in subparagraphs (a), (b), (c), (d) and (e) of the same paragraph, the punishment therein shall be increased".

[5]"The term of imprisonment shall be increased from one third to one half, and a fine of 25,000 euros shall be applied for each person, if the acts referred to in paragraphs 1 and 3: a) are committed for the purpose of recruiting persons to be destined for prostitution or otherwise for sexual or labour exploitation or concern the entry of minors to be employed in illegal activities in order to facilitate their exploitation; b) are committed for the purpose of making profit, even indirectly".

persons, who frequently find themselves in a, sometimes extreme, state of need" (Judgement No. 142/2017).

In the Court's opinion, the sharp punishment aggravations established in the paragraphs in question "are clearly linked" to this "multiharmful dimension": in essence, the common basis of these aggravating factors should, at least in principle, be sought in the fact that in these cases the harm to the public-institutional good of controlling migration flows is enriched by additional harms caused "first and foremost, though not exclusively," to individual goods belonging to the transported foreigners, who, finding themselves in a vulnerable condition, are in need of special protection.

Such a construction foreshadows the idea—that the Court will explicitly develop, more in detail, in one of the latest sections of the decision (4.5)—that the phenomenon of irregular transportation of migrants has two main forms, that are mirrored in the complex structure of Art. 12 Tuimm. Criminological analysis, in fact, makes it emerge how what is usually unitarily referred to (even within the Tuimm: Art. 4 par. 3) as "facilitation of illegal immigration" is actually composed of a variety of practices that are quite distinct from each other as regards both their structure and the reasons of their wrongness. Of these practices, the Court considers relevant to its reasoning the two that represent the extremes of the realization spectrum of the phenomenon: on the one hand, the conduct—subsumable under Art. 12 par. 1—of those who, individually and without profit motive (thus, for *lato sensu* altruistic reasons), merely help the foreigner to realize his/her purpose of illegally entering the territory of the state;[6] on the other hand, the conduct of those who, in an organised form and for profit, engage in migrant smuggling properly said, which would instead define the scope of the aggravating factors. In the first case, violated is only the interest of the state to control migratory flows, with the transported foreigner and his/her facilitator acting in unison, in full agreement; in the second case, in addition to the state interest, the interests of the transported persons are also put at stake: there is not perfect uniformity of purpose between them and those who transport them; the purpose of the foreigner, to enter the territory of the state, has a merely instrumental value for the smuggler, being only an opportunity of which s/he takes advantage in order to achieve a profit; the smugglers' conduct does indeed allow the foreigner to (attempt to) illegally enter the territory of the state, but this for him/her, or his/her family members, involves the payment of a price (economic and personal), which often may be very high: s/he becomes a cog in a mechanism that, once taken the initial decision to turn to smugglers, does not see him/her as a true agent; the

[6]It is barely worth pointing out that this altruistic facilitation, in which facilitators lack a profit motive, but do not act out of necessity, is different from the case in which foreigners, who have been rescued from a situation of distress in the high seas, are transported and delivered in a safe place, even against the will of state authorities. Cases of the latter type, sometimes referred to under the misleading label of 'humanitarian smuggling', do not actually constitute cases of facilitation or migrant smuggling at all. See, e.g., Allsopp (2016), pp. 47 ff.; Ead. (2017); Fekete et al. (2017); Landry (2017); Papanicolopulu (2017); Bernardi (2018), pp. 140 ff.; Carrera et al. (2019); Spena (2019c), pp. 1859 ff.; Zirulia (2020), pp. 140 ff.; Masera (2022).

aspiration to fulfil his/her desire compels him/her to place him/herself in the hands of people for whom s/he represents nothing more than a commodity, and who therefore act solely with a view to their personal gain, which only incidentally finds satisfaction through an activity—irregular transportation—that could also enable the foreigner to achieve his/her goal.

The role of the irregularly transported person is, thus, different in the two cases: in the case of mere facilitation, s/he benefits from the help s/he is given; s/he cannot be said to be a victim: on the contrary, his/her position is central to the perpetration of the deed, while his/her facilitator's role—as is entailed in his/her very denomination—is essentially ancillary, secondary, merely supportive; on the contrary, in the case of smuggling, the position of the migrant becomes decidedly passive, frequently entailing a form of victimisation, to the point of not being easily distinguishable from the position of the victim of human trafficking:[7] in the dynamics of the deed, s/he figures as a mere 'object' of smuggling, a source of profit, to which, once the payment of the price of the trip is obtained, the smugglers do not even have reason to pay particular attention.

3 Is the Distinction Between Mere Facilitation and Organised Smuggling Crystallised in Art. 12 Tuimm?

There is no doubt that, from a criminological perspective, facilitation in its 'individual' (i.e., committed by one single subject in favour of another single subject) and 'altruistic' (i.e., not committed for profit) form, on the one hand, and migrant smuggling properly said, committed unscrupulously and for profit, on the other hand, are different kinds of actions, both structurally and qualitatively; the Court, by underscoring this difference, correctly highlights two opposing configurations that, at its extremities, the phenomenon of the irregular transportation of migrants can take, and with that also underscores the considerable difference that can run between different politico-criminal reasons supporting its criminalisation.[8] Between these two extremes, however, there are some intermediate forms,[9] to which the Court does not draw attention: for instance, the conduct of individual *passeurs*, more or less occasionally performed, but nonetheless aimed at a profit, or the 'altruistic' facilitation, performed either by individuals or loosely organised groups of persons,

[7] The distinction between smuggled migrant and trafficked person, as is well known, is one of the most uncertain profiles of the subject matter. See, e.g., Piotrowicz and Redpath-Cross (2012), pp. 234 ff.; Militello (2018), pp. 86 ff.; Belloni and Tshabalala (2019) pp. 25 ff.

[8] Before the Court made it its own, by the way, the facilitation-smuggling dichotomy had been very effectively reconstructed by Escobar Veas (2019), pp. 226–241, who uses this distinction as a guide to make a critique of many existing European legislations (including the Italian one).

[9] For an illustration of the phenomenological variety of migrant smuggling, see, e.g.: Triandafyllidou and Maroukis (2012); Spena (2019d), pp. 11 ff., 20 f.; UNODC (2018); Punzo (2019), pp. 38 ff.

aimed at helping one or more foreigners (*e.g.*, whole families). These intermediate forms also raise problems of normative categorisation, which, however, could not be easily solved through the interpretation provided by the Court: they would undoubtedly be relevant under any of the aggravated configurations of Art. 12 Tuimm (either because of the profit motive, or because of the number of perpetrators, or because of the number of subjects transported), yet they lack the substance of migrant smuggling understood as an activity peculiar to criminal organisations.

The most problematic aspect of the Court's interpretive proposal thus begins to emerge: if, from a theoretical and politico-criminal point of view, the construction that underpins this proposal is surely of interest, it, however, does not fit perfectly with the existing law, or at least with the law existing in Italy; reading the existing Italian criminal law as if it already accommodated that criminological dichotomy, crystallizing it in corresponding normative contents, is an interpretive straining, which makes the Court's reasoning certainly more *arioso*, but also more questionable than it might otherwise have been.[10]

Actually, there is perspective from which the idea that the criminological premises discussed above are reflected in existing law is certainly tenable, that of inter- and supranational sources, which in fact provide several footholds in this regard. The Court is certainly right in stating that "the two criminological 'types' are kept quite distinct [...] from the supranational sources binding on our country".

It is undoubtedly true, for instance, that the "Palermo Protocol [i.e., *the special Protocol against the Smuggling of Migrants to the UN Convention against Transnational Organized Crime, signed in Palermo in 2000*] solely targets the phenomenon of international migrant smuggling, which is mostly run by large criminal organisations that derive huge profits from this activity". This can be inferred, in general, from Art. 4, which states that "[*t*]his Protocol shall apply, except as otherwise stated herein, to the prevention, investigation and prosecution of [*migrant smuggling and related*] crimes, where the offences are transnational in nature and involve an organized criminal group, as well as to the protection of the rights of persons who have been the object of such offences". Moreover, the genetic reason for the Protocol, as it emerges from its Preamble, is precisely made to descend from the "*Concern*[... *about*] the significant increase in the activities of organized criminal groups in smuggling of migrants and other related criminal activities [...],which bring great harm to the States concerned [*and which*] can [*also*] endanger the lives or security of the migrants involved» and the consequent need to «supplement[...] the United Nations Convention against Transnational Organized Crime with an international instrument against the smuggling of migrants by land, sea and air": it is, therefore, explicitly stated, in Art. 1, that the "Protocol supplements the United Nations Convention against Transnational Organized Crime[... *and*] shall be

[10]It is no coincidence that in Escobar Veas' article, which, as mentioned supra (nt. 8), constitutes somewhat the source of inspiration for this part of the judgment, the dualism facilitation-smuggling is indicated as a regulatory ideal to be developed *de iure condendo*, in order to make legislations—including Italian law—more harmonious and reasonable than they actually are.

interpreted together with the Convention".[11] Hence, the instrument refers to migrant smuggling as one of the businesses of interest to criminal organisations, which provides a key to the fact that—both in the very definition of the criminal conduct (Art. 3 subparagraph a) and for the purposes of its criminalisation (Art. 6)—it is required that the person acts for profit: excluding, therefore, what the Court calls altruistic facilitation (e.g., family or humanitarian facilitation).[12]

On the other hand, "the European Union's 'Facilitators Package' [- *i.e., the combined provisions of Directive 2002/90/EC and Framework Decision 2002/946/ JHA* -], while aiming to target both phenomena (with respect to the goal of controlling migration flows within, in particular, the Schengen area), calibrates its criminalisation and punishment obligations separately for the two types of conduct, limiting the obligation to adopt severe custodial penalties only for those attributable to international migrant smuggling":[13] more specifically, while for the facilitation of irregular immigration not committed for profit (Art. 1.1.a Directive 2002/90/EC, in conjunction with Art. 1.1 Framework Decision 2002/946/JHA) a mere duty of criminalisation is established, for the facilitation carried out for profit the obligation to criminalise is supplemented by an obligation to provide for the applicability of prison sentences, which eventually turns into a requirement that states impose a prison sentence of not less than a maximum of 8 years when the facilitation is carried out by a criminal organisation or with endangerment of the lives of the persons transported.

If traces of the dichotomy between facilitation and smuggling can be found in both of the instruments analysed, this does not mean, however, that these same instruments are characterized by a homogeneous politico-criminal inspiration. The different relevance recognized by the UN Protocol and the Facilitators Package to the link between criminal organisations and the facilitation of irregular immigration—genetic, structural and pervasive, in the first case, and merely aggravating and therefore eventual and superstructural, in the second—constitutes, in fact, the result of a more general difference of approach, which runs between the two

[11] "Art. 1 – *Relation with the United Nations Convention against Transnational Organized Crime*

1. This Protocol supplements the United Nations Convention against Transnational Organized Crime. It shall be interpreted together with the Convention.
2. The provisions of the Convention shall apply, mutatis mutandis, to this Protocol unless otherwise provided herein.
3. "The offences established in accordance with article 6 of this Protocol shall be regarded as offences established in accordance with the Convention."

[12] See United Nations—General Assembly, *Interpretive notes for the official records (travaux préparatoires) of the negotiation of the United Nations Conventions against Transnational Organized Crime and the Protocols thereto* [2000] A/55/383/Add. 1, §§ 88 e 92. See also Gallagher and David (2014), p. 366.

[13] The importance, in the Facilitators Package as in EU criminal policy in general, of the relationship between migrant smuggling and criminal organizations is underscored by Militello (2019), pp. 18 ff.

instruments, in the very way of conceiving the phenomenon of migrant smuggling/ facilitation and the states' reasons for countering it.

The Facilitators Package appears quite clearly driven by a state-centred approach, within which the criminalisation of the facilitation of illegal entry is essentially conceived as a strategy to tackle the more general phenomenon of irregular immigration: the first is a way of indirect criminalisation of the second.[14] As a consequence, the role of the transported subject is sketched in active terms, as a subject who performs, if not the criminal conduct (since there is no provision for self-facilitation), a conduct presupposed to it, namely that of irregular immigration. The facilitation of irregular immigration is thus constructed as a structurally ancillary and complicity act, the wrongful content of which consists of helping others—the foreigner not entitled to entry—to carry out his/her wrongdoing, i.e., irregular entry. The indicators of such an approach in the Facilitators Package are several: the term «facilitation» is explicitly used to name the crime; the criminal conduct is described as the act of "assist[*ing*] a person who is not a national of a Member State to enter [. . .] the territory of a Member State in breach of the laws of the State concerned on the entry [. . .] of aliens"; as mentioned above, it is not required that the 'facilitator' act for profit; as a consequence, there is no prohibition against criminalising 'altruistic facilitation', it being only left to states to exclude the application of sanctions in the case of conduct carried out for «the aim [. . .] to provide humanitarian assistance to the person concerned» (Art. 1.2 Directive 2002/90/EC).[15]

This state-centred approach, characteristic of the Facilitators Package, can be contrasted with the hybrid, more migrant-oriented approach of the UN Protocol,[16] which, in the normative galaxy orbiting the Palermo Convention, is paired with the Protocol against Trafficking, in a juxtaposition that makes vivid from the outset the idea that smuggling is here conceived as a crime that, if not necessarily multiharmful, nevertheless finds in multiharmfulness (in the contextual harm to the state interest in controlling flows and to the interests of the smuggled subject) its ordinary, paradigmatic framework of realization. The state's interest in controlling the migratory flows still remains central, but integrated into a broader view, in which widespread and structural consideration is also given to the interests of the smuggled subject. The latter does not stand as *Täter hinter dem Täter*, nor as the perpetrator of a presupposed unlawful conduct, but as the passive cog of a criminal mechanism that overpowers him/her. Not only that, as mentioned above, the conduct requires,

[14]See, e.g., Spena (2016), pp. 33 ff.; Id. (2019d), pp. 42 ff.; Id. (2019e), pp. 141 ff.; Mitsilegas (2019), pp. 68–85; Id. (2021), pp. 26 ff.; Id. (2022), pp. 142 ff.

[15]Which gives rise to the huge misunderstanding of so-called humanitarian smuggling, which, as noted above, is not smuggling at all: on this subject, in addition to the authors cited *supra*, in nt. 6, see also the *Communication from the Commission – Commission Guidance on the implementation of EU rules on definition and prevention of the facilitation of unauthorised entry, transit and residence 2020/C 323/01* (https://eur-lex.europa.eu/legal-content/EN/ALL/?uri=CELEX:52020XC1001(01). Accessed 30.9.2022).

[16]In addition to authors cited in nt. 14, see especially Gallagher and David (2014); see also Spena (2021), pp. 43 ff.

already in its basic form, the purpose of profit, indicating that it is considered, not so much as support for the smuggled person's irregular immigration, but as a market, a business run by criminal organisations; the smuggler's unlawful conduct is also constructed not in ancillary and complicity terms, but as autonomous conduct: not coincidentally, it is referred to as 'smuggling', not 'facilitation', indicating that the focus here revolves around what the smuggler does, and not what the smuggled does. The criminalisation of smuggling is not, therefore, properly a form of indirect criminalisation of the transported foreigner; the latter enters the picture as the object of smuggling; his/her role is constructed as objectual, not active or propulsive: as such s/he is in fact constantly referred to, as the "object" of the smugglers' conduct.[17] As a consequence, it is expressly established that "Migrants shall not become liable to criminal prosecution under this Protocol for the fact of having been the object of conduct set forth in article 6 of this Protocol" (art. 5). The basic idea is, in short, that even in those cases in which it is the foreigner's initiative to rely on smugglers, once s/he enters the machinery, s/he ends up losing true autonomy of action, becoming a mere 'asset', a 'commodity' for smugglers. This still does not mean that s/he must, always and necessarily, be conceived of as a victim of those who smuggle him/her[18]; there is no doubt, however, that, taken in this sense, migrant smuggling entails a substantial risk of victimization of smuggled migrants, which places it fairly close to human trafficking: all the more so since, in practice, it frequently happens that the foreigners relying on smugglers find themselves in a prior condition of vulnerability, which makes their interaction with those who will transport them unequal.

From the perspective of the Protocol, the smuggled migrant is, more specifically, in a condition of potential double victimization: not only the smugglers, taking him/her as an 'object' to be traded, show no regard for his/her interests; but also, the states often indulge in attitudes of similar disinterest, in pursuit of the objective—which, for them, is primary—of controlling migration flows. The transported foreigner risks, therefore, in addition to primary victimization, also secondary victimization, which in essence is realized when states use countering migrant smuggling as a strategy to tackle not so much organised crime, but irregular immigration.[19]

The same distinction between mere facilitation and organised migrant smuggling, which, as noted above, can be employed, all things considered fruitfully and despite the reported differences, in the reconstruction of the inter- and supranational legal framework, would, according to the Court, also be useful in making the general sense of the first four paragraphs of Art. 12 Tuimm:

> From the 'Legge Martelli' onward, the criminal norm on which the fight against illegal immigration has hinged (Art. 6, par. 8, of Decree Law No. 416 of 1989, and then Art. 12 Tuimm) has progressively differentiated, with ever greater sharpness [...], the punishment of two distinct classes of conduct: on the one hand, the aid to illegal entry into the territory of the state carried out in favour of individual foreigners, for broadly altruistic purposes; on the

[17] More extensively, Spena (2021), pp. 46 ff.

[18] Spena (2021), pp. 49 ff.

[19] Spena (2021), pp. 48 ff.

> other hand, the activity carried out for profit by organised criminal groups with respect to a more or less large number of migrants destined to be transported illegally to the territory of the state.
>
> The far greater sanctioning rigour established for the second class of conduct reflects the obvious distinction, on a criminological level, between [*these*] two radically different phenomena, as this Court had occasion to remark already in [*previous*] Judgment[*s* . . .].

According to the Court's view, par. 1 of Art. 12 thus criminalises mere facilitation of irregular immigration, the action of single individuals or at any rate of no more than two perpetrators (not of organisations), which, by attacking only the state's interest in controlling migratory flows, while not affecting any relevant interest of the person transported, has in the latter not a victim, but a 'beneficiary', who is helped to satisfy his/her desire to irregularly enter the territory of the state.

When, on the other hand, an irregular transportation of migrants is committed in one of the circumstances described in paragraphs 3 and 3 *ter* (singularly or, *a fortiori*, jointly: par. 3 *bis*), it takes on—according to the Court's view—the typical traits of the action of international criminal organisations, which act for profit and are not animated by particular restraint in their treatment of those they transport, thus becoming a multiharmful act, in which, the harm to the state good is accompanied by that to individual goods of the transported subject:

> Quite different appears, [*in fact*], the position of the foreigner in the structure of these two macro-hypotheses. In the case of the 'individual', or 'altruistic', facilitation described by Art. 12, par. 1, Tuimm, the foreigner whose unlawful entry is facilitated appears as a subject who in substance 'benefits' from the unlawful conduct, his/her interests remaining outside the focus of the protection provided by the provision, all focused on the legal good of the orderly management of migratory flows. Instead, in the case of several of the aggravated hypotheses envisaged by paragraphs 3, 3 *bis* and 3 *ter*, the foreigner undoubtedly becomes the holder of protected legal interests, constituting first and foremost the 'victim' of the criminal conduct: exposed to danger to his/her life or safety, or to inhuman and degrading treatment, or even to the risk of being initiated into prostitution or exploited in labour activities, and in any case—In the ordinary case where the conduct is carried out for the purpose of profit—compelled to shell out large sums of money in exchange for help in crossing borders.

Such a reconstruction of Art. 12 Tuimm, intriguing for its ability to make axiologically linear a discipline that at first glance would not appear to be so, nevertheless raises some concerns.

Problematic is, first of all, the idea that the aggravating factors of cross-border facilitation count as making the act multiharmful, all the more so if one understands it in the sense of a multiharmfulness against both state and individual interests. On this point, the Court's discourse is a bit ambivalent: sharper and more challenging statements are followed by tonal softenings, which sound like waning revisions of the argument that make it allusive, or evocative, rather than explicit and unambiguous.

At its first appearance, as we have seen, the thesis is that the "punishment increases" in question

> are clearly linked, in the legislator's perspective, to the multiharmful dimension of the hypotheses contemplated therein, whose horizon of protection far transcends that of the orderly management of migratory flows. To the point that this Court has had occasion to affirm, in relation to the provisions of paragraphs 3 and 3 *ter* of Art. 12 Tuimm, that they "are aimed primarily, though not exclusively, at protecting the persons transported, who are often in a state of need, even extreme need" (Judgement No. 142/2017).

Quite challenging statements, to be sure: all of the aggravating factors of cross-border facilitation would be characterized by a "multiharmful dimension"; this dimension would consist in their being "aimed *primarily, though not exclusively*, at protecting the persons transported, who are often in a state of need, even extreme need".

A first element of uncertainty immediately emerges: how should the phrase "primarily, though not exclusively", which the Court recalls from its previous decision, be understood? Taken literally, it would seem to mean that all of the aggravating factors in question have in the protection of transported persons their main purpose (*aimed primarily at protecting* ...), to which, however, additional (... *though not exclusively*) protective purposes should also be added, revolving around the state interest in migratory flow control, which remains in any case in the background of Art. 12; all these aggravating factors should thus be deemed multiharmful in the sense of adding to the protection of the state interest in migration flow control that of the interests of the person transported.

However, it does not take long to realize, and for that matter the Court itself makes it clear, that this reading can only apply to three of the aggravating factors in question:

> to the two aggravated cases covered by subparagraphs *b* and *c* of par. 3, which refer to the case where the person transported has been exposed to a danger to his/her life or safety, and even to inhuman or degrading treatment, respectively: hypotheses, both of which cannot fail to call to mind the dramatic images of journeys on makeshift and overcrowded boats, or in precarious hiding places in cold storage cells intended for the transport of goods, which often result in fatal events;

and to the aggravating circumstance referred to in par. 3 *ter*, subparagraph *a* ("for the purpose of recruiting persons to be destined for prostitution or sexual or labour exploitation, and bordering on the case of trafficking in persons referred to in art. 601 of the Criminal Code"), which actually "appears calibrated to the needs of protection of the foreigner much more than to the control of migratory flows, which also remains in the background of the criminal norm as in any other hypothesis regulated by art. 12 Tuimm".

Beyond these three easy cases, however, the possibility of explaining the aggravating factors of cross-border facilitation from the perspective of multiharmfulness becomes rather difficult, if not entirely impracticable. With some difficulty, one could perhaps also reconstruct in multiharmful terms the aggravating circumstance in par. 3(e), insofar as one can see a dangerousness—for the life and safety of persons (of those carried or of third parties), and more generally for the collective good of public order—inherent in the fact of using weapons or explosive materials as a means of making the conduct more effective: but this is an interpretation that the Court does not even consider, and that in any case, revolving the aggravating circumstance on the mere "availability" of weapons or explosive materials, would only serve to affirm a merely abstract, indeed presumed, dangerousness, such that recourse to the paradigm of multiharmfulness would end up being anything but informative.

None of the other aggravating factors, in any case, presents any foothold that would make it possible to read them in terms of multiharmfulness strictly understood. Not, for example, the aggravating circumstance in par. 3(a) ("the act concerns the illegal entry or stay in the territory of the State of five or more persons"), in the scheme of which there is no necessary interaction between harms to different goods, but, if anything, a greater intensity or magnitude of the harm caused to the same good already protected in par. 1.

The same can also be said for the aggravating circumstance referred to in the first part of par. 3(d): that the act was committed by three or more persons in complicity with each other does not add any additional profile of harmfulness with respect to the basic harm of migratory flow control, resolving itself, at best, in a deepening of that same harm.

The difficulty of applying the rationale of multiple harms is not diminished even if one looks at the aggravating provisions placed outside of par. 3. This happens, e.g., with the algebraic aggravation in par. 3 *bis*, which, being constructed in a manner dependent on the aggravating hypotheses of the previous paragraph, cannot add anything to them in terms of harmfulness: facts qualifying under this paragraph will be multiharmful only where they are already so by reason of their being relevant according to any of the subparagraphs of the preceding paragraph; the combined interplay of these subparagraphs does not produce 'new' multiharmfulness, but only the 'sum' of harms already relevant, on their own, under any of them: this 'sum' will prove to be multiharmful only as a sum of aggravations that, in at least one of those being added together, are themselves multiharmful.

Finally, the Court, albeit without any particular argumentative effort, adumbrates a multiharmful reading of the aggravating circumstance in subparagraph *b* of par. 3 *ter* (acts "committed for the purpose of making a profit, even indirectly"), when, in a passage quoted earlier, it points out that "in the ordinary case where the conduct is carried out for the purpose of profit[, *the person transported is*] forced to shell out large sums of money in exchange for help in crossing the borders". This is a plausible, but nonetheless merely empirical, assertion, unable to exhaust all the margins of application of the norm: in practice, situations may also arise in which the person transported cannot be said to be properly compelled to pay for the 'service' s/he uses[20]; in any event, the provision at issue, also read in the light of

[20]To give but one example, think of the form of smuggling that emerged, between 2017 and 2019, along the so-called 'ghost route' between Tunisia and southwestern Sicily, characterized by a small number of passengers (5/15 units), safe and concealed transit, as well as relatively short duration (4 h or so), and the provision of other benefits once the passengers reached Italian shores (food, clothing, but also forged documents and further transportation). Access to such services, which are more expensive than those usually practiced along the Central-Mediterranean route, is clearly restricted to wealthy 'clients' who are in conditions that it would be improper to describe as being of special vulnerability. See Punzo (2019), pp. 60 ff.

its normative context, militates against an interpretation in necessarily multiharmful terms, since it does not require, as an explicit or implicit element of the aggravating circumstance, a special vulnerability of the transported person.[21]

More adherent to existing law would then be to understand that expression ("primarily, though not exclusively") to mean that most, though not all, of the aggravating factors of cross-border facilitation protect interests of the person transported (even though it is exaggerated to say that the aggravating circumstances protecting the transported persons are the majority of those considered in paragraphs 3, 3 *bis* and 3 *ter* of Art. 12): a reading that in a later passage, already quoted above, the same court ends up making explicit.[22] In this way, however, the argument loses much of the force on which it seems to rely, and which would descend from the idea that the same axiological substance (the "multiharmful dimension" concerning both the state and the smuggled foreigner) unites (almost) all of the aggravating factors in question (except for the two under censure).

The path taken by the Court to attempt to recover this common axiological substance is to use a concept of multiharmfulness extended beyond its usual terms; this gives the argument a kind of sideways departure, which has the effect of making it more inclusive, though perhaps less harmonious and coherent: the "multiharmful dimension" characterizing the "other aggravated hypotheses provided for in Art. 12 Tuimm" (i.e., those other than the three easy cases mentioned above) should be sought "in a different direction": in particular, the

> aggravated cases referred to in par. 3 subparagraph *a* (act concerning the illegal entry or stay of five or more persons), subparagraph *e* (availability of weapons or explosive materials by the perpetrators of the act), as well as subparagraph *d* to the initial clause (act committed by three or more persons in complicity with each other) all appear to evoke, according to the likely intentions of the legislator, scenarios of involvement of criminal organisations active in international migrant smuggling: hypotheses with respect to which Framework Decision 2002/946/JHA requires the member state to adopt custodial sentences of not less than, in maximum, eight years.

This argumentative development, however, instead of simplifying the discourse, complicates it. A first perplexity, the least relevant one, arises on the dogmatic level, and it is as follows: even provisionally assuming that things are as they are claimed by the Court, that is, that all of the mentioned aggravating factors actually involve "scenarios of involvement of criminal organisations active in international migrant smuggling", in what sense would this be tantamount to making them multiharmful? If we understand the category of multiharmfulness in the proper sense, it seems to me that there would be no other way to make sense of this thesis than to argue that, whenever any of the said aggravating factors turn out to be applicable, the legal good

---

[21] Contrary to what could be argued instead about the UN Protocol: see Spena (2021), p. 51.

[22] "On the other hand, *in various aggravated hypotheses* covered by paragraphs 3, 3 *bis* and 3 *ter*, the foreigner unquestionably becomes the holder of other protected legal goods, constituting first and foremost the 'victim' of the criminal conduct" (§ 4.5, *Considerato in diritto*).

of public order is harmed in addition to the state interest in controlling migration flows, by reason of the alleged involvement of criminal organisations. However, this interpretation would make the Court's reconstruction rather weak and formalistic: the harm to public order, and thus the multiharmful nature of the aggravated act, should in essence be presumed, deriving it indirectly from the occurrence of factors not directly and necessarily related to it, which would only be relevant because they would suggest (but not necessarily entail) the involvement of criminal organisations.

All that remains, then, is to believe that the concept of multiharmfulness is understood here in an improper, non-technical sense ("in a different direction"), not to indicate the setback to several different legal goods in the overall harm caused through the crime, but rather to signal that the involvement of a criminal organisation in the realization of the act adds to it, in the perspective likely adopted by the legislator, a surplus of gravity, which helps explain the greater severity of the range of punishment.

Understood in this way, the thesis—again, assuming that its premise is well-founded (we will obviously have to return to it: *infra*, § 3.2.4)—would certainly be plausible: there is no doubt that the fight against criminal organisations, including through a toughening of criminal repression, has been one of the lines of criminal policy most vigorously pursued, in recent decades, both in Italy and at the inter- and supranational level, as indeed demonstrated, in relation to our specific topic, by the UN Protocol on Migrant Smuggling and, albeit in more nuanced and partial terms, the EU Facilitators Package (*supra*, § 3.1). The existence of a connection, of a relationship of implication, between aggravating factors of cross-border facilitation and organised crime would, therefore, be able to provide for a justification, also in view of the fulfilment of inter- and supranational obligations of criminalisation and (tougher) penalization, the considerable increase in penalties provided in paragraphs 3, 3 *bis* and 3 *ter*, giving the Court, among other things, a term of comparison with which to compare the two aggravating factors under dispute, in order to assess whether they too can be explained, and thus justified, by the same standard.

If we now re-connect this argumentative step with the previous one, the Court's argument, taken as a whole, would, therefore, be as follows: the "sharp punishment increases" prescribed by the considered subparagraphs would (almost) all find justification in a broadly understood concept of multiharmfulness, which, in some cases, would take the form of multiharmfulness in the proper sense, with aggression against the personal interests of the transported foreigners adding to the violation of the state interest in controlling the migratory flows (and here the aggravation would be justified by the importance of the personal goods harmed or put to danger), while, in other cases, would take the form of involvement of criminal organisations (and here the reasonableness of punishment aggravation would emerge as an aspect of the extreme seriousness with which states fight organised crime). Moreover, the combination of these two forms of multiharmfulness would make it possible to recognize in aggravated cross-border facilitation the features that criminological analysis shows as peculiar to migrant smuggling: namely, involvement of criminal organisations and scant regard, often resulting in outright victimization, of the persons transported.

This would equip the Court with an overall coherent account, in light of which to evaluate the two aggravating factors in dispute, being able to conclude in the sense of their unconstitutionality, due to the fact that, unlike the other factors taken into consideration in the same paragraphs, they would in no way succeed in fitting into this view of migrant smuggling as a multiharmful form of facilitation.

In fact, as we will see below, the reasons why the Court declares the two disputed aggravating factors unconstitutional are not really these: when specifically addressing the point, it makes a further sideways departure, leading it to use arguments that are substantially independent of those reconstructed thus far. It will have good reason to do so: taking its dogmatic reconstruction to its ultimate consequences, the unconstitutionality of both aggravating factors could not have followed at all. But we will return to this later on (*infra*, § 4). For now, there is still the question of whether, and within what limits, there is any basis for the argument that the aggravating factors of cross-border facilitation evoke "scenarios of involvement of criminal organisations active in international migrant smuggling", and thus serve to normatively crystallize this phenomenon. So far, we have taken it for granted; now it is a matter of making it the subject of specific consideration. To this end, one must first try to understand the Court's position correctly; which is not so simple: the wordings used by the Court are rather vague, and therefore require some effort to better define their scope. In principle, it seems to me that there are two versions of it, one weak and one strong.

In the weak version, that the aggravating factors of facilitation evoke "scenarios of involvement of criminal organisations active in international migrant smuggling" simply means that they are *compatible* with such involvement, that each of them leverages elements typically found in migrant smuggling carried out by such organisations: that, generally, when a migrant smuggling is run by criminal organisations, it has, among its characteristics, some of those that we find listed in Art. 12 Tuimm as aggravating factors of cross-border facilitation. The link between aggravating factors and criminal organisations is, therefore, in this sense, merely empirical and contingent: the occurrence of any of the aggravating factors in point is not necessarily indicative of the involvement of a criminal organisation, nor of the carrying out of an actual smuggling of migrants; there could be cases of facilitation that are aggravated but not related to the activity of criminal organisations; nonetheless, it is often the case that this connection exists.

This weak version can, in turn, be distinguished in two sub-versions: one, somewhat less weak, would have it that aggravated facilitation *normally*, though not necessarily, is a form of migrant smuggling, carried out by criminal organisations (whenever there is a finding, in a case of facilitation, of the occurrence of any of the aggravating factors listed in Art. 12, there is a high likelihood that it is a case of migrant smuggling run by criminal organisations); the other, somewhat weaker, would instead have it that smuggling of migrants, carried out by criminal organisations, normally presents the features of aggravated facilitation (the vast majority of cases of migrant smuggling run by criminal organisations are cases of facilitation characterized by the occurrence of some of the aggravating factors in Art. 12).

This second sub-version can be agreed upon without particular problems: it is certainly true that in migrant smuggling carried out by criminal organisations several of the aggravating factors set forth in Art. 12 generally occur:[23] normally these deeds involve the action of three or more agents, who, for profit, organise the irregular transportation of a plurality of foreigners; moreover, it often happens that the members of the criminal group organising or participating in carrying out the transportation, or some of them, have weapons or explosive materials; and it is just as often the case that, at some stage in the preparation or execution of the journey, the persons transported are subjected to inhumane and degrading treatment or put in danger of death; finally, it is certainly not uncommon for migrant smuggling managed by criminal organisations to be linked to forms of trafficking, and thus aimed at recruiting people, including minors, for sexual or labour exploitation.

One can even go so far as to assert (and this would already be a variant of the strong version we will see shortly) that a migrant smuggling operation run by criminal organisations necessarily entails at least the recurrence of the two aggravating factors of the number of at least three agents and the purpose of profit: some of the other aggravating factors will recur with extreme frequency, others only occasionally; but, without the first two, one could not even speak of migrant smuggling: these two factors conceptually participate in the definition of migrant *smuggling* (which doesn't exist without the purpose of profit) run by a criminal *organisation* (which doesn't exist without the complicity of at least three persons).

As regards, instead, the other variant of the weak version, the one I mentioned above as the less weak of the two, it is only within certain terms plausible: that aggravated facilitation normally is a form of migrant smuggling carried out by criminal organisations can be argued only with reference to facilitation aggravated by both the complicity of more than three agents and the profit motive; to say that when these two aggravating factors occur jointly, there will normally be migrant smuggling run by a criminal organisation, is an empirically sensible assertion.[24]

Outside of these cases, however, the argument does not hold up: e.g., a facilitation aggravated by only one of the factors considered in Art. 12 is never migrant smuggling carried out by criminal organisations, precisely because, as mentioned above, this type of smuggling always requires, necessarily, that at least the two aggravating factors of the number of agents and the profit motive be present. For the same reason, no multi-aggravated configuration of facilitation, which did not also include these two factors, could be said to imply smuggling of migrants carried out by criminal organisations.

---

[23] Cf. Punzo (2019), p. 38 ff.

[24] Which, however, does not detract from the fact that there can also be cases of facilitation aggravated by those two factors that are not migrant smuggling run by criminal organizations: nothing excludes, indeed, that, without acting like an organization, but simply improvising themselves as accomplices to take advantage of a propitious occasion, three or more persons, aware that they are contributing to an overall unitary fact, but each acting on his/her own behalf, contribute, with a view to making a profit, to helping one or more foreigners to enter the territory of the state irregularly (e.g., carrying them part of the way and then entrusting them to others).

In any case, within the limits specified so far, the weak version of the thesis of the link between the aggravated facilitation and organised smuggling of migrants can certainly be agreed upon. The fact is, however, that precisely because of its weakness, it is of little use for the Court's argumentative purposes: it is, indeed, a merely empirical, not normative thesis, which, by indicating only a possible link between those two terms—limited, moreover, to cases of multi-aggravated facilitation—is unable to provide an axiological foundation capable of cross-cutting the normative contents of paragraphs 3, 3 *bis*, and 3 *ter*, nor to justify the vigorous impact that each of them has on the severity of the punishment. And, while with respect to the multi-harmful aggravating factors in the strict sense this would have little argumentative impact (since here the contextual aggression of both state and individual interests could still make the punishment increase seem reasonable), it would instead end up depriving the Court's reasoning of demonstrative value with respect to the other aggravating factors: these factors, indeed, would not find in the evocation of «scenarios of involvement of criminal organisations active in the international smuggling of migrants» a common and necessary rationale, being applicable also to events that do not fall in that criminological paradigm.

Instead, the Court's argument gains its full argumentative force if it is understood in a strong sense: that the aggravating factors of facilitation evoke the said 'scenarios' would mean, in this view, that they *necessarily* imply the involvement of criminal organisations, that each of them leverages elements that are always and only found in the smuggling of migrants carried out by such organisations: that always, when a facilitation of irregular immigration is aggravated by some (even only one) of these circumstances, it possesses the traits of this type of smuggling. In this strong sense, the thesis would indeed point to an axiological foundation capable of uniting the aggravating factors of facilitation, in all their possible manifestations, within a single criminal policy framework, which, as mentioned above, would make it reasonable, also in light of the inter- and supranational commitments that burden our country, to impose a significantly harsher punishment than that provided for the crime in its basic form.

The fact is, however, that understood in this strong sense, the thesis would simply be untenable. As we have seen, the scope of the aggravating factors in Art. 12 goes well beyond migrant smuggling involving criminal organisations: therefore, it is not true that, necessarily, when the former are given, the latter will also be given; nor can it be said that to apply the aggravating factors in question to cases other than organised smuggling of migrants would be unreasonable, that these are marginal cases, mere glitches in the matrix, made inevitable by the open-ended texture of language, and yet easily manageable and eliminable through teleological interpretation. It would not be so easy to bypass the problem, for the simple reason that this area of further applicability is too central to the physiognomy of the aggravating factors at issue to be relegated to mere anomaly or dysfunction: aggravated facilitations of irregular immigration not amounting to organised smuggling of migrants are firmly located in the central, paradigmatic scope of application of the norms, as is made clear by the fact, already illustrated, that organised smuggling of migrants can never be spoken of when a single aggravating factor, or combination of aggravating factors that does not include number of participants and profit motive, comes into play. That each of the aggravating factors in Art. 12 can be applied separately, or again that the number of participants and the purpose of profit do not constitute necessary elements of the aggravated realization of facilitation, means that—from a normative, and not merely empirical—point of view, the ordinary case of aggravated facilitation is not organised smuggling of migrants.

After all, if the law really wanted to establish the link between aggravating circumstances and organised smuggling as structural and constitutive in the context of Art. 12 Tuimm, it had a very simple way of doing so: provide for it explicitly, e.g., along the lines of Art. 1.3 of Framework Decision 2002/946/JHA, where, as we have seen, there is a requirement for harsher penalization if "the crime is committed by a criminal organisation". Instead, in Art. 12 Tuimm, the concepts of organised crime or criminal association do not even appear. Which is not to say that the link between criminal organisations and smuggling, which undoubtedly exists from a criminological point of view, is not grasped by the law: it is grasped, e.g., in an explicit form, when Art. 416 par. 6 of the Italian criminal code establishes that it constitutes an aggravating circumstance of the crime of criminal association that it is directed to commit multi-aggravated facilitation within the meaning of par. 3 *bis* of Art. 12 Tuimm; that link is also grasped, in implicit form, thanks to the contextual applicability, to cases of migrant smuggling committed by criminal organisations, of Art. 12 Tuimm and Art. 416 It.c.c. What seems certain, however, is that the law does not use the system of aggravating factors of cross-border facilitation as a tool to give this link an explicit, specific and exclusive legal representation.

4 The Distinction Between Mere Facilitation and Organised Smuggling Is Irrelevant to the Constitutionality Question at Stake

It remains to be understood, at this point, how the doubts raised so far about the Court's proposed reconstruction of Art. 12 Tuimm might impact the outcome of the decision. If indeed the Court based its judgment of unconstitutionality on a comparison of the two censured factors with the others, reconstructed according to the paradigm of organised smuggling of migrants, having questioned this reconstruction should also cast doubt on the plausibility of the decision finally made.

However, the conception of aggravated facilitation under Art. 12 as organised smuggling of migrants is by no means a necessary premise of the Court's decision. An illustration of this is the fact that, had the Court applied that conception to its fullest extent, it would have had to draw, in relation to at least one of the two aggravating factors at issue, conclusions opposite to those drawn: indeed, of the aggravating circumstance of the use of "forged or altered or otherwise illegally obtained documents" (the third among those provided for in subparagraph *d* of par. 3) it can certainly be said, no less than of the others that the Court takes as paradigms of reasonableness, "scenarios of involvement of criminal organisations". It is true that the practice of document forgery is not peculiar to the manifestations of migrant smuggling that most take the media stage: migrants crammed into crumbling boats and thrown into the Mediterranean generally do not carry false documents, and in any case are not provided with them by smugglers; these forms of smuggling are not based on fraud, but on the brutality of being sent out to sea in search of rescue or an uncertain landing. In addition to these, however, smuggling can also take other forms,[25] among which, especially when it takes place by land or air, the use of fraud, and in particular the use of forged or illegally obtained documents, is certainly not uncommon. And when it takes a fraudulent form, smuggling generally requires, because of its executional characteristics, a considerable level of organisation, involving multiple people operating, with different roles, in different countries (typically, the one of departure and the one of destination):[26] there is, therefore, no doubt that the use of this mode is apt to evoke scenarios of involvement of transnational criminal organisations.[27]

It is no coincidence that the acts of "[*p*]roducing a fraudulent travel or identity document" and of "procuring, providing or possessing such a document", when "committed for the purpose of enabling the smuggling of migrants", constitute conduct of which Art. 6 of the UN Protocol—which, as noted above, deals with migrant smuggling precisely with a view to combating transnational organised crime—specifically requires the criminalisation.[28]

If the Court, despite its reconstruction, can conclude in the sense that this aggravating circumstance is unconstitutional, due to violation of the principles of reasonableness and proportionality of punishment, it is precisely because, on closer inspection, it does not derive this violation from that dogmatic-reconstructive premise, but from an essentially independent kind of argument. An argument that, as I will now try to show, merely applies the well-established criteria for assessing the reasonableness and proportionality of punishment directly to the content of the aggravating factors in question.

With regard, in particular, to the aggravating circumstance of the use of international transportation services (§ 4.4.1 of the *Considerato in diritto*), the Court argues, agreeably, that it does not add "any surplus of wrongness to the act"

> compared to the generality of the acts falling under the basic offense described in par. 1: such a way of committing the act does not offend any legal good beyond that protected by par. 1 (the orderly management of migratory flows), nor does it represent a particularly insidious kind of conduct or one that creates special difficulties of detection for the border police.

---

[25] See nt. 9.

[26] For further details, including reference to some case law from which the said features emerge clearly, see Spena (2019d), p. 13.

[27] A meaningful example of this is provided, again, by the 'ghost route', already mentioned in nt. 20.

[28] On the prominence that security and document control, and thus the related phenomenon of fraudulent smuggling, have in inter- and supranational law, see Gallagher and David (2014), pp. 512 ff.

Here the Court is applying intrinsic proportionality:[29] the disproportionality of the aggravated punishment, in this case, is not argued on the basis of a comparison with other crimes, let alone with the other aggravated hypotheses under Art. 12 Tuimm, but directly from the insignificance of the factor «use of international transportation services» in terms of the harmfulness or dangerousness of the conduct; the use of those services does not carry in itself any meaning—objective or subjective, actual or potential—capable of adding to the basic wrongness of the act of facilitation, so as to justify the aggravation effect: the Court thus stigmatizes an unreasonableness directly derived from the contents of the aggravating factor considered, not from its comparison with the other factors surrounding it; that the use of international transportation services "does not offend any legal good [...] nor does it represent a particularly insidious type of conduct or one that would create special difficulties of detection for the border police", are arguments that should have led the Court to deem the unreasonableness of the aggravated punishment even if the circumstance at issue had been the only one provided for in Art. 12.

Somewhat more complex, and in any case different, is the issue concerning the other aggravating factor at stake. Of this one can hardly be said that it does not carry a harmfulness/wrongness content capable of adding to that of the basic form of facilitation:

> There is no doubt, in fact, that the possession and use of documents that are totally or partially forged, or even only illicitly obtained (presumably, by means of an activity constituting other offenses), gives the conduct a harmful connotation additional to that proper to the basic offense. "Public trust," identified by the Criminal Code as the legal good of the entire class of public forgery offenses, actually calls forth the need to protect interests of great importance to the system and society as a whole, beginning with public order and security, which require the truthful identification of all persons in the national territory.

The judgment of unreasonableness/disproportionality, in this case, cannot follow straightforwardly from the intrinsic content of the aggravating factor. The question is whether such increased severity of punishment, which is justified in principle, is also justified in its amount. By this way, rather naturally, the discourse slides toward a systematic reading of the aggravating factor, in search of a parameter in the light of which to assess the reasonableness of the legislative choice, the so-called *tertium comparationis*: it is, in short, a matter of verifying the proportionality of the aggravating factor from a perspective that is more strictly distributive, and linked to the principle of equality, understanding it as the consistency of the sanctioning choice with respect to the system as a whole, having particular regard to the other sanctioning choices that the system makes in relation to similar wrongs.[30]

[29] On this possible meaning of proportionality of punishment, see, among many others: Palazzo (1998), pp. 350 ff., 362 ff.; Bartoli (2018), pp. 1540 ff.; Manes (2019), pp. 351, 354 ff.; Pugiotto (2019), pp. 785 ff.; Viganò (2021), pp. 266 ff.

[30] On this meaning of penal proportionality, see, also for further references: Pagliaro (1997), pp. 774 ff.; Palazzo (1998), pp. 350 ff.; Dodaro (2012), pp. 42 ff., 49 ff., 178 ff.; Bartoli (2018), pp. 1540 ff.; Manes (2019), pp. 344 ff.; Viganò (2021), pp. 233 ff., 261 ff.

If, however, we look at the way this reasoning is applied in this case, we easily see that, once again, there is a lack of reference to the other aggravating factors in Art. 12 and to the reading that sees in them a normative crystallization of the phenomenon of organised migrant smuggling; which is perfectly understandable: as we know (*supra* § 4), indeed, the aggravating factor in question would by no means be axiologically dystonic with respect to this interpretive construction at all; it would fit into it perfectly. If its unreasonableness and disproportionality are to be affirmed, the systematic comparison should rather be made—and this is precisely what the Court does—with the norms concerning crimes against public trust, which have the general function of criminalising wrongs of the same kind of that taken into specific consideration in the last part of subparagraph *d* of par. 3 of Art. 12 Tuimm.

In doing so, the Court then has good play in pointing out that

> the generality of the crimes of public forgery provided for in Chapters III and IV of Title VII of Book II of the Criminal Code are punished with penalties that, in the minimum, do not exceed the threshold of one year's imprisonment; and the same Art. 6, par. 6 *bis*, Tuimm, which criminalises the counterfeiting or alteration of residence permits or other documents related to the lawful presence of the foreigner in the national territory, provides for a range of punishment of one to three years of imprisonment. Only the crime of possession and manufacture of false documents valid for expatriation under art. 497 *bis* of the Criminal Code [...] establishes a minimum of two years and a maximum of five years of imprisonment, limited, however, to the possession of "false" documents: with the exclusion, therefore, of those that are authentic, but "illicitly obtained," also addressed by the aggravated hypothesis now under consideration.

The punishment increase provided for the case that a facilitation is committed using forged documents, etc. is, therefore, disproportionate, hence unreasonable, given the level of punishment generally established, in our system, in relation to acts of forgery against public trust:

> the provision of a minimum punishment of five years, and a maximum of fifteen years' imprisonment for an act ordinarily punishable by imprisonment from one to five years, only by reason of the use of counterfeited, altered or even only illegally obtained documents, presents, therefore, traits of absolute "intrasystematic" anomaly with respect to the sanctioning choices of both the Criminal Code and the special legislation. Such an anomaly must lead to a judgement of manifest disproportionality of the punishment provided for the aggravated hypothesis under consideration.

5 Concluding Remarks

Why, then, did the Court decide to embed its decision in such an articulate yet problematic discourse as the one we have critically reviewed above, without properly grounding that same decision in it? What can ever be the role of that reconstruction, if it does not serve to endow the decision with either a necessary premise or merely *ad adiuvandum* arguments? It is not easy to answer this question. It may be thought, however, that in so doing the Court intended to signal the abnormality to which repressive fury can lead, when the state's fight against irregular immigration becomes blind to the complexity of the events that are referred to by that label. That it thus wanted to show, by taking as an emblem the case at issue in the judgment *a quo*, how the figure of the smuggler, waved in the media as bogeymen to justify the compulsive recourse to increasingly severe criminalisation, can turn out to be a mere fetish, behind which, if one is willing to look without prejudice, it is not difficult to discern, many times, human vicissitudes of affection, hope, suffering. That the Court thus wanted to pass, in an almost subliminal form, a message addressed first to the legislature and then also to the judges: the punishment aggravations established in the currently existing Art. 12, given their very significant magnitude, are really justified only insofar as they apply to organised migrant smuggling.

References

Allsopp J (2016) The European Facilitation Directive and the criminalisation of humanitarian assistance to irregular migrants: measuring the impact on the whole community. In: Carrera S, Guild E (eds) Irregular migration, trafficking and smuggling of human beings. Policy dilemmas in the Eu. CEPS, Brussels, pp 47–56

Allsopp J (2017) Solidarity, smuggling and the European refugee crisis: civil society and its discontents. Diritto, Immigrazione e Cittadinanza 3:1–28. https://www.dirittoimmigrazionecittadinanza.it/archivio-saggi-commenti/saggi/fascicolo-n-3-2017/167-saggio-allsopp

Bartoli R (2018) Offensività e ragionevolezza sul sindacato di costituzionalità sulle scelte di incriminazione. Riv Ital Dirit Proced Penal 61(3):1540–1576

Belloni M, Tshabalala X (2019) On the key distinction between trafficking and smuggling. Views and implications from the horn of Africa and Southern Africa. Forum Crime Soc 10(1–2): 25–49. https://www.unodc.org/documents/data-and-analysis/bulletin/2021/V2102426.pdf

Bernardi S (2018) I (possibili) profili penalistici delle attività di ricerca e soccorso in mare. Diritto Penale Contemporaneo Rivista Trimestrale 1:134–144

Caputo A, Fidelbo G (2012) Reati in materia di immigrazione e di stupefacenti. Giappichelli, Torino

Carrera S et al (2019) Policing humanitarianism. Eu policies against human smuggling and their impact on civil society. Hart, Oxford

Ciervo A (2022) L'irragionevole sicurezza: la Corte costituzionale alle prese con il reato di favoreggiamento dell'immigrazione clandestina. AIC Osservatorio Costituzionale 3. https://www.osservatorioaic.it/images/rivista/pdf/2022_3_22_Ciervo.pdf

Di Martino A et al (2013) The criminalization of irregular immigration: law and practice in Italy. Pisa University Press, Pisa

Dodaro G (2012) Uguaglianza e diritto penale. Giuffrè, Milano

Escobar Veas J (2019) Smuggling of migrants is and should be established as an autonomous offence. Eur J Crime Crim Law Crim Justice 27(3):226–241

Fekete L et al (eds) (2017) Humanitarianism: the unacceptable face of solidarity. Institute for Race Relations, London. https://s3-eu-west-2.amazonaws.com/wpmedia.outlandish.com/irr/2017/11/10092853/Humanitarianism_the_unacceptable_face_of_solidarity.pdf

Gallagher AT, David F (2014) The international law of migrant smuggling. Cambridge University Press, Cambridge

Gatta GL et al (eds) (2021) Controlling immigration through criminal law. European and Comparative Perspectives on "Crimmigration", Hart, Oxford

Guild E (2010) Criminalization of migration in Europe. Human Rights Implications. CommDH/IssuePaper(2010)1. https://rm.coe.int/ref/CommDH/IssuePaper(2010)1

Guild E, Minderhoud P (eds) (2006) The legal measures and social consequences of criminal law in Member States on Trafficking and Smuggling in Human Beings. Brill, Leiden

Landry R (2017) Decriminalising "humanitarian smuggling". RSC Research in Brief 6. https://www.rsc.ox.ac.uk/publications/research-in-brief-decriminalising-humanitarian-smuggling

Manes V (2019) La proposizione della questione di legittimità costituzionale in materia penale e le sue insidie. In: Manes V, Napoleoni V (eds) La legge penale illegittima. Metodo, itinerari e limiti della questione di costituzionalità in materia penale. Giappichelli, Torino, pp 173–405

Masera L (2022) Soccorsi in mare e diritto penale nella stagione dei porti chiusi. Alcune riflessioni a partire dal caso di Carola Rackete. La Legislazione Penale 22.4.2022. https://www.lalegislazionepenale.eu/wp-content/uploads/2022/04/Masera-opinioni-LP-2022.pdf

Militello V (2018) La tratta di esseri umani: la politica criminale multilivello e la problematica distinzione con il traffico di migranti. Riv Ital Dirit Proced Penal 61(1):86–108

Militello V (2019) I traffici illeciti nel Mediterraneo e le organizzazioni criminali transnazionali. Una introduzione alla ricerca NESMeS. In: Militello V et al (eds) I traffici illeciti nel Mediterraneo. Persone, stupefacenti, tabacco. Giappichelli, Torino, pp 3–29

Militello V, Spena A (eds) (2015) Il traffico di migranti. Diritti, tutele, criminalizzazione. Giappichelli, Torino

Mitsilegas V (2015) The criminalisation of migration in Europe. Challenges for human rights and the rule of law. Springer, Cham

Mitsilegas V (2019) The normative foundations of the criminalization of human smuggling: exploring the fault lines between European and international law. New J Eur Crim Law 10(1): 68–85

Mitsilegas V (2021) The criminalisation of migration in the law of the European Union: challenging the preventive paradigm. In: Gatta GL et al (eds) Controlling immigration through criminal law. European and comparative perspectives on "crimmigration". Hart, Oxford, pp 25–46

Mitsilegas V (2022) EU criminal law, 2nd edn. Hart, Oxford

Pagliaro A (1997) Sproporzione "irragionevole" dei livelli sanzionatori o sproporzione "irrazionale"? Giurisprudenza Constitutionale 42(2):774–778

Palazzo F (1998) Offensività e ragionevolezza nel controllo di costituzionalità sul contenuto delle leggi penali. Riv Ital Dirit Proced Penal 51(2):350–384

Papanicolopulu I (2017) Immigrazione irregolare via mare, tutela della vita umana e organizzazioni non governative. Diritto Immigrazione e Cittadinanza 3:1–29. https://www.dirittoimmigrazionecittadinanza.it/archivio-saggi-commenti/saggi/fascicolo-n-3-2017/162-immigrazione-irregolare-via-mare-tutela-della-vita-umana-e-organizzazioni-non-governative-1/file

Piotrowicz R, Redpath-Cross J (2012) Human Trafficking and Smuggling. In: Opeskin B et al (eds) Foundations of international migration law. Cambridge University Press, Cambridge, pp 234–259

Provera M (2015) The criminalisation of irregular migration in the European Union. CEPS Paper in Liberty and Security 80. https://www.ceps.eu/wp-content/uploads/2015/03/Criminalisation%20of%20Irregular%20Migration.pdf

Pugiotto A (2019) Cambio di stagione nel controllo di costituzionalità sulla misura della pena. Riv Ital Dirit Proced Penal 62(2):785–810

Punzo V (2019) I traffici illeciti nel Mediterraneo. Aspetti criminologici e tendenze evolutive. In: Militello V et al (eds) I traffici illeciti nel Mediterraneo. Persone, stupefacenti, tabacco. Giappichelli, Torino, pp 31–66

Spena A (2014) Iniuria Migrandi: criminalization of immigrants and the basic principles of the criminal law. Crim Law Philos 8(3):635–657

Spena A (2016) Human smuggling and irregular immigration in the EU: from complicity to exploitation? In: Carrera S, Guild E (eds) Irregular migration, trafficking and smuggling of human beings. Policy dilemmas in the Eu. CEPS, Brussels, pp 33–40

Spena A (2017a) A just criminalization of illegal immigration: is it possible? Crim Law Philos 11(2):351–373

Spena A (2017b) La crimmigration e l'espulsione dello straniero-massa. Materiali per una Storia della Cultura Giuridica 47(2):495–513
Spena A (2019a) Il «gelo metallico dello stato»: per una critica della crimmigration come nuda forza. Rivista Trimestrale di Diritto Pubblico 2:449–462
Spena A (2019b) The double-deviant identity of the mass-foreigner and the lack of authority of the crimmigrationist state. New Crim Law Rev 22(3):301–317
Spena A (2019c) Smuggling umanitario e scriminanti. Riv Ital Dirit Proced Penal 62(4):1859–1907
Spena A (2019d) Migrant smuggling: a normative and phenomenological view from Italy. In: Militello V, Spena A (eds) Between criminalization and protection: the Italian way of dealing with migrant smuggling and trafficking within the European and international context. Brill, Leiden-Boston, pp 5–54
Spena A (2019e) L'incriminazione dello smuggling of migrants in Europa: una ricognizione comparatistica. In: Militello V et al (eds) I traffici illeciti nel Mediterraneo. Persone, stupefacenti, tabacco. Giappichelli, Torino, pp 141–163
Spena A (2021) Smuggled migrants as victims? Reflecting on the UN protocol against migrant smuggling and on its implementation. In: Forlati S (ed) The Palermo Convention at twenty. The challenge of implementation. Brill, Leiden-Boston, pp 43–57
Spena A, Marin L (2016) The criminalization of migration and European (dis)integration. Eur J Migr Law 18(2):147–156
Triandafyllidou A, Maroukis T (2012) Migrant smuggling. Irregular migration from Asia and Africa to Europe. Palgrave Macmillan, Basingstoke
UNODC (2018) Global study on smuggling of migrants. https://www.unodc.org/documents/data-and-analysis/glosom/GLOSOM_2018_web_small.pdf
Viganò F (2021) La proporzionalità della pena. Profili di diritto penale e costituzionale. Giappichelli, Torino
Zirulia S (2020) Non c'è smuggling senza ingiusto profitto. Diritto Penale Contemporaneo Rivista Trimestrale 3:143–177
Zirulia S (2022) La Corte costituzionale sul favoreggiamento dell'immigrazione irregolare: illegittima l'aggravante che parifica il trattamento sanzionatorio dei trafficanti a quello di coloro che prestano un aiuto per finalità solidaristiche. Sistema Penale 22 marzo 2022. https://www.sistemapenale.it/it/scheda/corte-costituzionale-2022-63-favoreggiamento-immigrazione-irregolare-aggravato-nota-zirulia#_ftnref7

Challenging the Hostile Environment for Search and Rescue at Sea: Reflections from the Sea Watch Litigation

Valsamis Mitsilegas

Abstract The article will analyse the creation of a hostile environment for civil society and NGOs assisting migrants and performing search and rescue at sea. The article will focus on the attempts by the state to neutralise NGO SAR activity through the use of administrative sanctions of detention of ships on health and safety grounds. The article will focus on the emergence of the Sea Watch litigation before the CJEU, and evaluate critically the ruling of the Court from a rule of law perspective.

1 Introduction

The recent past has witnessed the emergence of a 'hostile environment' against those who help migrants, and in particular against NGOs who conduct search and rescue at sea. By filling in the gap left by states in search and rescue at sea and in access to asylum, civil society and NGOs are increasingly being framed as a threat to state sovereignty.[1] The hostile environment has expressed itself primarily through the overcriminalisation of assistance to migrants,[2] via the prosecution of civil society actors for migrant smuggling offences.[3] The extensive use of criminal law on sjhaky normative foundations has been accompanied by efforts by state authorities to widen the net of enforcement by using other legal means—and in particular administrative law on health and safety and on the protection of the environment, in order to neutralise the efforts of civil society through measures resulting into the seizure

[1] Mitsilegas (2020).

[2] Mitsilegas (2019), pp. 68–85.

[3] Mitsilegas (2021), pp. 25–45.

V. Mitsilegas (✉)
Liverpool Law School, University of Liverpool, Liverpool, UK
e-mail: mitsilegas@liverpool.ac.uk

V. Militello, A. Spena (eds.), *The Challenges of Illegal Trafficking in the Mediterranean Area*, Legal Studies in International, European and Comparative Criminal Law 9, https://doi.org/10.1007/978-3-031-45399-1_7

and immobilisation of vessels in the ports of the host state.[4] A key example of this trend has been the actions of the Italian state vis-à-vis the NGO *Sea Watch,* which resulted into litigation before the Court of Justice of the European Union.[5] The case involved the conduct of health and safety inspections on, and the subsequent detention of, *Sea Watch* vessels which had conducted search and rescue activities at sea. The detention was ordered on the grounds of breaches of health and safety regulations.[6] *Sea Watch*—whose vessels had been certified to operate from the German authorities—brought legal action before the Italian courts challenging the legality of state action, arguing inter alia that the latter constituted in fact a roundabout means of attaining an objective of frustrating the search and rescue operations organised by Sea Watch in the Mediterranean Sea.[7] These actions generated a reference for a preliminary ruling by the Regional Administrative Court of Sicily asking the Luxembourg Court a number of questions including on the applicability of EU transport law on NGOs conducting search and rescue at sea, on the relationship between the law of the flag state which has certified the vessels with the flag state imposing inspections and sanctions and on the scope of the powers exercised in this context by the port state.

2 The Applicability of EU Law: The Transport Legal Basis

The first question by the referring court was whether Directive 2009/16 was to be interpreted, in view of its wording, the scheme of that directive and the objectives which it pursues, as including—or not including—ships which, while having been officially classified and certified by a body authorised to do so by the flag State and recognised at EU level as 'cargo' ships intended for use for commercial or trade purposes, are, in practice, exclusively and systematically intended for and assigned to activities relating to the search for and rescue of persons in danger or distress at sea.[8]

This is a central question seeking to ascertain whether ships which perform search and rescue at sea are subject to the same transport rules as cargo ships more generally, in view of the fundamentally different functions and objectives they perform. The CJEU answered in the affirmative, confirming the applicability of Directive 2009/16 on port state control of shipping which was adopted under a transport policy legal basis, to ships used by humanitarian organisations operating search and rescue at sea and stating that EU law precludes national legislation ensuring its transposition into domestic law from limiting its applicability only to

[4] Mitsilegas note 1 above. Minetti (2020) has characterised these trends as penal populism.

[5] Joined Cases C14/21 and C15/21, *Sea Watch*, ECLI:EU:C:2022:604.

[6] Paras. 46–49.

[7] Para. 49.

[8] Para. 54.

ships which are used for commercial activities.[9] This conclusion is open to challenge as it disregards the fundamental difference between the emergency activities of NGOs in search and rescue at sea and the activities of ordinary navigation. It is also contrary to the view of the referring court which indicated that it was inclined to consider that Directive 2009/16 is to be interpreted, in view of Article 3(4) and recitals 2–4 and 6 thereof, as well as the context of that provision and those recitals, as not applying to ships which, like *Sea Watch 4* and *Sea Watch 3*, are used for non-commercial or non-trade activities.[10]

3 The Law of the Sea and the Relationship Between International and EU Law

In developing its answers, the CJEU applied law of the sea and stressed the influence of international law of the sea in the interpretation of EU law. The Court stated that it was necessary to take account of the SOLAS Convention, to which all the Member States are parties, when interpreting Directive 2009/16[11] and reiterated that provisions of EU secondary legislation must be interpreted, to the greatest extent possible, in conformity both with the international conventions which are binding on the European Union and with the relevant rules and principles of general international law.[12] Directive 2009/16 must be interpreted, having regard to its objective and its content, by taking account not only of the SOLAS Convention but also of the Convention on the Law of the Sea[13] which is binding on the European Union and its provisions form an integral part of the EU legal order.[14] The CJEU continued by interpreting the objective of the Convention of the Law of the Sea,[15] whose legal regime seeks to strike a fair balance between the respective and potentially conflicting interests of States as coastal States and flag States.[16] The Court then examined in some detail the Convention provision on the duty to render assistance at sea and the related obligations in particular of the coastal state,

[9]Para. 86.

[10]Para. 55.

[11]Para. 91.

[12]Para. 92. The Court referred to its judgments of 3 September 2008, *Kadi and Al Barakaat International Foundation v Council and Commission*, C402/05 P and C415/05 P, EU:C:2008:461, para. 291, and of 27 February 2018, *Western Sahara Campaign UK*, C266/16, EU:C:2018:118, paras. 43–47).

[13]Para. 93.

[14]Para. 94.

[15]Para. 96.

[16]Para. 97. The Court referred to its judgments of 3 June 2008, *Intertanko and Others*, C308/06, EU:C:2008:312, paras. 58, and of 11 July 2018, *Bosphorus Queen Shipping*, C15/17, EU:C:2018:557, paras. 63 and 103–104.

considerations taken into account in the development of the Court's answers to the referring court.[17]

In an important finding, the Court then went on to interpret EU law in the light of international law of the sea and state that the systematic use of cargo ships for activities relating to the search for and rescue of persons in danger or distress at sea may not be regarded, solely on the ground that it results in those ships transporting persons in numbers which are out of all proportion to their capacity in that regard as derived from their classification and certification, and regardless of any other circumstance, as an unexpected factor for the purposes of EU law, permitting the port State to undertake an additional inspection.[18] In other words, overcrowding of ships undertaking search and rescue is not, by itself, a ground for additional state control. Such additional controls may only take place ex post, after entry into state territorial waters and after completion of the search and rescue operations, if ships are deemed to have been operated in a manner posing a danger to persons, property or the environment.[19]

In another limitation to the extent of the enforcement powers of the port state, the CJEU held that it follows from Article IV(b) of the SOLAS Convention that, as such, the presence of persons on board a ship by reason of *force majeure* or in consequence of the implementation, by the master of that ship, of his or her duty to render assistance at sea may not be taken into account for the purpose of ascertaining whether that ship complies with the provisions of that convention. However, the Court added, the fact remains that, under Article 98(1) of the Convention on the Law of the Sea, that duty must, as has been emphasised in paragraph 105 of this judgment, be implemented in so far as this can be done without serious danger to the ship, the crew or the passengers.[20]

4 Applying General Principles of EU Law: Sincere Cooperation

The relationship between the flag state and the port state has been at the heart of the Sea Watch litigation. A key question in this context was the extent to which the port state should accept the certification decisions undertaken by the flag state, and to what extent ex ante certification precluded further controls by the port state. This is essentially a question of mutual recognition and mutual trust. The Court allowed further inspections by the port state, but placed the latter under an obligation to report the detailed legal and factual elements capable of establishing the reasons why the fact that certain ships are, in practice, being systematically used for activities relating

[17]Paras. 105–109.

[18]Paras. 117 and 118.

[19]Para. 119.

[20]Para. 124.

to the search for and rescue of persons in danger or distress at sea, despite having been classified and certified as cargo ships by the flag State gives rise, on its own or together with other elements, to a danger to health, safety, on-board working conditions or the environment.[21] The act of making the control which may be carried out by the port State conditional upon the existence of clear grounds for believing that a ship or its equipment does not comply with the rule that a ship must be maintained, in all respects, in conditions such as to ensure that it remains fit to proceed to sea without danger to itself or to the persons on board is consistent with the rules of international law governing the division of powers between that State and the flag State.[22]

By contrast, a control which disregards that division of powers, such as the act, by the port State, of demanding that ships which are subject to a more detailed inspection hold certificates other than those with which they were issued by the flag State or that they comply with all the requirements applicable to ships covered by another classification, would be contrary, according to the Court, not only to the relevant rules of international law, but also to Directive 2009/–. Such a control would according to the Court ultimately be tantamount to calling into question the way in which the flag State has exercised its powers in the area of conferring its nationality on ships, as well as the area of classifying and certifying those ships.[23] Thus whereas additional inspection on ships operating search and rescue activities by the port state are allowed under certain conditions, the port state does not have the power to demand proof that those ships hold certificates other than those issued by the flag State or that they comply with all the requirements applicable to another classification.[24]

The Court expanded further on the relationship between the flag state and the port state. It established a duty of the port state to inform the flag state in writing of the circumstances and reasons which led to the inspection and the detention of a ship flying its flag, communicating to that State the report or reports drawn up following that inspection. This duty stems from both EU and international law applies regardless of the identity of the flag State and thus regardless of whether that State is another Member State or a non-Member State.[25] The Court evoked in relations between Member States the principle of sincere cooperation referred to in Article 4(3) TEU.[26] In view of that principle, the Member States are required to consult each other and to cooperate sincerely in the exercise of their respective powers of control, so as to ensure that the obligations under Directive 2009/16 are fulfilled by the competent State while safeguarding their effectiveness.[27]

[21] Para. 135.

[22] Para. 137.

[23] Para. 138.

[24] Para. 139.

[25] Para. 154. See also para. 155 on international law.

[26] Para. 156.

[27] Para. 157.

Thus the Court held that, in a situation where the ship which has been inspected and detained flies the flag of a Member State other than the port State, the latter State, must, in so doing, respect the classification and certifications granted by the flag State. For its part, the flag State must take account of the reasons which led the port State to inspect and then detain that ship, and aid it in its search for the most appropriate corrective measures to rectify the deficiencies found and the clear dangers or risks arising therefrom. Those two Member States must also both strive to adopt a common position as regards the measures to be taken by each of them, within the framework of their respective powers, as well as in the implementation of those measures.[28] The Court stated that those requirements are all the more important given that, as EU law currently stands, there are no provisions specifically governing the systematic activities relating to the search for and rescue of persons in danger or distress at sea at issue in the main proceedings.[29] The Court is thus reluctant to give a definitive judicial solution in the absence of legislative harmonisation and appears to be calling for further harmonisation in the field.[30]

5 The Rule of Law

A key feature of the Court's ruling is setting up rule of law parameters which are aimed to address state arbitrariness in the control of NGO ships conducting search and rescue at sea. Throughout the judgment, the Court imposed a number of rule of la requirements permeating all stages of intervention of the port state. Firstly, the Court required that the decision to insect must be fully reasoned and, and, as to the substance, justified both in law and in fact[31] with the Court proceeding to give detailed guidance as to the factors to be taken into account in the decision by the port authority.[32] Secondly, the Court only permitted ex post control: additional controls by the port state are only permitted after shisy have entered its waters and after all the operations relating to the transhipment or disembarking of persons to whom their respective masters have decided to render assistance have been completed if that State has established, on the basis of detailed legal and factual evidence, that there are serious indications capable of proving that there is a danger to health, safety, on-board working conditions or the environment, having regard to the conditions

[28] Para. 157.

[29] Para. 158.

[30] The Court has been criticised for failing to engage with existing EU sift law, namely Recommendation 2020/1365 addressing cooperation among Member States concerning operations carried out by vessels owned or operated by private entities for the purpose of SAR activities, https://verfassungsblog.de/ngos-in-distress/. Accessed on 10 August 2023.

[31] Para. 120.

[32] Para. 121.

under which those ships operate.[33] Thirdly, the Court held that, while the port State is required to ensure that all the deficiencies which have been confirmed or revealed by an inspection have been or will be rectified in accordance with the international conventions whose effectiveness that directive is intended to increase, they may not, by contrast, detain a ship unless such deficiencies pose a clear threat to safety, health or the environment.[34]

The detention of a ship cannot be ordered merely on the ground that an inspection carried out under Articles 11–13 of Directive 2009/16 enabled the port State to establish, with precision, that a ship had been operated in a manner posing a danger to persons, property or the environment. It is also necessary for that State to establish in a given case, first, that such a danger or future risk is a clear hazard and, second, that the deficiencies giving rise to that danger or risk, either individually or together, make the ship concerned unseaworthy.[35] The port State may not make the non-detention of those ships or the lifting of such detention subject to demands that ships subject to its jurisdiction hold certificates other than those with which they were issued by the flag State or that they comply with all the requirements applicable to ships covered by a classification other than their own.[36]

Fourthly, the Court held that the corrective measures which may thus be adopted by the port state in a given case must, in any event, be not only suitable and necessary to rectify the deficiencies which are clearly hazardous to safety, health or the environment and which make the ship unseaworthy on which that detention was based, but also proportionate to that end,[37] In this manner, the Court has placed enforcement action by the flag state under strict conditions of giving reasons and justification, and placed decisions limiting the rights of ships under a clear necessity and proportionality test.

6 Conclusion

Those who see the glass as half full, will stress the potential positive impact of the CJEU ruling in the *Sea Watch* litigation in protecting the search and rescue activities of NGOs at sea while placing limits to state arbitrariness and blanket enforcement. The Court allowed port state controls only after search and rescue operations have occurred; stated expressly that ship overcrowding by itself does not constitute a factor for additional controls; and placed a series of rule of law safeguards on the decision of the port state to conduct inspections and to detain ships, including the establishment of clear and detailed grounds and the giving of reasons for such

[33] Para. 126.

[34] Para. 144.

[35] Para. 147.

[36] Paras. 150–151.

[37] Para. 153. The Court further developed an unseaworthiness test in para. 148.

decisions. On the other hand, those who see the glass as half empty will note that the actual impact of the Court's ruling on the stance of state authorities on the ground is less clear. The Court placed ships operated by NGOs to conduct search and rescue at sea within the regulatory health and safety framework of ordinary cargo vessels, disregarding the fundamental difference in function between the two categories—it is doubtful whether ships who rescuer migrants in an emergency can follow the same health and safety rules as ships in ordinary navigation. Moreover, and notwithstanding the Court's evocation of the principle of sincere co-operation and the requirement for the port state not to second guess the certificate provided by the flag state, the judgment still leaves the port state with considerable leeway to continue to exercise health and safety inspections. While the rule of law safeguards provided by the Court are welcome, it is unclear whether these safeguards will address effectively the abuse of administrative proceedings by state authorities to create a hostile environment towards civil society and effectively neutralise the search and rescue activities of NGOs.[38] As the CJEU is arguably limited by the nature of the questions posed before it by national courts, it will be further litigation—asking specifically questions on the compatibility of national administrative measures with the right of access to asylum and with fundamental principles of criminal law—which may serve to place further limits to sate arbitrariness and to the hostile environment in the field.

References

Minetti M (2020) The facilitators package, penal populism and the rule of law: lessons from Italy. New J Eur Crim Law 11(3):335–350

Mitsilegas V (2019) The normative foundations of the criminalisation of human smuggling. Exploring the fault lines between European and International Law. New J Eur Crim Law 10: 68–85

Mitsilegas V (2020) Contested sovereignty in preventive border control: civil society, the 'hostile environment' and the rule of law. In: Bosworth M, Zedner L (eds) Privatising border control: law at the limits of the sovereign state. OUP

Mitsilegas V (2021) The criminalisation of migration in the law of the European Union. Challenging the preventive paradigm. In: Gatta GL, Mitsilegas V, Zirulia S (eds) Controlling immigration through criminal law. European and comparative perspectives on 'crimmigration'. Hart, pp 25–45

[38] It has been reported that such state practices continue in Italy notwithstanding the Court's judgment https://sea-watch.org/en/sea-watch-3-blockade/. Accessed on 10 August 2023.

Part III
Human Trafficking and Labour Market

The Problems of Trafficking in Human Beings in Spain. Criminal Regulations and Jurisprudential Treatment

Mirentxu Corcoy Bidasolo

Abstract In this work, it is intended to differentiate between smuggling, which protected migration policies, the employment and social rights of workers and trafficking, which protected human dignity. Indicative of the severity of these crimes is the fact that the Title 'Trafficking in Human Beings' comes after those that deal with crimes of torture and against the right of self-determination. Spain's criminal law at last distinguishes between people trafficking and the unlawful smuggling of migrants, in accordance with the various international instruments signed by Spain. One particularly important practical consequence of this legislative change is that in the application of the crime of trafficking in human beings, a sentence is passed for each individual trafficked, which is not the case in the application of the crime of immigration. For fights against Trafficking it is necessary to work on several levels: firstly, by taking action at the source by helping to create an improved social and economic situation in countries of origin; and secondly, by establishing measures to protect and help victims.

1 Introduction

For decades in Spain, the Criminal Code has confused illegal immigration with human trafficking. Organic Law 5/2010 introduced the crime of human trafficking, specifically in a single article, 177 *bis* of Title VII *bis*, which incorporates into Spanish law Framework Decision 2002/629/JHA of the European Council *on combating trafficking in human beings*. The incorporation of this directive occurred so late that it ended up overlapping with Directive 2011/35/EU of 5 April 2011 *on preventing and combating trafficking in human beings and protecting its victims*, which replaced the earlier Council Framework Decision.

M. C. Bidasolo (✉)
Department of Criminal Law and Criminal Sciences, University of Barcelona, Barcelona, Spain
e-mail: mcorcoy@ub.edu

V. Militello, A. Spena (eds.), *The Challenges of Illegal Trafficking in the Mediterranean Area*, Legal Studies in International, European and Comparative Criminal Law 9, https://doi.org/10.1007/978-3-031-45399-1_8

In light of this second directive, art. 177 *bis*[1] was modified by Organic Law 1/2015, addressing the phenomenon of human trafficking from the perspective not

---

[1] Art. 177 bis.

1. Any person who, be it in Spanish territory, from Spain, in transit through Spain or bound for Spain, using violence, intimidation or deception, or the abuse of power or the position of need or vulnerability on the part of the Spanish or foreign victim, or by means of delivering or receiving payments or benefits to achieve the consent of the person who has control of the victim, captures, transports, transfers, harbours or receives the victim, including the exchange or transfer of control over the victim, for any of the purposes described hereinunder shall be convicted of human trafficking punished with a penalty of 5–8 years imprisonment:

    (a) Forced labour or services, slavery or practices similar to slavery, servitude or begging.
    (b) Sexual exploitation, including pornography.
    (c) Exploitation to commit criminal activities.
    (d) The removal of internal organs.
    (e) The formalisation of forced marriages.

A situation of need or vulnerability exists when the person in question has no real or acceptable alternative other than to submit to the abuse.

2. Even if none of the means described in the section above is used, any of the actions indicated in the section above shall be deemed trafficking in human beings when they are carried out in relation to minors for the purpose of exploitation.
3. The consent of a victim of trafficking in human beings to the exploitation shall be irrelevant when any of the means set forth in the first section of this article has been used
4. The penalty one degree higher than that set forth in the first section of this article shall be applied when:

    (a) the life or physical or mental wellbeing of the victim of trafficking in human beings has been endangered;
    (b) especially vulnerable by reason of illness, pregnancy, disability or personal circumstance, or because they are a minor.

If more than one circumstance applies concurrently, the penalty imposed shall be in the upper half of the range.

5. The penalty one degree higher than that set forth in the first section of this article and absolute disqualification for 6–12 years shall be applied to anyone committing these acts taking advantage of their position as an authority, an agent of that authority or a public official. If in addition any of the circumstances set forth in Sect. 4 of this article apply concurrently, penalties in the upper half of the range shall be imposed.
6. The penalty one degree higher than that set forth in Sect. 1 of this article and special disqualification from any profession, office, industry or trade for the time of the sentence shall be imposed when the guilty party belongs to an organisation or association of more than two people, even if temporary in nature, that perpetrates such activities. If any of the circumstances set forth in Sect. 4 of this article apply concurrently, penalties in the upper half of the range shall be imposed. If the circumstance set forth in Sect. 5 of this article applies concurrently, the penalties in the upper half of the range indicated in this section shall be imposed.

    In the case of managers, administrators or persons in charge of such organisations or associations, penalties in the upper half of the range shall be applied and may be increased to that one degree immediately higher. In any event, the penalty shall be raised to that one degree immediately higher if any of the circumstances set forth in Sect. 4 or the circumstance set forth in Sect. 5 of this article applies concurrently.

only of combating crime, but also prevention and protection by including a wide range of measures relating to the protection of victims.

With the introduction of this crime, Spain's criminal law at last distinguishes between people trafficking and the unlawful smuggling of migrants,[2] in accordance with the various international instruments signed by Spain (United Nations protocols that supplement the United Nations Convention against Transnational Organised Crime, A/55/382/, of 2000, which are: the United Nations Protocol to Prevent, Suppress and Punish Trafficking in Persons, Especially Women and Children [A/RES/55/25, annex II] and the Protocol against the Smuggling of Migrants by Land, Sea and Air [A/Res/55/25, annex III]). If we consider the various legal rights protected in the crime of illegal people smuggling—migration policies and the employment and social rights of workers—and that protected in people trafficking—human dignity[3]—one particularly important practical consequence of this legislative change is that in the application of the crime of trafficking in human beings, a sentence is passed for each individual trafficked, which is not the case in the application of the crime of immigration.

Despite the improvement represented by the introduction of the crime of people trafficking, there remains a problem in relation to slavery/exploitation/servitude, as they are no longer set down as crimes but only as trafficking for the purpose of exploitation.[4] Consequently, these situations can only be punished as a crime when it has been previously proven that a crime of people trafficking has been committed. If it is not proven that exploitative conduct has taken place, they can only be described as crimes of prostitution or crimes against workers' rights. This in turn means that as

---

7. Pursuant to the terms set forth in article 31 bis, when a legal person is responsible for the crimes set forth in this article, the penalty imposed shall be a fine three to five times the profit obtained. Pursuant to the rules established in article 66 bis, judges and courts may also impose the penalties set forth in letters (b) to (g) in Sect. 7 of article 33.
8. Provocation, conspiracy and proposition to commit the crime of human trafficking shall be punishable by penalties lower by one or two degrees to that of the corresponding crime.
9. In any event, the penalties set forth in this article shall be imposed without prejudice to those that may apply, if appropriate, for the crime set forth in article 318 bis of this Code and other crimes effectively committed, including those that constitute the corresponding exploitation.
10. Sentences handed down by foreign judges and courts for crimes of the same nature as those set forth in this article shall produce the effects of recidivism, unless the criminal record has been cancelled or may be in accordance with Spanish Law.
11. Without prejudice to the application of the general rules in this Code, the victim of human trafficking shall be not liable to punishment for criminal infractions they may have committed while suffering exploitation so long as their participation in said infractions is the direct consequence of the situation of violence, intimidation, deception or abuse they have been subject to and that there is an adequate proportionality between said situation and the criminal act committed.

[2] The Supreme Court decision STS 188/2016, of 4 March 2016, establishes the distinction between migration and trafficking.

[3] Lopez Rodrìgueza and Arrieta Idikez (2019), pp. 20 ff.

[4] Unlike the various international instruments in which slavery is expressly prohibited, among others, in article 4 of the European Convention on Human Rights. This failing is evident in the 2019 Report of the Spanish General Attorney.

victims are not regarded as victims of people trafficking, they do not enjoy the rights, established in various European directives and in the Framework Protocol of 27 October 2011, that would otherwise pertain to them.

Alongside the penal intervention, various mechanisms have been established to prevent people trafficking. For example, the police have set up a website (www.policia.es/trata/), as has the Ministry of the Interior (www.interior.gob.es/web/servicios-al-ciudadano/trat), explaining the legislation, existing resources and ways of detecting human trafficking. In addition, the 2022 police website details all the national police activities related to people trafficking, including collaboration with INTERPOL. In just one of these operations, 216 people were arrested and 127 victims of people trafficking—subjected to forced labour and sexual exploitation—were rescued. In another operation (WEKA), in which twenty-four European and African countries participated, 195 people were arrested and 447 victims of trafficking were rescued. Collaboration with African countries such as Niger is helping to identify networks, even if on occasions migration is once again confused with trafficking.

An analysis of the data on the crime of human trafficking reveals that the victims may be of any nationality, though most of them are Spanish or legally resident in Spain, clearly distinguishing this crime from immigration. The statistics—which are limited, not up to date and generally restricted to trafficking for the purposes of sexual exploitation—show the victims are mainly Romanian, Spanish and Nigerian, though they are mostly Romanian, aged between twenty-three and twenty-seven and legally resident in Spain. Even though these nationalities are the most common, trafficking victims from as many as sixty countries have been identified according to Spain's General Attorney. One notable fact is that the nationality of the victims is to a large extent the same as that of the traffickers. An analysis of Spanish jurisprudence on trafficking also reveals that in a considerable number of sentences, the perpetrators are women engaged in trafficking generally for the purpose of sexual exploitation[5] but also for begging.[6] In many cases, these women had themselves been the victims of exploitation, placing them in the ambiguous position of both perpetrators and victims.

The extent and gravity of the problem of human trafficking is also revealed by the statistics, which show that in 2015 alone, 13,879 people at risk of sexual exploitation were identified, whereas in 2017 there were 10,111.[7] Most of the identified victims of trafficking for the purpose of sexual exploitation are Nigerian, are aged between eighteen and twenty-two and are not legally resident in Spain.[8] One characteristic

[5] Among others, see STS 77/2019, of 12 February 2019; STSJ Catalunya 123/2019, of 18 October 2019; SAN 1/2021, of 11 February 2021; SAN 19/2020, of 13 October 2020; SAP Castellón, 160/2020, of 9 June 2020; SAP Madrid 98/2020, of 27 February 2020; and SAP Badajoz 127/2018, of 17 July 2018.

[6] STS 306/2020, of 12 June 2020, purposes of sexual exploitation and begging.

[7] Figures supplied by the CITCO (Counter-terrorism and Organised Crime Intelligence Centre).

[8] CITCO statistic relating to 2017.

typical of these victims is that they are coerced through the use of voodoo.[9] In light of the deep-rooted belief that harm may befall their relatives, Spanish jurisprudence holds that threatening victims with voodoo is an effective way to coerce them even though, in another context, it would not be deemed ideal as a form of intimidation since these victims can go out and they retain their passports.

Curiously, despite the apparent proactive attitude of the police and the Ministry of the Interior, in the ministry's own statistics it is evident that hostess clubs are venues with the highest number of people at risk and yet little or nothing is being done about it. In other words, even though there is evidence that there are people at risk of sexual exploitation in some establishments open to the public, the police do not intervene. This evidence of exploitation is easily noted by 'clients', turning them into perpetrators of wilful crimes against sexual freedom, though it is possible to make reference in these cases to wilful ignorance. Nevertheless, the police take no action in this respect. Occasionally, as recorded in a police statement regarding the arrest of several people for sexual exploitation, the 'clients' beat and abused the victims if they did not do as the perpetrators asked, which they said was normal because: 'They had the right to do what they wanted with them'. This was another case where no action was taken with a view to investigating the conduct of these 'clients'.

We must add to the above trafficking in human beings for labour exploitation, with 12,419 cases of people at risk detected in 2016, 10,111 in 2017, 9315 in 2018, 8405 in 2019 and 3867 in 2020.[10] The reason for this significant drop in the number of people at risk remains unexplained, though it could, at least in part, be attributed to COVID. The victims of labour exploitation are mostly of Romanian (the majority), Portuguese, Spanish, and Lithuanian nationality, though there are some of Moroccan, Chinese, Brazilian and Paraguayan nationality. In some instances, these people are in enforced servitude to pay off debts, which they are under pressure to do, suffering injuries caused by hard or dangerous labour (scars, chronic disorders, back problems, loss of hearing and/or eyesight, respiratory and cardiovascular disease and even the amputation of limbs). The statistics do not reflect the situation of the Chinese, as they maintain a closed society, nor that of Sub-Saharans, who live in utter precarity, selling fake objects on the street using a blanket as their stall (known locally as *top manta*) and exploited by those who provide the goods.

One notable difference between forced sexual and labour exploitation is that in the first case, almost all the victims are women, whereas in the second, approximately 70% of victims are men. Moreover, there is evidence that trafficking for the purpose of sexual exploitation is generally carried out by criminal organisations who 'swap' their victims, moving them from one place to another. In contrast, enforced labour exploitation is mostly for seasonal work, independently of the cases not included in the statistics which, though they cannot be described as trafficking, are

---

[9] STS 1228/2017, of 29 March 2017: the accused forced the victims, of Nigerian nationality, to participate in a voodoo ritual to coerce them.

[10] Figures taken from the document "Trata y explotación de seres humanos en España. Balance Estadístico 2016–2020", CITCO, Ministerio del Interior.

instances of exploitation. As in the case of people trafficking for enforced sexual exploitation, the nationality of the perpetrators of trafficking for labour exploitation is largely the same as that of the victims. Underage victims of both sexual and labour exploitation have been identified, though they are limited in number.

People trafficking for the purpose of enforced begging is generally carried out by perpetrators of Bulgarian nationality, whereas trafficking for forced marriages is mostly perpetrated by people of Romanian nationality. The statistics on forced marriages do not include purchased 'marriage contracts' to which the woman, frequently underage, does not consent, and which arise in cultures related to the Islamic world. With regard to trafficking for forced criminal activities, the statistics only record people of Romanian nationality. Nevertheless, they do not take into account cases of people coerced in some way to carry drugs (mules), who are of Latin American nationality (Colombian, Equatorian, Bolivian or Peruvian).

The statistics differentiate between victims of sexual or forced labour exploitation and victims of trafficking in human beings for the purposes of sexual or labour exploitation. Actually, classification in one category or the other depends on the moment when the intervention occurred or whether it has been proven that capture, transfer or harbouring occurred prior to the exploitation. In general, the police conduct a larger number of interventions and identifications for exploitation than for trafficking and especially for sexual exploitation[11] due to the fact that this identification occurs at a time after the trafficking, which on occasion remains concealed and/or cannot be proven or the perpetrators identified.

Instances of forced labour are described as crimes against workers' rights (arts. 311 et seq.) and those of sexual exploitation as crimes of prostitution (arts. 187 et seq.). Consequently, they are not recorded as trafficking of human beings. Only if the existence of prior trafficking is proven is this punished as an instrumental crime leading to another, including crimes committed against workers' rights or of sexual exploitation, in art. 177 *bis*. In this respect, STS 101/2017, of 19 January 2017, is interesting, as it covers a victim forced into prostitution who had previously been brought to Spain and obliged to work without pay. The resolution states that even though the purpose of sexual exploitation had not previously been noted, she had been forcibly 'harboured' to 'work in conditions similar to those of slavery'.[12]

Indicative of the severity of these crimes is the fact that the Title 'Trafficking in Human Beings' comes after those that deal with crimes of torture and against the right of self-determination. It protects, preferentially, essential individual legal-penal rights such as the right to freedom and human dignity (SSTS 615/2014, of 24 October 2014, FJ 2°; and 910/2013, FJ 6°, of 3 December 2013). It also provides protection

[11] The report submitted by Spain's General Attorney in 2019 considers that sexual exploitation is the most common. I believe that this is because labour exploitation is more difficult to detect and also because labour exploitation is not categorised as exploitation. Santos Martin and Rìos Martin (2019), pp. 38 ff. refers to the precarity of current labour markets that places them, at least, on the verge of exploitation.

[12] Slavery is a form of trafficking in which prior acts of sale or transfer are not considered but solely the situation of exploitation.

in the context of financial, social or interpersonal inequality in order to prevent the objectification and commodification of the person, in contrast with the basic offence in art. 318 *bis*, in which the control of flows of migration by the state is protected.

2 Political-Criminal Matters

As mentioned, following the latest international conventions and agreements, we have moved from an exclusively criminological perspective, involving the criminalisation of conduct, to a victim-centric vision that places the emphasis on attending to the victim by protecting, or attempting to protect, their rights. In keeping with this, an integrated approach to the problem, which derives from the structural differences between poor and rich countries, is pursued. Consequently, to be even minimally effective, joint action by countries and public and private institutions working in this field is necessary.[13] The goal is to analyse the political and financial causes that give rise to people trafficking and to find solutions to mitigate them.

Such an approach calls for work on a number of levels: firstly, by taking action at the source by helping to create an improved social and economic situation in countries of origin; and secondly, by establishing measures to protect and help victims. This is especially important in the context of a criminal trial in which victims must testify, a situation that can represent a further victimisation but which is necessary in order to combat criminal organisations that traffic human beings. To avoid this secondary victimisation, they must be treated as subjects with rights rather than as a source of evidence. Consequently, they must be provided with financial and psychological support, as well as education and training, which takes time and hence the appropriateness of granting a residency card to those who do not already have one.

The case of trafficking victims forced into crime is especially problematic. In general, they are regarded as criminals and have even been described as members of a criminal organisation, not as victims. As a result, they are given prison sentences, often long ones, generally for the crime of drug dealing, and they do not receive the benefits established in the Statute on the Victims of Crime (Law 4/2015, of 27 April 2015), which details the rights in and out of court of victims of crimes committed or potentially pursued in Spain, regardless of whether they are adults or minors or legally resident or not.

Nevertheless, in the case of victims/perpetrators as well as that of other victims of forced sexual or labour exploitation, the police regard them essentially as sources of evidence and seek their collaboration in trials. The paradigmatic example of this is the so-called 'mules' who transport drugs from South America to Spain and are arrested at the airport on the grounds that they have acted voluntarily. It is true that

[13] Dìaz Barrado (2017), pp. 495–498, indicating that combating trafficking in human beings needs to extend beyond migration policy.

over 90% of the people who bring drugs into the country tell the same story: their family is very poor, they need the money to feed their family or to pay debts and so as not to lose their home. In any event, the 'mule' will be tried and in order to reduce their sentence or even be acquitted, they must prove that they really did act for these reasons and it is a one-off and not a habitual crime.

This treatment of victims of trafficking for the purpose of forced crime is due in large measure to ignorance of this type of trafficking in human beings and, fundamentally, to the non-existence of specific criteria for identifying them. In addition, this situation also affects victims of sexual exploitation who traffic drugs or even become controllers of other victims (known in Spanish as *mamis* [mums]). In cases where it is detected that the person is both a victim and a criminal, the procedure is closed. In the case of victims of sexual exploitation, if the crimes are directly related to this exploitation, they are deemed to be a victim and not a perpetrator.

In some cases of exploitation, not just those of exploitation for the purpose of forced crime, situations of need arise. A specific clause has been introduced into the Criminal Code exempting people subject to exploitation from punishment for crimes they have committed when their involvement in the crime is a direct consequence of the violence, intimidation, deception or abuse to which they are subject and this situation is proportional to the crime perpetrated. In any event, what is important is that the trafficked person has no need to go to trial when their trafficked status is verified. Both the victim of human trafficking captured for the sole purpose of committing criminal activities and the victim obliged to commit any crime even if trafficked for another purpose may be exempt from punishment if them meet the established requirements of direct consequence and proportionality.

With regard to the legal nature of this exemption from punishment, two solutions could pertain: (a) Exemption from criminal accountability, which would only affect those to whom this applies concurrently on the grounds that other people would have the option to report the events: (b) Cause of exclusion from criminal accountability, a thesis supported by the requirement to weigh rights, reference to the state of immediacy between the situation of exploitation and the act of defence, as well as the injustice that would arise from punishing the person who helps to defend the victim and those that would occur if it were deemed to be grounds for exemption from criminal accountability due to the limited accessory nature of the involvement.

The legislative technique used generates problems related to interpretation and judicial application. Thus, despite being encompassed within the crime of trafficking in human beings, it seems to be limited to criminal acts committed during the state of exploitation, with those acts committed during the process of trafficking being excluded *prima facie*. However, in accordance with the principle of not prosecuting victims, recognised in the Warsaw Convention and in Directive 2011/36/EU, there should be no problem in applying it to those crimes committed during the trafficking process, such as the use of false documentation.

The reality is that in judicial praxis the clause lacks the importance that it might be expected to have. Firstly, because unlike in neighbouring countries, certain conduct on the part of the victim of trafficking during the trafficking process and the exploitation phase are not categorised as crimes, making the exclusion of criminal accountability unnecessary. Such conduct includes, for example, exercising as a prostitute or entering Spain in an irregular manner, which are not of criminal relevance in Spain. Secondly, because the crimes perpetrated by trafficking victims during the exploitation phase very often occur before their status as a trafficking victim is accredited (an accreditation that must be judicial), thereby obstructing its application. This situation is facilitated by the fact that many of the crimes committed by trafficking victims, such as robbery and drug dealing, are easy to prosecute, as a result of which the trafficking victim may have been sentenced and even served their sentence before their status as a victim is recognised.

Lastly, there are the additional requirements for acquiring the status of a victim of trafficking—(a) that the acts are a direct consequence of the use of the means employed to commit trafficking (which do not necessarily have to be the same as those during the situation of exploitation); and (b) proportionality between the force, intimidation, deception or abuse employed and the criminal act—preventing the automatic application of exemption from criminal responsibility, as a result of which an oral trial is launched, thereby promoting the secondary victimisation of the victim. The requirement for proportionality implies restricting the scope of the exemption from criminal responsibility which, in principle, would apply to the perpetration of any crime by the victim.

In practice, however, this proportionality would, in the opinion of the Public Prosecutor, prevent its application to those victims of trafficking who in turn become, as a result of the situation of subjugation in which they find themselves, perpetrators or participants in new trafficking crimes. The same occurs in relation to those victims of trafficking who act as 'mules' and bring large amounts of drugs in Spain,[14] as their status as a criminal prevails over their situation as a trafficking victim. Consequently, there is a need for co-ordination between the prosecutor's office and investigating judges with a view to facilitating the suspension of those trials in which the accused person may be presumed a victim of trafficking until such time as the judicial process to determine their status as a victim is completed.

3 Trafficking of Human Beings: Spanish Legislation and Jurisprudence

The crime of trafficking in human beings is set forth as a mere activity, since it occurs when one of the typical acts is carried out, regardless of whether the various situations of exploitation have taken place or not (STS 420/2016, of 18 May 2016; STS 1226/2017, of 24 March 2017; and STS 615/2014, of 24 October 2014). However, reference to the purposes of exploitation means that inconsistencies may arise excessively between the subjective part in relation to the objective of the

[14] See Villacampa Estiarte (2016). Available online at http://www.usc.es/revistas/index.php/epc/article/view/3104.

offence, as a consequence of which this crime may behave as a mutilated result defined by law consisting of two acts or of incomplete outcome depending on whether the acts of the subsequent exploitation are committed by the same subject who was the perpetrator of the first phase or are committed by others, thereby giving rise to later crimes that cannot be attributed to the person who perpetrated the trafficking.

If we consider strictly the typical acts, some would lead to a categorisation of the offence as a result (*transport*, *transfer* and *capture* in cases in which announcements in the media are used) and others as a mere activity (*harbouring* and *receiving*), which would make it very difficult to assess the attempt. For a sector of the doctrine, punishment of the attempt would excessively widen the scope of the application of the crime and, in other instances, this attempt would be included in others of the typical acts. In art. 3 of Directive 2011/35/EU, of 5 April 2011, member states are called upon to adopt the necessary measures to ensure that attempting to commit the offence is punishable. With regard to this, it should not be forgotten that in accordance with art. 177 *bis*. 8, *manifested resolutions* are punished. These *manifested resolutions* are also termed *attempted forms of participation* or preparatory acts (conspiracy, proposition and provocation) to commit the crime of trafficking in human beings, representing a considerable widening of the scope of action of this criminal offence, a requirement not included in Directive 2011/36/EU.

Trafficking in human beings constitutes a common crime, as a result of which anyone may be a perpetrator, though in cases where the perpetrators are public officials or authorities these are deemed to be aggravated offences. The aggravating circumstance is applied when the perpetrator uses their position as an authority, an agent of that authority or as a public official, thereby abusing the greater facility provided by the position they occupy even when not in the exercise of their functions (STS 773/2006, of 10 July 2006; and STS 727/2004, of 10 June 2004). The penalty is also increased when the perpetrator is a member of a criminal organisation or group. For this to be applied, it is necessary: (a) For there to be two or more people. Mere agreement between several people is insufficient (STS 6-10-2003), as that would be a mere case of collusion; (b) It must be a stable and hierarchical network, even if basic and short-lived (STS 330/2010, 2–3; STS 951/2009, 9-2010, absolving; and SAP Madrid 3ª 333/2015, 19-5, finding guilty); (c) they must have co-ordinated material and human resources to bring foreign subjects to Spain (STS 1595/2005, 30–12); and (d) The organisation or association must be *dedicated* to carrying out these activities. The term 'dedication' requires at least two or more trafficking activities to be pursued. However, it will not be necessary for the dedication to trafficking by the organisation or association to be unique, as other activities that, generally, act as a cover for this activity may also be concurrent. In the case of predominantly or exclusively family clans, this aggravated sub-offence may be applied (SAP Madrid 3ª 615/2014, 24–10, FJ 2 °C) if its conditions are met.

It is possible to distinguish between four different phases in the crime of trafficking: capture or recruitment, transfer or transport, exploitation and exchange. Capture or recruitment means to attract a person in order to control them by material or intellectual means. To achieve this, generally deception is used, on occasions jointly with coercion. The deception consists of an offer of work in domestic employment, in shops, as models, etc. At that point, the victim supplies documentation that is taken away by the perpetrators, who retain it in order to make it difficult for the victim to escape. Documentation is also frequently forged. For deception to form the typical element of people trafficking, the deception must be appropriate in that it must be sufficient to mislead the victim. If it is not, the crime of trafficking in human beings is deemed not to occur. STS 3565/2017, of 5 October 2017, absolves the accused on the grounds that sufficient deception did not take place, as the presumed victim knew, at least in approximate terms, the reason why they were coming to Spain.

In the transfer or transport phase, the deceived or coerced individual is taken from one place to another using any means, even on foot. This conduct is important because not only is it a stage in trafficking, but also a change in place that facilitates estrangement, preventing contact with family and friends, one of the harms that underlie trafficking. Normally, transfer implies crossing borders, but this is not a necessary requirement. Lastly, the exploitation phase consists of obtaining financial benefits or other types of benefits through the forced participation of the victim in acts of prostitution, work, begging, etc. In this final phase, in cases where exploitation has not as yet occurred, penalties can be handed down for the prior conduct of harbouring and receiving, as set forth in art. 177 *bis*.

Generally, an exchange phase occurs in the context of exploitation, especially sexual exploitation. Organic Law 1/2015, through the incorporation of the provisions of art. 1-II of Directive 2011, introduces the conduct of 'exchanging or transferring control' of people subject to trafficking. This exchange or transfer of control may occur at the start of the trafficking or during it, with the victims used as commodities as if this conduct were simply another type of financial activity. Exchange means swapping some people for others, but it may also take place for other goods or compensation in kind (drugs, weapons, etc.) or services. Transfer means ceding the victim to another person, in principle for a price.

Normally, trafficking in human beings, like other conducts, is carried out to obtain a benefit, be it financial or otherwise. In addition to the obtaining of benefits, a distinction is drawn with regard to the subjective aspect between: (a) Labour exploitation: forced labour or practices similar to slavery. In this instance, the victim is subject to degrading working conditions that objectify the human being, either because they are owned as livestock is, or because they are denied all or the most elementary rights in the provision of labour by a free person (STS 196/2017, of 24 March 2017).[15] A frequent aspect of this type of exploitation, and in sexual exploitation, is 'debt bondage', in which the trafficked victim must repay through their exploitation the costs of their transfer and upkeep; (b) Sexual exploitation: the

[15] Prior to the inclusion of the crime of trafficking in the Criminal Code, in the Supreme Court Sentence of 30 July 2000, a penalty was handed down for a crime against workers' rights in the case of an Algerian in an irregular situation in Spain forced to sign a 'slavery' contract, the grounds for the sentence being that conditions clearly an assault on human dignity should not be imposed under any circumstances.

obligation to engage in conduct of a sexual nature (sexual aggression, sexual abuse, exhibitionism and prostitution, STS 1002/2016, of 19 January 2016; and STS 67/2017, of 15 March 2017), including pornography in which minors are used; (c) Begging exploitation, with the exploiter retaining all or part of the money collected by the victim of said exploitation; (d) Criminal exploitation: forcing the victim to commit any crime, with the exploiters retaining the benefit obtained. The most frequent offences are crimes against property and drug trafficking; (e) Exploitation for the purpose of organ removal: the conditions governing organ transplants are set forth in various sets of rules and regulations and in all of them financial compensation is forbidden.[16] In cases of exploitation for the purpose of organ removal, the perpetrator of the crime receives payment without consent given by the exploited person; (f) Exploitation for the purpose of forced marriage: this means marriage 'held without the full and free consent of at least one of the couple and/or when one or both of them lack the capacity to separate or put an end to the union due, among other motives, to coercion or intense social or familial pressure' (UN report 2-4-2014). In this report, a distinction is drawn between child and early marriages, though these could be encompassed, in the most serious cases, within the category of forced marriage.

The consent of victims of exploitation is irrelevant, whether they are minors or whether they are subject to any of the typical circumstances set forth in art. 177 *bis*—violence, intimidation, deception, abuse of a position of power or vulnerability—as this consent is null or vitiated. In cases where deception occurs, misleading the victim about the real purpose of the perpetrator, this must be sufficient to mislead (STS 3565/2017, of 5 October 2017). Also typical is the delivery or receipt of payments or benefits to obtain the consent of the person who had control over the victim. The particular feature of this type of exploitation—introduced by Organic Law 1/2015—lies in the fact that the means employed does not rest directly with the victim of the trafficking but with those who have control over the victim (parents, counsellors or guardians, in the case of minors, or the exploiters, above all in the case of adults).

When the victims are minors, consent is irrelevant even when none of the requirements referred to are met, but solely when the acts are carried out *for the purposes of exploitation* (STS 379/2015, 19 June 2015, FJ 1). This term refers in the basic act to the purposes of sexual or labour exploitation or for the purpose of committing criminal acts, with no mention of the removal of organs or forced marriages, so it is open to question whether they are included in this provision. Despite this impreciseness, the term 'exploitation' should be taken to mean all the purposes of trafficking as there is no qualifying adjective attached to it.

A series of aggravating circumstances are also set forth, the most important of which is endangering the life or the physical or mental wellbeing of the victim.

[16] Art. 156 bis CPE, introduced by Organic Law 1/2010, forbids not only financial compensation but also the removal of organs if prevailing legislation is not complied with (Law 30/1979 and Royal Decree 1723/2012).

Another aggravating circumstance is when the victim is 'especially vulnerable by reason of illness, pregnancy, disability or personal circumstance, or because they are a minor'. Regardless of the questions referring to the possible infringement of the principle that a person shall not be tried or punished for the same crime twice, the reference to the 'personal circumstance' is ambiguous, so it will be necessary to refer to vulnerability. In the case of minors under the age of eighteen, both aggravating circumstances should be applied in cases where they are children. With regard to pregnancy, it should be taken that the aggravating circumstance is to be applied in cases in which the exploitation or trafficking endangers the pregnancy.

4 Concurrency of Offences

Inasmuch as subjective rights—dignity and the right to self-determination[17]—are protected, the existence of more than one victim implies the application of a real concurrence of crimes.[18] Art. 177 *bis*. 9 details the concurrency clause—*without prejudice*—for crimes committed *with occasion* of human trafficking, which means that the real concurrence of crimes with respect to all those that are related will also be applied. Depending on the acts, in cases of violence murder or injury may also be concurrent. When intimidation is used, the concurrent circumstance would be illegal detention. Even when it would be possible with threats, they should be included as their typical component is precisely intimidation. For the self-same reasons, it would also be applicable to coercion in the case that violence is concurrent. Deception may mean that a crime of fraud is also implicated. The use of trafficked women as mules to bring drugs into the country is in real concurrence with the crime of drug trafficking (SAP Madrid, Sec. 17ª, 490/2011, of 13 April 2011). In cases of sexual exploitation, including pornography, the respective crimes in Title VIII shall be applied as means concurrent with trafficking (STS 101/2017, of 19 January 2017; STS 191/2015, of 9 April 2015; and STS 53/2014, of 4 February 2014). In STS 1229/2017, of 29 March 2017, punishments were handed down for the real concurrent crimes of people trafficking, illegal immigration, prostitution, rape and abortion. In many sentences in the case of sexual exploitation, it is described as being concurrent as an act with the crime of illegal immigration, in art. 318 *bis* (STS 471/2019, of 12 February 2019; STS 1020/2018, of 22 March 2018; and STS 1045/2017, of 15 March 2017). In cases of labour exploitation, this crime may be concurrent as an act with crimes relating to the rights of workers. In the case of minors or people deemed incompetent used for begging, the real concurrence would

[17] In art. 177 bis and in art. 4 of the Universal Declaration of Human Rights of 1948, as well as Title I of the Charter of Fundamental Rights of the European Union of 2000, dignity and the right to integrity are held to be protected fundamental rights.

[18] For all, STS 1226/2017, of 24 March 2017, for protecting personal legal rights such as freedom and dignity.

be with art. 232, which sanctions the use of minors for begging. In STS 2011/2018, of 20 March 2018, the court reproaches the public prosecutor for not also accusing the defendant of the crime of begging concurrently with the crime of people trafficking. In the case of the removal of internal organs, this would be concurrent with the offence of causing injury. However, with regard to the acts of the new crime of art. 156 *bis*, which deals with organ trafficking, the injuries could be described as preparatory acts or subsequent acts that are unpunished. In cases of forced marriages, they could be an instrumental crime leading to another in ideal concurrence with art. 218 and an instrumental crime leading to another in concurrence with the new offence of coercion, of art. 172 *bis*. 1, which addresses forced marriages. If the purpose were exploitation to commit criminal activities, it would be in real concurrence with the induced crime to be perpetrated or the crime of the indirect perpetrator in the case of children aged under fourteen. With regard to the crime of falsifying official documents (art. 390), both to facilitate fraudulent entry into Spain or to alter the victim's age, a concurrence of instrumental crimes occurs.

Following the abolition of clandestine immigration for work (art. 313.1), trafficking in human beings in art. 177 *bis* will be distinguished from the basic offence of illegal trafficking or clandestine immigration in art. 318 *bis*, as well as by the criminal legal right protected in: (a) that in art. 177 *bis*, it must always be committed without the consent of the passive subject or with vitiated consent, and is deemed to have taken place in all cases involving minors, whereas in art. 318 *bis* it is committed with the consent of people who are not citizens of a European Union member state except, if applicable, in the aggravated sub-offences of art. 318 *bis*. 3 (b); in art. 177 *bis*, the nationality of the victims is irrelevant, whereas in art. 318 *bis*, they must be citizens of a country that is not a member state of the European Union; (c) art. 318 *bis* does not require a specific purpose, but this is required in art. 177 *bis*; (d) in art. 177 *bis*, there is no transnational character required, but this is a requirement in art. 318 *bis* (STS 910/2013, FJ 6°). As these are different offences, there is the possibility, recognised in art. 177 *bis* itself, that the two could be concurrent crimes (STS 473/2019, of 12 February 2019, a sentence related to the concurrence of instrumental crimes leading to another crime, including crimes of trafficking in human beings, of prostitution and of illegal immigration of art. 318 *bis*).[19]

Slavery exploitation, be it for sexual, labour or begging purposes, is by its nature a permanent crime, so participation is possible in interventions that may occur at any time, and the statute of limitations does not start until the situation of slavery ends. Consequently, penalties should be established that vary depending on the length of time that the victim has been exploited, in line with the provisions for crimes of illegal detention or kidnapping.

---

[19] STS 298/2015, of 13 May 2015, FJ 5°, in an alleged case of the introduction into Spain of a person who was not a citizen of a European Union member state for the purpose of sexual exploitation, in view of the lack of accreditation that the victim of the sexual exploitation had not given consent, the case was downgraded to the cases described in art. 318 bis.

5 Procedural Problems

There is no need for borders to be crossed for it to be deemed that a crime of human trafficking has been committed (STS 910/2013, 3 February 2013, FJ 3°), as a result of which it can be perpetrated on Spanish territory—national trafficking—as well as from, in transit or bound for Spain—transnational trafficking. Directive 2011/33/EU (art. 10) abandons the principle of universality by referring only to those of territoriality and personality, without prejudice to what each member state might say (art. 23.4 of the Organic Law on Judicial Power). Notwithstanding this, it has been interpreted in case law that for jurisdictional competence to exist, it is sufficient for one of the acts to be carried out in Spain (STS 1020/2018, of 22 March 2018, affirms the territorial competence of one of the accused by virtue of carrying out the acts needed to transfer the victim to Spain, even when she lived in France and it was there that she was obliged to engage in prostitution).

Art. 177 *bis* 10 covers international recidivism, by virtue of which final convictions for these crimes in foreign countries shall be the equivalent of those handed down by Spanish courts for the purposes of the eighth aggravating circumstance in art. 22. However, due to the requirements of the principles of reintegration into society and res judicata, these convictions shall not be taken into account if the criminal record has been cancelled or may be in accordance with Spanish law.

This crime is governed by the—conditioned—principle of universality in art. 23.4. The abolition of the principle of double jeopardy, as established in art. 23.4 d) of the Organic Law on Judicial Power will be especially significant, above all when it refers to minors. In this crime, experience indicates that the pressure exerted on witnesses-victims of trafficking and exploitation is as a rule very intense, as a result of which recourse to pre-established evidence should be a frequent practice given the high probability that they will abscond, flee abroad or not appear at the oral trial, ordinarily as a result of fear of the potential consequences of testifying against their aggressors (STS 53/2014, of 4 February 2014, FJ 9°).

There is no need for an official complaint from the victim in order to proceed against this crime, as victims generally do not wish to file complaints out of fear of the trafficker or exploiter. The violence perpetrated during capture, transfer and harbouring and direct threats against the victim or their relatives carry more weight with the victim than their wish to collaborate with the authorities. When they do so, it is also very likely that they will not appear at the trial or will withdraw their statement. In other instances, their statement is deemed not credible due to the existence of spurious motives related to the obtaining of administrative benefits such as the granting of a residency permit.

If the victim makes an official complaint and appears at the trial, their testimony is sufficient proof of the charge if the following pertains:[20] (a) Objective credibility: the victim's statement must be logical (internal consistency) and have supplementary

[20] STS 473/2019, of 12 February 2019; STS 1228/2017, of 29 March 2017; STS 128/2017, of 29 March 2017; and STS 101/2017, of 19 January 2017.

corroboration in objective data of a peripheral nature (external consistency) (e.g. police officers in charge of the investigation, the people responsible for aiding, recovering and rescuing the victim to demonstrate their initial state and subsequent change, third parties, documentary evidence relating to the transfer of the victim, bank transactions, the state and situation of the victim's home or places where they were exploited, illnesses, treatment, injuries, sequelae, etc.); (b) Subjective credibility: the existence of spurious motives based on previous relationships with the active subject or other grounds (hatred, revenge, resentment, enmity, etc.) would exclude this subjective credibility. Moreover, it should be borne in mind that the obtaining of benefits of an administrative nature such as the granting of a residency permit due to collaboration with the police or court authorities, is regulated by art. 59 *bis*. 4 of the Organic Law on the Rights and Freedoms of Foreigners in Spain and their Social Integration (LOEX) and immigration regulations; (c) Persistence: the lack of fundamental changes in the various statements given by the victim. Material persistence in the incrimination. Specific details in the declaration and a lack of contradictions. Language, fear and threats can all create problems in this persistence.

6 Conclusions

The policies pursued in recent years should be positively evaluated, even though shortcomings in the system have been identified. Special attention continues to be paid to trafficking for the purpose of sexual exploitation, to the detriment of trafficking for other purposes, especially for labour exploitation. For example, the Second Integrated Plan to Combat Trafficking for the Purposes of Sexual Exploitation (2015–2018) was approved, once again ignoring other purposes associated with trafficking. One result of this is the lack of data concerning the real incidence of trafficking for purposes other than sexual exploitation in Spain, despite the fact that it is one of the destination or transit countries for victims of trafficking for the purposes of labour exploitation,[21] the limited number of identified victims[22] and the small number of cases that go to trial for these acts. This is exemplified by the 2017 report issued by Spain's General Attorney,[23] which reviews just one sentence for the crime

[21] Defensor del Pueblo. La trata de seres humanos en España: Víctimas Invisibles (Defensor del Pueblo 2012), p. 55; Accem, La trata de personas con fines de explotación laboral: un estudio de aproximación a la realidad en España (Accem 2006).

[22] The number of periods of reflection and recovery granted were 99 in 2013, 62, 12 in 2014, 95 in 2015 and 81 in 2016, whereas the number of residency authorisations granted were nineteen—four on the grounds of the personal circumstances of the victim—in 2013, 25—12 on the grounds of personal circumstances—in 2014, 38—19 on the grounds of personal circumstances—in 2015 and 127—30 on the grounds of personal circumstances—in 2016. See Greta (2018). Available online at https://rm.coe.int/greta-2018-7-frg-esp-en/16808b51e0.

[23] See Fiscalìa De Extranjería (2016). Available online at https://www.fiscal.es/documents/20142/160400/Diligencias+de+Seguimiento+del+delito+de+Trata+de+Seres+Humanos.+Fiscal%C3%

of trafficking for the purposes of labour exploitation and reports on only a small number of proceedings initiated for trafficking for the purposes of begging or forced marriage. Particularly significant is the failure to introduce an offence in which slavery/exploitation is punished, as this prevents convictions of trafficking in human beings when its existence is not proven. Moreover, this lacuna in the law also hinders victims from enjoying the rights established for the crime of trafficking of human beings.

Other problematic issues connected with the system arise due to the process of identifying victims and the complex procedure for granting residency and work permits to victims of trafficking, a process strongly conditioned by the victim's collaboration in the police investigation and criminal proceedings. The fact that it is immigration legislation that is responsible for recognising the victim's recovery and reflection period, which is accompanied by a series of rights intended to guarantee their assistance, is a clear reminiscence of the close link between irregular immigration and people trafficking. This connection between trafficking and irregular immigration that seems to underlie some provisions means that a large number of trafficking victims are left out of the system,[24] rather than extending the legal framework, albeit temporarily, to foreigners who enter Spanish territory in an irregular manner when it is impossible to ascertain whether the person concerned is a citizen 'voluntarily' and irregularly entering Spanish territory or whether the person is a victim of trafficking in the throes of being transported. Even though the illegal smuggling of foreigners and trafficking in human beings may be differentiated from a theoretical point of view, reality reveals them to be closely connected, hence it is impossible to grant adequate protection to people if we are ignorant of their situation.

Despite the major advances that have been made, there is still work to be done, as a phenomenon as complex as trafficking in human beings cannot be discouraged solely and exclusively by means of the criminal legal framework, nor by eliminating some of its determining factors. There is a need to adopt a comprehensive and coherent policy allocated sufficient resources so that it can be implemented and to ensure the necessary coordination takes place between the various public and private agents involved in pursuing this crime and protecting victims. To this end, doctrine[25] holds that a victim-centric approach is important, the kind of approach adopted by international instruments since 2005. With this strategy, we will be able to delve into the origin and cause of trafficking, which is closely connected with immigration.

ADa+de+Extranjer%C3%ADa+2016/467a2931-d770-fc6f-0941-62dc700467e8?version=1.1&t=1532605839480.

[24] During the period 2013–16, victims came mainly from Romania (306 victims), with up to fifty victims of Spanish nationality identified. See Greta, Report concerning the implementation of the Council of Europe Convention on Action against Trafficking in Human Beings by Spain. Second Evaluation Round, op. cit.

[25] Scarpa (2008), pp. 41 ff., detailing the various international instruments that take this perspective; and Villacampa Estiarte (2011), pp. 145 ff., which details an extensive body of literature on the subject.

Consequently, we must put in place policies that facilitate legal migration and increase co-operation between countries. In addition, mechanisms must be established to protect and assist victims.

The conduct of 'clients' in cases of sexual exploitation should also be taken into consideration, as in many instances, due to concurrent circumstances such as the age or incompetence of victims, the 'client' is aware of the lack of consent on the part of the victim and so the client's conduct should be categorised as a crime of rape. Moreover, with regard to labour exploitation, 'clients' may be aware of the circumstances in which victims work, so by purchasing products, undoubtedly at a price below market value, they are wittingly co-operating with the act of exploitation.

References

Accem (2006) La trata de personas con fines de explotación laboral: un estudio de aproximación a la realidad en España. Accem, Madrid

Defensor del Pueblo (2012) La trata de seres humanos en España: Víctimas Invisibles. Defensor del Pueblo, Madrid

Dìaz Barrado CM (2017) La lucha contra la trata de seres humanos en la Unión Europea: los componentes para una política propia. Rev Derecho Comunitario Eur 17:495–498

Fiscalìa De Extranjería (2016) Diligencias de Seguimiento del delito de trata. https://www.fiscal.es/documents/20142/160400/Diligencias+de+Seguimiento+del+delito+de+Trata+de+Seres+Humanos.+Fiscal%C3%ADa+de+Extranjer%C3%ADa+2016/467a2931-d770-fc6f-0941-62dc700467e8?version=1.1&t=1532605839480

Greta (2018) Report concerning the implementation of the Council of Europe Convention on Action against Trafficking in Human Beings by Spain. Second Evaluation Round. https://rm.coe.int/greta-2018-7-frg-esp-en/16808b51e0

Lopez Rodrìguez J, Arrieta Idiakez F (2019) La trata de seres humanos con fines de explotación laboral en la legislación española. Revista de la Facultades de Derecho y Ciencias Económicas y Empresariales 107:1–24

Santos Martin J, Rìos Martin P (2019) La tutela de la víctima de trata: una perspectiva penal, procesal e internacional. Bosch, Barcelona

Scarpa S (2008) Trafficking in human beings: modern slavery. Oxford University Press, Oxford

Villacampa Estiarte C (2011) El delito de trata de seres humanos. Una incriminación dictada desde el Derecho Internacional

Villacampa Estiarte C (2016) Trata de seres humanos para explotación criminal: ausencia de identificación de las víctimas y sus efectos. Estudios Penales y Criminológicos 36. http://www.usc.es/revistas/index.php/epc/article/view/3104

Organised Crime, Illicit Manpower Brokerage and Recent Italian Legislation

Antonio La Spina

Abstract The revised version of article 603 *bis* of the Italian criminal code (adopted in 2016) addresses illicit manpower brokerage and excessive labour exploitation. This chapter sketches a taxonomy comprising four different employment relationships, with or without manpower brokerage. The first refers to lawful activities that do not involve excessive labour exploitation. The second refers to illegal activities outside the domain of criminal law that also do not involve excessive labour exploitation. In the third set of cases, workers experience objectively excessive exploitation because they are forced by need, so explicit coercion exerted by illegal gang-masters or entrepreneurs is usually absent. Finally, excessively exploited workers of the fourth category constantly experience physical violence or threats systematically administered by criminal groups who are organised accordingly.

1 Italian Legislative Measures Against the Excessive Exploitation of Workers

The decree-law 138, which was adopted in 2011, introduced a new article 603 *bis* in the Italian criminal code. This provision was meant to fight the widespread phenomenon of illicit manpower brokerage which is endemic in the world of agriculture and is also present elsewhere, for example, in the building or the textile sectors. With regard to some productive sectors in Italy, this illegal gang-master system is called *caporalato*. Prosecutions based on the first version of art. 603 *bis* were rare.[1]

Therefore, a revised version of the article was soon introduced by law 199/2016. The rewriting was aimed at punishing both the gang-masters and the entrepreneurs

[1] Ferranti (2016).

A. La Spina (✉)
Department of Political Science, LUISS School of Government, Rome, Italy
e-mail: alaspina@luiss.it

V. Militello, A. Spena (eds.), *The Challenges of Illegal Trafficking in the Mediterranean Area*, Legal Studies in International, European and Comparative Criminal Law 9, https://doi.org/10.1007/978-3-031-45399-1_9

who employ the workers,[2] when they exploit them in an excessive way by taking advantage of their state of need. The normative text established a set of indicators to be used by prosecutors when detecting cases of excessive exploitation.

It is in the nature of an indicator to guide the search for evidence.[3] As was clarified in the revised version,[4] the occurrence of events to which the indicators enumerated by art. 603 *bis* refer does not always coincide with cases of excessive exploitation. Thus, the presence of some of the events does not necessarily imply an excessive exploitation, and conversely, in the absence of the indicated events, exploitation might nevertheless occur on some occasions in connection with other aspects of the work condition. Therefore, excessive exploitation must be ascertained on a case-by-case basis.

The exploiters must also be aware of the state of need of the worker and willingly take advantage of his or her weakness. Such a state of need does not concern the generic needs of persons who are not rentiers to earn something but rather a specific condition of socioeconomic weakness that severely restricts the worker's range of choices, who, in practice, is compelled to accept the proposed job even if he or she is going to be excessively exploited.[5]

According to other relevant provisions of law 199/2016, those people—such as entrepreneurs or brokers—who are involved in the crimes indicated by art. 603 *bis* and who decide to cooperate with the prosecutors are entitled to ask for a reduction of the sanctions that could be imposed on them.

Furthermore, the assets and the sums of money which were either used to accomplish the systematic exploitation of workers or generated through it must be confiscated. An alternative to the seizure of property of the firms involved, which is explicitly mentioned by law 199/2016, is judicial control: the owners and managers continue to stay in place to avoid risky interruptions of production that might jeopardise the income and the living conditions of the employees, while an administrator chosen by the court protects the workers and, at the same time, supervises the management of ongoing activities in order to guarantee that the firm sticks to the law. It is easy to see that tools of this kind resemble in a way those of Italian anti-mafia legislation.[6] On the one hand, the underlying assumption of the law is presumably that the imposition of extremely hard conditions of exploitation on some workers presupposes that the exploiters possess the ability to make the workers obey, when, in principle, they could refuse to undergo such conditions. On the other hand, the fact

[2] The employers were not explicitly addressed by the previous version. Now entrepreneurs can be sanctioned even if they recruit and exploit the workers directly, without the help of caporali.

[3] Ferranti (2016).

[4] Also by case-law presented by Vitarelli (2022), who discusses two decisions of the Court of Cassation: Sect. 4 no. 45615/2021 and no. 7861/2022.

[5] Vitarelli (2022), paras. 3–6; Cassation no. 45615/2021. On the state of need, a similar point is made by Braschi (2021), especially pp. 129–130.

[6] Apart from judicial control, the more intrusive judicial administration, as well as the even more intrusive appointment of a judicial commissary were deemed applicable in some cases: Barberio and Camurri (2020).

that art. 603 *bis* is an *ad hoc* norm—belonging to a section of the criminal code that is devoted to crimes against personal liberty—and that it is distinct from art. 600 that addresses slavery, means that in the mind of the Italian lawmakers who drafted both versions of art. 603 *bis*, certain behaviours that they were criminalising did not easily fall within the reach of the well-known measures concerning mafia-type groups.

After the entry into force of law 199/2016, an upsurge in judicial cases occurred,[7] with 260 ongoing proceedings detected in 2020.[8] Many of them were related to agriculture, but others concerned different fields. Moreover, the relevant events happened not only in the South but also in the Centre and in the North of Italy. Most of the workers exploited were migrants, but there were also several Italians.[9] This increase in cases is conspicuous when compared to the negligible amounts seen before 2016. However, the present absolute quantity of cases remains low, vis-a-vis the remarkable estimated diffusion of the phenomenon.[10]

Certain applications of law 199/2016 to sectors that are remote from the rural world (including the so-called Italian gig economy,[11] which typically takes place in and around urban areas) have been triggering the attention of the public. But the *caporalato* is still perceived as being very similar to—or even connected with—mafia-type organisations acting in traditional settings. This can sometimes, but not always, be true. In actual fact, manpower brokerage is a highly heterogeneous and constantly evolving reality.

2 The Need for Manpower Brokerage and the Organisational Aspects

Depending on the kind of productive activity they perform, some entrepreneurs require a certain type and a given number of workers, at a definite time. Such requests are a powerful factor of attraction for migrants.[12] Typical examples can be found in the seasonal work that takes place in agriculture.

However, as has already been stated, this by no means is the only economic sector involved. An entrepreneur can decide to recruit and supervise the workers he or she needs or can delegate these tasks to somebody else. The brokers/providers dedicate themselves to the search and management of suitable workers (who often must be transferred from distant areas and/or mobilised just in time), and their service is

[7] Such cases are discussed by Stoppioni (2019) and Santoro and Stoppioni (2018, 2019, 2020).

[8] Santoro and Stoppioni (2020), p. 221.

[9] Stoppioni (2019), Santoro and Stoppioni (2018, 2019, 2020).

[10] Mondi (2016); Orlando (2020).

[11] On this, Brambilla (2022) and Barberio and Camurri (2020), among others.

[12] Krissman (2004). If a productive sector sticks to a traditional labour intensive structure (as it frequently happens with agriculture in Southern Italy), more workers at cheap conditions of employment are needed in order to survive in competitive markets (Perrotta 2016).

valuable both to the employers (who solve their problem of manpower shortage) and the workers (who can earn something for a living). Therefore, this service—that can be extended to transportation, housing, surveillance of working activities, paperwork and so on—deserves to be fairly rewarded. Depending on the relevant legal norms in given places and times, manpower intermediation and provision can not only be a perfectly lawful business but also a helping hand for the parties involved. An efficient system of manpower brokerage and provision can be regarded as a desirable thing provided that the salary of the workers is proportionate to their effort and that their rights are effectively safeguarded, and this is something that policymakers could strive to achieve (in fact, in many countries the public sector itself supplies such brokerage). Moreover, in principle, a broker/provider should be eager to consider and protect the interests of the workers[13] because his or her earnings normally come from them.

It is also possible that given the existing regulations of the labour market and productive activities, there is a lack of compliance with administrative, fiscal and environmental norms (or other types of norms). This might occur at the expense of the worker, but it can also happen on the basis of genuine consent (given that the employee deems it convenient). If the latter applies, this could mean that the brokers, the workers, and the entrepreneurs that hire them are willingly cooperating in order to circumvent legal provisions. *Ex hypothesi*, such violations do not necessarily imply a breach of criminal norms (in Italy, more specifically, a breach of law 199/2016).

The vast majority of regulations are justified by the intent to protect workers, consumers, the environment and other relevant common goods. All existing rules are obviously supposed to be respected also outside the field of criminal law, even when the so-called informal (or invisible) economy and undeclared work are at stake. It is thus advisable that the relevant policymakers scrutinise the regulations and their effects to see whether they can be revised to more properly meet the needs of workers and employers, or whether there is some unreasonable burden in place that can be reduced or lifted. This would also increase compliance.

Is article 603 *bis* a tool meant to be used to fight against the informal economy as such? If *all* work relationships which take place in this domain imply a violation of the dignity of workers, the answer would be yes; but if this is not the case for a certain share of the invisible economy, the answer would instead be no. Indeed, we know that the declared intention of law 199/2016 is to hinder the excessive exploitation of workers that can take place in the informal economy as well as in borderline cases that *prima facie* appear to belong to the formal economy.[14]

A gang-master in principle can be an individual who personally stays in touch with a certain number of employers and workers and summons the latter when they are needed. However, depending on the quantity of contacts and the other tasks with which the gang-master deals (concerning transportation, housing, and so on), he or

[13] Some examples are indicated by Perrotta (2014).

[14] Ispettorato nazionale del lavoro (2019), pp. 6–7.

she will almost always not act alone. Some other people—such as watchers, lorry-drivers, and so on—will work with him or her on a continuous basis, and according to certain schemes and goals. The first version of art. 603 *bis* understandably spoke of organised activities imputed to criminal brokers, including the organisation of what the exploited workers do. The second version dropped this reference to the organisational dimension because it was not easy to find robust evidence related to it. But this, of course, does not mean that such dimension no longer exists or that it has become less important in the actual functioning of the *caporalato* or other forms of systematic exploitation of workers. Therefore, when we face the phenomena of excessive exploitation not only is it normally appropriate to speak of organised crime but the organisational side is also a crucial one with regard to both the organisation of the exploiters and the way in which they, in turn, organise the working activities and the life of their victims in more or less coercive ways.

The organisational element is again essential, even when there are no brokers/providers and a given entrepreneur directly recruits and manages some workers in order to severely exploit them. By definition, the entrepreneur runs his or her organisation, some of whose members are involved in the exploitation of workers, while some others at least know what is happening and tolerate it. The exploited workers must also in some sense be inserted into the pre-existing organisation. Even if the firm wants to stay in the formal economy and maintain an appearance of lawfulness, some of its members are devoting themselves to a complex criminal activity, and we again see a criminal organisation in action.

3 Criminal Organisations and Objectively Excessive Exploitation Without Intimidation

As I hinted at in the previous section, manpower brokerage can manifest in several forms. At least four distinct Weberian types can be drawn at a conceptual level (in the real world, as usually happens, some of the cases will not fit neatly in one and only one of these types). In the first type, we find lawful activities that do not imply an excessive exploitation of workers, who experience fair and decent working conditions. In the second, there is no compliance with certain legal provisions but, again by definition, there is no excessive exploitation of workers. Therefore, cases that belong to it do not fall within the range of the application of art. 603 *bis* c.p.

The third type indeed exhibits an excessive exploitation of workers performed by criminal organisations, and this is my main focus of interest here (together with the fourth type that I will present in Sect. 4). However, when looking at real cases, an external observer would detect an apparently spontaneous and voluntary adhesion by workers to the terms of the objectively exploitative informal agreements that they strike with brokers/providers or entrepreneurs. As anticipated, the workers are weak and experience a state of urgent need; thus, they not only accept but often actively seek opportunities that imply an excessive exploitation. *Ex hypothesi,* they will also try to maintain good relationships with gangmasters and entrepreneurs because they understand that if something doesn't go as expected for them, their substitution can be easy and quick. They will also fear that they will not be summoned again when new work arises.

Many workers that face exploitative working conditions come from abroad. Their travel and their temporary stay are frequently organised by the brokers/providers. When this third hypothetic type applies, it can be presumed that such migrants, as the resident workers, know in advance with sufficient approximation, and are ready to accept, the real salary that they will be given, the daily workload, the tasks and working rhythm, the strictness of surveillance, the safety conditions and some uncomfortable features of the dwellings that they will inhabit, which are supplied by brokers/providers or entrepreneurs. These things happen because the workers nevertheless expect a net improvement of their personal situation in comparison with what they are used to experiencing in their homeland. Therefore, their acceptance is based on their explicit consent (which is, in turn, dictated by their urgent basic needs), and their readiness to obey can be taken for granted. Recourse to coercion, physical aggression or threats in order to enforce the will of the exploiters will, in principle, not then be needed. Exploitation is programmed by criminal organisations and practically agreed upon by their vulnerable victims. Mutual coordination between the exploiters and the exploited persons—who become members of an organisation and are bound to its usual functioning and working routines—is supposed to be sufficient. Deviations from this hypothetical state of things that require the use of threats or violence, which could occur due to peculiar contingent circumstances, are seen as exceptional. Coercion exerted by the exploiters is virtually absent, and it can be said that workers are coerced only by their state of need. Therefore, in order to detect the presence of the relevant offences, prosecutors will have to rely on objective information about the gravity of exploitation that the workers recurrently undergo.[15]

It should be recalled at this point that unlike the first version of art. 603 *bis* c.p., the second version no longer actually requires as a necessary prerequisite for its application the demonstration—which can be difficult—of the fact that violence or threats have been inflicted on the exploited workers. Consequently, the penalties for the simple offence introduced in 2011 were significantly reduced in 2016.

Some of the exploited foreign workers are regular residents in or lawfully travel to Italy. When this is not the case, the brokers/providers of the third type of manpower brokerage either are also engaged (directly or in cooperation with other criminal groups) in smuggling migrants or will exploit foreigners that have independently reached the country and presently live there, such as refugees and asylum seekers.[16] The public rules and regulations (which also concern migration) that exist at a given

[15] Most of the time, prosecutions are not originated by reports made by the workers but rather by the activity of the labour inspectorate (which in Italy is remarkably understaffed) or by other judicial inquiries.

[16] Omizzolo (2020).

time must in some way be violated or circumvented, and this is a crucial element that criminal groups take into consideration in order to frame their relationships with exploited workers and the requests for cooperation directed to them.

4 Criminal Organisations and the Exploitation of Workers Backed by Intimidation

Even an agreement which was entered into under the pressure of a state of need can, under certain circumstances, become shaky afterwards. First of all, this can happen because one of the parties to the agreement—the exploiter—violates some of the informal clauses established in the agreement and engages in modes of exploitation which are much harsher than expected with regard to the heaviness of tasks, the subtraction of income and so on. For instance, the broker/provider can take for himself or herself a predatory share of the agreed salary that, in principle, should be received by the workers or can sell food, work tools and other necessary items at very expensive prices, thereby taking advantage of situations in which the exploited are compelled to buy from them.

Second, the exploiters can try to forcefully extract other extras from the workers which are extraneous to the agreement, such as sexual performance (especially with regard to women[17]) and bodily organs. This typically happens in the relationship of employment or during the trip of an incoming worker from her or his homeland.

Third, something which is external to the parties to the informal agreement could strengthen the position of the weak workers. Public institutions, some non-governmental organisations (NGOs), religious entities and so on can (among other things) supply financial, legal, and psychological assistance, provide comfortable accommodations and suggest approaches that help workers defend their rights. Workers might also choose to belong to a union. Self-organised movements of self-defence can emerge at the grassroots level and denounce the exploitation as unbearable.[18] If this happens, one possible outcome is that some workers will not accept such opportunities because they want to avoid being excluded by the recruiters in the future, who prefer more malleable and easily reachable people. Such reactions actually belong to the third type. However, if a criminal organisation of exploiters fears that the exploited can sooner or later change their minds or if there are already workers who are unionised, who organise collective movements or participate in them or who take advantage of what is supplied by public bodies, NGOs etc. and, therefore, overcome their state of need, the situation might shift into the fourth type. This would happen because the apparently spontaneous acceptance of the given conditions of exploitation by workers pushed by their state of need can no longer be

[17] Giammarinaro and Palumbo (2020); Palumbo and Sciurba (2015).

[18] Examples are given by Perrotta and Sacchetto (2014).

taken for granted. It can thus be expected that criminal organisations of exploiters will tend to switch to a tough and perceptible use of intimidation.

More generally, if an organisation of exploiters knows that those who are exploited could complain about broken pacts and unbearable pressures, or if the latter can be induced to resist and denounce their miserable situation by some favourable contextual conditions, then it becomes rational for the exploiters to monitor their victims and punish them when deemed necessary, sometimes by using direct violence but, most of the time, by creating an atmosphere of constant fear. Retaliation against resistant workers could also concern the economic side and working conditions, but these belong to the third type, while in the fourth type, we find the pervasive perception of being threatened as well as the possibility of physical attacks to persons or properties and other extremely severe sanctions. If we diachronically consider the life of criminal groups engaged in the excessive exploitation of workers, it could be the case that some of them begin as entities of the third type and, at a certain point in time, enter the fourth type. The reverse can also sometimes be true.

It must be remembered that the systematic use of intimidation is typical of certain offences. Art. 300 of the criminal code addresses slavery, which can be present even though the victims are paid in some way. What is distinctive here is the continuous subjection of the slave to the will of his or her master, who among other things can forcefully obtain sexual performances, bodily organs and other activities such as begging. However, such uninterrupted subjection—that excludes the possibility of a free choice for the slave—is difficult of conception with regard to the kind of exploited workers that have been discussed so far, who often live with their families, meet their friends and acquaintances, personally interact with public services or policemen, might belong to a union or participate in a collective movement, and so on. Therefore, it can be supposed that only a tiny fraction of cases of exploitation of the fourth type fall within the reach of art. 300.

Other provisions of Italian legislation address a notorious kind of criminal entity that is indeed able to generate the subjugation of their victims through the use of violence and intimidation. I am referring to mafia-type organisations and their characteristic way of behaving. It can be recalled that in the Sicilian case, the mafia was born in the rural world where its members were at the service of rich landowners who exploited their peasants. The latter were scared by homicides and other acts of violence orchestrated by mafia men and were forced to undergo their abuses. When the peasants began to organise themselves, several trade unionists were killed and most of them were intimidated by the mafia. This also happened with judges, policemen, priests, politicians and journalists.

Some of the brokers/providers and entrepreneurs that are devoted to the exploitation of workers belong to mafia-type organisations or are very close to them. In such cases, the application of anti-mafia legal instruments should be straightforward enough. Other organisations of exploiters that systematically use intimidation somewhat like mafia-type groups do not possess such connections. Would it be admissible on the basis of the legal norms that are presently in force to regard those belonging to this second set as autonomous mafia-type organisations from the point of view of the legal doctrine? This is a very interesting question. It must be noted that the first version of art. 603 *bis* was intended to tackle cases of excessive exploitation backed by violence and threats with robust sanctions. The second version of article 306 *bis* also considered the use of violence and threats as an aggravating condition. It was thus, in turn, meant to be invoked to punish cases of exploitation of the fourth type.

References

Barberio M, Camurri V (2020) L'amministrazione giudiziaria di Uber: un possibile cortocircuito tra il sistema giuslavoristico e le misure di prevenzione. Giurisprudenza Penale Web 7-8:1–20

Brambilla P (2022) Il reato di intermediazione illecita e sfruttamento lavorativo al banco di prova della prassi: spunti di riflessione sui confini applicativi della fattispecie alla luce della prima condanna per caporalato digitale nel caso Uber. Sistema Penale 3:149–170

Braschi S (2021) Il concetto di "stato di bisogno" nel reato di intermediazione illecita e sfruttamento del lavoro. Diritto Penale Contemporaneo 1:113–135

Ferranti D (2016) La legge n. 199/2016: disposizioni penali in materia di caporalato e sfruttamento del lavoro nell'ottica del legislatore. Diritto Penale Contemporaneo, 29 October. https://www.penalecontemporaneo.it/upload/FERRANTI_2016b.pdf

Giammarinaro MG, Palumbo L (2020) Le donne migranti in agricoltura: sfruttamento, vulnerabilità, dignità e autonomia. In: Osservatorio Placido Rizzotto (ed) Agromafie e caporalato. Quinto rapporto, FLAI-CGIL. Ediesse Futura, Rome, pp 81–114

Ispettorato nazionale del lavoro (2019) Circolare n. 5/2019 Art. 603 bis c.p. intermediazione illecita e sfruttamento del lavoro – attività di vigilanza – Linee guida 0000268, 28 February. https://www.ispettorato.gov.it/it-it/orientamentiispettivi/Documents/Circolari/Circolare-n-5-del-28022019-vigilanza-caporalato.pdf

Krissman F (2004) Sin Coyote Ni Patrón: why the 'migrant network' fails to explain international migration. Int Migr Rev 39(1):4–44

Mondi E (2016) La nuova disciplina del caporalato: misure di contrasto all'intermediazione illecita e allo sfruttamento del lavoro e attività di prevenzione dell'Inail. Riv Infort Mal Prof 2:297–318

Omizzolo M (2020) Sfruttamento lavorativo e caporalato in Italia: la profughizzazione del lavoro in agricoltura e il caso dei braccianti indiani nell'agro pontino. Costituzionalismo.it 2:1–36

Orlando S (2020) Il delitto di "caporalato" tra diritti minimi della persona e tutela del marcato del lavoro. Rivista Trimestrale di Diritto Penale dell'Economia 3-4:622–670

Palumbo L, Sciurba A (2015) Vulnerability to forced labour and trafficking: the case of Romanian women in the agricultural sector in Sicily. Anti-traff Rev 5:89–108

Perrotta D (2014) Vecchi e nuovi mediatori. Storia, geografia ed etnografia del caporalato in agricoltura. Meridian 79:193–220

Perrotta D (2016) Ghetti, *broker* e imperi del cibo. La filiera agro-industriale del pomodoro nel Sud Italia. Cartogr Soc 1(1):261–288

Perrotta D, Sacchetto D (2014) Migrant farmworkers in Southern Italy: ghettoes, caporalato and collective action. Workers World 1(5):75–98

Santoro E, Stoppioni C (2018) Sfruttamento, pregi e limiti della legislazione italiana. Rassegna Sindacale 1999–2020. https://www.collettiva.it/rassegna/2018/07/19/news/sfruttamento_pregi_e_limiti_della_legislazione_italiana-484599/

Santoro E, Stoppioni C (2019) Strategie per combattere lo sfruttamento lavorativo dopo l'entrata in vigore della legge 199/2016. http://www.adir.unifi.it/laboratorio/secondo-rapporto-sfruttamento-lavorativo.pdf

Santoro E, Stoppioni C (2020) Rapporto 2019 del Laboratorio sullo sfruttamento lavorativo e la protezione delle sue vittime di L'Altro Diritto & FLAI CGIL. L'Altro Diritto 4:220–233

Stoppioni C (2019) Intermediazione illecita e sfruttamento lavorativo: prime applicazioni dell'art. 603 *bis* c.p. Diritto, Immigrazione e Cittadinanza 2:69–94

Vitarelli F (2022) La cassazione sull'ambito di operatività del delitto di intermediazione illecita e sfruttamento del lavoro (art. 603 *bis* c.p.). Sistema Penale, 5 April 2022. https://www.sistemapenale.it/it/scheda/cassazione-2022-intermediazione-illecita-sfruttamento-lavoro-603-bis-cp

International and Domestic Perspectives to Combat Gangmaster Systems

Salvatore Orlando

Abstract Starting point of the paper is the description of the phenomenon of labour exploitation, which is intertwined with the global process of liberalization of the global labour market. In this context, a protection of workers can be traced back to legal instruments in combating human trafficking where the victim is a vulnerable person. To this end, I argue that domestic and international rules against labour exploitation define a sort of minimum statute of the worker, the violation of which may result in criminal law protection that otherwise cannot be guaranteed by other measures of an extra-criminal nature. The Italian legal system punishes not only the employer who exploits workers but also the 'caporale' (or gangmaster) who recruits labour for the purpose of allocating them to work for third parties under exploitative conditions, taking advantage of the workers' state of need. The paper then offers a comparative analysis with German criminal law, where unlawful intermediation of labour only plays a marginal role. Finally, I argue that the crime of labour exploitation intends to protect the entire labour market, defining the boundaries of the phenomenon within the so-called corporate crime. Evidence is, on the one hand, in Italy, the increasingly widespread application of the judicial administration and liability of entities under legislative decree 231/2001 and, on the other hand, in Germany, the tension towards labour market protection in the form of wage dumping.

1 The International Perspective in Combating Labour Exploitation

This contribution focuses on the international provisions on the fight against labour exploitation and then, from a comparative perspective, analyses the Italian and German legislations: this is with the intention of weighing up the advantages and

S. Orlando (✉)
Law Department, University of Palermo, Palermo, Italy
e-mail: salvatore.orlando@unipa.it

V. Militello, A. Spena (eds.), *The Challenges of Illegal Trafficking in the Mediterranean Area*, Legal Studies in International, European and Comparative Criminal Law 9, https://doi.org/10.1007/978-3-031-45399-1_10

disadvantages of the repressive instruments adopted on the issue, both nationally and internationally, which, as I have tried to highlight, have been strengthened as a result, on the one hand, of greater 'flexibility' in working conditions, according to capitalist dynamics that lead companies to the gain of competitive advantages, and, on the other, of a wider opening to migrant workers in the labour market.[1]

It is necessary, however, to start with figures.

Numbers do not lie and, in this context, numbers count. In Italy, the exploitation of the 'labour force', especially that of foreign origin, partly due to legislative approaches that pay little attention to integration policies in the labour market, emerges *as a normal form of employment* in various productive sectors: for example, it is estimated that between 400,000 and 430,000 agricultural workers are exposed to the risk of labour exploitation, through a 'caporale', subject to inadequate or disproportionate remuneration, which is counterbalanced by an absolute irregularity rate of the employment relationship that reaches estimated peaks of around 39%. Moreover, it is estimated that out of approximately one million agricultural workers, migrants make up around 28% of the total, of whom 15.5% would not even have a formalised employment relationship and 38.7% would not receive a union wage.[2]

On the other hand, in a global perspective, the International Labour Organisation (ILO) has estimated the presence of at least 25 million victims of labour exploitation with higher incidence in women (57%)—I.e. the most *vulnerable*—and a massive presence of minors (around 20%). In this context, about a quarter of labour exploitation occurs in domestic work, followed by the *construction* and manufacturing sector, and agriculture. One cannot overlook, in this context, also the data on *means of coercion* that show a massive recourse to *withheld wages*, threats, physical violence including sexual violence or narcotization (drugging).[3]

Thus, it cannot be denied that there is an intertwining of numerous factors that cause the phenomena of labour exploitation: however, it seems appropriate to point out how, on the one hand, global competition, including but not exclusively within the European Union, has led to the reduction of social safety nets in exchange for greater competitive advantages, with the consequent violation of workers' rights and, on the other hand, how, with regard to the humiliating forms of *human trafficking*, migration policies have been informed by safeguarding strategies, in which the migrant, who is formally recognised as having '*fundamental human rights*',[4] is first and foremost subject to containment and repression, considered a

---

[1] The contribution has to pay credit to a research carried out during my post-doctoral activities for EuMOSIT "Europe between Mobility and Security: the challenges of illicit trades in the Mediterranean Area". See Orlando (2020), p. 622.

[2] See Rapporto Eurispes (2019). See also V Rapporto Agromafie e caporalato edited by Osservatorio Placido Rizzotto (2019).

[3] See International Labour Organization (ILO) (2017).

[4] See, in Italy, for exemple, Art. 2 of the Legislative Decree 25 July 1998, n. 286 on "Testo unico delle disposizioni concernenti la disciplina dell'immigrazione e norme sulla condizione dello straniero".

criminal, while his/her *status* as a victim, as a vulnerable individual who may be exploited by criminal networks, is only minimally relevant.[5]

And so, the need to counter these insidious forms of labour exploitation has not escaped the attention of the international and European community, which has been concerned to enshrine a multiform, peculiar yet also generic *dignity of the worker*, as a declination or rather specification of the well-known category of human dignity.[6]

The main problem that has already been tackled at international level—and that the International Labour Organisation Report itself,[7] indeed, points out—Is that the range and forms of exploitation in general and of labour exploitation in particular can be boundless. From this point of view, the difficulty of a *reductio ad unum* of labour exploitation arises. This occurs at the very moment when the factual evidence, to be repressed as intolerable, must be transposed into legal terms, which can be done by means of an agreed positive formulation.

In regard to this, when the *Trafficking in Persons* Protocol additional to the UN Palermo Convention on Transnational Organised Crime defines exploitation, it also clarifies that it *"shall include, at a minimum, the exploitation of the prostitution of others or other forms of sexual exploitation, forced labour or services, slavery or practices similar to slavery, servitude or the removal of organs"*, Art. 3, (a). In the same way, Directive 2011/36/EU on *"preventing and combating trafficking in human beings and protecting its victims"* reiterates the same definition of exploitation, which would also include, as a minimum, forced labour or services. These are broad definitions: usual, but also necessary, when the focus of incrimination arises from the need to harmonise different regulatory systems between States. The breadth of the protection against labour exploitation and, in particular, of the *exploited person*, the symbolic victim of the crime, thus also rises to a general clause in the European Convention on Human Rights, which states in Article 4(2) that *"no one shall be required to perform forced or compulsory labour"*.

The normative reforms, at an international level, are part of a *multilevel protection* context[8] that, *inter alia*, concerns the absolute prohibition of slavery. In the perspective of combating forms of labour exploitation against the weaker sections of the population, there are also the Council of Europe measures, including the *Convention on Action against Trafficking in Human Beings,* signed on 16 May 2005 in Warsaw, the *Convention for the Protection of Minors against Sexual Exploitation and Sexual Abuse*, signed on 25 October 2007 in Lanzarote and, finally, the *Convention on the Prevention and Combating of Violence against Women and Domestic Violence*, signed on 11 May 2011 in Istanbul.

In any case, the common element to all the international instruments that variously impose obligations on States to criminalise exploitative conducts is the

---

[5] See Amnesty International (2012). See also European Union Agency for Fundamental Rights (FRA) (2019).

[6] Hassemer (2005), pp. 130–31.

[7] See above ILO (2017).

[8] Forlati (2013).

requirement of *abuse of the* victim's *vulnerable condition*: hence, reasoning with criminal law instruments, there would be no exploitation if not accompanied by taking advantage of or abusing the position of weakness of the subject of exploitation. The key point, therefore, of this approach is the focus of the expression at hand, as well as its translation and conversion in our domestic penal systems, so as to make it suitable both to hit the phenomena of exploitation and to differentiate the different degrees of offence to the individual freedom.[9]

In the European context, the expression is clarified as a situation in which *"the person has no real acceptable alternative but to submit to the abuse involved"* (Art. 1, (c), Council Framework Decision of July 2002 on combating trafficking in human beings (2002/629/JHA). There is indeed a victimological perspective, which in fact permeates the entire criminal matter in the European Union, and it is reflected in a definition that is only generic: it does not provide clarification on content and scope,[10] but claims to intercept the entire range of situations of weakness by reserving the choice of incrimination technique to the domestic lawmaker and eventually to the judge.

Yet, it seems only right ultimately to point out how the prospect of combating exploitation phenomena is not limited to the side of repression but is also projected into a dimension of guaranteeing the minimum safeguards that are due to the person as a worker: thus, the Directive (EU) 2019/1152 on transparent and predictable working conditions in the European Union intends to promote *"more transparent and predictable employment while ensuring labour market adaptability"* and *"lays down minimum rights that apply to every worker in the Union"*. In this respect, the reference to the Directive reminds us the emergence of a minimum standard to which national lawmakers will have to adapt. A violation of the above-mentioned Directive imposes a severe reaction of the legal system to which the protection of vulnerable individuals exposed to the risk of labour exploitation is entrusted.

2 The Italian Perspective: The Phenomenon of 'Caporalato'

An entirely new figure and to all intents and purposes internationally unknown has, however, emerged on the Italian scene: namely, 'caporalato' (i.e. *gangmaster system*). The phenomenon has old origins, as it has not thrived in a given market system or production sector and, historically, has also emerged as a *standard* way of recruiting workers to be exploited, especially where the legal system's nets of protecting employees struggle to be applied. In particular, the term 'caporale' (or *gangmaster*) is used to address a person who illicitly carries out an activity of intermediation in the labour market, recruiting labour for the purpose of allocating it

[9] Orlando (2020), p. 644.

[10] di Martino (2019), p. 20.

to third parties under exploitative conditions, taking advantage of the workers' being in need. Specifically, as operational protocols show, their role is, first, to intercept people willing to work in exploitative conditions and then, at a later stage, to transport them, by their own means, to the place of work, for a fee.[11]

It is therefore not surprising to note how the phenomenon found fertile ground in the agricultural sector and, in particular, in the most deprived geographical areas concentrated mainly in southern Italy.[12] It is a phenomenon, then, that has been linked inseparably with the huge migration flows that have affected Italy over the last two decades:[13] from this point of view, the arrival of an ever-increasing number of migrants has allowed local businesses to obtain labour by lowering wages, social security and welfare costs. A production system has been created that is able to rely on a tendentially unlimited supply of labour but, at the same time, must compete in a global market. As a result, it ends up stealing wealth from the state treasury and stimulating an underground economy, trying to gain competitive advantages. This makes possible offering goods and commodities at prices lower than the mere costs a company would have to bear to produce them in full compliance with the rules.

This production system, widespread, therefore, in various economic sectors, thus exposes the worker (be a foreigner or a citizen) to a condition of blackmail and, therefore, of weakness with regard to the 'caporale', who, pretending to exercise a beneficial social function, is not perceived as an oppressor. In this sense, one cannot overlook, in the outward manifestation, the further difficulty of identifying an individual offence in the absence of the victim's perception of any injury or damage and the related consensual acceptance of unfair working conditions.

2.1 The Demolition of Public Covenants in Labour Intermediation and the First Attempts to Combat the Phenomenon of 'Caporalato'

Nonetheless, the Italian lawmaker waited until 2011 before introducing an *ad hoc* offense into the national criminal system, which would fill a protection gap that had already emerged following the liberalisation process of the labour market inaugurated by an important sentence with which the Court of Justice condemned Italy in 1997 for breaching the European competition law.[14] Until that time, there was in fact a state monopoly in the exercise of intermediation activities, established and protected only by a criminal misdemeanor provided for by Laws No. 264 of 1949 and No. 1369 of 1960, which excluded private companies from any interference in

[11] Monticelli (2012), p. 575.

[12] Leogrande (2016).

[13] UNHCR – The UN Refugee Agency (2018). See also International Organization for Migration – IOM, World Migrations Report 2022.

[14] CoJ, VI, 11th December 1997, C-55/96, Job Centre c/Italy.

the intermediation between supply and demand in the labour market. On the assumption that such an activity integrated the concept of a *company*, which includes any economic business, regardless of its *status* and method of financing, the Court of Justice declared that public employment offices were in a so-called dominant position, the abuse of which is punished under Article 86 EC Treaty (now Article 102 TFEU): therefore, their activity, in a context of great economic ferment, had to be at least flanked, if not actually replaced, by the activity of private companies.

This reversal of perspective was embraced by the Italian legislation, enhancing an alleged autopoietic capacity of the market to generate optimal solutions in labour relations: first with a still only partial reform introduced with the *Pacchetto Treu*,[15] and then with the *Biagi Law*,[16] which definitively subverted the monopolistic regime in favour of the private one managed by previously authorised agencies.

And it is precisely from this point of view that the legislation on 'caporalato' must be framed. The Italian lawmaker, with a view of harmonising with international conventions and EU law, had already introduced offences such as trafficking in human beings (Article 601 of the Criminal Code). Now, his attention was focused on the unlawful intermediation activity of the so-called 'caporali' who, as mentioned, had established a widespread recruitment system in large areas of the peninsula.

It should be noted, in this regard, that the loss of state control in the encounter between labour supply and demand deprived the worker of an indispensable safeguard regarding the protection of their interests, previously guaranteed by a bureaucratic procedure managed by the employment agencies. In other words, the monopolistic system allowed for the protection of the worker both before and after recruitment by the employer, simultaneously avoiding any intimidation or abuse. The retreat of the state, whose presence in various economic sectors has become increasingly evanescent, has thus dictated a rethinking of the traditional approach to intervention in the matter, given that criminal law has been called upon to take the place of the public and regulatory sector, protecting with the threat of punishment at least some of the conduct of economic operators no longer subject to public regulation (the so-called *deregulation*): in my opinion, the progressive retreat of public regulation and the consequent weakening of the relative guarantees, rather than being managed through a system of control entrusted to public-private interaction, went hand in hand with the introduction of criminal law protection to *reassure public opinion* about state intervention. Criminal law thus took on the burden, or rather the responsibility, of the maintenance of the entire system of guarantees with obvious impacts also in terms of the effectiveness of the criminal law model to be put in place: suffice it to think that the incriminating cases devised by the new system of the *Biagi Law* were only in the nature of misdemeanor, having lenient penalties with the sole objective of sanctioning the failure to comply with labour law.

Thus, the repressive system having lent itself to abuses by the production system (i.e. employers and intermediaries) and in the wake of tragic criminal events, the

[15] Law 24th June 1997, n. 196 "Provisions on promoting employment".

[16] Legislative Decree, tenth September 2003, n. 276.

lawmaker finally intervened first in 2011 with the introduction of the offence referred to in Art. 603-*bis* of the Criminal Code concerning *"unlawful intermediation and exploitation of labour"*, and then with the amendment set out in Law No. 199/2016, with which an attempt was made to impress effective deterrence to the crime by broadening the area of criminal relevance.

The fieriness with which the lawmaker intervened in 2011 therefore immediately imposed a drastic re-designing of the entire punitive framework, eliminating those elements of typicality, that made the relevant unlawful conduct difficult to apply.

It should also be highlighted to what extent the reform of the offence is grounded in the changed repressive framework, the outcome of several regulations that have pushed towards labour market flexibility, putting the labour market and the exploited worker completely unprotected. From this point of view, I would like to draw attention to some recent legislation in the field of labour law: with Legislative Decree No. 81 of 15 June 2015, i.e. the so-called *Jobs Act*, a large number of criminal misdemeanors, which had been set up to protect the labour market, were decriminalised, including those provided for by the *Biagi Law*. This intervention, which was then followed by a further demolition of labour protections by Legislative Decrees 7 and 8 of 2016 that repealed, among others, the offence of unlawful interposition (Art. 18 *Biagi Law*), resulted in a glaring regulatory gap. In turn, the latter could not be filled by an offence such as that provided for in Article 603-*bis* of the Criminal Code, which was modelled along the lines of offences against individual liberty with typicality requirements that were difficult to ascertain.

Eventually, the new labour law framework and the criminal offense protected the worker either too much or too little: *too much* because they severely hit the hypotheses of 'black caporalato' and of very serious exploitation, with the risk, however, of a duplicity of protection for the possible concurrence with the offences under Articles 600 and 601 of the Criminal Code; *too little,* because the hypotheses of 'grey caporalato' and consensual slavery, not being able to integrate the typical elements of Article 603-bis of the Criminal Code, remained entirely without criminal protection.

2.2 New Repressive Paradigms in the Relationship Between Law and the Labour Market

For the reasons mentioned above, in 2016, the Italian lawmaker has therefore amended the criminal offence by significantly extending what is criminally relevant and the offence is then integrated when concurring the elements of (a) *taking advantage of the worker's state of need* and (b) *labour exploitation*, according to the indexes listed in paragraph 3 of Article 603-*bis*.

The reform has indeed provided the crime with lower penalties with custodial sanctions from one up to 5 years for each exploited worker and a fee from 500 up to 1000 euros and has widened, at the same time, the subjective scope punishing not only the 'caporale'"[17] but also the 'employer' "*if recruits uses, recruits or employs labor, including through the illicit activity, subjecting workers to exploitative conditions and taking advantage of their state of need*" (Art. 603-*bis*, par. 1, (b)). Meanwhile, the elements of violence and threat, if present, would increase the custodial sanction from 5 up to 8 years and a fee from 1000 up to 2000 euros for each exploited worker (Art. 603-*bis*, par. 2).

2.2.1 Genesis and Nature of 'Taking Advantage of the State of Need'

Authors have already given their contribution in defining the concept of *taking advantage of the state of need*: it is argued, in this regard, that it is not limited to an economic perspective, but suggests that the lack of means of subsistence, determined in relation to the economic-social context in which this deficit is appreciated, is relevant to the standard case; it has to be an unconscious condition for the victim which is intentionally used by the agent in order to establish or consolidate a formal or factual relationship of dependency. Therefore, the existence of a *relationship* in which a person exercises such *power* as to compress the personality of the worker (the weaker party) is essential, even if, as is claimed, his/her *status libertatis* is not affected.[18]

With the 2016 reform the requirement of the *state of need* was expunged in the face of the necessity to seal a threshold of criminal protection against the worker: in doing so, it was considered that the mere existence of the *state of need* had a strongly economic nature, the feature characterization of which lies, not only in the lesion of personal aspects, but also in those of a synallagmatic nature, due to the imbalance (and abuse of such an imbalance) of one of the contracting parties.

The offence of usury refers to the very same expression then indicating its aggravated form which is intended to criminally protect economic assets even if *against* the will of the victim: the legal system considers that the resulting imbalance on the part of the weaker party may legitimise an exception to the general principle that an asset cannot be criminally protected against the will of its owner.[19]

In a pathological contractual relationship then, criminal law legitimately intervenes to restore the regularity of private negotiations both, on the one hand, to protect the assets of the weaker party and, on the other, to generally protect the State's interest in the proper functioning of the credit market: in these hypotheses, the criminally relevant injury therefore affects the victim's patrimony.[20]

---

[17] In the light of Art. 603-bis, par. 1, (a) he/she is someone who "recruits labor for the purpose of allocating them to work for third parties under exploitative conditions, taking advantage of the workers' state of need".

[18] di Martino (2019), p. 41.

[19] Pagliaro (2003), p. 419.

[20] Ferranti (2016), p. 7. See also Merlo (2020), p. 535.

It is necessary, however, to distinguish between the *status* in which the worker finds him- or herself, which may also be only in his mind, and the action of *taking advantage* by the employer or 'caporale'—which instead must objectively be ascertained. Indeed, if the concept of *state of need* relates more properly to the subjective condition in which the worker must be in, a *quid pluris* is still required, which makes the fact reprehensible to perpetrators: their active conduct then consists of taking advantage of the subjective situation of the worker without his will being simultaneously annihilated. There must be an objective judgment, without there being a presumptive or implicit automatism by reason of the very acceptance of disproportionate contractual conditions.[21]

Therefore, in the final analysis, the real meaning of the expression *taking advantage of the state of need* assumes only a relative and not an absolute coercion to work and a degree of subjection that is also relative and, in any case, driven by economic and financial reasons: the offence aims to intercept a *grey area of criminal protection*, in which the exploited worker is not reduced to a *res,* but retains the power to freely determine his or her own situation, being able abstractly to escape the condition of exploitation. In other words, such a *grey area* lies somewhere between situations of mere transgression or violation of labour laws, in which the worker's state of need is not relevant, on the one hand, and forms of para-slavery 'caporalato' (so-called *'black caporalato'*) in which subjugation is such as to nullify any capacity for self-determination of the victim, on the other.[22]

2.2.2 Indexes of Exploitation Between Typicality and Protection of Workers' Rights

The other common element of the two offences (paragraphs 1(1) and (2)) referred to in Article 603-*bis* of the Criminal Code is therefore the exploitation of labour, the *meaning framework* of which is not defined or described, as would be required by a loyal, indeed due, respect for the principle of legality.[23]

In the Italian legal system, conditions of exploitation are instead inferred from the violation of labour laws, extra-legal or even of a purely private nature, and in particular (1) the repeated payment of remuneration in a manner that is manifestly different from the national or territorial collective agreements established by the most representative trade unions at national level, or in any case disproportionate to the quantity and quality of the work performed; (2) the repeated violation of the regulations on working hours, rest periods, weekly rest, compulsory leave, holidays; (3) the existence of violations of the regulations on safety and health in the

[21] This is a fundamental point, which is highlighted by di Martino (2019), p. 9; Padovani (2016), p. 50; Torre (2019), p. 95.

[22] Giuliani (2015), p. 139 talks about an "intermediate nature" of the crime of labour exploitation (Art. 603-bis).

[23] See Lo Monte (2013), p. 959; Piva (2017), p. 187; Di Giuseppe (2018), p. 146.

workplace; (4) the subjection of the worker to degrading working conditions, surveillance methods or demeaning housing situations.

In light of the aforementioned 'indexes', the crime of exploitation seems to regulate, even before punishing, the labour relations between the employer and the labour force employed, thus defining or rather, *indicating*, not so much the benefit of being protected, but the rights (of the workers) to be preserved within the production and industrial sector, made increasingly flexible by the process of globalisation and European liberalisation. In this sense, the offence referred to in Article 603-*bis* differs from related offences against individual liberty, which provide for more stringent requirements for their configurability with regard, in particular, to the degree of exploitation and offence to the victim's freedom of self-determination (Articles 600–601 of the Criminal Code).[24]

It is possible then, in my opinion, to discern in the indicators (as a central element of criminal offense) both a *probative orientation for the judge* who must ascertain their existence, but it is also possible to discern a *list of rights*, which tend to be inviolable, of a constitutional nature, insofar as they can be traced back to Article 4 of the Italian Constitution, in which injury legitimises the intervention of the State with penalties.

In other words, the very concept of exploitation postulates, in principle, a compression or rather a violation, temporally appreciable, of protected interests.[25] Thus, in the case of indexes, the violation insists precisely on the *minimum rights* of the worker to be protected in the workplace: consequently, those very rights that reveal the worker's dignity are criminally protected.

This is, in the Italian scenario, an innovative, even eccentric, way of defining the criminal misconduct. The 2011 and 2016 lawmakers formalized, through indexes, objective situations with a strong detrimental significance, as referred to in Article 4, paragraph 1 of the Constitution, promoting "*the minimum conditions that make this right effective*" and, on the other hand, as an immediate impact, the collective protection of *minimum working conditions* as "*a function that contributes to the material or spiritual progress of society*" (paragraph 2).

The judge, therefore, must take into account any element that proves the long-lasting injury to the abovementioned rights, i.e. where it ascertains that there are *situations that infringe the constitutionally recognised rights of workers*; thus with reference to individual indexes, for example: (1) the *right to proportionate remuneration* or (2) the *right to holidays*, and finally, (3–4) with reference to the entire category of workers, the *right to safe and healthy workplaces.*[26]

[24] See Gaboardi (2017), p. 65.

[25] That is also illustrated in the legislative Report on the reform of Art. 603-bis. See Giuseppe Berretta, Parliamentary Act (A.C.) n. 4008, Leg. XXVII.

[26] If only one index is present, then the crime is integrated, see Court of Cassation, Section V, n. 17939/2018.

2.3 And Paradigm Shift: From Repression to Prevention. A Form of Economic Crime

Lastly, a thorough analysis of the Italian regulations cannot disregard a further aspect: the 2016 lawmaker, pursuing that approach imposed by the European Union of protecting the competition market and encouraging the production sector, intended also to attribute responsibility to the company that exploits manpower, so as to guarantee, on the one hand, *accountability* of the companies and, on the other, the continuation of the economic activity in order to maintain the relevant employment levels.

From this point of view, an integrated approach has been adopted by means of economic measures, first of all by providing for the confiscation *"of the items that served or were intended to commit the offence and of that relating to the price, the product and the profit"* (Article 603-*bis*.2 of the Criminal Code) and of the extended confiscation (Article 16-*sexies* of Law Decree No. 306 of 1992) also of money, goods and other utilities of which the convicted person is the owner, even via a third party.

Even more significant was the inclusion of Article 603-*bis* of the Criminal Code in the list of offences subject to the administrative liability of the entity through an amendment to Article 25-*quinquies* of Legislative Decree No. 231 of 2001,[27] from which financial and disqualifying sanctions are imposed on the company with which the exploitative employer is entrusted. Moreover, the 2016 lawmaker has stated that *"if the interruption of the business activity could have negative repercussions on employment levels or jeopardise the economic value of the company"* the judge, rather than preventive seizure order pursuant to Article 321 of the Code of Criminal Procedure, must order *"the judicial control of the company where the offence was committed"* (Article 3, Law 199 of 2016).

Lastly, it should be noted that the lawmaker has included the renewed Article 603-*bis* of the Criminal Code among the predicate offences that can trigger the procedure referred to in Article 34 of Legislative Decree no. 159 of 2011, i.e. judicial administration.[28] This instrument reveals how the new law enforcement perspective is no longer oriented towards the identification of an individual offender, but in the pursuit of intercepting that range of criminal activities which, as mentioned, are interconnected with the very mode of production of the economic system. It is desired, in fact, to pursue the path of measures with a *not repressive but preventive purpose*, i.e. not to punish the individual entrepreneur, but to counteract the illicit contamination of healthy companies, subjecting them to judicial control with the

[27] Legislative Decree 8 June 2001, n. 231 "Disciplina della responsabilità amministrativa delle persone giuridiche, delle società e delle associazioni anche prive di personalità giuridica, a norma dell'articolo 11 della legge 29 settembre 2000, n. 300". Recently, see Selvaggi (2020), p. 719.

[28] Legislative Decree 6 September 2011, n. 159 "Codice delle leggi antimafia e delle misure di prevenzione, nonché delle nuove disposizioni in materia di documentazione antimafia, a norma degli articoli 1 e 2 della legge 13 agosto 2010, n. 136".

purpose of freeing them, as quickly as possible, from the criminal infiltration and return them to the free market once purified of the polluting elements.[29]

Hence, the punishment for the 'caporale', which is also potentially damaging to the victim and the economic system of reference, may well be based on an intervention, certainly invasive, which, according to the principle of proportionality, is capable of *reclaiming* the economic activity and removing the ascertained illegal contaminations.[30]

Furthermore, the repressive system which, on closer eyes, attempts to intercept a phenomenon unquestionably ascribable to the category of *corporate crime*, calls upon an *innovative approach of the punitive response* towards the 'caporale' and the exploitative employer, but moves away from the original axis of the incrimination, which found its legitimacy in the violation of the rights and dignity of the worker: inducing corporations to prevent, deter, and report misconducts of labour exploitation,[31] in my opinion, has shifted the target of the whole criminal system so as to broadly guard the labour market in general as well as the community of workers.

3 In Search of Hidden 'Caporali': The German Perspective and Labour Market Protection

The fight against labour exploitation in Germany is part of a complex repressive framework that, in some respects, does not appear, at first glance, unlike to the Italian system: this is, in particular, the result of the process of legal harmonisation in the area of human trafficking, in the context of the European Union.

From this perspective, first of all, the offence of human trafficking (*Menschenhanel*) today finds its own autonomous description in par. 232 *Strafgesetzbuch* ("StGB") and is included among the *"offences against personal liberty"* that contain, as far as it is of interest here, the offences of *forced labour* (par. 232b StGB) and *exploitation of labour power* (par. 233 StGB): therefore, the legal framework of the repressive system on labour exploitation is the result of a troubled path of reforms culminating in 2016[32] and it cannot be isolated from the entire legal framework provided for the protection of personal freedom provided within the German Criminal Code.

[29] See Tribunal of Milan, Section for Preventive Measures, 24 June 2016. In general, on the judicial administration, see Court of Cassation, Section VI, 7 July 2021, n. 30168 Court of Cassation, Section VI, 13 May 2021, n. 23330; Court of Cassation, Section V, 17 December 2020, n. 13388. See also Corso (2020), p. 106.

[30] See Quattrocchi (2020); Merlo (2022), p. 173.

[31] Oded (2011), p. 272.

[32] "Gesetz zur Verbesserung der Bekämpfung des Menschenhandels und zur Änderung des Bundeszentralregistergesetzes sowie des Achten Buches Sozialgesetzbuch", 11 October 2016, published on BGBl. I 2016, 2226.

In this sense, the purposes of protection of the incriminating provisions of Title 18 are multiple: however, the systematic placement among the *"offences against personal liberty"* provides this interest with a predominant importance within the plurality of interests protected by the offences, which also include economic and occupational freedom and physical integrity. In particular, the entire German repressive framework appears to revolve around the concept of *Selbstbestimmungsfreiheit*, i.e. the protection of the crime victim's freedom of self-determination.[33] The lawmaker has in any case shown itself to be sensitive to the *different grades and forms of injury* to the freedom of self-determination, according to the various factual nuances of the phenomena. In any case, however, in the attempt to provide firm protection for individual freedom, two typical elements are constantly maintained in the various forms of aggression referred to in the cases mentioned above: (1) the abuse of the condition of vulnerability, on the one hand, and (2) the definition of labour exploitation, on the other.

First of all, the concept of *abuse of the condition of vulnerability* always maintains (within Title 18 of the StGB) the same definition, which punishes conduct that is capable of undermining the victim's capacity for self-determination by exploiting one of the following two situations: a 'situation of personal or economic constraint' (*Ausnutzung ihrer persönlichen oder wirtschaftlichen Zwangslage*), which must be checked on a case-by-case basis depending on the subjective conditions of the victim, or a condition of vulnerability resulting from the victim's stay in a foreign country (*Ausnutzung [...] ihrer Hilflösigkeit, die mit dem Aufenthalt in einem fremden Land verbunden ist*), which occurs, for example, if the victim is not fluent in German or does not have the money to provide for his or her own food or accommodation.[34]

Having said that, with regard to the element of *labour exploitation*, unlike in Italy, paragraph 232(1)(2) StGB contains a definition, variously applicable to all criminal hypotheses in which that element is relevant: the provision therefore has a defining function while simultaneously not providing for an autonomous unlawful conduct of trafficking.

Specifically, there is *labour exploitation* when *"the activity, for reasons of ruthless profit-seeking, takes place under such working conditions as to be in obvious disproportion to those of workers, who perform an equal or in any case comparable working activity (exploitative working activity)"* (par. 232(1)(2) StGB).

In relation to the individual offences provided for in the title, the change from a crime of danger, i.e. section 232 StGB, to a crime of event, with higher maximum sentences, such as the crime of *exploitation of labour power* (*Ausbeutung der Arbeitskraft*, par. 233 StGB) is of extreme importance. The latter consists of five paragraphs and in paragraph 1 it punishes *"anyone who exploits another person, taking advantage of his or her personal or economic condition of difficulty and vulnerability. [...] 1. Through an employment activity as referred to in Section 232,*

---

[33] See Dölling (2022), para 232; Fischer (2018), para 232.

[34] Bürger (2017), pp. 171–172.

paragraph 1, subparagraph 2 [...]: 2. For begging; 3. For the commission of criminal acts".

Although the heading of the offence appears misleading which would make explicit reference to Article 2(2) of Directive 2011/36/EU, the offence of *exploitation of labour power* (par. 233 StGB) has been formulated in such a way as to intercept the fact that the offence of human trafficking would not be able to punish: in fact, unlike the provisions of paragraph 232 of the StGB, the victim's condition of exploitation is relevant without it being necessary to establish that the offender has induced or forced the victim to carry out a work activity. In other words, undermining the worker's will is not required except to the extent of taking advantage of his or her weakened condition: with the consequence that the victim may have undertaken the work activity on the basis of a free and voluntary decision.[35]

However, the rule has not found significant judicial application for a twofold reason: on the one hand, the decision not to include enslavement (*Sklaverei*) within the conduct of exploitation has been criticised, thus lowering the threshold of individual protection, directing it inversely towards aspects of economic nature; consequently, it has been pointed out that the rule does not connect with the usury offense in par. 291 StGB (*Wucher*), which assumes the abuse of a situation of weakness or duress of the victim (*die Zwangslage, die Unerfahrenheit, den Mangel an Urteilsvermögen oder die erhebliche Willensschwäche eines anderen*) as a prerequisite of punishment, while also giving provision for a milder punishment.[36]

However, as far as the specific phenomenon known as 'caporalato' is concerned, there is no corresponding German criminal offence, except within the limits of paragraph 5 of Sect. 233 StGb (*exploitation of labour power*), which punishes "with a custodial sentence of up to 2 years or with a fine, anyone who *facilitates* the commission of the offence referred to in paragraph 1, No. 1 by 1. *The intermediation of an employment activity;* 2. The renting out of rooms where the exploited person can stay".

Thus, the offence of *unlawful intermediation in the labour market* (*Vorschubleisten*) has only a residual function and is in fact a less serious form of labour exploitation to which a milder punishment follows. German authors consider that this is a case of independent aiding and abetting (*verselbstständigten Beihilfetatbestand*), which therefore allows the *facilitator* to be prosecuted as the author of the offence without the main incriminating offence actually being established, i.e. that there is actually a destination to work in 'exploitative conditions'.[37]

[35] See Renzikowski-Kudlich (2015), p. 45; Eisele (2019), para 233 StGB.

[36] See Eisele (2019), para 233 StGB. Para 291 StGB provides for a custodial sentence up to 3 years.

[37] See Renzikowski (2017), para 233 StGB.

3.1 Some Comparative Insights

The approach of the German criminal intervention in this area is therefore partly different from the Italian criminal law which, in order to meet the need for punitive measures against 'caporali', first created an autonomous criminal offence to combat only 'caporalato' and then unreasonably placed the 'caporale' and the employer on the same level of sentencing, making a provision based on two criminal offences in a relationship of *criminal progression*. It should also be noted that, in order to commit the conduct of unlawful intermediation in the labour market, it would not be necessary to establish the achievement or promise of an economic advantage (*Vermögenvorteil*) disproportionate to the (labour) service rendered, as provided, instead, by Sect. 291 StGB on the crime of usury.

In Germany, moreover, a fundamental role is played by par. 232b StGB, which punishes the so-called forced labour (*Zwangsarbeit*): here the criminal conduct is that of inducement (*Veranlassen*): (1) to labour exploitation; (2) to enslavement or (3) to begging. The offence punishes the exploitation of the labour of others, thus retaining the same definition for the explicit reference to par. 232(1)(2), by abusing a situation of limited freedom of self-determination or lack of discernment of the victim. From this perspective, authors[38] maintain that the purpose of protection (*Zweck der Norm*) is the interest of the individual personality in some of its declinations, among which the freedom of economic initiative (*berufliche und wirtschaftliche Betätigungsfreiheit*) as well as the individual property and the health of the victim are to be mentioned. Moreover, in the sense of protecting worker's health, case law[39] considers that the conditions of labour exploitation would not only be limited to disproportionate remuneration but would also concern health and safety at work. And, in this regard, it should be highlighted that although the protection of the individual is of paramount importance, it could also, in the most serious cases, lead to the violation of human dignity (*Menschenwürde*). The crime is intended to protect the labour market by combating the illegal use of foreign labour (to prevent the so-called *wage dumping*), thus departing from the cases set up to protect individual freedom, as provided—*mutatis mutandis*—for in the Italian Criminal Code (Art. 603-*bis*).[40]

4 Final Remarks. Corporate Crime and Labour Flexibility

The fight against labour exploitation has, therefore, recorded patchy trends: from an original repressive discipline focused on the protection of the individual's freedom of self-determination, which took its starting point from the international measures

[38] Ibid.

[39] BGH, 13.1.2010—3 StR 507/09, in NStZ, 2011, p. 157.

[40] Schröder (2017), p. 320.

on human trafficking, the lawmaker has reformulated—without denying its origins—the entire regulatory framework to protect the entire labour market—and, therefore, the principle of competition of the EU Law—defining the boundaries of the phenomenon within the so-called *corporate crime*.[41] Evidence is, on the one hand, in Italy, the increasingly widespread application of the judicial administration and liability of entities under legislative decree 231/2001 and, on the other hand, in Germany, the tension towards labour market protection in the form of wage dumping.

In any case, an attempt has been made to clarify how, in my opinion, the repression of 'caporalato', is the privileged ground for testing the relationship between fundamental rights and criminal law: between the freedom of enterprise and its limitations, in the wake of the very protection of the market and individuals.[42] In this sense, criminal policy—in this area—is an expression of the institutional approach that states have adopted in the face of modern economic dynamics in which, on the one hand, the demands of the free market and freedom of economic initiative clash with fair competition between enterprises and the individual protection of workers.

Today, therefore, for the reasons just mentioned, the legislation on 'caporalato'—by identifying a responsibility for the mode of production—has an intermediate nature between individual and collective protection, *shaping the paradigm of a new institutional response* in the framework of the current relations between law and economy. The phenomenon is so evident thatsome Italian authors speak of regulatory criminal law,[43] albeit within the framework of the so-called *Kernstrafrecht*.

In Italy, as well as in Germany, a meta-individual protection is therefore provided for the generality of workers in terms of fair and proportionate treatment or safe workplaces. The crime intends to protect State's interest in the emersion of black-labour market, which is detrimental not only to companies but also to the State treasury.

The European Union has, on several occasions, been concerned to provide protection for workers, while at the same time taking care of the needs of employers: evidence is the recent Directive (EU) 1152/2019/EU of the European Parliament and the Council of 20 June 2019 on *"transparent and predictable working conditions in the European Union"*, which laid down minimum rights that apply to all workers (Art. 1, par. 2), while ensuring the adaptability of the labour market (Art. 1). The Directive—reaffirming the principles on social rights, proclaimed in Goeteborg on 17 November 2017, with reference to the right to fair and equal treatment—introduced information obligations for employers, the violation of which must be

---

[41] In this sense, Merlo (2022), p. 184; Mongillo (2019), p. 649. See, in general, Gobert and Punch (2003); Wells (2001); Nelken (2012); Friedrichs (2007).

[42] See on liberal perspectives of Criminal Law, Hassemer (1989), p. 85; Roxin (2006), p. 715.

[43] De Rubeis (2018), para 4.

punished with effective, proportionate and dissuasive penalties, of an administrative and financial nature, or even *"other types of sanctions"*.[44]

Thus, in other words, the domestic and international rules against labour exploitation define a sort of minimum statute of the worker, the violation of which may result in criminal law protection that otherwise cannot be guaranteed by other measures of an extra-criminal nature.[45] This, however, must remain within the framework of the principle of subsidiarity,[46] according to an integrated system of protection—capable of intercepting phenomena of so-called corporate crime—in which criminal law is and must remain only the last possible resort.

References

Amnesty International (2012) Volevamo braccia e sono arrivati uomini. Sfruttamento lavorativo dei braccianti agricoli migranti in Italia. https://www.vociperlaliberta.it/images/stories/News_2012/italia_dic12_rapporto.pdf

Bürger S (2017) Die Neuregelung des Menschenhandels. Umsetzung unionsrechtlicher Vorgaben und Schaffung eines stimmigen Gesamtkonzept? ZIS 3:169–118

Corso SM (2020) Oltre il contrasto al "caporalato": dalla tutela della produzione alla tutela dell'occupazione. In: De Santis G, Corso SM, Del Vecchio F (eds) Studi sul caporalato. Giappichelli, Torino, p 87

De Rubeis A (2018) Bene giuridico e corretta definizione delle fattispecie. Sui rapporti tra riduzione in schiavitù intermediazione illecita e sfruttamento del lavoro. Cassaz Penal 12:4361–4391

Di Giuseppe MO (2018) Una legiferazione inutile in tema di contrasto allo sfruttamento del lavoro. Critica del Diritto 2:136–152

di Martino A (2019) Stato di bisogno o condizione di vulnerabilità tra sfruttamento lavorativo, tratta e schiavitù. Archivio Penale 1:1–48

Dölling D et al (2022) Gesamtes Strafrecht, 5th edn. Nomos, Baden Baden. para 232

Eisele J (2019) § 233 StGB. In: Schönke-Schröder, Strafgesetzbuch, Kommentar. C.H. Beck, p XXX

European Union Agency for Fundamental Rights (FRA) (2019) Severe labour exploitation: workers moving within or into the European Union. https://fra.europa.eu/sites/default/files/fra-2015-severe-labour-exploitation_en.pdf

Ferranti D (2016) La legge n. 199/2016: disposizioni in materia di caporalato e sfruttamento del lavoro nell'ottica del legislatore. www.archiviodpc.dirittopenaleuomo.org. Accessed 15 Nov 2016

Fischer T (2018) Strafgesetzbuch: StGB mit Nebengesetzen, 65th edn. C.H. Beck. para. 232

[44] See European Union Agency for Fundamental Rights (FRA) (2019), p. 93 underlines that "working conditions cannot be left to globalised labour market but require rigid monitoring and control. Criminal law provisions protecting the right of workers to fair and just working conditions from particularly severe violations are a cornerstone of any effective protection".

[45] See also Masera (2021), p. 186 who explains that nowadays "it is indispensable to ensure that the few guarantees that remain at the labour law level are actually respected [sanctioned with penalties], and the long process of liberalization of the labour market does not lead to a real exploitation of the weaker party in the relationship".

[46] See Roxin (2006), p. 733.

Forlati S (ed) (2013) La lotta alla tratta di esseri umani. Tra dimensione internazionale e ordinamento interno. Jovene Editore, Napoli

Friedrichs D (2007) Trusted criminals, vol III. Thomson Wadsworth, Belmont

Gaboardi A (2017) La riforma della normativa in materia di "caporalato" e sfruttamento dei lavoratori: corretto lo strabismo persiste la miopia. Legislazione Penale, 3 April 2017

Giuliani A (2015) I reati in materia di "caporalato". Intermediazione illecita e sfruttamento del lavoro. Padova University Press, Padova

Gobert J, Punch M (2003) Rethinking corporate crime. Cambridge University Press, Cambridge

Hassemer W (1989) Grundlinien einer personalen Rechtsgutlehre. In: Scholler-Philipps L (ed) Jenseits des Funktionalismus. Arthur Kaufmann zum 65. Geburstag, Heidelberg, p 85

Hassemer W (2005) Argomentazioni con concetti fondamentali. L'esempio della dignità umana. Ars Interpretandi 10:125–139

International Labour Organization (ILO) (2017) Global estimates of modern slavery. Forced Labour and Forced Marriage, Geneva

Leogrande A (2016) Uomini e caporali. Viaggio tra i nuovi schiavi nelle campagne del Sud. Universale Economica Feltrinelli, Milan

Lo Monte E (2013) Osservazioni sull'art. 603-bis di contrasto al caporalato: ancora una fattispecie enigmatica. In: Scritti in onore di M. Stile. Editoriale Scientifica, Napoli, p 959

Masera L (2021) Nuove schiavitù e diritto penale. In: Calore A, De Cesari P (eds) Schiavi, presente e passato. Giappichelli, Turin, pp 185–206

Merlo A (2020) La giurisprudenza tratteggia, ma ancora non definisce, i contorni del reato di intermediazione illecita e sfruttamento del lavoro. Foro Italiano 9:532–538

Merlo A (2022) Contrastare lo sfruttamento del lavoro attraverso gli strumenti della prevenzione patrimoniale: "Adelante con juicio". Diritto Penale Contemporaneo Rivista Trimestrale 1:173–193

Mongillo V (2019) Forced Labour e sfruttamento lavorativo nella catena di fornitura delle imprese: strategie globali di prevenzione e repressione. Rivista Trimestrale di Diritto Penale dell'Economia 3-4:630–675

Monticelli L (2012) Disciplina penale del collocamento e della intermediazione illecita. In: Gargani A, Deidda B (eds) Reati contro la salute e la dignità dei lavoratori. Giappichelli, Torino, p 575

Nelken D (2012) White-collars and corporate crime. In: Morgan R, Maguire M, Reiner R (eds) The Oxford handbook of criminology. Oxford University Press, Oxford, p 623

Oded S (2011) Inducing corporate compliance: a compound corporate liability regime. Int Rev Law Econ 31:272–283

Orlando S (2020) Il delitto di "caporalato" tra diritti minimi della persona e tutela del mercato del lavoro. Rivista Trimestrale di Diritto Penale dell'Economia 3-4:622–670

Osservatorio Placido Rizzotto Flai-CGIL, V Rapporto Agromafie e caporalato, 31st October 2019

Padovani T (2016) Necessario un nuovo intervento per superare i difetti di una riforma zoppa. Guida al Diritto 48:48–50

Pagliaro A (2003) Principi di diritto penale. Parte Speciale. Delitti contro il patrimonio, vol III. Giuffrè, Milan

Piva D (2017) I limiti dell'intervento penale sul caporalato come sistema (e non come condotta) di produzione: brevi note a margine della legge n. 199/2016. Archivio Penale 1:184–196

Quattrocchi A (2020) Le nuove manifestazioni della prevenzione patrimoniale: amministrazione giudiziaria e contrasto al caporalato nel caso Uber. Giurisprudenza Penale Web 6:1–17

Rapporto Eurispes, Agromafie, VI Rapporto sui crimini agroalimentari, 2019

Renzikowski J (2017) § 233 StGB. In: Münchener Kommentar zum StGB, vol IV. C.H. Beck

Renzikowski J, Kudlich H (2015) Reform der Menschendhandel in zweiten Anlauf – und immer noch nichts gelernt. ZRP 48(2):45–48

Roxin K (2006) Was darf der Staat unter Strafe stellen? Zur Legitimation von Strafdrohungen. In: Dolcini E, Paliero CE (eds) Studi in onore di Giorgio Marinucci. Giuffrè, Milano, p 715

Schröder F (2017) Das Rechtsgut der neuen Vorschriften gegen Menschenhandel (§§ 232-233b StGB). NStZ 6:320

Selvaggi N (2020) Criminalità organizzata e responsabilità dell'ente. Rivista Trimestrale di Diritto Penale dell'Economia 3-4:719–751

Torre V (2019) Lo sfruttamento del lavoro. La tipicità dell'art. 603-*bis* c.p. tra diritto sostanziale e prassi giurisprudenziale. Questione Giustizia 4:90–97

UNHCR – The UN Refugee Agency (2018) Global Trends. Forced Displacemet in 2017, Geneva, Switzerland. International Organization for Migration – IOM, World Migrations Report 2022

Wells C (2001) Corporations and criminal responsibility. Oxford University Press, Oxford

Part IV
Traffickings of Goods and Human Organs

Soft Drugs and Organized Crime: A Problematic Relationship

Licia Siracusa

Abstract The paper analyses the relationship between the criminal treatment of "soft" drugs and the fight against organised crime related to drug trafficking, with regard to European law, international law and national criminal law of some EU countries (Spain, Portugal, Greece, Germany and Italy).

Following an integrated approach, the essay analyzes the legislation in this matter, the phenomenology of trafficking and the initial effects that the anti-prohibitionist reforms of some North and South American jurisdictions have produced on the illicit market. The aim is to highlight the strengths and weaknesses of the decriminalization models, taking into account not only their theoretical profiles but also possible outcome on the fight against organised crime.

1 Personal Drug Use, Trafficking in Soft Drugs and Cannabis and Organized Crime

This paper deals with some "classic" issues of criminal thinking on drugs considered paradigmatic of the set of problems that pertain to the reasons and limits of penal intervention in this sector. It deals with the question of the penal treatment to be applied for personal consumption, trafficking of soft drugs and cannabis and the links between these aspects of the phenomenon and organized crime dedicated to drug trafficking.

The main differences between the national criminal systems examined here actually concern these issues. Similarly, it is precisely in the area of the importance to be given to the distinction between the different types of substances subject to trafficking and the criminal treatment for personal use conduct that the greatest differences between two opposing views of the problem of the criminal treatment

L. Siracusa (✉)
Law Department, University of Palermo, Palermo, Italy
e-mail: licia.siracusa@unipa.it

V. Militello, A. Spena (eds.), *The Challenges of Illegal Trafficking in the Mediterranean Area*, Legal Studies in International, European and Comparative Criminal Law 9, https://doi.org/10.1007/978-3-031-45399-1_11

of drugs are most strongly expressed: prohibitionism, on the one hand, and anti-prohibitionism, on the other.

As is well known, the prohibitionist model proposes criminalization *tout court* of the phenomenon of drug addiction and spread of drugs. Anti-prohibitionism, on the other hand, suggests forms of legalization—and sometimes even liberalization—not only of conduct consisting in use and possession of drugs, but also of activities related to offer of drugs.[1]

Halfway between the two opposite poles of the more radical versions of these approaches, there are a variety of nuanced and intermediate positions that advocate hybrid systems of regulation of the phenomenon.

The following analysis only focuses on some critical issues emerging from a comparative analysis of the national regulations examined and from criminological investigation of the phenomenology of such illicit trafficking in the Mediterranean area.

2 The Supranational Regulatory Context

In both the European and international contexts, criminal law constitutes one of the main instruments used by states to combat the phenomenon of the spread of drugs. Although the idea of an anti-prohibitionist paradigm shift in the strategy of combating the phenomenon is strengthening internationally, punishment of trafficking continues to represent a crucial option in the so-called "*Global war on drugs*",[2] also due to the massive presence of transnational criminal organizations.

With the exception of some forms of legalization of cannabis production for personal use recently introduced in America and in Spain, the prohibitionist approach can still be said to be prevalent internationally and in the panorama of European legal systems.

In the European context in particular, the legislative solutions adopted at national level by the individual EU states, despite the inevitable diversity of trends, reveal a substantial uniformity of punitive approach, largely also favored by implementation of indictment constraints imposed by the Union's regulatory sources and by international conventions.

The issue of combating the spread of drugs has, moreover, constituted a privileged action sector of cooperation between states at the international level since the first decades of the last century, and in Europe it was already one of the most important political priorities immediately after the birth of the European Union.

[1] On the opposition between prohibition and anti-prohibitionism, cf. Husak and De Marneffe (2005). Among the sources in support of the anti-prohibitionist outlook see, among others, Husak (1992); Husak (2003), pp. 21 ff. In favor of prohibition, instead, see De Marneffe (2003), pp. 34 ff.

[2] A famous expression coined by Richard Nixon in the early seventies to inaugurate the start of a policy of severe drug repression in the United States.

The first international act against drugs, the *International Opium Convention* (The Hague, 1912), limited itself to binding states to control of manufacture, import, sale, distribution and export of morphine, cocaine and their derivatives, without yet providing for specific harmonization measures of punishments for criminal offenses.[3]

In subsequent treaties, the option of imposing use of criminal law to combat the spread of drugs on national law was progressively affirmed. But it was only in 1961 that real obligations to incriminate conduct connected with production and dissemination of drugs were explicitly envisaged, with the signing in New York of the *Single Convention on Narcotic Drugs* (later amended in Geneva in 1972). It was followed, within a few decades, by the 1971 *Vienna Convention on Psychotropic Substances* and the UN *Convention against Illicit Trafficking in Narcotic Drugs and Psychotropic Substances* adopted in Vienna in 1988 and currently in force.

The latter text in particular outlines an "integrated" intervention model. It focuses on a *twin-track approach*: on the one hand, criminal repression of offer, through provision of incrimination constraints on every traffic profile (Article 3); and on the other hand, prevention and treatment of drug addiction, with adoption of measures for rehabilitative and therapeutic treatment of subjects suffering from it (Article 14, paragraph 4).

A similar approach was subsequently also adopted in Europe.[4] In fact, since the founding treaties of the European Union, policies of prevention of the spread of the phenomenon of drugs and for treatment of drug addiction have been accompanied by actions aiming to harmonize national criminal laws against illicit trafficking.[5]

In particular, the Framework Decision of 25 October 2004 no. 757/GAI imposed on states the obligation to penalize all conduct connected with trafficking in drugs and precursors (art. 2).[6] Among these, only personal consumption explicitly remained outside the scope of the criminal prosecution obligations envisaged (art. 2, sec. 2). On this point, the framework decision also leaves national legal systems free to opt for legal regimes other than criminal law.

---

[3]The Hague Opium Convention of 1912 was followed by two other International Conventions on Narcotic Drugs, signed in Geneva respectively in 1925 and 1931.

[4]The need for an integrated approach in the fight against drugs was also reiterated in the latest EU Action Plan on the fight against drugs 2021–2025, available in https://www.politicheantidroga.gov.it/media/3131/piano-dazione-eu-in-materia-di-droghe-2021-2025.pdf.

[5]Among the various interventions implemented by the EU in the years immediately following the entry into force of the Maastricht Treaty, we recall that in 1993 the European Monitoring Center for Drugs and Drug Addiction (EMCDDA) was established and in 1992 the first Directive on drug precursors was issued. (Directive No. 109, 14/12/1992, relating to manufacture and marketing of certain substances used in illicit manufacture of narcotic drugs or psychotropic substances; pages 0076–0082). In 1996, Joint Action No. 750 of 17/12/1996 was finally adopted, relating to harmonization of the laws and practices of the member states of the European Union for the purpose of combating illicit drug trafficking.

[6]Including the cultivation of plants from which drugs can be obtained (Article 2 letter b) for which the New York Convention of 1988 had instead only provided for adoption of milder measures (art. 14).

If compared, the two main supranational regulatory sources on drugs—the UN Vienna Convention and the Framework Decision just mentioned—appear highly similar in content. Both not only establish that any type of conduct in which the so-called "Drug cycle" is set in motion is to be punished, but also provide for harmonization obligations regarding the type of penalties to be applied, imposing recourse to imprisonment for the most serious offenses (respectively, art. 3 sec. 4 letter A) UN Convention; art. 4 of Framework Decision no. 757/2004 GAI[7]).

On the other hand, the approach of the two acts appears different with regard to both the phenomenon of *personal drug use* and the distinction between soft drugs and hard drugs. The choice of the Framework Decision to impose on states a constraint regarding proportioning of the penalties to the type and dangerousness of the substances trafficked is not reflected in the UN text.

Similarly, the conduct of personal use is expressly subtracted from the area of intervention of the penalization obligations only in European legislation, but not in the UN Convention, which is much severer on this point. Indeed, it attributes full criminal significance to mere use, although it does not exclude the possibility of reserving alternative legal treatment, rather than criminal sanction, for the simple consumer/offender. States are granted freedom to provide for hypotheses of "purchase, possession and cultivation" of substances intended exclusively for personal use instead of punishment, namely application of therapeutic treatment measures, education, post-health care hospital, rehabilitation or social reintegration (art. 3 sec. 4).

An overview indicates that the punitive type of strategy in relation to the supply of drugs adopted by both the international instruments considered is inspired by a double need for protection: (1) the protection of collective health, seriously endangered by the spread of drugs; (2) combating the breadth and variety of dangers against multiple legal assets (public order, fair competition in the markets, integrity of the state and the international community, etc.) generated by domination of the market by organized crime.

The fact that drug trafficking constitutes one of the main sources of supply for organized crime is in fact a datum that is not only historically established, but also overwhelmingly topical. The most recent studies on the subject, while highlighting ever greater diversification of the actors involved at the various levels of the drug market, reiterate that the sector remains firmly dominated by criminal organizations, both in Europe[8] and on a world scale.[9]

Precisely this is a historically preponderant factor in the development of international strategies to combat the phenomenon. Despite the variety of trends of the

[7]With the difference that only the European text goes so far as to also indicate the minimum and maximum extent of the custodial sanction to be provided.

[8]As recently stated by the European Monitoring Center on Drugs and Drug Addiction (EMCDDA) in the European Drug Report, pp. 4 ff.

[9]The World Drug Report, UNODOC (pp. 18 and 19) pointed out that despite the recent trend towards diversification of sources of profit and methods of action by organized crime, the drug market continues to be one of its main businesses.

individual positions, the choice between prohibitionism and anti-prohibitionism indeed had to deal with this peculiarity of the phenomenon. And it is likely that it could also influence the current debate within international institutions on the possibility of a general rethinking of criminal policies on drugs, and soft drugs in particular.

In the face of the important requests in this sense from many countries—especially in Latin America[10]—the resolution adopted by the United Nations on the margin of the last Special Session of the General Assembly on drug policies (UNGASS 2016) did not accept the proposal for a common strategy to decriminalize personal use of so-called "soft" drugs, while leaving open on this point the glimmer of a flexible interpretation of the treaties by individual states.[11]

Even in the recent decisions taken in Vienna by the United Nations General Assembly, resistance to the option of legalization for personal consumption and "controlled and legal" production of soft drugs has prevailed over anti-prohibitionist pressures.[12]

Against the background of the very delicate issue of a reform of the treaties in a more permissive direction, there is a host of complex questions, linked to the possible implications of the choice worldwide and the continuing uncertainties about the actual suitability of decriminalization for simultaneously triggering a double process, of contraction of illicit supply and demand and containment of the business of criminal organizations.

Moreover, the difficulty of assessing in such a short time the effects already produced by legalization of use and production/marketing of cannabis for recreational purposes, recently implemented in Uruguay, Canada and in some US states, should not be overlooked.

At the United Nations, the paucity of statistical data on the actual advantages brought about by the anti-prohibitionist model in the legal systems where it has already been adopted could in fact make the idea of such an epochal change of pace in favor of decriminalizing personal consumption of soft drugs and sale of such drugs appear premature.[13]

---

[10]The requests made by South American countries to resolve the economic and democratic political unsustainability of generalized action against the spread of drugs led to an anticipation of the Special Session of the United Nations General Assembly dedicated to drug policies (UNGASS 2016).

[11]UNGASS, Resolution adopted by the General assembly on 19th April 2016, A/Res/S-30/1, in https://undocs.org/A/RES/S-30/1.

[12]Resolution adopted by the General Assembly on 18 December 2019, A/Res/74/178/, in https://undocs.org/en/A/RES/74/178.

[13]In the World Drug Report 2019-1 UNODOC declared the absence of a direct correlation between legalization of the consumption of the marketing/production of cannabis, on the one hand, and contraction of the illegal market in the hands of organized crime, on the other (pp. 25 ff.). In this connection, it is observed that even in the absence of certain data on the final impact that legalization of this type of consumption has had in the legal systems in which it has come into force, the first studies show that in the States where it goes further back in time—Colorado and Washington—the

Given the complexity of the variables involved, the solutions to be adopted for the future, however, do not seem reducible to the schematic opposition between "prohibitionism and anti-prohibitionism". It is not at all easy to identify a synthesis between multiple protection needs, in a sector marked both by scientific uncertainties regarding the discrimination between use harmful to health and neutral use, and by regulatory ambiguities, regarding, for example, the distinction between conducts referable to exclusive use by the individual and unlawful conduct, supported by the purpose of making a profit and aimed at marketing the product.

From the criminal point of view, the legitimacy of criminal policies must certainly be assessed on the basis of compliance with fundamental principles and dogmatic categories. But in the reflection on the relationship between drugs and criminal law, the purely theoretical approach is not enough. It is inevitably accompanied by considerations related to the effectiveness of legislative choices in relation to the objectives set.

Thus, the persuasive capacity of principle-based approaches risks being sterilized by the imponderability of the effects attributable to a possible change in the punitive paradigm. Controlled liberalization could entail a risk that has already materialized in the tobacco sector and which would also seem to be taking shape in some of the foreign countries in which reforms of this type have already been implemented. That is to say, the transition from mere "tolerance" of consumption to legalization of it and to a controlled system of production of substances does not serve either to slow down diffusion of the substances themselves—especially among the younger sections of the population—or to contain the profits of organized crime. The latter has in particular proved to be largely able to adapt to the new regulatory framework and to carve out an illegal market, parallel to the lawful one, often economically more competitive for the consumer.[14]

3 US Legislation

As noted, the United States federal drug legislation is inspired by a rigid prohibitionist model. The 1970 *Controlled Substances Act* incriminates both conducts related to supply and personal consumption of drugs, without any distinction in treatment between types of substances.

However, following the growing consensus within American public opinion in support of forms of legalization of the use of soft drugs, and cannabis in particular, many states have recently adopted laws that allow and/or regulate use of cannabis for

illegal trade has not undergone any downturns and has remained substantially stable, also due to the cheaper prices it charges compared to those offered on the legal market.

[14] As has happened in the tobacco smuggling sector, which has remained flourishing, and is at times even slightly on the increase, both globally and in the Mediterranean basin, despite the decision of many legal systems to punish such conduct only administratively.

non-medical and recreational purposes.[15] The regulatory framework at the state level appears very varied: while some states have maintained a hyper-repressive approach and continue to punish even possession or consumption of small quantities of cannabis, in other states use of this type of drug is admitted either for exclusively medical purposes or if it concerns non-toxic forms of so-called "*cannabis light*."

As for those states that have introduced more permissive legislation, they allow possession and exchange of cannabis within a certain quantitative threshold (generally 28.5 gr.[16]), but only between adults and on condition that such conduct does not take place in public places.

In addition to recreational use, home cultivation of marijuana is also permitted in many states.

Decriminalization of non-medical consumption was then accompanied by legalization of the sale and production of cannabis, with the consequent decriminalization of all conducts inherent to the supply of the substance.

In particular, the production and marketing activities are regulated by ad hoc regulations and/or local regulations and are subject to a controlled regime of granting of specific licenses. The level and type of legal restrictions imposed for such permits and commercial establishments on the methods of sale varies, however, not only from state to state, but also within the same state, in counties and between city and city.[17]

4 The Legislative Solutions Adopted in Germany, Portugal, Spain and Greece

As for the solutions adopted at local level by EU states (specifically the subject of the research in which this paper is inserted), with regard to so-called "*personal*" consumption of drugs, the freedom of choice in this area granted to national legal systems by Framework Decision no. 757/2004 GAI has in fact led to a differentiation in the importance given to conduct connected to actual drug trafficking (production, cultivation, sale, distribution, transfer, import etc.), compared to that chosen for mere "*personal use*."

Indeed, in all the regulatory systems analyzed, while any behavior qualified? as "trafficking" is subject to criminal liability, simple use is not penalized and is often nothing more than an administrative offense.

[15] There are 17 states in which the recreational use of cannabis is currently permitted: Alaska, California, Colorado, Illinois, Maine, Michigan, Massachusetts, Nevada, Oregon, Vermont, Washington, Arizona, Montana, New Jersey, New Mexico, New York and Virginia. See World Drug Report-4, p. 87 and 88 and World Drug Report-3, p. 38.

[16] Only California does not set a maximum amount of the substance that can be possessed.

[17] On this point see the World Drug Report-1, p. 26. With regard to the different types of restrictions imposed, see pp. 44 ff. of the same report and pp. 39 ff. of the World Drug Report-3.

(a) In Germany, drug use is not a crime, whatever the type of substance it involves (*hard* or *soft* drugs) (sec. 29 BtMg[18]).

On the other hand, all other conducts connected to the "drug cycle" (cultivation, production, marketing, introduction without marketing, distribution, sale, transfer, purchase, etc.) are penalized. In this case too, the distinction between hard drugs and soft drugs is of no relevance.

However, only the act of consuming drugs is not punished, and not the complex of supporting behaviors that generally accompany it. The latter all fall within the sphere of application of the criminal law incriminating traffic—including possession.

However, *personal consumption* acquires more general importance in the application sphere, where if combined with the requirement of a modest quantity of narcotic, with regard to each of the activities belonging to the drug supply chain, it can give rise to non-punishment of the typical action, acquittal, or renunciation of criminal action by the judicial authority.[19] The extent of the abstract application scope of the exemption, however, contrasts with the limit of its optional nature, which makes its concrete application subject to the judge's discretion (sec. 29 para. 5 BtMg).

(b) In Portugal, the rigorous impress of drug use legislation saw a partial softening with the entry into force of Law no. 30/2000, which downgraded consumption, purchase and possession of narcotic drugs for personal use to an administrative offense, which takes place only if the quantity of drug subject to the conduct does not exceed the dose of the average consumption of 10 days (the quantity in grams is established by ministerial decree and varies according to the type of substance).

As for the distinction between soft drugs and hard drugs, it is a constitutive element of the crime of trafficking both in the basic case (art. 21 paras. 1 and 4 of Law Decree 15/1993), and in the attenuated case which punishes less serious trafficking: in both cases the penalty limits are differentiated according to the type of substances involved (respectively defined by tables I and III for hard drugs and IV for soft drugs).

(c) As for Spanish law, self-consumption is criminally unimportant. But the notion of *personal use* is indeterminate. The law does not provide any indication on the factual elements to be taken into consideration to consider it applicable. The indeterminacy that characterizes the concept of personal consumption also reverberates on the distinction between *penally illicit possession* and *penally lawful possession*: it is the "*purpose of personal consumption*" that distinguishes criminally irrelevant possession from that which instead is punishable (art. 368, sec. 1 Penal Code).[20] In this regard, jurisprudence uses a series of concrete indicators of the "*purpose of personal use*"; among these, the quantitative thresholds of the average

[18] German Narcotics Act—Gesetz über den Verkehr mit Betäubungsmitteln 28.07.1981, available in the Official Gazette of the Federal Republic of Germany with BGBl. I 1981, 681, 1187.

[19] However, the quantity is not defined by law and may vary from Land to Land.

[20] The action constitutes an administrative offense.

daily dose indicated in specific ministerial tables of the National Institute of Toxicology are of particular importance. So-called "*shared consumption*" or group consumption is also criminally irrelevant when the following elements occur in practice: (1) the quantity of drugs must be *insignificant*, that is, adequate for a minimum and sufficient consumption for a single encounter; (d) sharing in consumption must take place within a small group of consumers, as a sporadic act, without any risk of spreading the substances in public places or on public streets; (e) the people must be identifiable; (f) it must involve immediate consumption of drugs; finally, (g) it must be free of charge and non-profit.

Finally, with regard to the distinction between soft drugs and hard drugs, it is only indirectly relevant, not as a constitutive element of the type, but through a system of mitigating circumstances, including the fact that the substances subject to illicit trafficking *do not cause serious harm to the person* (article 369b of the criminal code).

Even in terms of the description of the material object of conducts, Spanish legislation suffers from indisputable vagueness. In this connection, it does not provide a definition of a narcotic substance, nor does it specify which drugs can fall into the category of those capable of causing serious damage to health. The judicial authority believes that in order to assess the narcotic quality of a substance, the following elements must be considered: it must (1) cause a tendency to increase the doses; (2) produce physical and psychological dependence; (3) produce serious deterioration of health.

(d) Greek legislation also punishes all conducts that make up the so-called "*drug cycle*" (art. 20 Law 4139/2013, modified by Law 4523/2018), including simple possession of substances and cultivation, as well as harvesting, of cannabis.

Unlike some of the legal systems taken into consideration (the Italian and Spanish ones), for Greek law simple use of drugs constitutes a crime. However, special penalties that are less severe than those provided for other traffic conducts are envisaged in cases where the purpose of individual personal use or use by family members exists.

In particular, a reduction of the sentence is applied in cases of: (1) distribution of small quantities of drugs to satisfy the daily need of the drug addict; (2) availability of non-profit drugs, for a person's own needs and those of their family, aimed at immediately satisfying these needs (Article 21, paragraph 1, Law no. 4139/2013, modified by Law no. 4523/2018); 3) availability of previously purchased drugs, serving exclusively to satisfy one's personal need.[21]

The penalty is also further reduced for those who obtain or possess a proportionate quantity of drugs justified by the aforementioned purpose exclusively for the

[21] For such cases, the maximum penalty of 3 years of imprisonment is envisaged, while trafficking which is not aimed at personal use is punished with imprisonment from 8 to 20 years (Article 20 of Law no. 4139/2013).

purpose of personal use. The same treatment is applied to those who use or grow cannabis exclusively for the purpose of personal consumption.[22]

The law does not set the quantitative thresholds necessary to define the purpose of personal use and leaves the judge with the task of identifying the factual elements that denote the existence of this purpose. Among these, Greek jurisprudence generally attributes importance not only to the quantity of substance possessed, but also to other indices, such as the type and purity of the substance, the frequency and time of use, the average daily dose and the specific needs of the consumer.

Finally, the Greek legislator gives no importance to the distinction between soft drugs and hard drugs in criminal treatment of the respective forms of trafficking, as evidenced by the fact that use and cultivation of cannabis for personal use are also criminal actions, although they are punished less severely than other types of conduct belonging to the drug cycle.

5 Italian Law

The Italian legislation on narcotics conforms to the prohibitionist approach prescribed by supranational, international and European sources. Indeed, it provides for an all-out intervention of the criminal instrument on the side of "trafficking" of doping substances but not criminalization of personal consumption behaviors that remain outside the area of criminal relevance and are only subject to administrative sanctions (art. 75 Decree of the President of the Republic no. 309/1990[23]).

Moreover, the Italian legal system has long since abandoned the more radical version of the prohibitionist model focused on *tout court* criminalization of the drug phenomenon and drug addiction itself to embrace a more balanced punitive option, inspired by the logic of the twin-track approach: (1) severe repression of behaviors connected with the supply of drugs, on the one hand, (2) taking charge of the consumer's health through provision of rehabilitation programs and addiction treatment, on the other.

In this framework of legislative policies inspired by demands for protection of collective and individual health, use of drugs continues to be frowned upon—not simply tolerated—by the legal system, which indeed sanctions it on an administrative level. The different legal treatment of the consumer (subject to administrative sanctions) compared to the trafficker then reverberates on the typification of the range of conducts pertaining to the notion of "traffic" and criminally relevant pursuant to art. 73 Consolidated Law on Drugs (TU STUP). Each of the activities potentially capable of increasing circulation and diffusion of drugs is considered

---

[22] The penalty in this case is 5 months' imprisonment (art. 29 sec. 1, Law 4139/2013).

[23] The subject of narcotics is regulated by the Decree of the President of the Republic of 9 October 1990 no. 309 ("Consolidated Law on the discipline of narcotic drugs and psychotropic substances, prevention, treatment and rehabilitation of related drug addiction states"; hereinafter, TU STUP).

criminally illicit. Sale, trade, transfer, production, manufacture and cultivation of drugs, import and export are criminalized.

Conversely, in addition to simple use, considered in and of itself, import, purchase, receiving, export and possession remain outside the area of application of criminal laws and are subject to administrative sanctions (art. 75 para.1 TU STUP), when marked for personal use.[24] However, art. 75 TU STUP does not expressly mention unauthorized cultivation of plants from which narcotic substances are obtained, which therefore falls within the offense referred to in art. 73 TU STUP, even if for personal use.

The unreasonable difference in treatment between cultivation, which is criminally unlawful, and other conducts preparatory to use, not criminally relevant if not aimed at increasing the drug market because they were carried out for personal use, has triggered a lively conflict in application.

A first orientation of the courts recognizes that cultivation has a greater harmful potential than other preparatory or ancillary conducts for personal consumption, as it makes it possible to increase the volume of drugs in circulation, through diffusion and proliferation of the cultivated product.[25]

Other jurisprudence, on the other hand, gets round the irrationality of the legislation and restricts application of the incriminating penal law to cases of cultivation that actually risk harming public health.[26]

On this point, the United Sections of the Court of Cassation have recently subordinated the criminal relevance of cultivation to its concrete risk potential. Harmlessness would concretely be inferred *a contrario* from the modest size, the domestic nature of the activities carried out, the lack of indices about the insertion of the products obtained in the marketing circuit and finally the objective intention to limit them to personal use.[27]

As for the distinction between soft drugs and hard drugs, it was restored following the declaration of constitutional illegitimacy of the rules that had equated criminal treatment of soft drugs with that of hard drugs (Constitutional Court, sent. no. 32/2014[28]). The ruling restored consistency to the national legislation both in terms of compliance with the principle of proportion and reasonableness and as regards congruity with the constraint imposed by EU legislation to diversify the penalties in relation to the type and dangerousness of drugs.

---

[24] For an in-depth analysis of the interpretative problems concerning "personal use", we refer to the extensive literature on the subject, and in particular Gambardella (2014), pp. 19 and 20.

[25] Among the many, Cass. pen., sentence of 10 February 2016, n. 10,169; Cass. pen., sentence of 10 May 2016, n. 25,057; Cass. pen., sentence of 27 October 2015, no. 44136.

[26] Ex multis, Cass. pen., sentence of 21 October 2015, no. 2618/2016; Cass. pen., sentence of 22 February 2017, no. 36037.

[27] Cass. pen., SU, sentenza 16 aprile 2020, n. 12,348. See the comment by Argirò (2020), pp. 1447 ff.

[28] The difference in punishment between hard drugs and soft drugs, previously in force, was abolished by the so-called "Fini-Giovanardi" law (Law no. 49/2006, conversion of Legislative Decree no. 272/2006).

6 Points of Contact and Divergences Between the European Systems Examined

Among the European legislations examined, numerous points of contact can be identified, in part due to implementation of the harmonization constraints imposed by EU sources.

In compliance with the requirements of framework decision no. 757/2004 GAI, almost all the national legal systems taken into consideration are inspired by a "*moderate*" type of prohibition that does not consider the consumer an *offender* and restricts the area of criminal intervention to conduct relating to drugs "traffic." Unlike the *pure* and rigorous version applied by the laws of some US states, the European version of prohibition therefore only incriminates supply of substances and not the related demand.

Mere consumption is in fact criminally irrelevant in Italy, Germany, Spain and Portugal; and in most cases it constitutes an administrative offense (Italy, Spain, Portugal). The exception is Greece, which makes it a crime, although it provides for significantly less severe penalties than those to which other traffic conducts are subject.

In countries that place it outside the area of intervention of criminal law, consumption of drugs is, however, something which is still frowned on by the legal system, even if it lacks the social negative value sufficient to make it worthy of a criminal sanction; it is seen as behavior, that is, which is not *neutral*, and yet does not risk causing harm to society such as to justify its *criminal* punishment.

The prevalence among the EU states analyzed of a perspective that tends towards prevention, rather than repression of demand, is confirmed by the fact that the decision to downgrade consumption to a simple administrative offense (Italy, Spain and Portugal) is often accompanied by the provision of measures aimed at stimulating implementation of rehabilitation treatments for regular consumers.

The substantial uniformity of the solutions adopted at national level with regard to the legal treatment of the drug user also extends to the decision to exclude criminal action for other behaviors distinct from consumption, considered in and of itself, but preparatory or connected to it.

In Italy and Portugal, these activities are categorically indicated. In particular, Portuguese legislation qualifies consumption, purchase and possession for personal use as administrative violations. On the other hand, the range of conduct that the Italian legislation considers criminally lawful is wider, if carried out for the purpose of personal use: import, purchase, reception, export and possession.

On this point, the solution adopted by the German legal system differs: it sees personal use as a cause of non-punishment of the behavior, or as a condition of non-prosecution and renunciation of the prosecution of criminal action, valid for all conducts related to the so-called "Drug cycle" but applicable at the discretion of the judge, with the exception of mere consumption.

Finally, the Spanish penal code does not punish use of drugs, considered in and of itself, if carried out in public or in a public place; at most it constitutes an administrative offense. As for conduct ancillary to personal use, it is envisaged that the concept of personal use is relevant exclusively in relation to possession, and not with regard to the other types of conduct that characterize drugs traffic.

The latter therefore constitute a crime even when univocally and exclusively aiming at personal consumption of the narcotic substance.

In other words, possession is the only one among the conducts expressly indicted in Spain as pertaining to traffic that does not constitute a crime, if aimed at personal consumption.

A particular case is that of Greece, which, as we have seen, also punishes simple consumption and emphasizes personal use exclusively on the side of the penalty, with a significant reduction both for those who distribute or dispose of small quantities of drugs for the purpose of satisfying their personal needs, or that of their family members, and for those who obtain or possess drugs for the sole purpose of making personal use of them. In particular, Greek law expressly includes use and cultivation of cannabis for personal consumption among the less severely punished conducts.

In line with the prohibitionist approach of the respective legislations, none of the legal systems studied envisages forms of legalization of production and marketing of soft drugs and cannabis. With the exception of the model proposed by the "*cannabis social clubs*" in Spain, whose lawfulness has recently been questioned by the Supreme Court, also because of the lack of adequate legislation at the state level, cannabis production and cultivation for non-medical purposes are generally prohibited.

Regarding the distinction between soft drugs and hard drugs, it is relevant in Spain, Portugal and Italy. On the other hand, no difference in penalties for the conducts punished with variation in the type, nature and harmfulness of the trafficked substance is envisaged in Germany and Greece.

Finally, with regard to the penal relevance of organized crime engaged in drug trafficking, it is significant that if the provision of more severe penalties for trafficking conducted by subjects belonging to criminal groups is common to all the legal systems examined, no fewer than three of the national legislations taken into consideration (Italy, Spain, and Portugal) contemplate for these types of criminal associations ad hoc incriminating rules, distinct and special with respect to the more general rules punishing organized criminal groups.

7 An Overview of the Legislations Adopted at National Level to Combat Organized Crime Dedicated to Drug Trafficking

With regard to the fight against organized criminal groups involved in drug trafficking, the solutions adopted by the national legal systems examined essentially go in two directions. A first case is that of legal systems which, for trafficking carried out by organized criminal groups, provide for aggravating circumstances or autonomous and more serious incriminating rules than the corresponding single-subject situations. The second case, which actually only refers to Italian legislation, is the paradigm of organized crime aimed at drug trafficking.

In particular, in the Spanish and Greek legislations, the punishment of an organized criminal group is subject to the actual fulfillment of one or more activities in the drug cycle by subjects belonging to it. Thus, in Spain, art. *369b código* penal incriminates more severely conducts pertaining to illicit trafficking committed by subjects belonging to an organized criminal group and diversifies the penalties according to the role played by the latter in the criminal organization, contemplating for the leaders, the promoters and the organizers more severe penalties than those reserved for simple participants. Even with respect to this incriminating situation, as in cases of a single subjects carrying out typical conduct, an increase in the penalty is then established where the trafficked substances are particularly dangerous.

A similar solution can be found in the Greek legislation, which establishes an increase in the penalty for the case of trafficking carried out by a member of an organized criminal group, as defined by articles 187 and 187 A of the Greek penal code—that is to say, a structured and stable group, composed of three or more people and having the purpose of committing more than one crime.

Halfway between the two models—the one contemplating an autonomous idea of associative crime marked by the specificity of the trafficking purpose or the introduction of aggravating circumstances/increases in the sentence in cases of involvement of organized and structured criminal groups—we find the German solution and the Portuguese one. In this connection, the German legislation punishes more severely a wide range of conducts (marketing, cultivation and production), when carried out by a member of a criminal association (sec. 30 BtMg) and also punishes with a sentence of not less than 5 years cultivation, introduction and transport of significant quantities of drugs by a participant in a *gang*, employing minors under the age of 18 and using weapons (sec. 30, letter (a) BtMg).

The Portuguese system, on the other hand, like the Italian one, provides for an ad hoc incriminating framework that is not based on the idea of criminal association but on that of the structured criminal group. Indeed, anyone who promotes, founds or finances or collaborates with, joins or supports or commands or directs a criminal group, stable over time and with its own organic structure, aimed at committing drug trafficking offenses, is punished more severely.

Finally, the Italian solution is unique: as is well known, it autonomously punishes the criminal association aimed at drug trafficking (Article 74 TU STUP) through a specific incrimination within whose sphere of application only criminal organizations set up with the primary or exclusive purpose of drug trafficking fall.[29] Simple

[29] As is well known, one of the major application problems relating to the case in question concerns the relations of the same with the mafia-type criminal association. For a criticism of the prevailing jurisprudential orientation that between the two cases identifies a formal concurrence of crimes, see the recent article by Birritteri (2018), pp. 168 ff.

establishment of a criminal association marked by the specific nature of the criminal program is also punished, regardless of the actual implementation of the latter.

The Italian peculiarity of widening the range of the indictment to conducts of simple participation in an association, even if not accompanied by the carrying out of the criminal purpose, must be ascribed to the specificity of the legal tradition of our country, which has been strongly marked by the phenomenon of organized crime. The particular criminal context in which the penal responses to combat drug trafficking managed by criminal organizations have been worked out has undoubtedly shaped its contents.

The different approach followed in other national legal systems is instead, in many cases, the result of implementation of the model adopted by European legislation, which has formulated a precise definition of an organized criminal group. Transposing almost verbatim the homologous provision contained in the Palermo UN Convention on transnational organized crime, framework decision no. 841/2008 JHA on the fight against organized crime exhaustively describes the constitutive requirements of the criminal organization. These consist in the structured and stable nature of the association, in the presence of at least two associates and in the criminal program being aimed at perpetration for profit of crimes punishable with loss of liberty or with a security measure depriving people of their freedom for a period of not less than 4 years or with a more severe sentence (Article 1 paragraph 1[30]). This definition is taken up in framework decision no. 757/2004 GAI on illicit drug trafficking in the part in which it enjoins states to sanction more severely conducts relating to drug trafficking committed by an organized criminal group (Article 4 paragraph 3).[31]

In particular, the positive effects in terms of harmonization of the laws of the member states due to the impact of European legislation on internal laws can be seen above all in the national regulations adopted after the two framework decisions mentioned above, respectively, in the fields of organized crime and narcotics. This is the case, for example, of art. 369b of the penal code, introduced with Ley Orgánica no. 5/2010. Almost with the same wording as framework decision no. 841/2008 JHA are the definitions of organized criminal group contained in the Greek and Portuguese legislations. These systems also conform to the paradigm imposed by framework decision no. 757/2004 GAI in the field of narcotics of not envisaging penalties for criminal associations engaged in drug trafficking but establishing more serious penalties than the basic crime for cases in which the typical conduct of such trafficking is linked to an organized criminal group.

Despite the variety of individual national responses, however, it appears undeniable that European legislation has played a crucial role in strengthening internal

[30] On these issues see the important contributions by Militello (2011), Militello (2013), Militello (2021).

[31] Actually, the framework decision on drugs explicitly refers to the definition of an organized criminal group contained in joint action no. 98/733/JHA concerning criminalization of participation in a criminal organization in the Member States of the European Union, later replaced by framework decision no. 841/2008 JHA relating to the fight against organized crime.

measures to combat the phenomenon of organized crime involved in drug trafficking. It has indeed allowed national legal systems to take decisive steps towards adopting a more modern political-penal approach, capable of combining, in this sector too, the more traditional forms of offense to personal property with incriminating cases of criminal associative phenomena, in relation to which the arguments that fuel the inexhaustible debate around the reasons for punishment in the field of drugs inevitably fade, and almost vanish, leaving room for other evaluations of rationality with respect to the aims pursued.

Indeed, there is no doubt that the dimension of organized crime represents a distinct and specific problem with respect to the more general one on the basis and limits of the penal fight against drug trafficking. Hence the importance of considering this particular aspect of the phenomenon as a magnifying glass through which to look at the complexity of the individual issues involved, identifying their mutual connections.

8 The Merits of the Italian Solution

As for the other types of associative crime present in the legal system, also with regard to criminal association aimed at drug trafficking, the Italian legislation does not describe in an exhaustive and complete manner the structural elements of the criminal association. It punishes the very existence of the association, regardless of the implementation of the criminal program. Membership of the association does not automatically entail participation in the planned offenses, nor is the actual carrying out of such offenses required for the purposes of punishment of participation alone.

For this reason, jurisprudence has the task of better defining the constitutive characteristics of the case: from the symptomatic indices of the *pactum sceleris* to the endurance of a minimum of organizational structure.

The elasticity of the structural elements required for the criminal association undoubtedly has the advantage of allowing easy adaptation of the incriminating case both to the fluidity of criminal organizations and to the new types of organized crime emerging in practice. The offense can occur even in the absence of a complex, stable and ramified organizational structure and not merely occasional predisposition of people aimed at implementing the criminal program is sufficient. This makes it possible to apply the most severe penalties provided for by the law both to more embryonic forms of manifestation of the associative phenomenon, and for more sophisticated organized criminal structures—that is, from small gangs of pushers to real networks of organized criminal groups.

The system is thus capable of adhering promptly to the complexity and changeability of the operating methods of organized crime in the narcotics sector. In this connection, from the empirical-criminological point of view, criminal organizations involved in drug trafficking show that they possess considerable flexibility, are able to agree on transactions or to forge authentic alliances between associations, different in origin and size and finally, often, are able better to exploit the new sales channels offered by the dark web.

These trends also seem to concern the European context. Recent criminological studies have in fact shown that in Europe too, alongside organized criminal groups of the traditional type, large and hierarchically structured, smaller criminal organizations are operating, characterized by a reticular physiognomy, of a cellular type, whose *modus operandi* reduces the use of violence to the minimum and favors the use of other means of persuasion, such as bribery or co-optation.[32]

In this complex scenario, the open scheme typical of associative crime seems to adapt better to the Protean criminal reality of drug trafficking than the rigid figure of the organized criminal group, typified in European legislation and implemented in national criminal legislations. The fact is that the applicability of the latter to new forms of organized crime is enormously reduced by the need for all the structural requirements to be present in practice (minimum number of participants, stability, etc.) and is in any case subject, in the case of drugs, to the condition that one or more planned offenses have actually been committed—that is one or more conducts typical of drug trafficking.

In addition to greater flexibility and adaptability to concrete situations, recourse to the framework of the associative type also brings further advantages. It makes it possible, for example, to have recourse to the investigative tools provided for criminal association crimes and to measures for freezing and confiscating the related illicit proceeds. And this undoubtedly facilitates interception of the dynamics of traffic and overall strengthens the system's ability to adequately combat the phenomenon.

9 Phenomenology of the Trafficking of Soft Drugs and Cannabis in the Mediterranean

The cannabis and soft drugs market is one of the most flourishing in the world drug trafficking scene.

In this connection, recent UNODOC studies attest that around 200 million people around the world used cannabis in 2019[33] and that the recent introduction of forms of legalization of the offer in some US states, Canada and Uruguay has not significantly affected the volumes of illicit trafficking of this substance, which remains substan-

[32] See the interesting article by Punzo (2019), pp. 43 ff.

[33] According to the World Drug Report-2, p. 21, it is about 4% of the world population aged between 15 and 64 years.

tially stable globally.[34] Similar trends are recorded with regard to the European context, where cannabis is one of the most consumed and widespread drugs.[35]

Despite the high levels of domestic production, the European demand for cannabis and derived products—including synthetic cannabinoids—is still largely satisfied through import of the substances from foreign countries, which generally use Europe not only as an arrival point for traffic but also as a transit place for drugs to be sent to other continents.

The Mediterranean area further represents an important crossroads for trafficking of cannabis and hashish but also of other narcotic substances, especially cocaine and synthetic drugs. The scope and dangerousness of trafficking in so-called "light" drugs in this area are also increased by the fact that criminal organizations controlling these routes not only often traffic different types of substances simultaneously,[36] but in addition use the facilities, means and human resources set up for the drug market in other types of illicit trafficking too, such as tobacco smuggling, arms trafficking and especially human trafficking.

In addition to their ability to maximize returns through simultaneous exploitation of people and means for multiple illicit purposes, the particular flexibility of these organizations is also manifested in their tendency to fragment themselves into smaller and more agile groups, capable of operating as true networks on a transnational level between the European continent and Africa.

These peculiarities of the ways of acting of organized crime in the sector considered here make illicit drug trafficking in the Mediterranean area a complex phenomenon, difficult to intercept and counter. The strong involvement of criminal networks, combined with their extraordinary ability to adapt to market needs, plays an important role in balancing the interests that are taken into consideration, when it comes to sifting through the different legislative approaches to the problem, also with regard to the soft drugs sector.

Any legislative option in favor of more or less market-driven forms of legalization must in fact take into due account the consequences that such a paradigm shift could generate on the side of combating the business of criminal organizations. And from this point of view, the matter is complicated not a little, due to the numerous variables affecting the evaluation of the political/criminal appropriateness of the chosen legislative models.

---

[34] Word Drug Report-1, pp. 14 ff.

[35] As reported in A review and assessment of EU drug policy, Directorate General for Internal Policies, Policy Department C: citizens' rights and constitutional affairs, Civil Liberties, Justice and Home Affairs, pp. 25 and 38 and in the Relazione europea sulle droghe, pp. 16 ff. and (2022), pp.26 ff.

Cannabis use in Europe is estimated to be around five times higher than that of other drugs: see Relazione europea sulle droghe, p. 41.

[36] In the World Drug Report-4 UNODOC, pp. 20 ff. it is noted that so-called "Polydrug trafficking", i.e. the ability of organized criminal groups to manage the trafficking of different substances simultaneously and to establish transnational supply networks, significantly contributes to increasing the complexity of the world drugs market.

Although, reasoning in the abstract, the need to subtract important slices of the market from the criminal organizations involved in trafficking could make it seem appropriate to resort to forms of legalization of offer, similar to those experienced overseas, the concrete realization of this possibility nevertheless remains very problematic. There are several factors that get in the way.

First, there is the difficulty of predicting the actual capacity of such a reform to achieve the desired result of containing the illicit market. The first empirical evidence on the effects of legalization of cannabis in Canada and Uruguay has shown that the possibility of obtaining the substance on the legal market has not led to a significant reduction in purchases on the illegal market. Both restrictive regulation of access to consumption (limited places and opening hours and age group limitations) and the high price of available substances have certainly contributed to making the illicit offer still attractive.[37]

Secondly, the option of a more permissive regulatory framework must be able to appear legitimate in the same way as the arguments of a theoretical nature that outline the foundation and limit of criminal intervention in the field of drugs.

Indeed, on the criminal side, the strong request for protection of public order and security that is expressed in the fight against organized crime involved in trafficking represents only one of the many interests at stake. The aim of protecting collective health and also the life and health of individuals, considered individually equally remains a priority in this context.

To follow the path followed by some US states of regulating production, sale and dissemination of certain drugs on a legal basis, possibly by introducing a controlled system of prices and state licenses, it is therefore necessary to rethink some of the reasons that justify the penalties for conduct related to the cycle of soft drugs. If the idea that consumption of soft drugs can go unpunished is present in many legal systems, there is no such uniformity of views with regard to conduct of transfer of such substances.

A change in the legislative approach on the subject of supply of soft drugs is therefore possible only on condition of overcoming the idea that on a large scale consumption of these types of substances constitutes behavior harmful to the health of the community, although not particularly dangerous for the health of the individual user; and more generally, abandoning the prospect that the spread of drugs still represents, beyond the actual detrimental scope of the individual transfer behaviors, a socially harmful phenomenon to be prevented and avoided, including through use of criminal sanctions. On this basis alone, state involvement in the distribution of these types of drugs might appear legitimate.

Returning to the European context which was the starting point, it would be risky to imagine forecasts about the possibility that this legislative change may in the future take place both in the systems examined here and at the level of the European Union. Although there are signs of important cultural and custom changes underway in favor of the anti-prohibitionist option, at least with reference to drugs with remote

[37] Fischer et al. (2021), p. 61.

or only serial dangerousness, the action of states does not seem to go in this direction.

10 Balance Sheets and Perspectives *de iure condendo*: The Weight of Lightness

Despite the international push towards introduction of models of legalization of supply of cannabis for recreational use, several factors are therefore acting against a change of pace in the criminal law approach of European states towards the phenomenon of soft drugs: (1) of a *technical* nature, relating to the principles and reasons for criminalization of the conduct involved; (2) of a *scientific* nature, concerning the effects of drug addiction on individual and collective health; (3) of a *regulatory* nature, connected to the obligations imposed by supranational, European and international sources; and finally (4) of a *political-utilitarian* nature, relating to assessment of the capacity of the various regulatory solutions to effectively combat criminal organizations that manage trafficking.

(1) With regard to the arguments of principle that are generally evoked for or against the prospect of legalizing supply of cannabis and soft drugs for non-medical use, it is evident that in the context of EU countries these profiles take on different meanings and nuances with respect to the debate taking place overseas. In this connection, on the level of the theoretical reasons that legitimize use of the criminal instrument in the field of drugs, the differences between common law and civil law appear to be considerable and significant.

In continental European countries, the discussion on the appropriate penalties for conduct relating to drug trafficking goes far beyond the schematic contrast between paternalistic prohibitionism and anti-prohibitionism of anti-paternalistic inspiration, to which the problem of the relationship between drugs and criminal law in the Anglo-Saxon context is generally linked.[38]

The criminal reflection worked out in the legal systems considered here, and more generally in the systems of continental Europe, in fact considers that the consumption of drugs should be considered in the perspective of the legal assets to be protected and the types of conduct that risk damaging them. From this point of view, the spread of drugs reveals that it is capable of causing damage both to the individual, exposed to the health and life risks associated with addiction, and to the

[38] On the subject of the principles of criminalization typical of Anglo-Saxon culture, one inevitably has to make reference to the four volumes of Feinberg (1984); Feinberg (1985); Feinberg (1986); Feinberg (1988).

In Italian criminal law, for a critical analysis of the themes of penal paternalism, see Spena (2014), pp. 1209 ff., and also, among the now numerous contributions on the theme, Romano (2008), pp. 984 ff.; Cadoppi (2011), pp. 223 ff., Cornacchia (2011), pp. 239 ff.; Pulitanò (2011), pp. 489 ff.; Cavaliere (2013), pp. 421 ff.

community, due to the dangers to the safety of others and to public health that arise from unlimited use of drugs.

The circulation of drugs thus constitutes a phenomenon that the legal system disapproves of because it is dangerous for individuals and for society—it is something that is not considered "colorless" by the legislator but as something that the law can aim to prevent, including through the use of criminal sanctions.

In particular, all the legal systems analyzed here recognize the harmful effect of conducts that increase the spread of drugs (production, import, sale, etc.) and at the same time believe that the option of denying criminal relevance to personal use is legitimate and reasonable, or that it could be downgraded to a mere administrative offense. The individual consumer is seen, indeed, as a potential victim of a crime in which the reasons for punishing that are valid for the conduct of the seller are not necessarily reflected in the complementary conduct of the buyer.

This way of approaching the problem with regard to drug use in general is also valid—perhaps even more so—with respect to the particular hypothesis of use of those types of drugs whose dosed intake is shown to cause no significant damage to the health of the individual, and is not believed in the long run to be able to harm public health, seen as an asset with diffuse ownership, rather than a mere sum of the health of individuals. In accordance with the principles of proportion and *extrema ratio*, the lower negative value of the conduct of taking soft drugs compared to consumption of hard drugs can therefore abstractly legitimize their being moved from the area of the administrative offense to the area of total lawfulness, criminal and extra-criminal, without this undermining the overall rationality of the prohibitionist approach.

A possible choice in favor of decriminalization of personal use conducts does not make decriminalization of the correlative offer equally mandatory, as specified. The latter may in fact continue to appear deserving of a criminal sanction, based on the fact that its ability to increase the circulation and diffusion of narcotic substances in the community actually puts it at risk of damaging the set of collective assets referred to above.

What has just been said confirms the premise made explicit at the beginning of this reflection about the fact that the significance of the problem of criminal intervention in the field of drugs is not limited to the quantity of freedom to be granted to the individual user.

The real critical issue in the relationship between criminal law and drugs is represented, rather, by the difficulty of establishing whether in this sector there are reasons that legitimize limitations on the freedom of self-determination of the individual, in view of the protection of other assets, such as life or public health. In fact, it appears evident that a prohibitionist type of legislative solution requires that in the balance between the various assets at stake, some are identified whose need for protection is capable of justifying the heavy interference of the punitive power of the state in the sphere of autonomy of the citizen.

However, the considerations made up to now on the prohibitionist choice do not completely clarify the reasons for the irrationality of legalization of the sale of only the drugs that are least harmful for health.

On the contrary, from a logical point of view it does not seem possible to identify a radical incompatibility between a type of legislation that allows controlled distribution of soft drugs, on the one hand, and the theoretical principles that underlie the criminalization choices made by the European countries examined, on the other.

Based on the scheme of crimes with abstract dangerousness that offend collective goods, the sale of soft drugs and cannabis, subject to precise limits and a system of legal controls, does not reach the threshold of offensiveness and social negativity necessary to justify the imposition of the criminal prohibition.[39] The provision of forms of sale regulated by law and supervised by the state appears, on the other hand, to be consistent with the criminal reasons that legitimize the decision to punish trafficking relating to the most dangerous substances.

Allowing sale of soft drugs in compliance with certain restrictions is not in fact the same as admitting legalization *tout court* of the supply of any type of doping substance. Even under a more permissive regime regarding soft drugs, distribution of hard drugs could continue to constitute a criminal offense, and there would be no obstacles to penalizing sale of soft drugs that is carried out in such a way as to break the rules imposed by law, or is not controlled by the public authority.

The constraints imposed on the transferor of substances admitted by the legislator and the system of marketing authorizations would serve to prevent the occurrence of the dangers associated with an indiscriminate spread of the drugs traded. In other words, they would act as a legal parameter for determining a permitted risk threshold, justified by the lower harmful potential of these drugs compared to hard ones. Beyond this threshold, however, as is obvious, the realization of the serial dangerousness of the individual transfer conducts would be sufficient to justify their criminal relevance.

(2) With regard to the scientific factors that could hinder the introduction of forms of legalization of cannabis or other soft drugs, what has just been said regarding the fact that a controlled distribution system subject to precise restrictions on the quantity and quality of substances—at least with regard to the lightest of soft drugs, namely cannabis—would correspond to the logic that a diffusion contained within permitted risk thresholds is less dangerous for public health, compared to unlimited and out-of-control circulation.

(3) In the set of impediments to possible anti-prohibitionist reforms on the side of soft drugs, the regulatory constraints of a supranational source appear perhaps to be among the most difficult to overcome.

As initially highlighted, international sources on the subject seem to allow states little room for maneuver in terms of legalizing the supply of soft drugs. Both the UN Convention against illicit drug trafficking and the Framework Decision of n. 757/2004/JHA establish obligations to criminalize supply of drugs without any distinction between soft drugs and hard drugs. And in particular, only the European text

---

[39] Among the voices in favor of legalization of sale of soft drugs, see Cavaliere (2014), pp. 596 ff. And Ferrajoli (1991), pp. 133 ff.

expressly removes personal consumption from the area of intervention of criminal law, leaving national legislators free to choose whether and how to punish it.

Despite the absence of an explicit prohibition on the hypothesis of legalization of production, sale and distribution of soft drugs, without a revision of international treaties and European legislation on the subject, in the European countries examined here—and more generally in the context of states of the European Union—implementation of reforms similar to those that have taken place overseas would be difficult to reconcile with the content of these supranational sources.

(4) Finally, with regard to the effects that legalization of cannabis could generate on the front of the fight against organized crime, the question becomes more complex, given the difficulty of measuring empirically and *ex post* the effectiveness of the chosen solutions and of evaluating *ex ante* their suitability for the purpose.

At present, there is no objective evidence that regulation of the distribution of soft drugs determines an automatic contraction of the illicit market managed by criminal organizations. As already reported several times, the available statistics do not make it possible to establish a direct correlation between legalization of marketing and/or production of cannabis, on the one hand, and reduction of the size of the illegal market in the hands of organized crime, on the other.

Rather, in the American states that have experienced legislation of this type for the longest time, both levels of consumption (except for the slight increase recorded in the period immediately following the entry into force of the reforms) and the business of organized criminal groups have remained unchanged. The latter have in fact resisted the impact of the birth of a legal market, making the illicit one more competitive, by offering far lower prices than those practiced by legal distribution.[40] If the prediction of such a trend were also to come true with regard to trafficking in the Mediterranean, there would be the risk that in this specific territorial context, criminal organizations would be able to maintain their turnover unchanged, by implementing compensatory mechanisms both between types of trafficked substances, and between the different types of illicit trafficking that are part of their criminal agenda.

In the geographical area of southern Europe, due to the ability of criminal groups to act simultaneously on several fronts, both from the point of view of the variety of drugs trafficked, and from the point of view of the diversification of managed trafficking, it could in fact happen that lower revenues from the cannabis and other soft drugs market would be offset by the simultaneous intensification of trafficking in hard drugs and the increase in other illicit trafficking managed (weapons, tobacco, human beings).

[40] However, the collection of analyzable data from the vast basin of the numerous US states that have embarked on the road to legalization is only at the beginning. The widespread implementation of permissive legislation in North America was defined by Fischer et al. (2021), p. 60, "a real "natural experiment" which for the first time will make it possible to carry out a comparative evaluation of the prohibitionist model and the anti-prohibitionist one, based on empirical bases and not only on prognostic judgments.

Finally, in the criminological context considered here, it cannot be excluded that other side effects should be added to the side effects just mentioned, similar to those already manifested in European countries that have introduced systems for legalized sale of soft drugs. We refer in particular to the so-called "back-door" effect and the phenomenon of the increase in the illicit offer intended for minors.

As for the "back-door" phenomenon, this is a problem that has emerged in the Netherlands, where, since the law allows coffee shops to hold stocks of cannabis not exceeding a certain amount established by law,[41] it often happens that in order to satisfy demand and keep up with the market, the managers of these establishments turn to the illegal market, with the consequence that the legal and illegal offers end up increasing each other.[42]

Finally, among the problems associated with anti-prohibitionist reforms, the possibility should not be overlooked that once the sale of cannabis has been legalized—albeit under certain conditions—traffickers will be able to intercept the consumption demand of the younger sections of the population to which the law would prohibit access to legal sale.[43]

References

Argirò F (2020) Commercializzazione di cannabis light e coltivazione domestica tra contrasti giurisprudenziali e inerzia normativa. Diritto Penale e Processo 8:1447

Birritteri E (2018) Il concorso tra associazione per delinquere di stampo mafioso e associazione finalizzata al traffico di stupefacenti: alla ricerca di una razionale repressione del fenomeno. Diritto Penale Contemporaneo 1:168–178

Cadoppi A (2011) Paternalismo e diritto penale. Criminalia 6:223–237

Cavaliere A (2013) Paternalismo, diritto penale e principi costituzionali: profili di teoria generale. I-Lex 20:421–441

Cavaliere A (2014) Il controllo del traffico di stupefacenti tra politica criminale e dogmatica. Diritto Penale e Processo 5:586–601

Cornacchia L (2011) Placing care. Spunti in tema di paternalismo penale. Criminalia 6:239–277

De Marneffe P (2003) Against the legalizion of Heroin. Crim Justice Ethics 22:34–40

Feinberg J (1984) The moral limits of the criminal law. Harms to others. Oxford University Press, Oxford

Feinberg J (1985) Offense to others. Oxford University Press, Oxford

---

[41] A total of 500 g.

[42] See the report Cannabis Legislation in Europe. An overview, p. 15, as well as the previously mentioned study A review and assessment of EU drug policy, p. 145. On this point, see MacCoun (2011), pp. 1899–1910.

[43] Prohibition of access to the lawful market could also encourage use by minors of hidden networks from the so-called "Darknet" and home cultivation. That the drug market is exposed to inscrutable rebound effects is shown by what happened during the restrictions on taxes around the world for containment of the Covid-19 pandemic. The inability to access traditional forms of illicit procurement did not trigger a contraction in supply and demand but instead increased online purchases of modest quantities of cannabis, both on the legal market and through the dark web. On this point see the World Drug Report-5, p. 17.

Feinberg J (1986) Harm to self. Oxford University Press, Oxford
Feinberg J (1988) Harmless wrongdoing. Oxford University Press, Oxford
Ferrajoli L (1991) Proibizionismo e diritto. In: Mancioni L (ed) Legalizzare la droga. Una ragionevole proposta di sperimentazione. Feltrinelli, Milan, p 133
Fischer B, Daldegan-Bueno D, Reuter P (2021) Toward a post-legalization criminology for cannabis: a brief review and suggested agenda for research priorities. Contemp Drug Probl 1: 58–74
Gambardella M (2014) La nuova disciplina in materia di stupefacenti. Cassaz Penal 9:1–38
Husak D (1992) Drugs and rights. Cambridge University Press, Cambridge
Husak D (2003) Four points about drug decriminalization. Crim Justice Ethics 22:21–29
Husak D, De Marneffe P (2005) The legalization of drugs: for & against. Cambridge University Press, Cambridge
MacCoun RJ (2011) What can we learn from the Dutch cannabis coffeeshop system? Addiction 106:1899–1910
Militello V (2011) Criminalità organizzata transnazionale e intervento europeo fra contrasto e garanzie. Rivista Trimestrale di Diritto Penale dell'Economia 4:821–837
Militello V (2013) I nuovi modelli di incriminazione delle organizzazioni criminali all'interno dell'Unione Europea. In: Bargi A (ed) Il doppio accertamento dei fatti di mafia. Giappichelli, Torino, pp 23–56
Militello V (2021) La convenzione di Palermo sul crimine organizzato (UNTOC): un punto di svolta vent'anni dopo. Discrimen 4:1–5
Militello V, Spena A, Mangiaracina A, Siracusa L (eds) (2019) I traffici illeciti nel Mediterraneo. Persone, stupefacenti, tabacco. Giappichelli, Turin, p 43
Pulitanò D (2011) Paternalismo penale. In: Bertolino M, Eusebi L, Forti G (eds) Studi in onore di Mario Romano. Napoli, Jovene, I, p 489
Punzo V (2019) I traffici illeciti nel Mediterraneo. Aspetti criminologici e tendenze evolutive, In: Militello V, Spena A, Mangiaracina A, Siracusa L, I traffici illeciti nel Mediterraneo. Persone, Stupefacenti e tabacco, Giappichelli, Torino, pp 31–66
Romano M (2008) Danno a sé stessi e paternalismo penale. Rivista Italiana Diritto e Procedura Penale 51:984–1003
Spena A (2014) Esiste un paternalismo penale? Un contributo al dibattito sui principi di criminalizzazione. Rivista Italiana Diritto e Procedura Penale 3:1209–1248
UNGASS (2016) Resolution adopted by the General assembly on 19th April 2016

Trafficking in Cultural Property. An Evolving International Legal Framework

Arianna Visconti

Abstract Trafficking in cultural property has long been considered mostly a social, economic and cultural problem, instead of a proper criminal one. Only at the turn of the century the focus really started shifting on the need for penal suppression. This chapter, after a brief analysis of the reasons behind this delay, including the 'grey' (not 'black') nature of the international market in artworks and antiquities, will focus on the most recent developments in international and EU law aimed at preventing and combating cultural property trafficking, as well as on the reasons that prompted this significant change in attitude by both national and international policymakers.

1 Introduction

Theft, looting and, in general, trafficking in artworks and antiquities is a phenomenon likely as ancient as human society itself, as security measures adopted by Egyptian builders to defend against tomb robbing as far back as the Early Dynastic Period (c. 3150–c. 2613 BCE), or the relief from the Arch of Titus showing the spoils of Jerusalem being carried triumphantly to Rome after the sack of 70 CE, clearly testify. The combination of economic, artistic and symbolic value[1] typical of these particular objects has traditionally made them a marker of high social status and explains why they have always been coveted by rulers, conquerors, the wealthy and the powerful. While grave-robbing and theft were usually considered as crimes even in ancient times, attitudes about war booty or the looting of monuments and necropoleis of extinguished or 'alien' civilizations have been quite permissive for most of human history.

[1] See e.g. Forrest (2010), pp. 3–13.

A. Visconti (✉)
Department of Private and Public Economics Law, Università Cattolica del Sacro Cuore, Milan, Italy
e-mail: arianna.visconti@unicatt.it

V. Militello, A. Spena (eds.), *The Challenges of Illegal Trafficking in the Mediterranean Area*, Legal Studies in International, European and Comparative Criminal Law 9, https://doi.org/10.1007/978-3-031-45399-1_12

A real care for ancient remains and artworks, also in the form of embryonic and fragmented protective legislation, started to emerge with the advent of Humanism and the Renaissance,[2] with the Papal States taking a leading role since the Fifteenth Century.[3] Later on, with the advent of the Enlightenment,[4] scholars such as Antoine Chrysostome Quatremère de Quincy[5] affirmed the importance of preserving artworks and ancient remains to the benefit not only of the countries and populations possessing them, but, more broadly, based on the universal value of civilization and the principle of *fraternité*, of the whole humankind. Quatremère de Quincy also stressed the intrinsic harm caused to an artwork or antiquity by removing it from its context, be it by way of trade or of looting, thus also strongly opposing the Napoleonic practice of plundering conquered countries and bringing such prized war spoils to France, to add to the grandeur of the Republic and, later, of the Empire (often under a varnish of legitimacy provided by peace treaties such as the one of Tolentino).[6]

Following the fall of Napoleon and the Restoration, the 1815 mission of Antonio Canova in France, which resulted in the recovery of most (albeit not all) the heritage taken from Italy, as well as the ensuing restitution by the Papal States themselves, for reasons of consistency, of a large number of manuscripts taken in 1622 from the Palatine Library of Heidelberg University and donated, the year after, to Pope Gregory XV, helped consolidate a general principle according to which cultural property looting in wartime should be considered prohibited and, when enacted, should give rise to a right to see the artworks returned after the end of hostilities.[7] It must however be observed how such principles were never extended to countries and populations outside the Western world: actually, the very same decades which saw the progressive emergence of an international humanitarian law aimed at mitigating the consequences of war for Western civilians, civilian property, and cultural heritage,[8] also saw a significant further expansion of European colonialism and, with it, the theoretical as well as practical exclusion of 'uncivilized' peoples from the horizon of this slowly developing new set of principles.[9]

---

[2] See R O'Keefe (2006), pp. 5–8.

[3] First with the 1462 *Cum almam nostrum Urbem Bull* by Pope Pius II, and subsequently with the 1474 *Cum provida Bull* by Pope Sistus IV; in 1686 Pope Innocent XI forbade, with the so-called *Editto Altieri*, any export of artworks or antiquities from the Papal States except in case of governmental permission. See e.g. Haskell (1981); Borio di Tigliole (2018), pp. 3–9.

[4] See R O'Keefe (2006), pp. 8–17.

[5] See Quatremère de Quincy (1815) (first edition 1796), in particular pp. 3–87. For an analysis of the lasting influence of Quatremère de Quincy's work see also Scovazzi (2011), pp. 344–347.

[6] *Traité de paix entre la République française, représentée par le général Bonaparte, et le pape Pie VI.* Acte donné à Tolentino, 19 February 1797, in particular art. XIII. See also Scovazzi (2011), pp. 343–344.

[7] See further Scovazzi (2011), pp. 347–350, who also remarks on the fact that the States which had defeated Napoleonic France «refrained from looting the looter».

[8] See also R O'Keefe (2020).

[9] See broadly e.g. Van Beurden (2017).

First attempts to codify said principles into international law were made by the end of the Nineteenth Century and the beginning of the Twentieth, with the 1899 and 1907 Hague Conventions on the laws and customs of war.[10] The considerable destruction and displacement of cultural property during World War I, albeit followed by the provision of restitution obligations in the ensuing peace treaties,[11] proved the weakness of this legal framework, so that, in the following decades, the League of Nations promoted several attempts to provide stronger protection to cultural heritage, both in wartime and in peacetime, none of which, however, came to fruition before World War II erupted.[12]

In the aftermath of a conflict which resulted (also) in the most massive destruction and looting of cultural heritage ever recorded in human history, renewed efforts were made to strengthen international humanitarian law rules specifically aimed at the protection of artworks and antiquities in times of war;[13] efforts which eventually succeeded with the adoption, in 1954, of the Hague Convention for the Protection of Cultural Property in the Event of Armed Conflict (henceforth 1954 Hague Convention).[14] However, the need to add a separate and specific Protocol (henceforth First Protocol),[15] which could be optionally signed, or not, by States Parties to the Convention, shows how the issues related to the removal and international circulation of movable (or mobilized) items of cultural property, its regulation, and possible remedies to illegitimate acts, were destined to remain amongst the thorniest ones.

Subsequently, only after long and complex negotiations the United Nations Educational, Scientific and Cultural Organization (UNESCO)[16] was able to adopt, in 1970, a Convention on the Means of Prohibiting and Preventing the Illicit Import,

---

[10] Convention (II) with Respect to the Laws and Customs of War on Land and its annex: Regulations concerning the Laws and Customs of War on Land, The Hague, 29 July 1899, in force 4 September 1900 (see in particular arts 28, 47 and 56); Convention (IV) respecting the Laws and Customs of War on Land and its annex: Regulations concerning the Laws and Customs of War on Land. The Hague, 18 October 1907, in force 26 January 1910 (see in particular arts 27 and 56). See further, e.g., Toman (1996), pp. 10–13; R O'Keefe (2006), pp. 22–34; Forrest (2010), pp. 67–69. It is to be noticed that there is a general consensus amongst scholars on the idea that the practice of taking properties during military operations could not be considered a violation of international law prior to the adoption of these two treaties. On customary IHL rules specifically addressing the protection of cultural property in times of armed conflict see e.g. Forrest (2010), pp. 127–130; Francioni (2020).

[11] For further details see e.g. Scovazzi (2011), pp. 352–353.

[12] For a summary see e.g. Toman (1996), pp. 14–19; R O'Keefe (2006), pp. 35–61; Forrest (2010), pp. 69–73.

[13] See further e.g. Toman (1996), pp. 20–21; R O'Keefe (2006), pp. 61–91; Forrest (2010), pp. 73–76; Scovazzi (2011), pp. 353–355.

[14] Adopted on 14 May 1954, in force 7 August 1956, 249 UNTS 240. For a detailed analysis see e.g. Toman (1996), pp. 21 ff.; R O'Keefe (2006), pp. 92–195; Maugeri (2008), pp. 25–41; Forrest (2010), pp. 78–104.

[15] Protocol for the Protection of Cultural Property in the Event of Armed Conflict, The Hague, 14 May 1954, in force 7 August 1956, 249 UNTS 358, on which see further Toman (1996), pp. 331 ff.; R O'Keefe (2006), pp. 195–201; Forrest (2010), pp. 104–108.

[16] See broadly Vrdoljak and Meskell (2020).

Export and Transfer of Ownership of Cultural Property (henceforth 1970 UNESCO Convention),[17] aimed specifically at curbing the worldwide illicit trafficking in artworks, antiquities and collectibles. Nonetheless, for reasons that will be discussed below, this treaty proved to be less effective than it had been hoped, besides completely failing to address the issue of removals of cultural property in colonial times, which remains quite open and problematic today.[18] As, anyway, the issue of 'historical depredations' (such as Nazi looting of artworks and antiquities[19] and colonial takings) is beyond the scope of this analysis (also considering the strict non-retroactivity principle governing criminal law at both national and international level), this chapter will focus on present-day trafficking in cultural property and the international legal framework currently addressing it.

The discussion will start with a brief analysis of the main empirical features of this phenomenon, which have contributed to obscure for a long time its criminal dimension and which keep hindering today efforts aimed at preventing and suppressing it. We will then address the reasons behind the complete marginalization of criminal law[20] in the aforementioned 1970 UNESCO Convention and the focusing on private law issues of restitution in the ensuing complementary 1995 UNIDROIT Convention on stolen or illegally exported cultural objects (henceforth 1995 UNIDROIT Convention).[21] As the end of the Twentieth Century saw a shift in this paradigm and the emergence of a new awareness about the proper criminal dimension of trafficking in cultural property, the chapter will then discuss the reasons for this change in attitude, the role played by the United Nations Office on Drugs and Crime (UNODC) and by UNESCO itself through non-binding documents, and the main relevant provisions introduced firstly in international humanitarian law, and then in European Union law. The new push to criminalize offences against cultural heritage eventually culminated with the adoption of a proper, and at last viable, suppression treaty by the Council of Europe in 2017,[22] which will be discussed in some detail. Conclusively, we will try and provide an overview of ongoing progresses and remaining open questions in the international fight against trafficking in cultural property.

---

[17] Adopted in Paris on 14 November 1970, in force 24 April 1972, 823 UNTS 231. See further PJ O'Keefe (2007); Forrest (2010), pp. 166–196; Stamatoudi (2011), pp. 31–66.

[18] See e.g. Van Beurden (2018); Savoy (2022).

[19] On which see e.g. Redmond Cooper (2021).

[20] See also Manacorda (2011); Visconti (2021a).

[21] Adopted in Rome on 24 June 1995, in force 1 July 1998, 34 ILM 1322. See further Forrest (2010), pp. 196–219; Stamatoudi (2011), pp. 66–111; Prott (2021).

[22] Council of Europe Convention on Offences relating to Cultural Property, adopted in Nicosia on 19 May 2017, in force 1 April 2022, CETS No. 221 (henceforth 2017 Nicosia Convention). This treaty was preceded, as we will discuss, by an earlier attempt by the Council of Europe itself—the European Convention on Offences relating to Cultural Property, adopted in Delphi on 23 June 1985, ETS No. 119 (henceforth 1985 Delphi Convention)—which, however, never entered into force, having failed to achieve the minimum required number of three ratifications. See further Visconti (2015), pp. 275–276; Boister (2018), p. 225.

2 Trafficking in Cultural Property: A Criminological Overview

Till the very end of the Twentieth Century trafficking in cultural property was not commonly considered as a 'proper' criminal phenomenon. Concerns about it were mostly confined to international organizations charged with the preservation and enhancement of culture and cultural heritage, such as UNESCO, ICOM (the International Council of Museums) or ICOMOS (the International Council on Monuments and Sites), devoid of specific criminological and criminal law competences and of any mandate to address penal issues. The empirical study of this traffic was, in turn, basically the province of a small number of culture and preservation specialists and professionals—most of whom archaeologists, given the relevance of clandestine excavations and looting of archaeological sites in feeding the illicit trade in cultural objects, and the dramatic loss of not only important artworks and artefacts, but also of irretrievable and oft irreplaceable context information, which gets destroyed in the course of such unlawful and unprofessional searches.[23]

Notwithstanting this relevant harm to collective interests, the topic has nonetheless been long considered a niche one also amongst criminology and criminal law experts,[24] and the problem used to not alarm public opinion—not even in countries victims of significant depredation of their heritage. In truth, even nowadays, when the issue has achieved, as we will see, a certain worldwide consideration for its proper criminal dimension, it remains the province of a comparatively small number of researchers and scholars, criminological analysis remains underfunded and mostly carried out through short-term and ad hoc programmes, and the subsequent unavoidable poor understanding of the organization and working of this illicit trade ends up undermining effective criminal policy formulation and implementation.[25]

Even with this necessary premise, there are some few conclusions, based on existing research and data, about the main features and causes of trafficking in cultural property, which it is possible and, actually, necessary to draw in view of an informed discussion of existing international legal instruments and trends.

2.1 Transnational Dimension, Dark Figure, and the Grey Market

Firstly, trafficking in cultural property has always been transnational in nature, driven by a demand coming from countries comparatively poor in cultural heritage, but rich in resources to be spent in its acquisition and, thus, resulting, on balance, net

[23] See e.g. Brodie (2006).

[24] See also Chappell and Hufnagel (2019), pp. 3–6.

[25] See further Mackenzie (2009); Brodie et al. (2022).

importers of artworks and antiquities (so-called 'market States'). Said demand meets with an 'offer' from usually poorer, often underdeveloped, countries, which are however quite rich in cultural items and which thus result in being (mostly unwilling) net exporters (so-called 'source countries'). In-between, the so called transit countries are those which—like Switzerland, the United Kingdom, Hong Kong etc.—perform the role of hubs in the international market of artworks and antiquities, importing and (re)exporting a significant amount of cultural property, sometimes also easing the (apparent or effective) 'legalisation' of items of unlawful provenance, thanks to 'favourable' rules about time limitations, acquisitive prescription, position of a 'good faith' purchaser, and so on.[26]

The distinction between 'source' and 'market' States, albeit conceptually useful to distinguish between countries with very different interests in (and thus also, usually, very different models of regulation of) the trade in cultural property, should, however, not be over-emphasized. As stated above, artworks and antiquities are attractive not only for their aesthetic or historic value, but also because of their rarity, or even uniqueness, and of the social status which goes with their possession. Thus it is actually *comparative* scarcity what drives the transnational movement of cultural 'goods': Italy[27] or China[28] provide a good example of this, as they are traditionally, and with good reason, considered source countries par excellence, having long been victims of extensive looting and smuggling of their national heritages, but at the same time they represent also flourishing markets for imported 'exotic' cultural items.

Generally speaking, crimes against cultural property include a wide range of offences, as diverse as art and antiquities thefts, looting of archaeological sites, frauds and forgeries, acts of vandalism or iconoclasm, as well as illicit import and export of cultural objects, receiving and laundering of 'tainted' items, etc.[29] Notwithstanding the increasing efforts made in recent decades to try and assess the real extent of illicit dealings in cultural property,[30] at present it remains true that «there are no reliable statistics describing either the material volume or monetary value of

[26] On this distinction see further, e.g., Merryman (1986); Mackenzie (2005), in particular pp. 8–88; Forrest (2010), pp. 136–140; Mackenzie et al. (2020), in particular pp. 1–39.

[27] As testified by the number of cultural objects of unlawful foreign provenance (mostly coming from Asia, Middle Eastern countries, and South America) frozen by the Carabinieri Command for the Protection of Cultural Heritage (the specialized police unit instituted in 1969, which also keeps detailed and specific criminal statistics about offences against cultural heritage) and returned yearly to their countries of origin. See e.g. Carabinieri (2020), according to which, in 2019, 594 ex voto paintings were returned to Mexico, 796 archaeological items were returned to China, and two ancient books were returned to European countries.

[28] See Huo (2015), pp. 11–12.

[29] For a general overview see e.g. Conklin (1994); Alder and Polk (2007); Durney and Proulx (2011); Passas and Bowman Proulx (2011); as well as, broadly, Hufnagel and Chappell (2019).

[30] See, amongst others, Mackenzie (2005), pp. 10–14; Fisman and Wei (2009); Ní Chonaill et al. (2011); Brodie et al. (2013); Sargent et al. (2020).

the trade»;[31] nor, therefore, do we have any factual basis for the (frequently heard) claim that trafficking in cultural property is the third or fourth most large illicit trafficking.[32] This lack of precise knowledge and reliable data reflects structural features of the traffic in cultural property and, more broadly, of the art and antiquities market, and it is therefore intimately connected to enduring problems in its prevention and repression.[33]

The causes of the present huge dark figure (i.e., the number of offences which are actually committed, but never reported or otherwise discovered) of cultural heritage crime are many. Firstly, quite often cultural property disappears from unregistered and/or unmonitored sites, its very existence unknown to the authorities. Secondly, the art and antiquities market, albeit legal per se (and thus not a 'black market', differently from what happens with other kinds of transnational traffic), is intrinsically opaque, so much so that it is commonly defined as a 'grey market', with a licit and an illicit dimension strictly interwoven.[34]

The subculture of this market is a fundamental component of its 'greyness', as it mostly follows a 'don't ask, don't tell' policy, where even subjects not actively involved in the traffic too often turn a blind eye on suspicious goods, and forget to ask the right questions about provenance and ownership. In fact, the ingrained practice of confidentiality about deals and the people involved in them,[35] together with an (only recently and very slowly evolving) rather cavalier attitude towards provenance information,[36] traditionally eases the circulation on the market of both genuine objects of unlawful provenance and of fakes and forgeries,[37] and has even given rise to increasing concerns about money laundering opportunities.[38]

---

[31] Brodie (2011a), p. 411.

[32] See also Calvani (2009) pp. 29–30: «It is very difficult to gain an exact idea of how many items of cultural property are stolen throughout the world and it is unlikely that there will ever be any accurate statistics. National statistics are often based on the circumstances of the theft (petty theft, theft by breaking and entering or armed robbery), rather than the type of object stolen. To illustrate this, every year, the Interpol General Secretariat asks all member countries for statistics on theft of works of art, information on where the thefts took place, and the nature of the stolen objects. On average, we receive 60 replies a year (*out of 187 member countries*), some of which are incomplete or inform us that no statistics exist (difficulties in comparison of available data *collected in different countries*)». According to the last available report (INTERPOL 2021) the situation has not improved much, as only 72 countries provided the requested data. For a critical evaluation of often repeated 'figures' about cultural property trafficking see also Balcells (2019).

[33] See also Brodie et al. (2022).

[34] See e.g. Bowman (2008); Lane et al. (2008), pp. 250–257; Massy (2008); Tijhuis (2011); Mackenzie and Yates (2016).

[35] Which has induced some authors to consider that of the art and antiquity market a 'culture of secrecy': see Renfrew (2000); Mackenzie (2011a), p. 141.

[36] See also Mackenzie (2005), in particular pp. 23–62 and 157 ff.; Gerstenblith (2019); Gerstenblith (2020).

[37] See further, e.g., Naylor (2008); Mackenzie and Davis (2014); Malnati (2018).

[38] See e.g. Van Duyne et al. (2015); Hardy (2020). It is worth mentioning that Directive (EU) 2018/843 of the European Parliament and of the Council of 30 May 2018 amending Directive (EU) 2015/

Actually, the scenario we have just sketched not only increases the opportunities for cultural property crime and trafficking, but also provides potential and actual offenders with a wide range of very effective neutralizations[39] and helps maintaining the varnish of social prestige and positive reputation which, in turn, contributes to keeping the less savoury aspects of the trade largely below the radar of public opinion and policymakers both.[40]

Even the fragmented and partial data we have to rely on, however, appear to justify the overall conclusion reached by some empirical studies, according to which a significant share of the antiquities currently traded on the market, or appearing in catalogues of museums, collections, and the like, are of illicit or, at best, dubious provenance.[41] All in all, cultural property trafficking appears to be a widespread phenomenon,[42] which, albeit almost impossible to measure in quantitative terms (exact number of stolen, looted or smuggled artefacts, and their market value), causes major harms to cultural heritage worldwide, due to the related loss of unique items, context information, and irretrievable historical, anthropological and scientific knowledge.

2.2 *Intersections with White-Collar Crime, Organized Crime, and Terrorism*

The transnational and intrinsically opaque nature of the art and antiquities market, and the related difficulties in discovering, investigating, and prosecuting offences

849 on the prevention of the use of the financial system for the purposes of money laundering or terrorist financing (OJ L 156, henceforth Fifth Money Laundering Directive) expanded the scope of application of EU AML rules in the art and antiquities market beyond «high value dealers» to any «persons trading or acting as intermediaries in the trade of works of art, including when this is carried out by art galleries and auction houses, where the value of the transaction or a series of linked transactions amounts to 10.000 € or more», independently on the payment method (art. 1(1)(c)(i)).

[39] The expression 'techniques of neutralization' is used by criminologists to define a set of strategies by which people who commit illicit or deviant acts temporarily neutralize those internal restraints which would normally keep them from such actions (Sykes and Matza (1957)). For an empirical analysis of the techniques of neutralization most commonly used in the art and antiquities market see Mackenzie (2005), pp. 205–226; Brodie (2021).

[40] See also Mackenzie (2011a).

[41] See e.g. Gill and Chippindale (1993); Chippindale and Gill (2000); Brodie et al. (2013), pp. 23–25.

[42] Even if they represent only the proverbial 'tip of the iceberg', the last available data by INTERPOL (2021) paint a dark picture: in 2020 a total of 35.749 artworks and antiquities were reported as stolen worldwide (and the fact that European countries appear to be the most affected, with 27.710 items, basically confirms the bias in criminal statistics due to systematic underreporting or complete lack of data in many countries); reported illicit excavations worldwide amounted to 2.042; cultural objects of unlawful origin (possibly years or even decades old) seized by law enforcement agencies worldwide amounted to 857.742.

against cultural property, highlight how cultural property trafficking shares some significant traits with white-collar crime.[43]

Firstly, in the international chain of traffic, the links following the theft, pillage or looting of cultural property, and its immediate smuggling, are generally «committed by a person of respectability and high social status» in the course of their legitimate occupation,[44] that is by dealers in antiquities and works of art, gallerists, auctioneers, etc. (with all the related problems of 'double standard' at both regulatory and enforcement level),[45] who are also the ones making the most money from the trafficking itself. Besides, these offences are often interwoven with many other typically 'white-collar' ones, namely corruption[46] (for instance to ease the illicit export from countries of origin where sometimes corruption and bribery are endemic),[47] tax evasion, and money laundering (since cultural objects are eminently valuable and portable).[48]

Since the 1990s, besides, growing concerns about the possible involvement of organized crime in the illicit trade in cultural property started to emerge in the international community. The timing coincides with the drafting and negotiation of the United Nation Convention against Transnational Organized Crime[49] (henceforth UNTOC), which marked a generalized increase in the attention paid to organized crime worldwide; besides, an assumption started to circulate, about the attractiveness of cultural property trafficking for organized criminal groups, given its profitability, the lower risks of discovery and sanctioning, the possibility to take advantage of existing transnational smuggling rings and logistics used for other traffics (such as drugs, weapons, human beings etc.).

As a consequence, international organizations have increasingly taken for granted a significant involvement of such criminal organizations in cultural property trafficking,[50] which is also one of the main reasons for the growing interest in the subject

---

[43] See e.g. Alder and Polk (2007), pp. 347–356; Mackenzie (2005), pp. 193–226; Mackenzie (2011a).

[44] EH Sutherland (1983), p. 7.

[45] See specifically, e.g., Mackenzie (2005), in particular pp. 193–226; Mackenzie (2011a); Mackenzie and Davis (2014), p. 156; Balcells (2015); Mackenzie et al. (2020), in particular pp. 77–114.

[46] See e.g. Alder and Polk (2007), p. 352; Brodie et al. (2000), pp. 16–17; Lane et al. (2008), p. 251.

[47] Empirical studies have evidenced a correlation between (estimated) rates of illicit export of cultural properties and the level of corruption in the exporting country as measured by survey-based indexes: see Fisman and Wei (2009), pp. 88–95.

[48] See Bowman (2008), pp. 231–232, and note 38, above.

[49] Adopted by resolution A/RES/55/25 of 15 November 2000 at the fifty-fifth session of the General Assembly of the United Nations, New York, Doc A/55/383, in force 29 September 2003, 2225 UNTS 209. See broadly Boister 2018, pp. 126–145.

[50] See e.g. ECOSOC Resolution 2004/34 and ECOSOC Resolution 2008/23, both on Protection against Trafficking in Cultural Property; ECOSOC Resolution 2010/19, on Crime Prevention and Criminal Justice Responses to Protect Cultural Property, Especially with Regard to its Trafficking; ECOSOC Resolution 2011/42, on Strengthening Crime Prevention and Criminal Justice Responses to Protect Cultural Property, Especially with Regard to its Trafficking; and finally the Resolution of the same title adopted by the UN General Assembly at its 89th plenary meeting, on 19 December

and the recent push towards a greater criminalization of offences against cultural heritage, including by making an increasing use of UNTOC in this field.[51] Considering, however, the aforementioned gaps in available empirical knowledge, which are even more significant in a field (the analysis of organized crime) which traditionally suffers of a number of research difficulties (including a never-ending definitional debate) of its own,[52] a slightly more cautious approach appears worth recommending.[53]

From a precautionary perspective, there is certainly reason to assume this market as extremely attractive for organized criminal groups. As Mackenzie[54] notes, «antiquities are a relatively scarce commodity» which can command «high prices» and, at the same time, they are both generally easy to appropriate, due to the «low or non-existent levels of security at local sites», and «relatively portable» (all factors which may fuel the supply side of the market); on the other hand, the demand appears steadily high in traditional market countries; also, the level of market regulation can be extremely low, and law enforcement appears often defective. All of this contributes to make the antiquities market «a high risk market in terms of opportunities presented to organised criminals» (be they traditional organized criminal groups, or networks constituted *ad hoc* for the purposes of exploiting a vulnerable cultural heritage).[55] More broadly, cultural property trafficking generally requires the involvement of a plurality of subjects (thieves and looters, smugglers, receivers and facilitators, traders, buyers) and, thus, at least a minimum of organization;[56] besides, as observed, it is a typically transnational phenomenon.

On the other hand, however, we still lack reliable data about the actual involvement of 'traditional' organized criminal groups, and «while there are many features that the illicit traffic in antiquities seems to share with other forms of organized crime, there are a number of features that immediately stamp this traffic as different»—mainly, the possibility of building a very profitable traffic with a really minimal amount of organization, as well as the great asymmetry between the source and market sides of the trafficking (with the illegality, and occasional violence, almost entirely on the side of the former, and a largely legitimate trade on the side of

---

2011 (A/RES/66/180), which all express alarm at «the growing involvement of organized criminal groups in all aspects of trafficking in cultural property».

[51] See also Sect. 3.2, below.

[52] See in particular Dietzler (2013).

[53] See also Manacorda and Chappell (2011), pp. 3–5.

[54] Mackenzie (2011b), pp. 76–80.

[55] Also, recent studies have shown the existence of some kind of overlapping between areas of flourishing drug industry and archaeologically rich sites, and it's quite possible that, in regions traditionally characterized by a heavy territorial control by organized criminal groups, looters couldn't operate without at least an implicit consent by said groups. For an overview see Bowman (2008), pp. 230–232.

[56] See e.g. Polk (2000); Chappell and Polk (2011); Alderman (2012); Campbell (2013); Dietzler (2013); Polk and Chappell (2019); Sargent et al. (2020), in particular p. 87.

the latter).[57] Thus, when speaking of trafficking in cultural property, «the term "organized" refers largely to networks whose task is to handle the numerous changes that take place from the time of the theft (or the clandestine excavation) to the time the objects reach the final users (major collectors, museums, art institutions, etc.); while these networks have coordinated activities and even use the same channels, this does not necessarily denote the involvement of "traditional" criminal associations and even less so the presence of a "Mafia"».[58]

This preliminary evidence should certainly suggest an increase in national and international authorities' commitment to the prevention and suppression of cultural property trafficking, including, when needed, through a more incisive use of criminal law, but, at the same time, it does not appear enough to support recurring invocations for 'emergency policies'.[59] A consensus might instead be reached[60] on the fact that the kind of transnational criminal networks involved in this traffic do often satisfy the loose definition of «organized criminal group» adopted by UNTOC[61] and might thus justify advocacy for its application, whenever appropriate.

Finally, by the beginning of the new century, after the 2001 and 2005 terrorist attacks against, respectively, the US and UK, and following the extensive ensuing conflicts and unrest in the Middle-East, with their consequent large-scale destruction and scattering of cultural property, a new concern entered the political debate:[62] the idea that trafficking in looted antiquities can be used to finance terrorist groups and armed militias.[63]

From a criminological perspective, it must be admitted that we have even less hard evidence of links between cultural property trafficking and terrorism[64] than we have about the involvement of Mafia-like criminal groups. When it comes to the financing of terrorism and civil wars, we can only rely on correlations (increased

---

[57] Chappell and Polk (2011), pp. 103–106 (quote at p. 104).

[58] Nistri (2011), p. 184.

[59] See also Manacorda (2011), p. 23.

[60] See e.g. Chappell and Polk (2011), p. 103; Alderman (2012), pp. 604–605; Dietzler (2013), p. 339; Borgstede (2014).

[61] Art 2(a) defines an organized criminal group as «a structured group of three or more persons, existing for a period of time and acting in concert with the aim of committing one or more serious crimes or offences established in accordance with [the] Convention, in order to obtain, directly or indirectly, a financial or other material benefit»; art 2(c) defines a «structured group» as «a group that is not randomly formed for the immediate commission of an offence and that does not need to have formally defined roles for its members, continuity of its membership or a developed structure».

[62] See UN Security Council Resolution S/RES/1267 (1999) (Afghan conflict); UN Security Council Resolution S/RES/2195 (2014) (on terrorism in Africa); UN Security Council Resolution S/RES/2199 (2015); UN Security Council Resolution S/RES/2322 (2016); UN Security Council Resolution S/RES/2347 (2017). See also the Preamble of the 2017 Nicosia Convention.

[63] See e.g. Schindler and Gautier (2019).

[64] UN Security Council, Twenty-third report of the Analytical Support and Sanctions Monitoring Team submitted pursuant to resolution 2368 (2017) concerning ISIL (Da'esh), Al-Qaida and associated individuals and entities, 15 January 2019, S/2019/50, p. 19; see also Dehouck (2019), pp. 17–21.

archaeological looting in territories affected by war and controlled by armed paramilitary groups),[65] as well as on some historical well documented examples (like the final stages of the Khmer Rouge guerrilla rule in Cambodia).[66]

This is not to say that present concerns, albeit possibly exaggerated,[67] are totally unfounded. On the contrary, the very 'gray' nature of the art and antiquities market, with its lack of transparency, traditional and heavy 'pollution' by objects of illicit or questionable provenance, mingling of legal and illegal actors, and lack of regulatory consistency amongst States, makes it, in general terms, the perfect 'crossroad' for very different criminal typologies, from smuggling to insurance fraud, from tax evasion to money laundering, from bribery to financial fraud,[68] and thus also attractive to organized and terrorist groups. What remains, however, presently impossible to assess is the extent to which cultural property trafficking does actually contribute to the financing of terrorist groups, and how relevant the purpose of profiting from this traffic really is—when compared with ideological reasons and political strategies, as well as with the sheer amount of criminal opportunities provided by any situation of unrest—in influencing the destruction and scattering of cultural heritage in conflict zones.

2.3 Globalization, E-Commerce and New Online Criminal Networks

The development of a flourishing e-commerce of artworks and antiquities has caused a growth and acceleration in transactions, widening even further the transnational dimension which is intrinsic to this market, and consequently multiplying difficulties for national law enforcement agencies. And while the development of new technologies, such as apps based on image recognition software,[69] platforms that allow for

[65] See e.g. Brodie (2011b); Kila (2015), in particular pp. 182–194; Brodie (2018); Schindler and Gautier (2019), p. 332; ASOR 2020. The recent increase of Middle-Eastern antiquities on the international—and particularly on the digital—market, with a shift of the model of trade from «low-volume but high-cost objects to a trade which is higher in volume but lower in quality», is also considered consistent with the idea that trafficking is (also) financing local armed groups: see Polk and Chappell (2019), pp. 409–412.

[66] See Mackenzie and Davis (2014).

[67] For a critical analysis (which, however, supports the conclusion of an increase in illegal traffic of cultural objects from conflict areas) see Sargent et al. (2020).

[68] See also Adam (2017), in particular pp. 146–148 and 188–190.

[69] See e.g. the Italian Carabinieri's iTPC mobile app, (https://www.beniculturali.it/mibac/multimedia/MiBAC/documents/feed/pdf/Comunicato%20stampa%20iTPC-imported-44388.pdf, accessed 10 August 2023) or INTERPOL's ID Art mobile app (https://www.interpol.int/Crimes/Cultural-heritage-crime/ID-Art-mobile-app#:~:text=The%20ID%2DArt%20mobile%20app,objects%20from%20134%20member%20countries, accessed 10 August 2023). Both can be used also by the general public to check suspicious items against the respective databases of stolen or missing cultural property (*Banca dati dei beni illecitamente sottratti* and Stolen Works of Art

shared monitoring of the market,[70] or AI tools capable of recognizing items of suspicious origin based on 'red flags',[71] may provide new and effective investigative tools, issues of (lack of) jurisdiction, complexity of transnational investigative and judicial cooperation, gathering of evidence in view of prosecution and trial, seizure and confiscation of cultural property of unlawful origin, obviously multiply on this new global online market.

The increase in online sales appears significant and steady, and it involves both e-commerce websites following a consumer-to-consumer business model (such as eBay), and business-to-consumer platforms (e-galleries and online auctions); social networks and instant messaging apps have also proven to be a significant channel.[72] In fact, one peculiarity of online trafficking in cultural property appears striking. While «it is suspected that the darknet is being used to transact trafficked antiquities, [...] no evidence has been produced. One explanation may be that there is no need to use the darknet when trafficked antiquities can be sold openly on publicly accessible websites with seemingly little risk to the vendors».[73] The widespread online sale of illicit or at least suspicious artefacts seems thus to confirm once more the overall lack of public awareness about cultural property trafficking and its harmful implications, as well as the 'privileged' status of the art and antiquities market.

Worryingly, however, «online galleries and auction platforms», by «bring[ing] geographically distant buyers and sellers together in electronic space», «make it financially viable to trade in low-value and potentially high-volume material», meaning that «minor archaeological sites or cultural institutions, which previously may not have been worth looting and thus left intact by criminals, can now be viewed in a more lucrative light and targeted accordingly. The resultant trade in small, portable, and easy to conceal antiquities is less likely to make headlines than that in major works of ancient art, but it is more difficult to police and arguably more destructive to the historical record».[74] Besides, online auctions appear to take advantage of no or minimal provenance provisions:[75] actually, «on the internet poorly-provenanced and unprovenanced objects consistently command higher prices than objects with a pre-1970 provenance».[76] Thus, online sales and re-sales have the potential to offer a new and effective tool to provide antiquities of unlawful

Database), as well as to record their own artworks and antiquities according to a uniform inventorying standard in order to ease investigations in case of future theft or loss.

[70] See e.g. the CircArt Project (2018–2021), addressing trafficking in Egyptian and Sudanese antiquities: https://www.britishmuseum.org/our-work/departments/egypt-and-sudan/circulating-artefacts (accessed 10 August 2023).

[71] See e.g. the KIKU app being presently developed in Germany: Hickley (2021).

[72] See Brodie (2017); Al-Azm et al. (2019); ASOR (2020), pp. 15–17.

[73] Brodie (2017), p. 6.

[74] Brodie (2017), p. 5.

[75] See e.g. Brodie (2015); Mackenzie et al. (2020), p. 69.

[76] Mackenzie et al. 2020, p. 109; see further Brodie (2015).

origin with an appearance of legitimacy, as they produce, in a few, inexpensive and quick passages, a digital provenance paper trail.[77]

Finally, online sales also contribute feeding the illicit trafficking in antiquities looted from countries ravaged by armed conflicts and political instability, as recent reports have confirmed.[78] In particular, the immediacy of online exchanges appears to favour the development of 'loot to order', that is a practice where criminals offer large artefacts (e.g. mosaics, architectural elements, coffins) still *in situ* and find buyers before making the effort to remove the object.[79] Finally, the recent analysis of illicit trade in Middle-Eastern antiquities on social media groups has lent further credence to the hypothesis that terrorist and paramilitary groups use (also) cultural property trafficking as a way of financing their activities, as it revealed the involvement of individuals associated with Syrian-based groups like Hay'at Tahrir Al Sham (HTS), Hurras Al-Din, the Zinki Brigade and other non-Syrian based Al-Qaeda or Islamic State in Iraq and Syria (ISIS) affiliates.[80]

2.4 The Slow Evolution of International and EU Law towards Actual Criminalization of Offences Related to Trafficking

The increase in knowledge and, even more, concerns about trafficking in cultural property and its possible intersections with other forms of criminality, considered more serious and alarming, which we have outlined in the previous chapter, contributes to explain the reasons why, starting from the end of last century, a new trend emerged amongst national and international policymakers, promoting a larger use of criminal law provisions and penal sanctions in the prevention and suppression of offences against cultural heritage. A trend that we are now going to summarize with respect to the different branches of international law involved in cultural heritage regulation and protection.

2.4.1 The Failure of the 1954 Hague Convention and the Evolution of International Humanitarian Law

The specific rules for the protection of cultural property in times of armed conflict enacted with the 1954 Hague Convention focused mainly on the prevention of direct

[77] See also Fabiani and Marrone (2021).

[78] See e.g. Al-Azm et al. (2019); ASOR (2020), pp. 15–17.

[79] See Al-Azm et al. (2019).

[80] See Al-Azm et al. (2019).

and indirect harm caused by military operations,[81] while issues of possible dispersion remained, as already observed, to some extent marginal. Article 4(3) obliges State Parties «to prohibit, prevent and, if necessary, put a stop to any form of theft, pillage or misappropriation of, and any acts of vandalism directed against, cultural property», at least by their own troops (while it is contested whether the obligation also covers prevention of like actions by third parties, such as civilians or enemy militias),[82] and to «refrain from requisitioning movable cultural property situated in the territory of another High Contracting Party». However, the obligation «to prevent the exportation», in accordance to local national laws,[83] «from a territory occupied» is relegated into the aforementioned separate (First) Protocol, which got fewer ratifications, and at a slower rate.

Moreover, the 1954 Hague Convention and First Protocol do not provide for very demanding obligations of criminalization. In fact, the only norm that «comes within the punitive province»[84] is article 28, which requires contracting States to «take, within the framework of their ordinary criminal jurisdiction, all necessary steps to prosecute and impose penal or disciplinary sanctions upon those persons, of whatever nationality, who commit or order to be committed a breach» of the Convention. The provision fails to enumerate and detail specific criminal offences, thus leaving ample latitude for very different transpositions into national laws, besides being in itself too general and allowing for the use of disciplinary sanctions in the framework of military law.[85] As for the abovementioned export prohibition, paragraph III article 11(a) of the First Protocol rather generically requires States to «take all necessary measures to ensure [its] effective application», thus in fact leaving the Parties totally free to choose what kind of sanctions—if any—should be introduced to this effect.[86]

The Iran-Iraq conflict in the 1980s and the First Gulf War and the Balkan Wars of the 1990s highlighted the many shortcomings of the existing body of international humanitarian law[87] and thus provided a new push for a more intensive use of criminal law to prevent and punish also offences against cultural heritage in wartime,

---

[81] This is even more true for the specific rules introduced in 1977 in the corpus of Geneva Conventions, which only deal with intentional destructive attacks against «historic monuments, works of art or places of worship which constitute the cultural or spiritual heritage of peoples»: see arts 53 and 86(4)(d) of the Protocol I Additional to the Geneva Conventions of 12 August 1949, and relating to the Protection of Victims of International Armed Conflicts, (adopted 8 June 1977, in force 7 December 1978, 1125 UNTS 3, and art. 16 of the Protocol II Additional to the Geneva Conventions of 12 August 1949, and relating to the Protection of Victims of Non-International Armed Conflicts, adopted 8 June 1977, in force 7 December 1978, 1125 UNTS 609. See further Toman (1996), pp. 377–397; R O'Keefe (2006), pp. 202–233; Forrest (2010), pp. 108–110.

[82] See R O'Keefe (2006), pp. 132–133; Forrest (2010), pp. 91–92.

[83] See Toman (1996), p. 344; R O'Keefe (2006), p. 198; Forrest (2010), p. 105.

[84] Manacorda (2011), p. 27.

[85] See Manacorda (2011), p. 27.

[86] See Forrest (2010), p. 108.

[87] See e.g. Keane (2004), pp. 20–28; R O'Keefe (2006), pp. 236–240.

including, to some extent, actions capable of feeding international trafficking. While the 1998 Rome Statute instituting the International Criminal Court[88] had no immediate effect on the illicit trade, as it only provides for an offence of intentional attack against cultural property (article 8(2)(b)(ix) and 8(2)(e)(iv)),[89] the Second Protocol added in 1999 to the Hague Convention[90] encompasses a broader set of relevant penal provisions. In fact, it obliges contracting States to criminalize, amongst others, the «extensive [. . .] appropriation of cultural property» (art 15(1)(c)) and its «theft, pillage or misappropriation» (art 15(1)(e)). These behaviours are deemed «serious violations» of the Protocol,[91] and, differently from the 1954 Convention, each State Party is bound to «adopt such measures as may be necessary to establish [them] as criminal offences under its domestic law [. . .] and to make such offences punishable by appropriate penalties» (art 15(2)).

It must be however observed that other offences conducive to illicit trafficking in cultural property are subject to less stringent obligations of criminalization:[92] according to article 21, the contracting parties undertake to «suppress», when «committed intentionally», any «illicit export, other removal or transfer of ownership of cultural property from occupied territory in violation of the Convention or [the] Protocol», but they remain free to choose between «such legislative, administrative or disciplinary measures as may be necessary». Nonetheless, as concerns for the possible instrumentality of cultural property trafficking to financing of terrorism grew, several States (e.g. Italy,[93] Germany,[94] the United Kingdom[95]), when adopting implementing legislation, opted for introducing penal provisions and sanctions to suppress these offences, too.

[88] Statute of the International Criminal Court, adopted Rome, 17 July 1998, in force 1 July 2002, 2187 UNTS 90. See further e.g. Klamberg (2017).

[89] See specifically R O'Keefe (2006), pp. 331–232 and 343–344; Maugeri (2008), pp. 245–336; Hall (2018). In 2016 the Court issued the first conviction under art 8(2)(e)(iv): *The Prosecutor v. Ahmad Al Faqi Al Mahdi* (Judgement) ICC-01/12–01/15.

[90] Second Protocol to the Hague Convention for the Protection of Cultural Property in the Event of Armed Conflict, adopted 26 March 1999, in force 9 March 2004, 38 ILM (1999) 769. See Keane (2004), pp. 27–36; Forrest (2010), pp. 110–121.

[91] See R O'Keefe (2006), pp. 274–287; Manacorda (2011), pp. 28–29.

[92] See R O'Keefe (2006), pp. 287–288; Manacorda (2011), p. 29.

[93] Law n 45 of 16 April 2009, art 11 (punished with imprisonment).

[94] Act on the Protection of Cultural Property (KGSG) of 31 July 2016, arts 28(3), 32(1.2) and 83 (1.3 and 1.4), prohibition of import and placing on the market of cultural property removed due to an armed conflict in violation of sec I(1) of the First Protocol to the Hague Convention (sanction: imprisonment or a fine), and arts 21(3), 32(1.2) and 83(1.2), prohibition of export of cultural property previously unlawfully imported in Germany from a conflict zone (sanction: imprisonment or a fine). There are however no provisions directly punishing the illegal export from an occupied territory.

[95] Cultural Property (Armed Conflicts) Act 2017, art 17 (punished with imprisonment or a fine, or both).

Besides, the Model Law on the Protection of Cultural Property in the Event of Armed Conflict[96] developed by the ICRC Advisory Service on International Humanitarian Law in 2019 to support the implementation of the Second Protocol in common law jurisdictions, recommends the use of imprisonment or a fine as punishment for individuals guilty of illicit export, removal, or transfer of ownership of cultural property from an occupied territory (article 16(2)(a)); it also suggests the adoption of corporate liability for the same offences (to be punished with a fine: article 16(2)(b) and (3)) and recommends the adoption of said criminal law provisions even in case the State is only party to the 1954 Convention and First Protocol (note 34).

2.4.2 The Inadequacy of International Regulation of the Transnational Circulation of Cultural Objects and the Renewed Efforts by UNESCO and UNODC

In the wake of the extensive decolonization process started after World War II, several source countries began expressing a need for a transnational response to the illicit trade.[97] Eventually, after long and difficult negotiations,[98] the abovementioned 1970 UNESCO Convention was adopted, with the purpose of providing minimum shared public law rules on the international circulation of cultural property. In truth, however, the extremely different interests and positions of the negotiating States[99] led to a not-so-workable compromise.[100] Even in recent years, despite an increase in ratifications by market States, this Convention cannot be considered to have bridged the gap between strict (but often quite ineffective in practice) protectionist legislations in source countries, and the liberal approach prevailing in most importing States, which favour minimum, or no, import barriers, 'light' regulation on circulation, short time limitations, extended protection for 'good faith' possessors, and no specific criminal law provisions.[101]

In addition to a large body of provisions on social, educational, civil, economic, and institutional measures, and others referring to international cooperation, the 1970 UNESCO Convention binds States Parties to consider «illicit» any «import, export or transfer of ownership of cultural property effected contrary to the provisions adopted under [the] Convention» (article 3), which sets an obligation (article 6(b)) of prohibiting exportation of cultural objects «unless accompanied by the [...] export certificate» provided for in article 6(a). Parties are also required (article 7(b)

---

[96] Online at https://www.icrc.org/en/document/protection-cultural-property-event-armed-conflict-model-law (accessed 10 August 2023).

[97] See also Forrest (2010), pp. 131–135.

[98] See also R O'Keefe (2006), pp. 7–8.

[99] See Abramson and Huttler (1973).

[100] See R O'Keefe (2006), p. 7; Forrest (2010), p. 167.

[101] See also Merryman (1995); Posner 2007; Blake (2015), pp. 12–22.

(i)) «to prohibit the import of cultural property stolen from a museum or a religious or secular public monument or similar institution in another State Party [. . .], provided that such property is documented as appertaining to the inventory of that institution» (export restrictions are thus far more stringent than limitations to importing).[102] Finally, contracting States have to oblige antique dealers to keep a register of traded objects, complete with information on provenance, and to inform the purchaser of possible export prohibitions (article 10(a)).

Each of these provisions must be backed up by sanctions, but the Convention leaves it to each contracting State's discretion to decide between criminal or administrative ones (articles 8 and 10(a)). On the whole, «the fulcrum of the system controlling the illicit circulation of cultural assets lies [. . .] in instruments of an administrative or private law nature [. . .], even when the transfer itself involved acts of penal significance, such as theft»,[103] and the 1970 UNESCO Convention has therefore been rightly considered as marginalizing criminal law as a tool to fight illicit trafficking in cultural property.[104]

A quick comparative glance[105] demonstrates, in fact, a wide range of different approaches to criminalization of, respectively, unlawful export and unlawful import by contracting States. While some of them (like the US) did not even adopt a specific implementing legislation,[106] or opted for very limited and specific implementing provisions (like the UK),[107] others chose to criminalize only unlawful export (like

[102] At least in the interpretation and implementation of the 1970 UNESCO Convention which prevails in market States: see Forrest (2010), pp. 176–181.

[103] Manacorda (2011), p. 32.

[104] The same approach to criminalization is to be found also in the later UNESCO Convention on the Protection of the Underwater Cultural Heritage, adopted 2 November 2001, in force 2 January 2009, 41 ILM 40, whose main purpose is to offer tailored protection to cultural property to be found on seabed. Art. 14 mandates contracting parties to «take measures to prevent the entry into their territory, the dealing in, or the possession of, underwater cultural heritage illicitly exported and/or recovered», where recovery was contrary to the Convention itself; when it comes to enforcement, art. 17(1), while requesting States Parties to impose sanctions for violations of measures taken to implement the 2001 Convention itself, only requires said sanctions to be «adequate in severity to be effective in securing compliance with [the] Convention and to discourage violations wherever they occur». Contracting States are thus completely free to opt for the use of administrative sanctions. See also PJ O'Keefe (2002), pp. 111–112.

[105] See R O'Keefe (2006), pp. 98 ff.; for an updated overview, more specifically focused on comparison of penal legislations, see also Manacorda and Visconti (2024).

[106] As the 1983 Convention on Cultural Property Implementation Act (CPIA), 19 US Code §§ 2601–2613, made very limited additions to domestic law and contains no specific penal provisions. See also Fincham (2007); Nafziger (2010), pp. 766–767; Gerstenblith (2016).

[107] See in particular the Dealing in Cultural Objects (Offences) Act 2003.

Spain,[108] India,[109] China,[110] Egypt,[111] as well as, till 2016, France[112] and, till 2022, Italy),[113] while others yet (such as Canada,[114] Cambodia,[115] Algeria,[116] Australia[117] and, more recently, Germany)[118] adopted an approach of equal criminalization of both unlawful export and unlawful import, thus revealing how different positions in the international market of art and antiquities, as well as, in some instances, different internal legal 'traditions', keep influencing the actual implementation of the alleged 'uniform' public law standards provided by the 1970 UNESCO Convention, especially (albeit not only) in penal matters.

Later efforts by UNESCO focused, through a cooperation with the United Nations International Institute for the Unification of Private Law (UNIDROIT), mostly on issues of recovery of trafficked cultural property, that the 1970 UNESCO Convention was structurally unable to properly address. This led to the adoption of the 1995 UNIDROIT Convention on Stolen or Illegally Exported Cultural Objects, conceived as complementary to the 1970 UNESCO Convention, with the specific purpose of introducing minimum uniform private law rules to address issues of restitution and return.[119] This treaty, albeit aimed at contributing to the fight against illicit trafficking in cultural property, can have only a very indirect effect in this respect: its own Preamble acknowledges that its «implementation [...] should be accompanied by other effective measures for protecting cultural objects», amongst

---

[108] See the Law n 16 of 25 June 1985 on Spanish Historic Heritage, and related amendments.

[109] See the 1972 Antiquities and Art Treasures Act.

[110] See the 1982 Law on Protection of Cultural Relics, and related amendments, as well as the Chinese Penal Code. See further Huo (2015).

[111] See Law n 117 of 1983, amended by Law n 3 of 2010 (Antiquities Protection Law).

[112] See the Cultural Heritage Code (*Code du patrimoine*) 2004, and related amendments; in particular, with Law n 925 of 7 July 2016 arts L111-8 and L111-9 were introduced, prohibiting, respectively, import of cultural objects from a State party to the 1970 Convention in the absence of an export certificate (when required by the law of said country), and import, export, transportation of, or any dealing in, cultural objects illicitly exported from a country according to a UN Security Council resolution. Infringements are punished with the same sanctions applicable to unlawful exports (art. L114-1(I)).

[113] See Lgs. Decree n. 42 of 22 January 2004 (Cultural Heritage Code), and related amendments, and the comprehensive reform of Italian cultural heritage criminal law enacted with Law n 22 of 9 March 2022, which introduced a new felony of unlawful import in art. 518 decies Penal Code (punished with a less serious penalty than unlawful export, presently art. 518 undecies Penal Code). This reform was directly influenced by both Regulation EU 2019/880 and the 2017 Nicosia Convention, which are discussed below.

[114] See the 1985 Cultural Property Export and Import Act (CPEIA).

[115] See the 1996 Law on the Protection of Cultural Heritage (LPCH). While it provides an outline of the strategy adopted by the country, its actual scope of application is influenced by several layers of often overlapping implementing regulations (not accessible in translation). See Carrano (2010).

[116] See the comprehensive 1998 Law for the Protection of Cultural Heritage.

[117] See the Protection of Movable Cultural Heritage Act 11/1986 (PMCHA).

[118] See arts 31–39, 40–47 and 85–86 KGSG (note 94, above).

[119] See note 21, above; see also Prott (1996).

which, however, meaningfully penal tools are not mentioned, and it will therefore not be the subject of further discussion here.

As previously mentioned, a real change in attitudes and pace emerged only in the 2000s and, even more, 2010s. In particular, UNODC started being directly involved in the development of new strategies to combat trafficking in cultural property. A first line of intervention focused on the employment of UNTOC in this field,[120] given the large number of ratifications of the treaty. The idea of a specific additional Protocol was discarded, due to the difficulty in re-mobilizing the international community over an issue still perceived as marginal by many States.[121] The path actually taken was to encourage and support UNTOC contracting parties in employing this treaty to tackle criminal offences against cultural property.[122] This was to be done particularly by inviting them to make such offences into «serious crimes» in the meaning of article 2(b) UNTOC, thus for the States Parties to make them punishable «by a maximum deprivation of liberty of at least four years or a more serious penalty», in order to bring them («where the offence is transnational in nature and involves an organized criminal group»: article 3(1)), within the UNTOC's scope of application. This, in turn, would make available for use UNTOC provisions concerning, amongst others, criminalization and other measures against laundering of proceeds of crime, seizure and confiscation, extradition, special investigative techniques, and measures to enhance the transfer of evidence and cooperation with law enforcement authorities.

A recommendation to this effect is also present in the second tool developed under the auspices of UNODC: the International Guidelines for Crime Prevention and Criminal Justice Responses with Respect to Trafficking in Cultural Property and Other Related Offences, adopted by the UN General Assembly on 18 December 2014 with Resolution 69/196.[123] Albeit not binding in nature (or, rather, because of this), the Guidelines have the potential to be a useful instrument for the improvement of national criminal laws and their harmonization (guidelines 15–27), and the development of further bilateral or multilateral agreements, particularly with regard to police and judicial cooperation (guidelines 30 and 32–47). A further advantage of this soft-law instrument resides in its not being limited to penal measures,[124] as it also includes a broad set (guidelines 1–12) of pre-penal (educational, social, administrative) preventive measures intended to both reduce crime rates and facilitate

[120]See ECOSOC Resolution 2004/34; Report of the Conference of the Parties to the United Nations Convention against Transnational Organized Crime on its fifth session, Vienna, 18–22 October 2010, CTOC/COP/2010/17, and Resolution 5/7 of 2010; UNODC/CCPCJ/EG.1/2009/2; UNODC/CCPCJ/EG.1/2012/4. See also Res. 10/7 adopted at the Conference of the Parties to the United Nations Convention against Transnational Organized Crime on its tenth session, Vienna, 12–16 October 2020.

[121]See Manacorda (2011), p. 43.

[122]See e.g. Manacorda (2011), pp. 42–45; Borgstede (2014); Blake (2015), pp. 48–50.

[123]See specifically guideline 13.

[124]See also Visconti (2013).

investigations when an offence is committed, which, as we will see, also influenced the shape of the 2017 Nicosia Convention.[125]

A like strategy was adopted by UNESCO: as the many shortcomings of the 1970 UNESCO Convention could no longer be ignored while, at the same time, proceeding to negotiate a new convention would have been too long, complex and uncertain, UNESCO promoted the introduction of a set of Operational Guidelines (henceforth OG), adopted by consensus on 18 May 2015 by the Meeting of States Parties to the 1970 UNESCO Convention. Regarding article 8 of the 1970 UNESCO Convention and, thus, issues of criminalization, paragraph 65 OG stresses the need for criminal sanctions to be adopted at the domestic level. While «the Convention does not specify what sort of sanctions are to be applied» by States Parties, they are nonetheless «encouraged to penalize offences against cultural property, committed in violation of the Convention, by introducing penal sanctions against the perpetrators of such offences». Besides, paragraph 66 OG, in turn, requires contracting States who are also signatories of the UNTOC[126] to consider offences related to illicit trafficking in cultural property as «serious crimes» pursuant to article 2 UNTOC, while paragraph 67 OP encourages States to also take the 2014 UN Guidelines into account in implementing the 1970 Convention.

Thus by the mid-2010's a tight net of international soft-law tools had emerged, which would pave the way for the adoption and entry into force, in a few more years, of a proper suppression treaty devoted to the fight against cultural property trafficking.

2.5 *The Evolution of European Union Law*

Due to the founding Treaties' constraints, the European Union has limited competence in the matter of harmonization of cultural heritage law, basically confined to issues of circulation strictly linked to the functioning of the common market.[127] Thus, between the 1990s and the first half of 2010s, the only two issues addressed by EU secondary law have been export of cultural 'goods' outside the Union's borders,[128] and the return of illegally exported items amongst Member States.[129] Yet, in

[125] See also Mottese (2018).

[126] Adopted by resolution A/RES/55/25 of 15 November 2000 at the fifty-fifth session of the General Assembly of the United Nations, New York, Doc A/55/383, in force 29 September 2003, 2225 UNTS 209.

[127] See Stamatoudi (2011), pp. 112–132.

[128] Council Regulation (EEC) No 3911/92 of 9 December 1992 on the export of cultural goods, OJ L 395, repealed by Council Regulation (EC) No 116/2009 of 18 December 2008 on the export of cultural goods, OJ L 39.

[129] Council Directive 93/7/EEC of 15 March 1993 on the return of cultural objects unlawfully removed from the territory of a Member State, OJ L 74, repealed by Directive 2014/60/EU of the European Parliament and of the Council of 15 May 2014 on the return of cultural objects unlawfully

recent years, the European Union started to share international concerns about links between trafficking in cultural property and other serious crimes, particularly organized crime, money laundering, and terrorism.[130]

The first steps in attempting to control cultural property trafficking on the demand side were made with Regulation EC 1210/2003 and Regulation EU 1332/2013.[131] The former[132] introduced the prohibition of importing and trading cultural objects having illegally left Iraq after 6 August 1990; the latter[133] introduced within Regulation EU 36/2012 a like provision with respect to artefacts having illegally left Syria after 9 May 2011, a deadline which was later moved up to 15 March 2011.[134] Eventually, this new path led to the adoption, in 2019, of a new Regulation on the import of cultural property from all non-member States.[135]

The new rules prohibit the importation of items «removed from the territory of the country where they were created or discovered in breach of the laws and regulations of that country» (article 3.1, applicable since 28 December 2020 according to article 16) and introduce a system of import licensing for 'cultural goods' deemed at higher risk of trafficking (archaeological findings and parts of dismembered monuments; articles 3(2) and 4, Annex Part B), as well as of mandatory importer's statements for further types of cultural objects (articles 3(2) and 5, Annex Part C).[136] Even if these provisions cannot be mandatorily backed by criminalization obligations, given the EU's lack of direct criminal law competences (article 83 TFEU) which requires penalties to be introduced by Member States through national legislation and leaves them free to chose their nature (criminal, administrative, or civil), the Regulation

removed from the territory of a Member State and amending Regulation (EU) No 1024/2012 (Recast), OJ L 159.

[130] See European Commission (2019), in particular pp. 108–115. See also Urbinati (2018); Dehouck (2019); Zagato (2021).

[131] See specifically Urbinati (2018), in particular pp. 57–59.

[132] Council Regulation (EC) No 1210/2003 of 7 July 2003 concerning certain specific restrictions on economic and financial relations with Iraq and repealing Regulation (EC) No 2465/96, OJ L 169.

[133] Council Regulation (EU) No 1332/2013 of 13 December 2013 amending Regulation (EU) No 36/2012 concerning restrictive measures in view of the situation in Syria, OJ L 335.

[134] With Council Regulation (EU) 2015/827 of 28 May 2015 amending Regulation (EU) No 36/2012 concerning restrictive measures in view of the situation in Syria, OJ L 132.

[135] Regulation (EU) 2019/880 of the European Parliament and of the Council of 17 April 2019 on the introduction and the import of cultural goods, OJ L 151. See also Schreiber (2021); de Jong (2021).

[136] According to art. 16, these latter provisions shall apply from the date on which the centralized electronic system referred to in article 8 (to be used for the storage and exchange of information between the competent authorities of the Member States, in particular regarding import licences and importer statements) will become operational, or at the latest from 28 June 2025. The European Commission has recently adopted the necessary preliminary rules, with the Commission Implementing Regulation (EU) 2021/1079 of 24 June 2021 laying down detailed rules for implementing certain provisions of Regulation (EU) 2019/880 of the European Parliament and of the Council on the introduction and the import of cultural goods, OJ L 234, on which see Giardini (2021).

requires them to be supported by «effective, proportionate and dissuasive» penalties (article 11).

Thus, it seems likely that several Member States (especially those who have chosen, or will choose in future, to also ratify the 2017 Nicosia Convention) will opt for introducing new criminal offences.[137]

3 The Long Road towards a Suppression Treaty

Notwithstanding the prevailing 'blindness', at the time, of the international community to the criminal stature of cultural property trafficking, it was actually in the 1980s and the 1990s that the first significant attempts at encouraging some measure of harmonization of national penal laws were made, even if, as we are going to discuss, a set of exogenous and endogenous factors would undermine any possibility of success till the mid-2010s.

3.1 The First Attempt by the Council of Europe: The 1985 Delphi Convention

The first international treaty specifically and consistently aimed at criminalizing acts that impinge upon cultural property, both movable and immovable, was adopted and opened to signature on 23 June 1985 in Delphi by the Council of Europe (CoE).[138] The structure of this treaty and its workings (had it ever entered into force) appear rather complex, a feature that likely contributed to its fate.

A first group of offences against cultural property[139] (theft, appropriation through violence or menace, and receiving of the two previous offences' objects: article 3 and Appendix III) were subject to a proper obligation of criminalization. A second group of offences (mainly including other acts of illicit appropriation and dispersion) were instead permitted to be made by States Parties into criminal offences, so that other contracting parties could not object. Finally, States Parties could at any time declare that they would deem offences against cultural property any other harmful act or omission not listed within the Convention. Contracting States were also to commit themselves (article 12) to «take the necessary measures for adequate sanctioning» (being able to choose amongst custodial and noncustodial sanctions, including fines,

[137] This is for instance the choice recently made by Italy: see note 113, above, and Visconti (2021b), in particular pp. 347–348 and 354.

[138] See note 22, above. See also Nafziger (1985), pp. 840–841; Manacorda (2011), pp. 37–38; Boister (2018), p. 225; Mottese (2020), pp. 26–28.

[139] Defined in a very detailed list in Appendix II(1), according to art. 2, which also granted contracting States the possibility to unilaterally add to said list.

bans, and disqualifications). A set of detailed provisions regulated jurisdiction, plurality of proceedings, application of *ne bis in idem* principle, letters rogatory, and restitution of cultural property (articles 6–19).

The 1985 Dephi Convention never entered into force (and has now been rendered outdated by the 2017 Nicosia Convention, discussed below), having failed to reach the minimum number of (just) three ratifications (article 21): in fact, it collected only six signatures, none of which by a primary market country.

The reasons for this failure are likely twofold: firstly, the conflict between source States' and market States' interests in, and legal approaches to, cultural property circulation was still too sharp in the 1980s and 1990's, and it was not yet counterbalanced by a shared awareness of, and concern for, the interlinked criminal dimension of illicit traffic in cultural property; secondly, criminal law was, and remains today, the branch of any legal system more strictly related to State's sovereignty, and the 1985 Delphi Convention probably asked too much in terms of concessions to an external 'interference'.[140]

3.2 *The 1990 Model Treaty*

A few years later, in 1990, the Eighth UN Congress on the Prevention of Crime and the Treatment of Offenders adopted a model treaty «for the prevention of crimes that infringe on the cultural heritage of peoples in the form of movable property».[141] According to the Preamble, the Model Treaty's stated purpose was «combating criminal activities which involve movable cultural property through the introduction of measures for impeding illicit transnational trafficking in movable cultural property whether or not it has been stolen, the imposition of appropriate and effective administrative and penal sanctions and the provision of a means for restitution».

Different from other UN model treaties, it was never adopted and thus remained purely a template for international agreements concerning actual criminalization obligations.[142] Its most interesting features are the parallel presence of an offence of illicit export and one of illicit import (articles 2(a) and 3(a)), the intended punishment of intentional acquisition of, or dealing in, stolen or illicitly imported cultural property (articles 2(b) and 3(b)), the specific consideration given to the criminalization of «international conspiracies» (articles 2(c) and 3(c)), and the intended possibility to apply sanctions not only to physical persons, but also to legal ones (articles 2 and 3).

[140] See also Bieczyński (2017), p. 262.

[141] Eighth United Nations Congress on the Prevention of Crime and the Treatment of Offenders, Havana, 27 August-7 September 1990: report prepared by the Secretariat (United Nations publication, Sales No E.91.IV.2), chp. I, sec B.1, annex.

[142] See Manacorda (2011), pp. 36–37; Mackenzie (2009), pp. 10–14; Boister (2018), pp. 227–228.

Even though this document is not binding, it is considered a model for bilateral and multilateral agreements, and it has achieved renewed visibility in recent years, mostly thanks to recommendations by the UN Economic and Social Council (ECOSOC)[143] and by the Expert Group on protection against trafficking in cultural property;[144] eventually, a recommendation for States to «consider», in bilateral cooperation, «making use of the model treaty for the prevention of crimes that infringe on the cultural heritage of peoples» was included also in the 2014 UN Guidelines (guideline 14). It can thus be considered as having exercised an enduring influence on later efforts by the international community to introduce uniform criminal law standards.

3.3 *The 2017 Nicosia Convention*

As observed above, by the mid-2010s concern about the possible involvement in cultural property trafficking of organized and terrorist criminal groups had come to a boil and, coupled with a rising awareness about the links between offences against cultural heritage and a broader set of economic and white-collar crimes, it prompted renewed efforts by the CoE to promote a specific criminal law convention.

The new Convention on Offences relating to Cultural Property[145] was adopted in Nicosia on 19 May 2019 and opened to signature to all CoE member States, as well as to non-members having participated in its elaboration; it is also opened for accession to further non-member States (article 28). The stated purpose was that of filling criminalization gaps left open by other existing cultural heritage treaties.[146] Albeit defined by some «modest»,[147] it is likely that its simpler structure and more limited scope, together with a better coordination with existing relevant conventions, contributed to make it more acceptable by prospective parties. In fact, on first April 2022 it entered into force, having reached (and surpassed) the minimum required

[143] ECOSOC Resolution 2003/29; ECOSOC Resolution 2004/34; ECOSOC Resolution 2008/23; ECOSOC Resolution 2010/19; ECOSOC Resolution 2011/42, adopted by the General Assembly as Resolution 66/180, United Nations A/RES/66/180.

[144] Report on the Meeting of the Expert Group on Protection against Trafficking in Cultural Property held in Vienna from 24 to 26 November 2009, UNODC/CCPCJ/EG.1/2009/2; Report on the Meeting of the Expert Group on Protection against Trafficking in Cultural Property held in Vienna from 27 to 29 June 2012, UNODC/CCPCJ/EG.1/2012/4.

[145] See note 22, above. See also the annexed Explanatory Report to the Council of Europe Convention on Offences relating to Cultural Property, CETS No 221. For a detailed discussion see Mottese (2020). See also Bieczyński (2017); Boister (2018), pp. 225–227; Fincham (2019).

[146] See Explanatory Report, Chap. I; Bieczyński (2017), p. 262; Fincham (2019), pp. 323–325.

[147] Boister (2018), p. 225.

number of five ratifications, of which at least three by CoE member States (article 27).

Its broad definition of 'cultural property' (article 2) covers both movable and immovable items (the latter basically for purposes of criminalization of destruction and damage: article 10) and draws amply on definitions provided by earlier conventions (the 1970 UNESCO Convention, with respect to the former,[148] and the 1972 UNESCO World Heritage Convention,[149] with respect to the latter).[150] With respect to provisions concerning police and judicial international cooperation, the 2017 Nicosia Convention mostly relies on pre-existing «relevant applicable international and regional instruments and arrangements agreed on the basis of uniform legislation or reciprocity» (article 19). As previously observed, it also largely builds on the 2014 UN Guidelines, as it provides for a broad set of non-penal preventive measures (articles 20–21), aimed at integrating and supporting criminal ones.[151]

In general terms, the number of criminal offences has been drastically reduced in comparison to the 1985 Delphi Convention and mostly focused on movable objects and behaviour instrumental to trafficking (including falsification of provenance documentation: article 9), with the 'thorniest' issues left free for parties to be made into administrative instead of criminal offences.[152]

---

[148] Art. 2(2)(a) of the 2017 Nicosia Convention indeed almost exactly matches the definition and list of cultural property to be found in art. 1 of the 1970 UNESCO Convention, including the requirement of formal identification of the protected items as cultural property («any object, situated on land or underwater or removed therefrom, which is, on religious or secular grounds, classified, defined or specifically designated by any Party to this Convention or to the 1970 UNESCO Convention on the Means of Prohibiting and Preventing the Illicit Import, Export and Transfer of Ownership of Cultural Property, as being of importance for archaeology, prehistory, ethnology, history, literature, art or science»).

[149] Convention Concerning the Protection of the World Cultural and Natural Heritage, adopted in Paris on 16 November 1972, in force 15 December 1975, 1037 UNTS 151. See further Francioni (2008); Forrest (2010), pp. 224–286.

[150] Art. 2(2)(b) of the 2017 Nicosia Convention echoes the definition of «cultural heritage» by art. 1 of the 1972 World Heritage Convention, by including «monuments», «groups of buildings» and «sites», to which it adds any «structure of any other kind, whether situated on land or underwater, which is, on religious or secular grounds, defined or specifically designated by any Party to this Convention or by any Party to the 1970 UNESCO Convention as being of importance for archaeology, prehistory, ethnology, history, art or science»; it also covers any such immovable artefact which «is listed in accordance with Article 1 and Article 11 (paragraphs 2 or 4) of the 1972 UNESCO Convention concerning the Protection of the World Cultural and Natural Heritage».

[151] See specifically Mottese (2018).

[152] As a summary of substantive criminal law provisions (Chap. II), we may observe that criminalization is required for: (art. 3) theft and other forms of unlawful appropriation of movable cultural property, which can anyway be ensured also by way of unspecific penal provisions; (art. 4) unlawful excavation of cultural property and unlawful removal of archaeological movable cultural property, when committed intentionally, for which is however given States parties the possibility to opt for non-criminal sanctions; (art. 5) intentional illegal importation of movable cultural property (ditto); (art. 6) intentional illegal exportation of movable cultural property; (art. 7) acquisition of stolen, illegally exported, illegally imported or illegally excavated movable cultural property made with knowledge of its unlawful origin, with a recommendation to also consider criminalizing negligent

With specific respect to the international circulation of artworks and antiquities, article 6(1) binds contracting States to criminalize «illegal exportation», meaning the intentional export of movable cultural property whose exportation is prohibited according to domestic law, or which is carried out without the authorisation required under national law.[153]

Like (almost) all other offences listed by the 2017 Nicosia Convention, unlawful export, according to article 14(1), shall be punishable by «effective, proportionate and dissuasive» penal sanctions, which, in this case, are bound to include penalties of deprivation of liberty that may give rise to extradition.[154] Also provided for, in respect to this and any other criminal offence introduced according to the 2017 Nicosia Convention, is the accessory penalty of confiscation, both of items instrumental to the commission of the crime and of proceeds of crime (or property whose value corresponds to such proceeds: article 14(3)). Forfeiture of cultural property seized in the course of criminal proceedings is meant to be instrumental, whenever appropriate, to its restitution to the State of origin (article 14(4)). Besides, for this (and any other) criminal offence established in conformity to the 2017 Nicosia Convention, States parties are mandated to introduce (criminal, administrative, or civil) liability of legal persons for the benefit of which the offence was committed (article 13).

When it comes to import of cultural property, the 2017 Nicosia Convention appears, however, less decisive and innovative. Illegal importation is defined under article 5(1) as import of movable cultural property, the importation of which is prohibited pursuant to the State Party's domestic law on the grounds that such property has been either (a) stolen in another state, or (b) unlawfully excavated or retained (according to article 4 of the Convention), or (c) exported in violation of the

behaviours; (art. 8) intentional placing on the market of stolen, illegally exported, illegally imported or illegally excavated movable cultural property made with knowledge of its unlawful origin, with a recommendation to also consider criminalizing negligent behaviours; (art. 9) falsification of documents relating to movable cultural property made with the intent of presenting the item has having a licit provenance; (art. 10) intentional unlawful destruction and damage of movable or immovable cultural property, for which is however given States parties the possibility to make exceptions for cases of destruction or damage by the owner or made with the owner's consent; (art. 11) aiding or abetting of the aforementioned offences (for which is however given States parties the possibility to make exceptions for cases of unlawful excavations), as well as attempts at committing them. See also Bieczyński (2017), pp. 265–269; Boister (2018), pp. 225–226; Fincham (2019), pp. 326–331.

[153] Contracting States are also invited, but not bound, to criminalize intentional (re)export of illegally imported movable cultural property (art. 6(2)), in order to stop trafficked cultural property from leaving the country. See also Explanatory Report, para 53.

[154] According to art 2 of the European Convention on Extradition (adopted 13 December 1957, entered into force 18 April 1960, ETS No 24) extradition is to be granted in respect of offences punishable under the laws of the requesting and requested parties by deprivation of liberty for a maximum period of at least 1 year or by a more severe penalty. There are some offences which are however exempted from this requirement: namely, lower penalties are allowed, according to art. 14(1), for unlawful excavations (art. 4(1)(a)) as well as for illegal import of cultural property recovered or exported in breach of the laws of its country of origin (art. 5(1)(b-c)).

law of the state that has classified, defined or specifically designated the cultural property as such.

Thus, unlawful importation under the 2017 Nicosia Convention has a potentially broader scope of application than under article 7(b) of the 1970 UNESCO Convention,[155] as any stolen object is taken into account; no prior inventorization of the object is required (indeed, illegally excavated objects are expressly included); and there is a clear and unequivocal correlation between exportation effected contrary to the laws of the country of origin and illegality of the import in the territory of a State party. Nonetheless, while article 5(1) presupposes that States parties have domestic legislation in place prohibiting the import of such objects, it does not compel them to introduce such prohibitions if they are not already provided for.[156]

Additionally, when looking at enforcement strategies, in this instance there is no relevant change in attitudes from the 1970 UNESCO Convention, as discussed above. While contracting States are bound to provide sanctions for unlawful importation where committed intentionally by a person who knew the cultural property to have been stolen, excavated, or exported in violation of the law of another State (article 5(1)), the option of criminal liability, albeit introduced as first choice, is by no means mandatory: according to article 5(2), States parties may, at the time of signature or when depositing the instrument of ratification or accession, reserve the right to provide for non-criminal sanctions. Further, article 14(1) omits any requirement for penalties amounting to deprivation of liberty and susceptible to give rise to extradition, even in the case that importation of unlawfully excavated or unlawfully exported cultural objects is a criminal offence under domestic law.

Nonetheless, as previously observed, it seems likely that at least current and prospective States parties to the 2017 Nicosia Convention which are also members of the European Union will implement penal provisions concerning illicit import, given the combined push by the Convention and the abovementioned Regulation EU 880/2019.

Finally, a note on jurisdiction: article 12 requires contracting States to establish their jurisdiction over criminal offences against cultural heritage referred to in the 2017 Nicosia Convention not only based on ordinary principles of territoriality (i.e. when the offence is committed in their territory, or «on board a ship flying the flag of that Party», or «on board an aircraft registered under the laws of that Party»)

---

[155] According to which State parties undertake «to prohibit the import of cultural property stolen from a museum or a religious or secular public monument or similar institution in another State Party to this Convention after the entry into force of this Convention for the States concerned, provided that such property is documented as appertaining to the inventory of that institution». Many contracting parties to the 1970 UNESCO Convention thus opted for restricting import prohibitions to inventoried cultural property stolen from cultural or religious institutions, often also failing to introduce specific provisions and instead choosing to just make use of existing, unspecific offences punishing the dealing in any item of a criminal origin. See above, Sect. 3.2.

[156] See Explanatory Report, para 46.

and nationality (i.e. when the offence is committed by one of their nationals),[157] but also based on the principle *aut dedere aut judicare*, in order to ensure that parties that cannot or will not extradite an alleged offender have the legal ability to undertake investigations and proceedings domestically.[158]

4 Conclusion. Ongoing Progresses and Open Questions

So: success at last? The entry into force of the 2017 Nicosia Convention, a long-awaited proper suppression treaty, is certainly a positive signal. The prevention and fight of cultural property trafficking has always greatly suffered from the complete lack of even a minimum of uniform penal standards and from the related problems affecting police and judicial cooperation. Criminals in the art and antiquities market have traditionally been extremely skilled in exploiting all available regulatory gaps and non-uniformities between national legal frameworks, and the new CoE treaty is an important step towards filling those gaps and reducing that lack of uniformity. Nonetheless, its actual efficacy will depend on many factors and cannot be overestimated, at present.

Looking at ratifications and signatures not (yet) followed by ratifications, indeed, what immediately strikes the eye is the *complete* absence of major market and transit States. A situation worryingly akin to the status of ratification of the 1995 UNIDROIT Convention, whose very limited efficacy in the (different, but related) field of return and restitution of illegally exported and stolen cultural objects[159] depends, in fact, mostly on the still limited number of ratifications (just 53 after almost 30 years since its adoption) as well as on the insignificant number of market countries amongst contracting parties.[160] Thus, like the 1995 UNIDROIT Convention, the 2017 Nicosia Convention presently appears to be basically ‘preaching to the converted’: unless it will prove able, in future, to gather ratifications also from the other side of the international market, its fate seems destined to be a very modest one indeed, helping States with a pre-existing interest in, and often also an already solid tradition of, protection of (their national) cultural heritage to strengthen it even further (on paper, at least), with, however, no appreciable effects on curbing the transnational trafficking in cultural property.

---

[157] In this case, however, prospective States parties have the possibility to declare, at the time of signature, ratification, acceptance, approval or accession, that they reserve the right not to apply, or to apply only in specific cases or conditions, jurisdiction based on the nationality principle: see art. 12(3).

[158] See also Explanatory Report, paras 73–81.

[159] See e.g. Forrest (2010), pp. 218–219; Stamatoudi (2011), pp. 109–111.

[160] Amongst such we may count Denmark, Finland, and to some extent Italy and, even more, China, given its growing role as (also) importer of artworks and antiquities, but no major, or at least really relevant, net-importer or hub of the international trade has ratified the 1995 UNIDROIT Convention, yet.

Obviously, these are still early days, so it would not be proper to give up all hopes of future improvements in the availability of market countries to bind themselves to this new suppression convention. Reasons to remain optimist mostly relate to the proven and ever growing concerns about involvement of organized crime and terrorist groups in cultural property trafficking. Nonetheless, at present the best hope to reinforce international cooperation in criminal investigations and prosecutions of offences against cultural heritage appears to still lie on the aforementioned possibility, and international push, to make effective use of the UNTOC in this field, too.

Finally, it will never be repeated enough how criminal law can effectively prevent and sanction only harmful behaviours which are comparatively *rare*. When cultural property trafficking is as prevalent as it currently appears to be, even discounted the many gaps in available information that we highlighted in the first part of this discussion, an excessive focus on punishment will unavoidably result in a cheap show of symbolic expression (often at the expenses of individual liberties and fundamental rights), more than in practical results.

To make criminal law provisions work, an adequate investment must be made in educational, economic, organizational, civil and administrative measures, from widespread inventorying of cultural property to 'neighbourhood watching' over monuments and archaeological sites, from licensing of dealers to the implementations of codes of conduct and the strengthening of administrative regulation and remedial sanctions, and so on (not to mention reduction of armed conflicts and improvement of economic and social conditions for local communities in source countries, which, at present, appear a very remote scenario indeed). This, in turn, requires a willingness to find adequate resources and to follow a (legal, as well as economic) solidarity principle[161] between States, including those at the two ends of the market. A change of attitude which, unfortunately, still appears a work very much in progress.

References

Abramson RD, Huttler SB (1973) The legal response to the illicit movement of cultural property. Law Policy Int Bus 5:932–970

Adam G (2017) Dark side of the boom. The excesses of the art market in the 21st century. Lund Humphries, London

Al-Azm A, Paul KM, Graham S (2019) Facebook's black market in antiquities. Trafficking, terrorism, and war crimes. Antiquities Trafficking and Heritage Anthropology Research (ATHAR) Project. http://atharproject.org/wp-content/uploads/2019/06/ATHAR-FB-Report-June-2019-final.pdf

Alder C, Polk K (2007) Crime in the world of art. In: Pontell HN, Geis G (eds) International handbook of white-collar and corporate crime. Springer, New York, pp 347–357

[161] For a discussion of the importance of adopting a solidarity principle in the approach to transnational issues concerning cultural heritage see Visconti (2021c).

Alderman KL (2012) Honor amongst thieves: Organized crime and the illicit antiquities trade. Indiana Law Rev 45(3):601–627

ASOR (2020) The state of illicit trade and looting of Libyan antiquities 2011–2020. https://www.asor.org/wp-content/uploads/2021/03/CHI-Report_Libya-Illicit-Trafficking_Full_Compressed_2021-03-25.pdf

Balcells M (2015) Art crime as white collar crime. In: Kila JD, Balcells M (eds) Cultural property crime. An overview and analysis of contemporary perspectives and trends. Brill, Leiden-Boston, pp 96–110

Balcells M (2019) One looter, two looters, three looters. . . The discipline of cultural heritage crime within criminology and its inherent measurement problems. In: Chappell D, Hufnagel S (eds) The Palgrave handbook of art crime. Palgrave Macmillan, London, pp 33–53

Bieczyński MM (2017) The Nicosia Convention 2017: a new international instrument regarding criminal offences against cultural property. Santander Art Cult Law Rev 3(2):255–274

Blake J (2015) International cultural heritage law. Oxford University Press, Oxford

Boister N (2018) Transnational criminal law, 2nd edn. Oxford University Press, Oxford

Borgstede G (2014) Cultural property, the Palermo Convention and transnational organized crime. Int J Cult Prop 21(3):281–290

Borio di Tigliole R (2018) La legislazione italiana dei beni culturali. Giuffrè, Milan

Bowman BA (2008) Transnational crimes against culture. Looting at archaeological sites and the "grey" market in antiquities. J Contemp Crim Justice 24(3):225–242

Brodie N (2006) An archaeologist's view of the trade in unprovenanced antiquities. In: Hoffman BT (ed) Art and cultural heritage. Law, policy and practice. Cambridge University Press, Cambridge-New York, pp 52–63

Brodie N (2011a) Congenial bedfellows? The academy and the antiquities trade. J Contemp Crim Justice 27(4):408–437

Brodie N (2011b) The market in Iraqi antiquities 1980-2009 and academic involvement in the marketing process. In: Manacorda S, Chappell D (eds) Crime in the art and antiquities world. Illegal trafficking in cultural property. Springer, New York-Dordrecht, pp 117–133

Brodie N (2015) The Internet market in pre-columbian antiquities. In: Kila JD, Balcells M (eds) Cultural property crime. An overview and analysis of contemporary perspectives and trends. Brill, Leiden-Boston, pp 237–262

Brodie N (2017) How to control the internet market in antiquities? The need for regulation and monitoring. Antiquities Coalition Policy Brief. https://traffickingculture.org/app/uploads/2019/02/Brodie-2017-Policy-Brief.pdf

Brodie N (2018) The illegal excavation and trade of Syrian cultural objects: a view from the ground. J Field Archaeol 43(1):74–84

Brodie N (2021) Cuneiform exceptionalism? Justifying the study and publication of unprovenanced cuneiform tablets from Iraq. In: Oosterman N, Yates D (eds) Crime and art. Sociological and criminological perspectives of crimes in the art world. Springer, Cham, pp 103–117

Brodie N, Doole J, Watson P (2000) Stealing history: the illicit trade in cultural material. The McDonald Institute for Archaeological Research, Cambridge

Brodie N, Dietzler J, Mackenzie S (2013) Trafficking in cultural objects: an empirical overview. In: Manacorda S, Visconti A (eds) Beni culturali e sistema penale. Vita e Pensiero, Milan, pp 19–30

Brodie N, Kersel MM, Mackenzie S, Sabrine I, Smith E, Yates D (2022) Why there is still an illicit trade in cultural objects and what we can do about it. J Field Archaeol 47(2):117–130

Calvani S (2009) Frequency and figures of organized crime in art and antiques. In: Manacorda S (ed) Organised crime in art and antiquities. ISPAC, Milan, pp 29–39

Campbell PB (2013) The illicit antiquities trade as a transnational criminal network: characterizing and anticipating trafficking of cultural heritage. Int J Cult Prop 20(2):113–153

Carabinieri TPC (2020) Attività operativa 2019. https://media.beniculturali.it/mibac/files/boards/388a5474724a15af0ace7a40ab3301de/file_pdf/Attivita_Operativa_2019.pdf

Carrano J (2010) Cambodia: preserving cultural heritage. https://www.jurist.org/commentary/2010/02/cambodia-preserving-cultural-heritage/#:~:text=In%201996%2C%20the%20Cambodian%20legislature,be%20used%2C%20and%20the%20appropriate
Chappell D, Hufnagel S (2019) Art crime: exposing a panoply of theft, fraud and plunder. In: Chappell D, Hufnagel S (eds) The Palgrave handbook of art crime. Palgrave Macmillan, London, pp 3–32
Chappell D, Polk K (2011) Unravelling the "Cordata": just how organized is the international traffic in cultural objects? In: Manacorda S, Chappell D (eds) Crime in the art and antiquities world. Illegal trafficking in cultural property. Springer, New York-Dordrecht, pp 99–113
Chippindale C, Gill DWJ (2000) Material consequences of contemporary classical collecting. Am J Archaeol 104(3):463–511
Conklin JE (1994) Art crime. Praeger, Westport
de Jong AM (2021) The cultural goods import regime of Regulation (EU) 2019/880: four potential pitfalls. Santander Art Cult Law Rev 7(2):31–50
Dehouck MRJ (2019) Balancing markets, morals and law: The fight to regulate illicit trafficking in cultural goods and the EU Regulation on the import of cultural goods. Art Antiq Law 24(1): 1–38
Dietzler J (2013) On 'organized crime' in the illicit antiquities trade: moving beyond the definitional debate. Trends Org Crime 16:329–342
Durney M, Proulx B (2011) Art crime: a brief introduction. Crime Law Soc Change 56(2):115–132
European Commission (2019) Illicit trade in cultural goods in Europe. Characteristics, criminal justice responses and an analysis of applicability of technologies in the combat against the trade. Final report. Publications Office of the European Union, Luxembourg
Fabiani MD, Marrone JV (2021) Transiting through the antiquities market. A social network analysis of auctions. In: Oosterman N, Yates D (eds) Crime and art. Sociological and criminological perspectives of crimes in the art world. Springer, Cham, pp 11–28
Fincham D (2007) Why US Federal criminal penalties for dealing in illicit cultural property are ineffective, and a pragmatic alternative. Cardozo Arts Ent Law J 25(2):597–1279
Fincham D (2019) The blood antiquities Convention as a paradigm for cultural property crime reduction. Cardozo Arts Ent Law J 37(2):299–336
Fisman R, Wei SJ (2009) The smuggling of art and the art of smuggling: uncovering the illicit trade in cultural property and antiques. Am Econ J Appl Econ 1(3):82–96
Forrest C (2010) International law and the protection of cultural heritage. Routledge, London-New York
Francioni F (2008) The 1972 World Heritage Convention: a commentary. Oxford University Press, Oxford-New York
Francioni F (2020) Custom and general principles of international cultural heritage law. In: Francioni F, Vrdoljak AF (eds) The Oxford handbook of international cultural heritage law. Oxford University Press, Oxford, pp 531–550
Gerstenblith P (2016) The legal framework for the prosecution of crimes involving archaeological objects. U S Att'ys Bull 64(2):5–16
Gerstenblith P (2019) Provenances: real, fake, and questionable. Int J Cult Prop 26(3):285–304
Gerstenblith P (2020) Provenience and provenance intersecting with international law in the market for antiquities. N C J Int Law 45(1):457–495
Giardini G (2021) A commentary to Commission Implementing Regulation (EU) 2021/1079 of 24 June 2021 laying down detailed rules for implementing certain provisions of Regulation (EU) 2019/880 of the European Parliament and of the Council on the introduction and the import of cultural goods. Santander Art Cult Law Rev 7(2):183–192
Gill DWJ, Chippindale C (1993) Material and intellectual consequences of esteem for Cycladic figures. Am J Archaeol 97(4):601–659
Hall J (2018) Les défis culturels de la Cour pénale internationale. In: Lagrange E, Oeter S, Uerpmann-Wittzack R (eds) Cultural heritage and international law. Springer, Cham, pp 209–235

Hardy SA (2020) Criminal money and antiquities. An open-source investigation into transnational organised cultural property crime. In: Benson K, King C, Walker C (eds) Assets, crime and the State: innovation in 21st century legal responses. Routledge, London, pp 154–167

Haskell F (1981) La dispersione e la conservazione del patrimonio artistico. In: VV.AA., Storia dell'arte italiana, part. 3, Situazioni momenti indagini, vol. 3, Conservazione, falso, restauro. Einaudi, Turin, pp 5–35

Hickley C (2021) In the battle against antiquities trafficking, Germany develops app to identify looted cultural heritage. The Art Newspaper, 5 June 2021. https://www.theartnewspaper.com/2021/01/05/in-the-battle-against-antiquities-trafficking-germany-develops-app-to-identify-looted-cultural-heritage

Hufnagel S, Chappell D (eds) (2019) The Palgrave handbook on art crime. Palgrave Macmillan, London

Huo Z (2015) Legal protection of cultural heritage in China: a challenge to keep history alive. Int J Cult Prop 22(4):2–10

INTERPOL (2021) Assessing crimes against cultural property 2020. Survey of INTERPOL member countries. https://www.interpol.int/en/content/download/16751/file/2020%20Assessing%20Crimes%20Against%20Cultural%20Property.pdf

Keane D (2004) The failure to protect cultural property in wartime. DePaul J Art Technol Intell Prop Law 14(1):1–38

Kila JD (2015) From crimes against art to crimes against cultural property: new perspectives and dimensions in art crime. In: Kila JD, Balcells M (eds) Cultural property crime. An overview and analysis of contemporary perspectives and trends. Brill, Leiden-Boston, pp 167–205

Klamberg M (ed) (2017) Commentary on the law of the International Criminal Court. Torkel Opsahl Academic, Brussels

Lane DC, Bromley DG, Hicks RD, Mahoney JS (2008) Time crime: the transnational organization of art and antiquities theft. J Contemp Crim Justice 24(3):243–262

Mackenzie S (2005) Going, going, gone: regulating the market in illicit antiquities. Inst Art Law, Leicester

Mackenzie S (2009) Protection against trafficking in cultural property. Background paper for the meeting of the Expert group on protection against trafficking in cultural property - Vienna, 24–26 November 2009, UNODC/CCPCJ/EG.1/2009/CRP.1

Mackenzie S (2011a) Illicit deals in cultural objects as crimes of the powerful. Crime Law Soc Change 56(2):133–153

Mackenzie S (2011b) The market as criminal and criminals in the market: reducing opportunities for organised crime in the international antiquities market. In: Manacorda S, Chappell D (eds) Crime in the art and antiquities world. Illegal trafficking in cultural property. Springer, New York-Dordrecht, pp 69–85

Mackenzie S, Davis T (2014) Cambodian statue trafficking networks: an empirical report from regional case study fieldwork. In: Manacorda S, Visconti A (eds) Protecting cultural heritage as a common good of humanity: a challenge for criminal justice. ISPAC, Milan, pp 149–164

Mackenzie S, Yates D (2016) What is grey about the 'grey' market in antiquities. In: Beckert J, Dewy M (eds) The architecture of illegal markets: towards and economic sociology of illegality. Oxford University Press, Oxford-New York, pp 70–86

Mackenzie S, Brodie N, Yates D, Tsiroginnis C (2020) Trafficking culture. New directions in researching the global market in illicit antiquities. Routledge, London-New York

Malnati L (2018) La falsificazione dei reperti archeologici nel commercio clandestino. In: VV.AA. L'arte non vera non può essere arte. Edizioni Efesto, Rome, pp 69–73

Manacorda S (2011) Criminal law protection of cultural heritage: an international perspective. In: Manacorda S, Chappell D (eds) Crime in the art and antiquities world. Illegal trafficking in cultural property. Springer, New York-Dordrecht, pp 17–48

Manacorda S, Chappell D (2011) Introduction. In: Manacorda S, Chappell D (eds) Crime in the art and antiquities world. Illegal trafficking in cultural property. Springer, New York-Dordrecht, pp 1–15

Manacorda S, Visconti A (2024) Article 8, 1970 UNESCO Convention. In: Chechi A, Jakubowski A, Vrdoljak AF (eds) 1970 UNESCO and 1995 UNIDROIT Conventions: A commentary. Oxford University Press, Oxford. (forthcoming)

Massy L (2008) The antiquity art market: between legality and illegality. Int J Soc Econ 35(10): 729–738

Maugeri AM (2008) La tutela dei beni culturali nel diritto internazionale penale. Crimini di guerra e crimini contro l'umanità. Giuffrè, Milan

Merryman JH (1986) Two ways of thinking about cultural property. Am J Int Law 80(4):831–853

Merryman JH (1995) A licit international trade in cultural objects. Int J Cult Prop 4(1):13–60

Mottese E (2018) Preventive measures in the Council of Europe Convention on offences relating to cultural property: an overview. Santander Art Cult Law Rev 4(2):121–142

Mottese E (2020) La lotta contro il danneggiamento e il traffico illecito di beni culturali nel diritto internazionale. La Convenzione di Nicosia del Consiglio d'Europa. Giappichelli, Turin

Nafziger JAR (1985) International penal aspects of protecting cultural property. Int Lawyer 19(3): 840–841

Nafziger JAR (2010) United States. In: Kono T (ed) The impact of uniform laws on the protection of cultural heritage and the preservation of cultural heritage in the 21st century. Brill, Leiden-Boston, pp 757–771

Naylor R (2008) The underworld of art. Crime Law Soc Change 50(4–5):263–291

Ní Chonaill S, Reding A, Valeri S (2011) Assessing the illegal trade in cultural property from a public policy perspective. RAND Corporation, Santamonica-Arlington

Nistri G (2011) The experience of the Italian Cultural Heritage Protection Unit. In: Manacorda S, Chappell D (eds) Crime in the art and antiquities world. Illegal trafficking in cultural property. Springer, New York-Dordrecht, pp 183–192

O'Keefe PJ (2002) Shipwrecked heritage: a commentary on the UNESCO Convention on underwater cultural heritage. Institute of Art Law, London

O'Keefe PJ (2007) Commentary on the 1970 UNESCO Convention on the means of prohibiting and preventing the illicit import, export and transfer of ownership of cultural property, 2nd edn. Institute of Art & Law, Builth Wells

O'Keefe R (2006) The protection of cultural property in armed conflict. Cambridge University Press, Cambridge-New York

O'Keefe R (2020) Cultural heritage and international humanitarian law. In: Francioni F, Vrdoljak AF (eds) The Oxford handbook of international cultural heritage law. Oxford University Press, Oxford, pp 43–74

Passas N, Bowman Proulx B (2011) Overview of crimes and antiques. In: Manacorda S, Chappell D (eds) Crime in the art and antiquities world. Illegal trafficking in cultural property. Springer, New York, pp 51–67

Polk K (2000) The antiquities trade viewed as a criminal market. Hong Kong Lawyer 82:82–92

Polk K, Chappell D (2019) Policing and prosecution of heritage crime: revisiting the 'Cordata' – just how organised is the international traffic in cultural heritage? In: Mitsilegas V, Hufnagel S, Moiseienko A (eds) Research handbook on transnational crime. Edward Elgar, London, pp 403–412

Posner EA (2007) The international protection of cultural property: Some skeptical observations. Chic J Int Law 8(1):213–231

Prott LV (1996) UNESCO and UNIDROIT: a partnership against trafficking in cultural objects. Unif Law Rev 1:59–71

Prott LV (2021) Commentary on the UNIDROIT Convention, 2nd edn. Institute of Art & Law, Builth Wells

Quatremère de Quincy AC (1815) Lettres sur le préjudice qu'occasionneroient aux Arts et à la Science, le déplacement des monumens de l'art de l'Italie, le démembrement de ses Ecoles, et la spoliation de ses Collections, Galeries, Musées, etc., s.n., Rome

Redmond Cooper R (ed) (2021) Museums and the Holocaust. Institute of Art & Law, Builth Wells

Renfrew C (2000) Loot, legitimacy and ownership: the ethical crisis in archaeology. Duckworth, London
Sargent M, Marrone JV, Evans A, Lilly B, Nemeth E, Dalzell S (2020) Tracking and disrupting the illicit antiquities trade with open-source data. RAND Corporation, Santa Monica
Savoy B (2022) Africa's struggle for its art. History of a postcolonial defeat. Princeton-Oxford, Princeton University Press
Schindler HJ, Gautier F (2019) Looting and smuggling of artifacts as a strategy to finance terrorism. Global sanctions as a disruptive and preventive tool. Int J Cult Prop 26(3):331–342
Schreiber H (2021) Regulation (EU) 2019/880 and the 1970 UNESCO Convention – a note on the interplay between the EU and UNESCO import regimes. Santander Art Cult Law Rev 7(2): 173–182
Scovazzi T (2011) Diviser c'est détruire: ethical principles and legal rules in the field of return of cultural property. Riv Dir Int 2:341–395
Stamatoudi I (2011) Cultural property law and restitution. A Commentary to international conventions and European Union law. Edward Elgar, Cheltenham-Northampton
Sutherland EH (1983) White-collar crime. The uncut version. Yale University Press, New Haven
Sykes GM, Matza D (1957) Techniques of neutralization: a theory of delinquency. Am Sociol Rev 22:664–670
Tijhuis EAJG (2011) The trafficking problem: a criminological perspective. In: Manacorda S, Chappell D (eds) Crime in the art and antiquities world. Illegal trafficking in cultural property. Springer, New York, pp 87–97
Toman J (1996) The protection of cultural property in the event of armed conflict. UNESCO - Dartmouth Publishing, Aldershot
Urbinati S (2018) The European Union legal framework and the fight against the illicit trafficking of cultural property coming from situations of armed conflict. Santander Art Cult Law Rev 4(2): 51–70
Van Beurden J (2017) Treasures in trusted hands. Negotiating the future of colonial cultural objects. Sidestone Press, Leiden
Van Beurden J (2018) Decolonisation and colonial collections. An unresolved conflict. BMGN Low Count Hist Rev 133(2):66–78
Van Duyne PC, Louwe L, Soudijn M (2015) Money, art, and laundering: coming to grips with the risks. In: Kila JD, Balcells M (eds) Cultural property crime. An overview and analysis of contemporary perspectives and trends. Brill, Leiden-Boston, pp 79–95
Visconti A (2013) Le prospettive internazionali di tutela penale: strategie sanzionatorie e politico-criminali. In: Manacorda S, Visconti A (eds) Beni culturali e sistema penale. Vita e Pensiero, Milano, pp 139–159
Visconti A (2015) Cultural property trafficking. In: Boister N, Currie RJ (eds) Routledge handbook of transnational criminal law. Routledge, London-New York, pp 264–279
Visconti A (2021a) The illicit trade in cultural objects. From marginalization to the current surge in attention by transnational criminal policymakers. In: Boister N, Gless S, Jessberger F (eds) Histories of transnational criminal law. Oxford University Press, Oxford, pp 220–235
Visconti A (2021b) Fighting cultural property trafficking: the Italian criminal law framework and its forthcoming reform. Art Antiq Law 26(4):317–354
Visconti A (2021c) Between "colonial amnesia" and "victimization biases": double standards in Italian cultural heritage law. Int J Cult Prop 28(4):551–573
Vrdoljak AF, Meskell L (2020) Intellectual Cooperation Organisation, UNESCO, and the culture conventions. In: Francioni F, Vrdoljak AF (eds), The Oxford handbook of international cultural heritage law. Oxford University Press, Oxford, pp. 13–39
Zagato L (2021) The EU contribution against the illicit trafficking of cultural goods. Recent developments. In: Traviglia A, Milano L, Tonghini C, Giovanelli R (eds) Stolen heritage. Multidisciplinary perspectives on illicit trafficking of cultural heritage in the EU and the MENA region. Edizioni Ca' Foscari, Venice, pp 51–70

The Criminal Policy on Trafficking in Cultural Goods

Riccardo Ercole Omodei

Abstract In recent years the international community has shown interest in intervening to combat the flourishing illegal art market, so much so that it has acted several times with hard and soft law instruments, albeit with unsatisfactory results. This is also due to the fact that the fight against illegal trafficking has hitherto been considered as a sub-sector of the war on organised crime, taking the tools of intervention from this. An illegal trade, however, such as the trade in cultural goods, which has absolutely peculiar characteristics compared to other illicit markets, does not lend itself to such a crime-fighting technique, becoming useful ground to reflect upon for an autonomous rewriting of the discipline of combating illicit trafficking. Considering illegal markets not as battlegrounds for criminal associations, but as physiological centres of exchange driven by the logic of profit, can make it possible to outline holistic law enforcement regulations that are more effective and more respectful of individual rights.

1 Introduction

The international community is increasingly intervening through *ad hoc* instruments in the fight against various types of trafficking. As of today, in addition to the conventions and protocols already in force on, among other things, drugs, trafficking in human beings, smuggling of migrants and arms, the possibility of regulating trafficking in dangerous waste and cultural goods is also being discussed.

This awareness is certainly to be welcomed as it provides states, defenceless in the face of such complex transnational phenomena, with indispensable tools for confronting prosperous illicit markets. Nevertheless, the trend to regulate the phenomenon suffers from a significant lack of perspective, according to which the

R. E. Omodei (✉)
Law Department, University of Palermo, Palermo, Italy
e-mail: riccardoercole.omodei@unipa.it

V. Militello, A. Spena (eds.), *The Challenges of Illegal Trafficking in the Mediterranean Area*, Legal Studies in International, European and Comparative Criminal Law 9, https://doi.org/10.1007/978-3-031-45399-1_13

anti-trafficking discipline is always conceived as a sub-sector of the fight against organised crime.

This is made clear by the method chosen at the international level to counter specific trafficking, strongly linked with the criminal organisation. In some cases, this assimilation is evident—as for the Additional Protocols to the Palermo Convention on Organised Crime—while in others it is less conspicuous but nonetheless present, as for the UN Convention against Illicit Traffic in Narcotic Drugs.

This connection, it would be better to say dependence, of the matter of trafficking with that of criminal association is presumably based on two different reasons. On the one hand, the difficulty of differentiating the two phenomena on a criminological level, also given the absolute vagueness of the notion of criminal organisation. On the other, there is the appeal that the Palermo Convention has acquired in the international context, and the political consensus that has been created around it.

The aim of this paper is to show the limits of this approach in the fight against the various types of trafficking and, even more so, in the specific sector of illegal trade in cultural goods characterised by certain peculiarities that make it difficult to fit into the classic schemes of organised crime. Starting from the premise, which is taken for granted, that the fight against trafficking is conceived in the international system as a sub-sector of the war on organised crime, I will proceed as follows. Firstly, the two reasons underlying the assimilationist choice will be refuted, and it will be demonstrated that they are inconsistent. Next, the peculiarities of trafficking in cultural goods will be briefly analysed and recent instances of reform will be discussed. After showing how even in the area of illicit trade in cultural goods the trend of assimilation between the two issues appears strong, the sanctioning distortions of this criminal policy will be investigated by looking closely at the Italian legal system that has recently intervened in the area of crimes against cultural property.

Finally, the possible positive consequences that a criminal policy to combat trafficking independently of the criminal organisation might entail will be mentioned.

2 A Needed Clarification: What Is Organised Crime (from the Law Point of View)?

The basic assumption of this paper is that the criminal policy related to trafficking in cultural goods, and broadly speaking related to every kind of trafficking, is overly influenced by strategies against criminal organisations. I also argue that this confusion is primarily due to two different reasons; one of these is the unclear notion of organised crime.

Considering this, before proceeding with the analysis, it is appropriate to say a few words on this disputed notion.

As is well known, the concept of criminal organisation, although already appearing at the beginning of the twentieth century, was theorised in greater depth in post-World War II America in relation to the criminal phenomenon of the Sicilian Mafia. This gave rise to a definition characterised by elements such as hierarchy, use of violence and the tendency to obtain a monopoly position in illegal markets.[1] Such a narrow definition, tailored to the idea of Cosa Nostra, was immediately criticised in favour of a concept of organised crime reinterpreted in terms of illicit enterprise. From a structural point of view, organised crime became simple partnership among illegal entrepreneurs. In the 1990s, the boundaries of the notion in question became even vaguer, as the idea of the illicit enterprise was replaced by that of the network, seen as a self-organising structure, completely flexible, capable of adapting to changes and new opportunities.[2]

Such a broad definition, that leaves *readers unsure as to what it means*,[3] is not able to precisely mark the boundaries of the organised criminal group. It therefore happens that any organised criminal activity, such as, for example, illicit trafficking that consists of different stages and different actors is easily qualified as organised crime. Hence, this latter notion became almost useless.

I am convinced that a more precise notion of organised crime, and of its structure, can be found in the field of criminology,[4] but nevertheless I believe that, regardless of the concept that criminology embraces, law, and especially criminal law, cannot but conclude for a more precise and delimited notion.

It is indeed undeniable that the legal definition must serve the typical purposes of the law. In the field of criminal law, a definition serves to answer the question: what makes a conduct wrong? If a conduct is wrong when it is harmful, the legally relevant concept is aimed at preventing and punishing conducts that are harmful *per se*. Therefore, the concept of criminal group should be able to identify harmfulness different from (and independent of) that envisaged by the specific criminal activities in which the group is involved. Indeed, when criminal law punishes participation in a criminal organisation, it aims at punishing the existence of an autonomous, stable and enduring entity, organised with the objective of engaging in activities of a criminal nature. The criminal organisation is punished because it has a distinct organisational apparatus that is clearly separated from the preparatory (and executive) activities relating to individual offences.

I am aware that I am still a long way from a satisfactory definition of organisation, a difficulty well highlighted by those who have delved into the UN and EU definitions on the subject,[5] but I believe I have sufficiently proved what I was interested in proving: in the field of criminal law, the concept of organisation must

---

[1] This is the idea of the pioneer of the modern criminological study of organised crime: Cressey (1969).

[2] For an in-depth reconstruction of the concepts mentioned and appropriate bibliographical references, see Mann (2020) pp. 3–17; Varese (2017), pp. 27–56; Finckenauer (2005), pp. 63–83.

[3] Varese (2017), p. 27.

[4] On the criminological distinction between organised criminal activity and organised crime see Finckenauer (2005) pp. 76 f.; Hagan (2006), pp. 134 ff.

[5] On the two different definitions see the articles by Militello (2017) and Polimeni (2017).

be something different from the mere complexity that denotes ramified criminal phenomena such as trafficking. What the legislator intends to punish through the notion of criminal organisation is something different, more structured, than the chain of connections, the network, that characterises trafficking. Both the phenomena are organised activities, but the criminal group is something more than the network of the trafficking.

It is worth specifying that obviously the two phenomena can overlap and that perhaps a criminal organisation may have a competitive advantage in managing trafficking or a phase of it, but we have to bear in mind that we are speaking of different realities.

Before moving to the features of the market and to the instances of reform related to the field of trafficking in cultural goods, I would like to spend a few words on the other reason why the two topics (trafficking and organised crime) often overlap: the appeal of the Palermo Convention. Indeed, it must be recognised that in the face of a still-present resistance of states to binding themselves with international criminal law instruments towards specific incrimination choices, the topic of the criminal organisation succeeds in acting as a veritable *passe-partout*, capable of overcoming the reluctance of even the most hesitant systems.

Beyond these reasons, which cannot be analysed here but which are probably linked to the idea of organised crime nowadays perceived as a major threat to society,[6] it seems plausible that basing possible new conventions against trafficking on the ground already laid by such an important instrument as the Palermo Convention could represent a simpler and more easily achievable path to international harmonisation.

Nevertheless, the risk inherent in such a course of action is that the application of repressive law enforcement tools typical of the organised crime sector will be over-extended to areas that do not necessarily present the same characteristics, and thus the same risk, as the criminal organisation.

I shall return to the possible distortions of this approach later, citing the example of Italian legislation; here, I would only like to emphasise that greater awareness on the need of an autonomous criminal policy could be of considerable benefit both to legislation on trafficking and to that on organised crime.

[6] Recently, Mann (2020) has insisted on this function of the concept of war on organised crime as a necessary condition for the development of an extensive architecture of law, policing, surveillance and intelligence.

3 The Features of the Cultural Goods Market

According to recent but rough estimates, due to the dark figure of the crime and the inherent variability of the value of the objects trafficked, the cultural goods market can generate earnings of more than 2.2 billion USD per year,[7] and is often characterised by its transnational dimension. Indeed, this trafficking usually involves several states and consists of various illicit steps, characterised in turn by the presence of different criminal actors.

To simplify, three phases can be identified in the illicit circulation of cultural goods.[8]

The first, relating to their apprehension, is the moment in which the criminal nature of the action is most evident, as the goods are attracted into the illicit circuit through manifestly criminal conduct, such as theft or illegal excavation. Subsequently, the extensive phase of ‘cleaning up’ of its illicit origin begins, which may involve various intermediaries in different parts of the globe. It is worth pointing out that the people involved in trafficking, at this time, change faces, often characterised as being art experts of international fame and standing, and that it is possible that the individual operating in this role is unaware of the illicit origin of the good.

This more or less complex intermediation, however, allows the object to reach its destination, i.e. the final buyer, who is willing to pay a huge amount of money to acquire that unique piece of art.

From this inevitably incomplete sketch, the main feature of this type of trafficking emerges. Unlike other illicit trades, such as drugs or human beings, in the cultural goods case, not only are the traded goods legitimate, but the overlap between the licit and illicit market is almost total. The illicitly acquired goods indeed exploit the same channels as the licit ones *ab origine*.

Of this mixed, grey nature, of the market, the main actors of all the reported phases are first and foremost aware. In a not recent but relevant study,[9] there emerges the pervasiveness of the phenomenon of looting, which 98% of the interviewed archaeologists are aware they have to live with. At the same time, the overwhelming majority of intermediaries, even the most reputable ones, are not only aware of the mixed nature of the market in which they operate, but are not inclined to investigate the provenance of the object in depth, often contenting themselves with the more

[7] According to Campbell (2013), p. 114.

[8] In this regard see Campbell (2013), passim, who however identifies four different phases, differentiating a first intermediation phase and a second intermediation phase. Since the intermediaries can be multiple, we have opted here for a general second phase including all possible intermediate steps of cleaning up the good between the moment of apprehension and the final purchase by the collector/museum. For the necessary bibliography, please refer to the cited contribution.

[9] I am referring to a 2008 study based on 2400 interviews with archaeologists around the globe, cited in Passas and Bowman Prouls (2011), p. 61.

than dubious qualification of 'belonging to a private collector'.[10] Indeed, the neutralisation mechanisms typical of so-called white collar crimes are present, whereby the perpetrator is often unaware that he is engaging in criminal conduct, or in other words, does not grasp, more or less consciously, the criminal nature of the act performed.[11]

The possibility of handling goods of unlawful origin is therefore usually perceived as an inevitable risk of the activity performed, often accompanied by the idea that not investigating further the dubious origin of that object, far from constituting a criminal act, is rather a deserving conduct, as it saves the goods from a deplorable end. Finally, it can be said that the illegal market in cultural goods is partly an apparently legal market involving people of considerable international renown and social status.[12]

The people operating there mostly tend to act autonomously, exploiting their technical knowledge and the network of contacts at their disposal, with a more or less vague awareness of the illicit origin of the goods. In such a context, large-scale organised crime, normally operating in the more canonical illicit markets, seems to limit itself to episodic 'intrusions' in the first phase of the trafficking under consideration.

This characteristic has also been observed by recent criminological studies in peculiar illegal trade in cultural goods connected with international terrorism. I am referring to the well-known trafficking of archaeological finds from Syria and Iraq by Islamic State. According to the results of this research,[13] the trafficking of antiquities was not managed by the terrorist organisation itself, but by individual looters and intermediaries from outside IS, who simply paid tributes to the Islamic State in return for their activities,[14] and otherwise acted independently through their own network.

---

[10] In relation to one of the most important transit markets, the UK, see Mackenzie (2011), p. 69 ff. and the bibliography cited therein.

[11] Just as, according to some literature, corporate structures drive the white collar worker to commit the crime through the provision of the context, the means and the incentive to commit the crime, leading the perpetrator to feel no remorse for that illicit action, perceived as routine and natural, in the same way, the cultural goods market represents the perfect context for annihilating the counter-push to crime of the criminal law, since it is characterised by huge profits, the absence of a victim, and therefore the lack of confrontation with the victim or a real scene of the crime, and a very high possibility of 'getting away with it'. In addition, this market is dominated by a small circle of professionals, closed to external control as they are protected by their technical knowledge, thus allowing the reiteration of practices, if not illegal, certainly irregular, within the ambiguity of which criminal practice can proliferate. On this feature of white collar crimes, see, among others, Gobert and Punch (2007), pp. 98 ff.

[12] See v. Chappell and Polk (2011), pp. 99 ff.

[13] I am referring to Sargent et al. (2020). The European Commission's final report also recently concluded on the fluid nature of the market in question, while not denying possible intrusions of traditional organised crime, see Brodie and Yates (2019), pp. 68 ff., 108 ff.

[14] Sargent et al. (2020), pp. 25–26. In the same report, a possible greater involvement of ISIS emerges at a later stage, with the followers themselves engaged in the excavation activity, but this does not change the final judgement of the authors, who conclude by recognising the illegal trade in

I do not intend to deny any form of organisation to the criminal process under study, which, on the other hand, is characterised by a high degree of complexity, being structured in the same way as a veritable criminal network, without a management centre, where the independent actors are all motivated exclusively by the aim of unjust profit. I just want to remark that this kind of organisation is not the one that justifies the adoption of the classical tools against Organised Crime.

Obviously, I also do not want to deny that in some cases criminal organisations operate in this market, but this is not the rule.

4 The Interest of the International Community in the Phenomenon and the Possible Interventions

Having clarified the features of the illegal market, I can now turn to the regulatory attempts developed in recent years. The issue of the protection of cultural property has acquired a very important dimension in the supranational context. This is borne out by the dense web of international treaties[15] that have been concluded since the 1954 Hague Convention on the Protection of Cultural Property in the Event of Armed Conflict.

Nevertheless, if we exclude humanitarian law and international criminal law related to armed conflicts, we can say that, so far, criminal law has played a minor role in this area, which has been dominated by public and private international law.[16] Thus, it is no coincidence that the two most relevant conventions on this subject are the UNESCO Convention on trafficking in cultural goods[17] and the UNIDROIT treaty[18] on stolen or illegally exported cultural objects.

question as peculiar in nature compared to other trades, precisely because of the absence of a ramified criminal organisation as a rule.

[15] Looking only at the European continental context, the following can be mentioned here: the European cultural convention, signed in Paris in 1954; the European convention on the protection of archeological heritage (London, 1969) and the new version of this treaty signed in La Valletta in 1992; the Convention for the protection of the architectural heritage in Europe (Granada, 1985) and the Council of Europe framework convention on the value of cultural heritage for society (Faro, 2011).

[16] As scholars have already pointed out, international criminal law—thanks above all to the work of the international criminal courts—played a crucial role in fostering protection of the cultural heritage. Recently see, also regarding the different approaches that animate international criminal law, Frulli (2020), pp. 100 ff.

[17] Convention on the means of prohibiting and preventing the illicit import, export and transfer of ownership of cultural property (Paris, 1970).

[18] Convention on stolen or illegally exported cultural objects (Rome, 1995). On the complementary relationship between the two conventions, see Prott (1996) and Prott (2009).

Therefore, when facing the issue of the illicit circulation of cultural property, international law still relies essentially on private law tools and possibly on administrative sanctions.[19]

Luckily, things look different today. This change of direction is reflected in recent international regulations. The new dimension of the criminal phenomenon is testified by the UN *Guidelines for Crime Prevention and Criminal Justice Responses with Respect to Trafficking in Cultural Property and Other Related Offences*[20] which strongly encourages Member States to review their criminal legislation related to trafficking in cultural goods by criminalising a lot of different kinds of conducts related to this illicit procedure, and by the so-called Convention of Nicosia of the CoE on *Offences relating to cultural property*.[21] This is the first hard law tool of criminal law that has entered into force on the subject, so it may represent a clear turning point in protection of the cultural heritage.

It is not my intention to deal with the discipline dictated by the Nicosia Convention,[22] For the purposes of my argument I would just like to emphasise that this international act is scarcely influenced by the issue of organised crime and represents an attempt to recognise the autonomy of criminal policy in combating trafficking.

Indeed, the legislation envisaged seems to be modelled on the need to counter the various conducts that are part of trafficking, taking into account their criminological peculiarities, and not on countering the criminal organisation that may act in such trafficking. In a proper balancing of the two phenomena, the criminal organisation is not the focus of this legislation, but neither it is excluded altogether. Indeed, after the trafficking-fighting discipline was structured in an autonomous manner, a specific aggravating circumstance has been provided for to counter any organisation operating in the art market.

Unfortunately, the path mapped out by the Council of Europe seems to have little appeal among the international community. To date, although it has entered into force, the number of ratifications is indeed particularly low (only 6).

Despite considerable progress in international legislation on the protection of cultural property, in criminal matters the reluctance of the legislator is still particularly evident. The jealousy with which parliaments guard their power in criminal matters still seems far from disappearing, although in some regional areas—I am thinking primarily of the European one—this dogma is slowly but steadily being eroded. Outside the regional contexts, however, we are still a long way from such a situation, and to overcome the resistance of individual legal systems, the threat of organised crime is frequently invoked. This is mainly due to the fact that organised crime is not conceived anymore as a domestic threat but as a major problem for the international community that demands global responses. Thus, states are more

[19]On the different impact of criminal law in the two different areas of cultural heritage protection: Manacorda (2011).

[20]Resolution adopted by the General Assembly on 18 December 2014.

[21]https://www.coe.int/en/web/conventions/full-list?module=treaty-detail&treatynum=221.

[22]In relation to this topic, see the essay by Visconti in this volume.

willing to cede parts of their sovereignty on this topic. It is therefore clear that being able to establish, or at least find, a close link between a specific topic and the fight against organised crime can be a useful shortcut to major international legislation.

This is also what is happening in the field of trafficking in cultural goods, where the applicability of the Palermo Convention has long been invoked by many. Indeed, both the doctrine[23] and the international community[24] have expressed themselves in favour of this conclusion in recent years, considering it to be the most convenient way to achieve an effective fight against the criminal phenomenon of the illegal trade in works of art.

Such a course of action, which certainly has the merit of following a path already well-trodden in international law, nevertheless presents two pitfalls. On the one hand, the risk is that of extending an unprecedented and exceptional apparatus of regulatory, investigative and police measures, well-tailored on the needs of the criminal organisation counter action, to sectors that do not need such instruments and where the rights of individuals would therefore be unnecessarily endangered.

On the other hand, this mere uncritical reproduction of a criminal policy envisaged for the criminal organisation runs the risk of presenting itself as an ineffective law enforcement tool, not adapted to the specific needs of individual trafficking.

The two risks mentioned are both present in the Italian anti-trafficking legislation to which, therefore, the analysis must now turn. A look at the Italian legislation will allow me to clearly show the distortions of a criminal anti-trafficking policy excessively linked to the war on organised crime, thus revealing that the path mapped out by the Nicosia Convention is to be preferred.

5 The Italian Case

A look at the Italian regulatory experience in combating trafficking can be particularly useful. Indeed, the philosophy of combating criminal organisation in it seems to be particularly present.

I will focus on the following trafficking: smuggling of migrants, trafficking in human beings, drug trafficking and hazardous waste trafficking. In all these cases, the Italian legislation to combat them is deeply linked to the regulations on criminal organisations.

I will be brief: in two ways trafficking policy is influenced by the need to fight organised crime. On one hand, we have the hypothesis of smuggling of migrants, human and drug trafficking, and on the other we have waste trafficking.

---

[23] On this point see Borgstede (2014) and Visconti (2021), pp. 230 ff.; Critical about this option Manacorda (2011), pp. 42–45.

[24] The Conference of the Parties on two occasions called for the need to extend UNTOC to the trafficking of cultural property: Resolution 5/7 of October 2010 and Resolution 10/7 of October 2020.

In the former, the legislator not only introduces a specific criminal offence concerning trafficking,[25] but also provides for a criminal offence to punish the criminal association dedicated to that type of trafficking. But why does a system that already includes a general offence dedicated to criminal association[26] feel the need to intervene with new association offences that add nothing in terms of typifying the conduct? and why does it continue to do so despite the obvious problems of concurring offences that are posed by case law?.[27]

The answer can only be found by observing the relevant procedural and prison regulations. The fact is that all these special associative offences are included in the increasingly dense list of crimes subject to a special regime of trial and penal execution. These lists, contained in Article 51, para. 3 *bis* of the Italian Code of Criminal Procedure and Article 4 *bis* of the Law n. 354/1975 (so called Penitentiary Law), entail, for the offences included in them, considerable deviations from the ordinary procedural and prison guarantees.[28] This exceptional criminal justice system, which arose in connection with, and is justified by, the mafia type association, should not be subjected to extension and its steady growth is perhaps the clearest proof of how the Italian legislator conceives trafficking only in connection with the

[25] The criminal offence of trafficking usually contains an extensive list of alternative punishable conducts with the intention of striking at all the different conducts that make up the illegal cycle, from production to use of the object.

[26] The Italian legal system has a provision capable of punishing all criminal associations composed by more than three persons and aimed at committing an indeterminate number of crimes (art. 416 Criminal Code). The applicability of this offence is not limited to a specific category of crimes, since the association may be aimed at committing any kind of crime. In addition to this 'general' provision, the Italian legal system also includes another "general" offence that, however, only applies when the association uses a mafia method, as defined in Article 416 bis of the Criminal Code.

[27] I will try to outline a problem that stems directly from the proliferation of the association offences in the trafficking sector. The increase in the number of associative offences carries a considerable risk of violating ne bis in idem. In fact, as practice has shown, in the presence of a single criminal organisation operating in several illicit markets, the defendants may be charged with the different associative rules. To give an example, if a criminal group sells both drugs and smuggled cigarettes, the members of the group will be charged with both the offence of association dedicated to drug trafficking and the offence of association for the purpose of smuggling cigarettes, with an obvious double charge in respect of the same action (the criminal association).

[28] There are many differences between the rules governing this special trial and prison regime and the ordinary ones. On the criminal trial side, for example, the office in charge of preliminary investigations will be different (with longer deadlines for carrying out investigations), but there are also differences with regard to the regulations on wiretapping, the presumption of adequacy of pre-trial detention in prison and the evidence procedure. On the other hand, with regard to prison treatment, it is a matter of subjecting the convicted person to the so-called "hard prison regime", where obtaining rewards and benefits is precluded.

It is evident that this regime, which waives some fundamental guarantees, can only be justified in the presence of major public order interests, as in the case of mafia association and terrorism, but is difficult to justify in other contexts. Its continued expansion, therefore, is a source of concern for the jurist.

criminal organisation, while at the same time showing the risks to the rights of the individual that such a criminal policy strategy entails.

In the case of waste trafficking, however, this dependence is even more pronounced. In this case, the Italian legislator chose to introduce a single provision which, however, presents peculiar characteristics. Indeed, this is not the usual criminal offence concerning trafficking (characterised by a list of alternative punishable conducts, necessary to punish the entire cycle of illegal trade) but a criminal offence that appears to focus on the requirement of organisation, as if it were an associative offence. Despite being formally a one-subject criminal offence, it seems to focus on the organisational structure stably dedicated to trafficking in waste, a rationale we have seen underpinning the notion of criminal organisation that is useful for criminal law.

And indeed, in Italy, doctrine has long debated the nature of this offence:[29] whether it should be a single-subject or necessarily a multi-subject one. The question has therefore been raised as to whether the law wanted to introduce a new associative offence with this provision.

Once again, the influence of the notion of a criminal organisation is felt in the area of trafficking. Indeed, in this case, it is so marked that it directly affects the conformation of the specific criminal offence of illegal waste trafficking, which seems aimed at punishing criminal association and not mere trafficking.

This offence is designed to tackle criminal organisations and this is clear if we look at the applicable procedural and prison regime. Indeed, it is the same regime provided for organised crime by Article 51 para. 3 *bis* of the Code of Criminal Procedure and Article 4 *bis* of the Penitentiary Law.

In conclusion, we can state that the Italian legal system completely assimilates criminal policy on illicit trafficking with that on criminal organisation, leading to an uncontrolled expansion of the special law enforcement instruments envisaged for criminal associations, waiving the defendant's fundamental rights.

A fleeting glance at the recent reform of offences against cultural property may provide further confirmation on this point.

The recent Law No. 22/2022[30] has profoundly changed the face of Italian criminal law on the protection of cultural property. The amendment has rewritten the entire criminal law framework from the bottom up, making it more consistent with the constitutional and international significance of cultural heritage, and ensuring a particularly extensive form of direct protection of this legal asset with significant penalties. An entire title has been inserted into the Criminal Code, VIII-bis, containing a long list of incriminating offences specifically dedicated to the cultural heritage, which provide for considerably higher penalties than those previously imposed for the same conducts of dispersing or damaging cultural goods.

However, if we look at the trafficking of cultural objects, little has been done. Indeed, no catch-all offence has been introduced to combat the entire cycle of illegal

[29] To date, jurisprudence and doctrine consider it a one-subject criminal offence.

[30] For a first commentary on the law, see Demuro (2022).

trade, while just a few specific offences, such as theft and laundering of cultural goods, have been provided for. Little attention was therefore paid to trafficking when the reform was passed, despite the fact that during the parliamentary debate the tone was quite dissimilar. The reform project on this point was indeed considerably different, since it provided for the introduction of a criminal offence specifically dedicated to trafficking in cultural goods and modelled on Article 452 *quaterdecies* of the criminal code.[31]

The proposed article therefore had the same defects of criminal policy as for the criminal offences commented on above, since it found its justifying reason in combating criminal organisations and not illegal trafficking. As proof of this, the offence of trafficking in cultural goods was included in the list of exceptional cases contained in Article 51 para. 3 *bis* of the Code of Criminal Procedure and Article 4 *bis* of the Penitentiary Law.

Not having approved this provision is certainly a virtue of the recent reform. Introducing an article identical to the one currently in force on waste trafficking would have entailed a further expansion of the already vast area of combating criminal organisations, to the detriment of the rights of individual defendants.[32] At the same time, the failure to approve it has shown all the limits of the current criminal policy against illegal trafficking: with the disappearance of the reference to organised crime, the fight against trafficking shows the lack of an autonomous dimension. Having always thought of trafficking in terms of combating criminal organisations has inevitably distorted its contents, which are now absolutely lacking. This deficiency emerges in the Italian discipline on combating trafficking in cultural goods, which is detached from the logic of tackling organised crime and today is shown to be absolutely deficient. Faced with the need to delineate a policy to combat illicit trafficking that was independent of criminal organisations, the Italian legislator preferred to take a step backwards, refraining from outlining a comprehensive criminal law framework that could address the problematic definition of trafficking in works of art.

The Italian legislation is therefore a vivid example of how the international approach to combating illicit trafficking, overly dependent on the fight against organised crime, can lead to two major distortions: on the one hand, excessive recourse to exceptional instruments typical of the fight against organised crime; on the other hand, the absolute deficiency of the anti-trafficking criminal policy which, deprived of the tools to fight organised crime, appears bare in content. Therefore, separating the fight against trafficking from the fight against organised crime may prove to be a useful way to reflect more seriously on an effective policy modelled on the specific trafficking.

---

[31] I.e. the criminal offence of trafficking of hazardous waste.

[32] On the risks linked to the expansion of the discipline against organised crime to the area of illegal trafficking in the Italian legal system, see Omodei (2021), pp. 994 ff., Omodei (2020), pp. 98 ff.

6 Concluding Remarks: How to Tackle the Trafficking Phenomenon?

So far, it has been shown that the current international approach to combating trafficking is particularly deficient, and in doing so, the example of the Italian legal system has also been cited. In these closing remarks, I must dwell on two different issues that have to be examined in depth in the future in order to arrive at an incisive criminal policy.

The first one is a specifically criminological problem and relates to what is an illicit traffic, and what are its characteristics. As seen above, this analysis should not be developed around the notion of organised crime, but it should be aimed at a more general understanding of the market and its transactions. From this point of view, illicit traffic can be analysed for what it actually is: market exchanges that stand in violation of the law.[33] Thus, we should be willing to abandon the idea, as already done in the field of economic sociology,[34] that illicit trafficking is *a parasitic phenomenon at the fringes of economy*,[35] the fruit of the exclusive action of criminal organisations, acknowledging instead that it is *an integral part of capitalist accumulation*.[36] In this way, we can finally free ourselves from the idea of a perennially emergency phenomenon that characterises anti-trafficking policies, like all regulations against organised crime, in favour of a wide policy, not only criminal, which takes greater account of the dynamics of the market and the peculiarities of the traffic that forms part of it.

The first outcome of this change of point of view is that anti-trafficking policies cannot be only criminal but must embrace the various areas of law. An exclusively criminal policy to combat a phenomenon that is a physiological expression of every market will inevitably prove to be fallacious.

The second issue is strongly linked to the previous one and deals with the structure of the criminal policy against trafficking. I would like to make it clear that I am not concluding in favour of a single criminal offence applying to all trafficking. Each phenomenon has its own peculiarities, and these must be taken into account in the criminal provisions. What I want to emphasise here is that anti-trafficking criminal policies can, indeed must, have a common foundation. In fact, seeing the traffic as that set of transactions aimed at feeding an even partially illegal market, the fight against it becomes the fight against each individual transaction of the market.

The single criminal provision, therefore, should be able to hit all the actors that take part in the specific illegal procedure and all their actions. It is evident that it is not a simple operation. In fact, it would be necessary to identify a criminal offence

[33] And like every financial transaction, the trafficking is demand-driven and profit-driven.

[34] See Beckert and Dewey (2017).

[35] Ivi, p. 3.

[36] Ibid.

(or several criminal offences) making it possible to sanction all the different phases of the wrongful act, which in such complex phenomena can be characterised by a large number of actors and relevant actions or omissions. It is a question of tackling, with the unreactive weapons of law, a very dynamic and fickle phenomenon, which grows, changes and proliferates at the pressing pace of modern economies.

Given these features, dynamically combating the phenomenon, and thus suppressing all possible transactions that can be carried out, is a titanic task that is difficult to achieve. It is indeed inconceivable that the legal system could criminalise all the conducts in the trafficking cycle, and above all repress a significant portion of the market through law enforcement agencies, so as to discourage its growth linked to the demand for illegal goods. Thus, a common requirement of any criminal policy aiming at combating illicit trafficking is the repression of its static dimension, i.e. possession of the trafficked good.

This would obviate the need for law enforcement agencies to catch the fleeting moment of the individual stage of trafficking (production, transfer, export, etc.) and thus such a dynamic and elusive phenomenon would become, in the eyes of criminal law, a static conduct that is easier to detect.

I am therefore convinced that a serious criminal policy in this regard must necessarily come to terms with criminalisation of possession of the trafficked good. Nevertheless, proposing to build the criminal policy upon possession offences is not something revolutionary or new. Indeed, possession crimes are proliferating in many western countries, and they are considered one of the pillars of the so-called *war on crime*.[37] Hence the "possession paradigm" is not an innovation of trafficking-oriented criminal policy, but it also perfectly matches the idea of the war against criminal organisations.

The change of perspective that I am proposing, in order to be useful, should bring something new. Actually, it does, because it may lead away from the distortions typically linked with possession offences.

Usually, possession offences are criticised in at least two different respects. Firstly, the censures focus on the structure of the crime. Indeed, they are obviously not result crimes, but they also scarcely fit in with the idea of conduct crimes. Possession offences are very often addressed as crimes without conduct, given that it is not easy to find an action or a criminally relevant omission in the possession of an object.[38] The criticism, however, is easily overcome by resorting to the category

---

[37] See Dubber (2002). Concerning this kind of offences, some scholars talk about a case of overcriminalization: Husak (2008), pp. 45 ff.

[38] This is particularly opposed in civil law jurisdictions, due to the alleged conflict of such hypotheses with the principle of materiality. Above all, see Lagodny (1996), pp. 322 ff.

The idea of the possession offence as a conductless offence is very common also in the common law jurisdictions. See, among others, Dubber (2005), pp. 103 ff., that use the expression "attendant circumstance offence".

of status offences, according to which possession is not a conduct but is a *state of affairs* corresponding to the power to dispose of a given object.[39]

Secondly, scholars censure possession offences from the point of view of the harm principle.[40] According to this opinion, possession of an object is unlikely to harm or endanger a legal asset worthy of protection, and thus its criminalisation would contravene the recalled principle. Indeed, the legislator often does not take the trouble to describe the details of the punished conduct of possession of a particular thing, but merely criminalises it, following the logic of all-out war on crime. Devoid of any mark of dangerousness, the conduct thus (poorly) described comes across as enacting over-soon protection with respect to a relevant legal asset, which cannot be affected in any way by the offence.

To date, this interpretation constitutes the most well-founded criticism of possession crimes, and has represented, especially in the continental European panorama and even more so in the Italian one, the main reason behind scholars' mistrust of this type of offence.

The problem of the harmless nature of the possession paradigm could be, in my opinion, surmounted with the new perspective of the criminal policy here suggested. In fact, in a trafficking-oriented criminal policy the aim of possession offences is no longer mere prevention of serious crime but combating the illicit market. This purpose will require knowledge of the market and its function, on the basis of which criminal norms will be shaped. Thus, the possession offence will be structured in line with the nature of the market and its weakness, so as to create an endangerment crime as close as possible to the harm to the protected legal asset.

To avoid being too vague, a concrete example from the illicit market in cultural goods might be useful. In this market punishing mere possession of a cultural object may be particularly problematic. This is because cultural property is not a dangerous object *per se*, nor is its circulation illegal. Hence, the idea of punishing just possession of cultural goods, even if unlawful, would represent an excessive and unjustified anticipation of protection of the legal asset involved. Moreover, such a wide and vague offence would be dangerous. Indeed, faced with a market where the cultural good is, under certain conditions, freely exchangeable, the emptiness of the formula adopted runs the risk of lending itself to major application distortions and, at the same time, of dissipating the system's energies to the benefit of the agents feeding the grey market in cultural goods.

A market-oriented criminal policy could help in both directions. A criminological analysis of the market shows that the nerve centre of the entire trade is represented by the various intermediaries, who allow goods of illicit origin to enter the legal market and circulate freely within it. At this stage of the market, the one that also registers

---

[39] This solution is particularly usual in common law jurisdictions, see among others Ashworth (2011); Dubber and Hörnle (2014), pp. 206 ff.; but it is also present in the continental scenario. Please refers to Eckstein (2001) and, for the Italian legal system, Salvadori (2016).

[40] Harm principle is here understood as that criterion which requires that every offence must violate at least a legally protected interest. On this European-rooted principle, in comparison with the Anglo-Saxon systems, see Eser (1966).

the highest profits, the need to criminalise possession therefore becomes particularly pressing. Thus, criminalization should focus on this phase and the criminal policy should be based on the idea of striking these criminal actors.

I cannot go further on the content of a possible criminal offence.[41] For this I would have to refer to a specific legal system and to the principles and rules governing the circulation of cultural goods in that legal order.[42] I would just like to point out in these closing remarks that with better knowledge of the market and its weak points, the criminal anti-trafficking policy could identify more circumscribed crimes and thus be more respectful of the principles governing criminal law. In order to do so, however, it is necessary to change perspectives and abandon the still pervasive emergency view of organised crime.

To sum up, current anti-trafficking policies, for a variety of reasons, are modelled on the emergency pattern of the fight against organised crime. This approach entails significant distortions for citizens' rights and, in addition, is not very effective. The need therefore arises for an autonomous crime policy on trafficking that is able to take into account the peculiarities of the phenomenon and act at the nerve centres of the market. The trafficking of cultural goods, because of the characteristics it possesses, represents a useful opportunity to attempt this change of perspective.

References

Ashworth A (2011) The unfairness of risk-based possession offences. Crim Law Philos 5:237–257

Beckert J, Dewey M (2017) The architecture of illegal markets. Towards an economic sociology of illegality in the economy. Oxford University Press, Oxford

Borgstede G (2014) Cultural property, the Palermo Convention and transnational organized crime. Int J Cult Prop 21:281–290

Brodie N, Yates D (2019) Illicit trade in cultural goods in Europe. European Publication Office, Bruxelles

Campbell P (2013) The illicit antiquities trade as a transnational criminal network: characterizing and anticipating trafficking of cultural heritage. Int J Cult Prop 20:113–153

Chappell D, Polk K (2011) Unraveling the "Cordata": just how organized is the international traffic in cultural objects? In: Manacorda S, Chappell D (eds) Crime in the art and Antiquites world. Springer, New York, pp 99–116

[41] I explored the issue of the criminalisation of possession of cultural goods in relation to the Italian legal system in a recent article, Omodei (2022).

[42] Given the dependence of anti-trafficking legislation on general cultural heritage regulations, it is impossible to go into more detail here. The differences in terms of circulation are in fact still considerable even between neighbouring legal systems. For example, the Italian and German legal systems start from extremely divergent points on the circulation of cultural goods. While in fact German law enshrines, in Article 20 of the Kulturgutschutzgesetz of 2016, the freedom of movement of cultural property (Kulturgutverkehrsfreiheit) unless otherwise provided for, the Italian system starts from the opposite assumption: it does not provide for a general freedom of movement but specifies in Art. 53 et seq. of the Code of Cultural Heritage and Landscape (D. Lgs. n. 42/2004) a long series of limitations for the circulation of cultural objects.

Cressey DR (1969) Theft of a nation: the structure and operation of organized crime in America. Harper & Row, New York
Demuro GP (2022) I delitti contro il patrimonio culturale nel codice penale: prime riflessioni sul nuovo titolo VIII bis. Diritto Penale Contemporaneo Rivista Trimestrale:1–26
Dubber DM (2002) Policing possession: the war on crime and the end of criminal law. J Crim Law Criminol 91:831–995
Dubber DM (2005) The possession paradigm: the special part and the police power model of the criminal process. In: Duff R, Green S (eds) Defining crimes. Essays on the special part of the criminal law. Oxford University Press, Oxford, pp 91–118
Dubber DM, Hörnle T (2014) Criminal law. A comparative approach. Oxford University Press, Oxford
Eckstein K (2001) Besitz als Straftat. Duncker & Humblot, Berlin
Eser A (1966) The Principle of "Harm" in the Concept of Crime. Duquesne Law Rev 4:345–417
Finckenauer J (2005) Problem of definition: what is organized crime? Trends Organ Crime 8:63–83
Frulli M (2020) International criminal law and the protection of cultural heritage. In: Francioni F, Vrdoljak AF (eds) The Oxford handbook of international cultural heritage law. Oxford University Press, Oxford, pp 100–120
Gobert J, Punch M (2007) Because they can. Motivation and intent of white collar crimes. In: Pontell H, Geis G (eds) International handbook of white-collar and corporate crime. Springer, New York, pp 98–124
Hagan F (2006) "Organized Crime" and "organized crime": indeterminate problems of definition. Trends Organ Crime 9:127–137
Husak D (2008) Overcriminalization. The limits of the Criminal Law. Oxford University Press, New York
Lagodny O (1996) Strafrecht von den Schranken der Grundrechte. Mohr, Tubinga
Mackenzie S (2011) The market as criminal and criminals in the market: reducing opportunities for organized crime in the international Antiquities market. In: Manacorda S, Chappell D (eds) Crime in the art and Antiquites world. Springer, New York, pp 69–86
Manacorda S (2011) Criminal law protection of cultural heritage: an international perspective. In: Manacorda S, Chappell D (eds) Crime in art and antiquities world. Springer, New York, pp 17–48
Mann M (2020) Policing and politicising organised crime. Routledge, London & New York
Militello V (2017) The notion of organised crime in the EU law. In: Carnevale S et al (eds) Redefining organised crime. Hart, Oxford, pp 191–221
Omodei RE (2020) Il ruolo dell'organizzazione criminale nel contrasto al traffico di tabacchi lavorati esteri. Rivista Trimestrale di Diritto Penale dell'Economia 1–2:91–127
Omodei RE (2021) Il traffico di beni culturali: un caso studio delle distorsioni e dei limiti nel contrasto ai traffici illeciti. Riv Ital Dirit Proced Penal 3:975–1021
Omodei RE (2022) Note critiche sui nuovi reati a tutela del patrimonio culturale: incoerenze normative e questioni aperte. Lex Ambiente 2:1–26
Passas N, Bowman Prouls B (2011) Overview of crimes and antiquities. In: Manacorda S, Chappell D (eds) Crime in the art and Antiquites world. Springer, New York, pp 51–68
Polimeni G (2017) The notion of organised crime in the United Nation Convention against transnational organised crime. In: Carnevale S et al (eds) Redefining organised crime. Hart, Oxford, pp 57–74
Prott L (1996) UNESCO and UNIDROIT: a partnership against trafficking in cultural objects. Revue De Droit Uniform 1:59–71
Prott L (2009) The UNIDROIT Convention on stolen or illegally exported cultural objects – ten years on. Revue De Droit Uniform 14:215–237
Salvadori I (2016) I reati di possesso. ESI, Napoli

Sargent M et al (2020) Tracking and disrupting the illicit antiquities trade with open-source data. RAND Corporation, Santa Monica
Varese F (2017) What is organised crime? In: Carnevale S et al (eds) Redefining organised crime. Hart, Oxford, pp 27–56
Visconti A (2021) The illicit trade in cultural objects. In: Boister N et al (eds) Histories of transnational criminal law. Oxford University Press, Oxford, pp 220–235

Trafficking in Human Organs: A Portuguese Perspective

Sónia Fidalgo

Abstract Until September 2019, the Portuguese legal system did not provide for a crime of trafficking in human organs. Law no. 102/2019, of 6 September, adapted the Portuguese legal system to the provisions of the Council of Europe Convention against Trafficking in Human Organs, adopted in Santiago de Compostela, on 25th March 2015. With this law, Article 144-B—*Trafficking in human organs*—was added to the Portuguese Criminal Code. In these few pages I will refer to the international legal framework of the trafficking in human organs. I will then refer to the evolution of the legislation in Portugal on this matter and point out some interpretative doubts regarding the criminal offence under analysis.

1 The Problem

In the last 50 years organ transplantation has become widespread throughout the world, which has prolonged and improved the quality of life of hundreds of thousands of patients.[1] However, despite the progress of transplantation medicine all over the world, the worldwide demand for organs exceeds the supply. In this context, what has been called transplant tourism developed.[2] In fact, due to the shortage of organs, some patients seek transplantation opportunities outside the regulatory framework of the national transplantation system. The scarcity of organs available for transplantation has stimulated human trafficking for the purpose of

[1] In Portugal, the first organ transplant was performed with a kidney from a living donor, on July 20, 1969, at the Hospitals of the University of Coimbra. More than a decade later, in 1980, the first kidney transplants from a deceased donor were performed. Other organ transplants followed, such as liver, heart, pancreas, lung, as well as tissue and cell transplants (see Silva 2019, p. 86).

[2] See, among others, Kelly (2013), pp. 1317 ff.

S. Fidalgo (✉)
Faculty of Law, University of Coimbra, Coimbra, Portugal
e-mail: sfidalgo@fd.uc.pt

V. Militello, A. Spena (eds.), *The Challenges of Illegal Trafficking in the Mediterranean Area*, Legal Studies in International, European and Comparative Criminal Law 9, https://doi.org/10.1007/978-3-031-45399-1_14

organ removal and, of course, it has also stimulated the trafficking in human organs itself.

In this scenario, transplants are often performed in clandestine, improvised clinics, without regard to standards of safety and hygiene. There are also cases, however, in which transplants are performed in clinics or hospital units that are already established and with a high degree of sophistication. In both situations, organs from donors that are not adequately screened from a clinical point of view are normally used. In some cases, the donors may have communicable diseases, which can jeopardize the health—and even the life—of the recipient. In addition to the freedom of the donors, their health is also often affected, as they often suffer serious complications due to the lack of medical follow-up in the postoperative period.[3]

Until September 2019, the Portuguese legal system did not provide for a crime of trafficking in human organs. Law no. 102/2019, of 6 September, adapted the Portuguese legal system to the provisions of the Council of Europe Convention against Trafficking in Human Organs, adopted in Santiago de Compostela, on 25th March 2015.[4] With this law, Article 144-B—Trafficking in human organs—was added to the Portuguese Criminal Code. The addition of this article to the Criminal Code has not yet given rise to a debate among legal scholars in Portugal.[5] In these few pages I will refer to the evolution of the legislation in Portugal on this matter and point out some interpretative doubts regarding the criminal offence under analysis.

2 International Legal Framework

The fight against the commercialization of the human body and its parts has been the focus of attention from numerous international organizations. The diplomas that refer to this issue are many and diverse, and come from the most varied sources: the United Nations, World Health Organization, Council of Europe and European Union.[6] Within the legal framework of the fight against trafficking in human organs and tissues and, more generally, against the commercialization of the human body and its parts, the Council of Europe Convention on Human Rights and Biomedicine

---

[3] See Regulation of the Portuguese Medical Association no. 498/2020, of 26 May 2020.

[4] Portugal signed the Convention on 25 March 2015, in Santiago de Compostela, and approved it by Resolution of the Assembly of the Republic no. 236/2018, of 7 August; ratified by Decree of the President of the Republic no. 48/2018, of 7 August. The Convention entered into force in Portugal on March 1, 2019.

[5] In Spain, for example, where the crime of trafficking in human organs was added to the Spanish Criminal Code in 2010 (LO 5/2010, of 22 June) and amended in 2019 (LO 1/2019, of 20 February), the debate on trafficking in human organs has been very intense. See, among others, Díaz-Maroto y Villarejo (2011), pp. 275 ff., González de Murillo (2012), pp. 87 ff., Gómez Rivero (2013), pp. 113 ff., and Pérez Ferrer (2020), pp. 91 ff. In Italy, see among others, Tigano (2015), pp. 1801 ff.

[6] In detail on the international normative framework, see Pérez Ferrer (2020), pp. 96 ff.

must be highlighted.[7] Article 21 of the Convention prohibits financial gain, by establishing that the human body and its parts shall not, as such, give rise to any financial gain.[8] These provisions of the Convention were further elaborated and complemented by the Additional Protocol concerning the Transplantation of Organs and Tissues of Human Origin.[9] Article 21 of this Additional Protocol also establishes the prohibition of financial gain, and Article 22 expressly establishes that organ and tissue trafficking shall be prohibited.

Both the Convention and the Additional Protocol establish that Parties shall provide appropriate judicial protection to prevent or to put a stop to any unlawful infringement of the rights and principles set forth in these legal instruments (Article 23 of the Convention and Article 24 of the Additional Protocol); and that Parties shall provide for appropriate sanctions to be applied in the event of infringement of the provisions contained in those legal instruments (Article 25 of the Convention and Article 26 of the Additional Protocol). Nevertheless, neither the Convention nor the Additional Protocol provide for the criminalisation of such acts.

The Council of Europe Convention against Trafficking in Human Organs, of 2015, constitutes, therefore, a new historic milestone in this legal framework. According to Article 1, the purposes of the convention are: (a) to prevent and combat the trafficking in human organs by providing for the criminalisation of certain acts; (b) to protect the rights of victims of the offences established in accordance with the Convention; (c) to facilitate co-operation at national and international levels on action against the trafficking in human organs.

Therefore, this Convention complements the provisions of other international legal instruments, such as the Convention on Human Rights and Biomedicine (referred to above), as well as the Council of Europe Convention on Action against Trafficking in Human Beings, of 16 May 2005.[10] It is true that this Convention already provided for the criminalisation of trafficking in human beings for the purpose of the removal of organs (Article 4 and Article 16). However, the problem of trafficking in organs goes beyond the problem of trafficking in people for the purpose of removal of organs. Trafficking in human organs is often an autonomous problem, so such conduct must be considered separately.

---

[7] The Convention for the Protection of Human Rights and Dignity of the Human Being with regard to the Application of Biology and Medicine—Convention on Human Rights and Biomedicine—was opened for signature on 4 April 1997 in Oviedo (Spain) and entered into force on 1 December 1999. Portugal signed the Convention on 4 April 1997 and approved it by the Resolution of the Assembly of the Republic no. 1/2001, of 3 January, ratified by the Decree of the President of the Republic no. 1/2001, of 3 January. The Convention entered into force in Portugal on December 1, 2001.

[8] See Marques (2021), pp. 473 ff.

[9] Portugal approved this Protocol by the Resolution of the Assembly of the Republic no. 24/2017, of 16 February, ratified by the Decree of the President of the Republic no. 14/2017, of 16 February. The Protocol entered into force in Portugal on September 1, 2017.

[10] Portugal signed this Convention on 16 May 2005, and approved it by the Resolution of the Assembly of the Republic no. 1/2008, of 14 January, ratified by Decree of the President of the Republic no. 9/2008, of 14 January. The Convention entered into force in Portugal on June 1, 2008.

Bearing in mind that Portugal ratified the convention without any reservations, the obligation was assumed to take the necessary legislative measures to establish the following acts, when committed intentionally, as criminal offences under domestic law: (1) the removal of human organs from living donors, where the removal is performed without free, informed and specific consent (Article 4 (1) (a) first part); (2) the removal of human organs from deceased donors, without the removal being authorised under domestic law (Article 4 (1)(a) second part); (3) the removal of human organs from living or deceased donors, where, in exchange for the removal of organs, the living donor, or a third party, has been offered or has received a financial incentive or comparable advantage (Article 4 (1)(b)(c)); (4) the use of illicitly removed organs for the purposes of implantation or purposes other than implantation (Article 5); (5) the illicit solicitation, recruitment, offering and requesting of undue advantages (Article 7); (6) the preparation, preservation, storage, transportation, transfer, receipt, import and export of illicitly removed human organs (Article 8).

The Convention leaves each Party the option of criminalising the removal/ implantation of human organs from living or deceased donors where this is performed outside of the framework of the domestic transplantation system, or where the removal / implantation is performed in breach of the basic principles of national transplantation laws or rules (Article 4 (4) and Article 6).

3 National Legal Framework Until 2019

In Portugal, the harvesting and transplantation of organs and tissues of human origin are regulated by Law no. 12/93, of 22 April.[11] This law expressly provides that such acts can only be carried out in hospital units, under direct medical supervision, in accordance with the respective leges artis (Article 3). The law also provides for the free donation of organs and expressly prohibits their commercialisation (Article 5).

This law provides for the possibility of organ harvesting either from living donors (Chap. II—Article 6 ff.), or from deceased donors (Chap. III—Article 10 ff.). Organ harvesting from a living person may only be carried out in cases where a deceased donor organ is not available and there is no alternative therapeutic method of comparable efficacy (Article 6). Harvesting from deceased donors is thus the rule. In Portugal, the so-called model of dissent is followed: all people who have not manifested their status as non-donors to the Ministry of Health are considered potential donors (Article 10).[12]

[11] Last amended by Law no. 75-B/2020, of 31 December.

[12] Decree-Law no. 244/94, of 26 September, regulates the organization and operation of the National Non-donor Registry. On this model of dissent, see Costa (1993), pp. 225 ff.

Concerning harvesting from a living donor, the consent of the donor and the recipient must be free, clarified, informed and unequivocal, provided before a doctor, with the donor's consent being given in writing and freely revocable (Article 8).

Article 16 of Law no. 12/93 states that violators of the provisions of this law shall incur civil, criminal and disciplinary liability, under the general rules of the law. This provision would have been unnecessary, if not for the fact that we must bear in mind that this law of 1993 does not provide for any type of crime. Moreover, this law expressly revoked Decree-Law no. 553/76, of 13 June—which regulated the harvesting of organs from deceased donors—and which established as criminal offences a series of actions related to organ harvesting and transplantation (Article 9 (a) (b) (c)).[13] Those acts, since 1993, have no longer belonged to the catalogue of criminal offences of the Portuguese legal-penal system. This means that from 1993 to 2019 no criminal offence specifically related to organ harvesting and transplantation was contained in the Portuguese legal system.

As a result, Portuguese legal scholars had been discussing the need to provide for the criminalisation of certain acts committed in the scope of organ transplantation, whether in the case of post-mortem or inter vivos donation.[14] I am referring, in particular, to the commercialization of organs. Although such commercialization is expressly prohibited by Article 5 (1) of Law no. 12/93, the commercial trade in human organs was not expressly criminalised in Portugal until 2019. The Portuguese legal system established (and still provides for) several administrative offences (contraordenações) and administrative sanctions (coimas) for the violation of the transplantation rules. These are, for instance, the administrative offences and sanctions set out in Articles 21 and 22 of Law no. 36/2013, of June 12, in case of violation of the rules established to ensure standards of quality and safety for human organs intended for transplantation into the human body.[15] Conduct that violates the principle of gratuitousness, as well as any conduct that violates the rules on consent (Article 21 (4)(a) and (j)), constitute administrative offences. But, until 2019, such conduct would not constitute any criminal offence specifically related to trafficking in human organs.

With the ratification of the Convention against Trafficking in Human Organs, new obligations arise for the Portuguese state regarding the criminalisation of some acts related to the trafficking in human organs.[16] It is true, however, that the majority of the acts referred to in the Convention had already found expression in Portuguese criminal law, whether through Law no. 20/2008, of 21 April, which establishes the system of criminal responsibility for crimes of corruption committed in international

[13] See Faria Costa (1993), p. 232.

[14] See Faria Costa, ibid.

[15] This Law no. 36/2013 (last amended by Law no. 2/2015, of 8 January) transposed into national law the Directive 2010/53/EU, of 7 July 2010, on standards of quality and safety of human organs intended for transplantation.

[16] See supra footnote 4 and point II.3.

trade and private activity,[17] or through some of the criminal offences provided for in the Criminal Code.

In fact, the removal of a human organ might constitute a criminal offence under the terms of the Portuguese Criminal Code, and have been so even before the 2019 revision.

It is worth mentioning that harvesting for transplantation does not come under Portuguese criminal law as it relates to medical-surgical procedures and treatments. The Portuguese Criminal Code treats medical activity in a differentiated and privileged manner, through the specific rules relating to medical-surgical procedures and treatments: Article 150 of the Criminal Code (Medical-surgical procedures and treatments), Article 156 of the Criminal Code (Arbitrary medical-surgical procedures and treatments) and Article 157 of the Criminal Code (Duty of explanation) embody this legal-criminal regime.[18] According to Portuguese legislation, the criminal law for medical-surgical procedures and treatments "is analysed in two fundamental statements: first, the proclamation of the atypical nature of medical-surgical procedures and treatments in the direction of the offences against physical integrity and homicide; second, the punishment of arbitrary medical-surgical procedures and treatments as a specific crime against freedom".[19]

[17] This Law no. 20/2008 (last amended by Law no. 58/2020, of 31 August) transposed into national law the Council Framework Decision 2003/568/JHA, of 22 July 2003, on combating corruption in the private sector.

[18] Article 150 (Medical-surgical procedures and treatments) establishes that: "(1) Any procedure or treatment, which, to the best of medical experience and knowledge, is considered advisable and is duly and correctly performed in accordance with leges artis by a doctor or other legally authorized person, with the intention of preventing, diagnosing, eliminating or alleviating illness, suffering, injury or bodily fatigue, or mental disorder, shall not be construed as an offence against the person; (2) Any person referred to in paragraph 1 who, for the purposes provided for therein, performs any procedure or treatment which violates the leges artis and thus creates a danger to life or a risk of serious bodily injury or to health, is subject to a term of imprisonment of up to 2 years or a fine of up to 240 days, save where the law provides elsewhere for a more severe sentence". Article 156 (Arbitrary medical-surgical procedures and treatments) establishes that: "(1) Any person referred to in article 150 who, for the purposes provided for therein, performs any procedure or treatment without the consent of the patient is subject to a term of imprisonment of up to 3 years or a fine; (2) Such conduct is not punishable when consent: (a) Can only be obtained when any delay would involve a danger to life or a serious risk of bodily injury or to health; or (b) Has been given for one procedure or treatment and another different one has been performed due to its becoming necessary, to the best of medical experience and knowledge, to avoid a danger to life or a risk of serious bodily injury or to health; and that under no circumstances could it be safely concluded that such consent would be refused; (3) An agent who, through gross negligence, falsely represents the prerequisites of consent is subject to a term of imprisonment of up to 6 months or a fine of up to 60 days; (4) Criminal proceedings shall not be commenced in the absence of complaint". Article 157 (Duty of explanation) establishes that: "For the purposes of article 156, consent is only effective when the patient has been duly informed of the diagnosis and the nature, range, scope and possible consequences of the procedure or treatment, save where such information would imply the communication of circumstances that, if divulged to the patient, would endanger life or be likely to cause grave damage to the patient's physical or mental health".

[19] Andrade (2012a), § 1.

According to Portuguese law as it stands, a medically advisable medical-surgical procedure or treatment, carried out by a doctor, for therapeutic purposes and according to the leges artis, does not constitute any type of offence against physical integrity. And such procedure / treatment will be atypical even in cases where it fails in its objectives, that is even if it aggravates the injury or disease (or causes the patient's death). The production of undesirable results (death, aggravation of the disease or injuries) will only be relevant as a typical corporal offence (or homicide) when it comes about as a consequence of the violation of leges artis.[20]

On the other hand, a medical-surgical procedure or treatment will be atypical from the point of view of the offence against physical integrity regardless of the patient's consent. The absence of the patient's consent is only relevant for the purposes of Article 156 of the Criminal Code—Arbitrary medical-surgical procedures and treatments—which is a crime against personal freedom (it is not a crime against physical integrity).[21] The legal interest protected by the incrimination of Article 156 is thus the "freedom to dispose of one's body and one's life".[22]

Organ transplants are authentic medical-surgical procedures, atypical from the perspective of Article 150 of the Criminal Code on the side of the recipient or beneficiary. On the donor's side, transplants constitute typical bodily harm, since, in relation to the donor, the intervention in question is not intended to be therapeutic.[23]

Therefore, according to Portuguese law, the non-consensual removal of a human organ from a living person constitutes an offence of bodily harm (Article 143 of the Criminal Code).[24] If it is a case of deprivation of an important organ, the offence will be that of serious bodily harm (Article 144 of the Criminal Code).[25]

Within certain limits, the non-consensual removal of a human organ from a deceased person is likely to constitute an offence of desecration of a corpse (Article 254 (1)(b) of the Criminal Code).[26]

There are still situations related to organ trafficking that could be offences related to the crime of trafficking in persons, which, since 2007,[27] expressly provides for punishment of the conduct of trafficking in persons for the purpose of the removal of organs (Article 160 of the Criminal Code).[28]

Considering that one of the ways of combating trafficking is to combat the demand for the services or organs of the trafficked person, Portuguese criminal

---

[20] See Costa Andrade (2004), p. 450, and, the same author (2012b), § 9.

[21] See Fidalgo (2008), p. 42, and, the same author (2019), p. 21.

[22] Figueiredo Dias (1973), p. 33.

[23] See Andrade (2012b), § 56; Brito (2007), p. 503. For further developments, see Faria (1995), pp. 52 ff.

[24] See Faria (2012a), § 8.

[25] See Faria (2012b), § 11.

[26] See Faria (1999), §§ 11 and 18.

[27] Law no. 59/2007, of 4 September.

[28] On the Portuguese crime of trafficking in human beings, see Carvalho (2012), §§ 11 ff.; Rodrigues (2017), p. 43 ff., and the same author (2018), pp. 27 ff.

law also provided for the punishment of the person who uses these services or organs (the recipient), in the knowledge that the other person was a victim of trafficking in human beings (Article 160 (6) of the Criminal Code).[29]

On the other hand, the values derived from the commission of the typical illegal acts of trafficking in human organs or tissues are considered benefits for the purposes of the crime of money laundering (Article 368-A (1) of the Criminal Code).[30]

However, from the comparison between the material content of the criminalisation obligations contained in the Convention and the Portuguese criminal law system, Portuguese lawmakers concluded that such content did not find full correspondence to the criminal offences that already existed. It was considered that the Portuguese criminal law system did not enshrine "trafficking in human organs, with the axiological density provided for in the Convention, as an autonomous incrimination".[31] Thus, a new criminal offence—trafficking in human organs—was added to the Criminal Code in 2019, to ensure conformity of the domestic legal system to the requirements of the Convention.

4 The Criminal Offence of Trafficking in Human Organs

Article 144-B—Trafficking in Human Organs—of the Criminal Code states the following:

"1. Whoever removes a human organ:

   (a) From a living donor, without his free, informed and specific consent, or from a deceased donor, where unavailability for donation has been validly expressed; or
   (b) When, in exchange for the removal, the living donor or a third party is promised or given a pecuniary or non-pecuniary advantage, or has received such an advantage,

   is subject to a term of imprisonment from 3 up to 10 years.

2. The same penalty shall apply to whomever, having knowledge of the conduct provided for in the preceding paragraph:

   (a) By any means, prepares, preserves, stores, transports, transfers, receives, imports or exports a human organ removed under the conditions provided for therein; or
   (b) Uses a human organ, or parts, tissue or cells thereof, for transplantation, scientific research or other non-therapeutic purposes.

[29] See Carvalho (2012), §§ 26 ff.

[30] On the Portuguese crime of money laundering see, among others, Anabela Miranda Rodrigues (2015), pp. 213 ff., and Caeiro (2017), pp. 267 ff.

[31] Explanatory memorandum of the Proposal of Law no. 182/XIII, of 31 January.

3. Whoever, with the intention of obtaining for himself or a third party a pecuniary or non-pecuniary advantage, solicits, entices or recruits a donor or recipient for the purpose of removal or transplantation of a human organ, is subject to a term of imprisonment from 3 up to 10 years.
4. Any persons listed in Article 150 (1) who remove, transplant or allocate a human organ to a recipient other than the one who is eligible, violating the leges artis or contrary to the general criteria for transplantation in relation to clinical urgency, immunogenic compatibility or preference and priority, are subject to a term of imprisonment from 1 up to 5 years, where a more severe punishment is not applicable under any other legal provision.
5. The penalties provided for in the preceding paragraphs shall be increased by one-third, in their minimum and maximum limits, if the act was committed in an organised manner or if the victim is especially vulnerable.
6. The penalty shall be subject to special mitigation whenever the perpetrator, up until the close of the trial at first instance, materially assists in the obtaining or production of conclusive evidence for the identification of other responsible parties."

The legal type of crime is extensive and very complex. This is not the appropriate place for a commentary on each of the paragraphs of Article 144-B. I will only make two kinds of consideration: one regarding the legal interest protected by criminalisation and another regarding the decision by the Portuguese legislature to criminalise the removal and implantation of human organs where this is performed outside of the framework of the domestic transplantation system, or is performed in breach of essential principles of transplantation rules.

The Portuguese legislature included this type of crime in the chapter of offences against physical integrity.[32] It is true that the removal of an organ without the consent of the donor violates the donor's physical integrity. But, in my opinion, it was not physical integrity—or rather it was not essentially physical integrity—that was the legal interest that the legislature wanted to protect with this new crime. In fact, as we have already seen, such conduct would already constitute (one of) the (traditional) criminal offences of physical harm.

In several aspects of Article 144-B, physical integrity does not appear to be the legal interest to be immediately protected. Moreover, physical integrity is definitely not the legal interest protected in Article 144-B (1)(a), in which the law punishes an agent who removes a human organ "from a deceased donor when the unwillingness to donate has been validly demonstrated".

The criminal offence of trafficking in human organs (Article 144-B (1)) is therefore a complex type of crime, which aims to protect various legal interests[33]:

---

[32] Chap. III (Crimes against physical integrity), of Title I (Crimes against persons), of Book II (Special Part), of the Criminal Code—Articles 143 ff.

[33] The consideration of the crime of organ trafficking as a complex crime may have important implications for the resolution of problems of concurrence of offences (see Dias (2019), pp. 363 ff., 1151 ff. and 1168 ff.).

certainly, physical integrity, but above all freedom, in its dimension of freedom to dispose of the body, including the freedom to dispose of the body after death, by prohibiting the removal of organs from it.

What is more, the idea of protecting confidence in the functioning of the national transplantation system itself is definitely also present in the cases set out in Article 144-B (4) of the Criminal Code, – which provides for the punishment of doctors or other legally authorised persons[34] "who remove, transplant or allocate a human organ to a recipient other than the one who is eligible (to receive it), violating the leges artis or contradicting the general criteria for transplantation in relation to clinical urgency, immunogenic compatibility or preference and priority"—although it cannot be excluded that the protected legal interest here is also physical integrity.

Article 144-B (4) is an expression of the decision of the Portuguese legislature to punish the removal and implantation of human organs where this is performed outside of the framework of the domestic transplantation system, or is performed in breach of essential principles of transplantation rules. As we have already seen, the law provides for the punishment of doctors or other legally authorised persons "who remove, transplant or attribute a human organ to a recipient other than the one who is eligible, violating the leges artis". It is not clear how to interpret this medical act in violation of leges artis. In my opinion, violations of the leges artis that are extrinsic or exogenous to the process desired and designed by the doctor (such as a careless movement during the handling of the scalpel that affects an organ outside the surgically intervened part of the body, or the leaving of foreign bodies in the area of the body operated on) will not be included here.[35] These will be normal negligent offences to be treated in general terms, of offences to physical integrity by negligence (Article 148 of the Criminal Code).

The violations of the leges artis that are typically relevant here take the form of recourse to transplantation procedures consciously undertaken by the doctor in violation of the rules established for this practice. Thus, such conduct will only be punishable under this rule when the agent acts with intention (dolo), and his intention has to include intervention in violation of the leges artis or the aforementioned contravention of the general criteria for transplantation.

5 Conclusion

Despite the doubts regarding the systematic insertion of the new law into the Criminal Code and the difficulties of compatibility—concurrence of offences—between the new criminal offence and the criminal offences already existing in the Portuguese legal system before the 2019 amendments, making for autonomous

[34] See supra, footnote 18, Article 150 (1).

[35] In the same sense, in relation to Article 150 (2) of the Criminal Code, see Costa Andrade (2012b), § 36.

provision for a criminal offence of trafficking in human organs was the right decision. The passage of time will allow Portuguese legal scholars to pronounce on the merits and weaknesses of its classification as a crime, and the courts will be able to clarify the difficulties of its being employed in the solutions of one of the problems of life.

References

Andrade MC (2004) Consentimento e Acordo em Direito Penal (Contributo para a Fundamentação de um Paradigma Dualista), reprint. Coimbra Editora

Andrade MC (2012a) Artigo 149° (Consentimento). In: Figueiredo Dias G (ed) Comentário Conimbricense do Código Penal. Parte Especial, t. I, 2nd edn. Coimbra Editora, p 420

Andrade MC (2012b) Artigo 150° (Intervenções e tratamentos médico-cirúrgicos). In: Figueiredo Dias G (ed) Comentário Conimbricense do Código Penal. Parte Especial, t. I, 2nd edn. Coimbra Editora, p 457

Brito TQ (2007) Os crimes contra a integridade física. In: Direito Penal – Parte Especial: lições, estudos e casos. Coimbra Editora, p 483

Caeiro P (2017) Contra uma política criminal 'à flor da pele': a autonomia do branqueamento punível em face do branqueamento proibido. In: Estudos em Homenagem ao Prof. Doutor Manuel da Costa Andrade, vol I. Instituto Jurídico da Universidade de Coimbra, p 267

Carvalho AT (2012) Artigo 160° (Tráfico de pessoas). In: Figueiredo Dias G (ed) Comentário Conimbricense do Código Penal, Parte Especial, t. I, 2nd edn. Coimbra Editora, p 676

Costa JF (1993) O valor do silêncio do legislador penal e o problema das transplantações. Boletim da Faculdade de Direito 69:225

Dias JF (1973) O problema da ortotanásia: introdução à sua consideração jurídica. In: As técnicas modernas de reanimação. Conceito de morte. Aspectos médicos, teológico-morais e jurídicos, Porto - Ordem dos Advogados, p 29

Dias JF (2019) Direito Penal Parte Geral. Questões Fundamentais. A Doutrina Geral do Crime, vol I, 3rd edn. Gestlegal

Díaz-Maroto y Villarejo J (2011) El delito de tráfico de órganos humanos. In: Díaz-Maroto y Villarejo J (ed) Estudios sobre las reformas del Código Penal (operadas por la LO 5/2010, de 22 de junio, y 3/2011, de 28 enero). Civitas, p 275

Faria PR (1995) Aspectos jurídico-penais dos transplantes. Universidade Católica Portuguesa – Editora

Faria PR (1999) Artigo 254° (Profanação de cadáver ou de lugar fúnebre). In: Figueiredo Dias G (ed) Comentário Conimbricense do Código Penal. Parte Especial, t. II. Coimbra Editora, p 653

Faria PR (2012a) Artigo 143° (Ofensa à integridade física simples). In: Figueiredo Dias G (ed) Comentário Conimbricense do Código Penal. Parte Especial, t. I, 2nd edn. Coimbra Editora, p 298

Faria PR (2012b) Artigo 144° (Ofensa à integridade física grave). In: Figueiredo Dias G (ed) Comentário Conimbricense do Código Penal. Parte Especial, t. I, 2nd edn. Coimbra Editora, p 338

Fidalgo S (2008) Responsabilidade penal por negligência no exercício da medicina em equipa. In: Publicações do Centro de Direito Biomédico 13. Coimbra Editora

Fidalgo S (2019) Responsabilidade penal médica por negligência. Revista Gestão Hospitalar – APAH 17:20

Gómez Rivero MC (2013) El delito de tráfico ilegal de órganos humanos. Revista Penal 31:113

González de Murillo S (2012) Tráfico de órganos humanos y lesiones. Cuadernos de Política Criminal 107:87

Kelly E (2013) International organ trafficking crisis: solutions addressing the heart of the matter. Boston Coll Law Rev 54:1317

Marques R (2021) Artigo 21° (Proibição de obtenção de lucros e utilização de partes do corpo humano). In: Convenção para a Proteção dos Direitos do Homem e da Dignidade do Ser Humano face às Aplicações da Biologia e da Medicina – 20 anos de vigência em Portugal. Instituto Jurídico da Faculdade de Direito da Universidade de Coimbra, p 473

Pérez Ferrer F (2020) Nuevos desafios del delito de tráfico de órganos en el ordenamiento jurídico-penal español tras la reforma de la LO 1/2019, de 20 de febrero. Cuadernos de Política Criminal 132:91

Rodrigues AM (2015) O sentido político-criminal da harmonização do crime de branqueamento no direito internacional penal e no direito penal da União Europeia. Alguns problemas de configuração típica. Os exemplos dos direitos português, da região administrativa especial de Macau e brasileiro. Revista Portuguesa de Ciência Criminal 25:213

Rodrigues AM (2017) Tráfico de seres humanos – uma questão de política criminal ou de segurança internacional? In: Estudos em Homenagem ao Prof. Doutor Manuel da Costa Andrade, vol II. Instituto Jurídico da Universidade de Coimbra, p 43

Rodrigues AM (2018) O crime de tráfico de seres humanos à luz do princípio da legalidade. In: Conferência Internacional – 18 de Outubro – Dia Europeu contra o tráfico de seres humanos. Instituto Jurídico da Faculdade de Direito da Universidade de Coimbra, p 27

Silva A (2019) Tráfico de órgãos humanos – benefícios e desafios da nova Convenção sobre o Tráfico de Órgãos Humanos e sua implementação no ordenamento jurídico português. Revista do CEJ 1:85

Tigano V (2015) La repressione del traffico di organi prelevati da vivente: verso il nuovo Art. 601 Bis C. P. Riv Ital Dirit Proced Penal 4:1801–1841

The manufacturer's authorised representative in the EU is Springer Nature Customer Service Centre GmbH, Europaplatz 3, 69115 Heidelberg, Germany. If you have any concerns regarding our products, please contact ProductSafety@springernature.com

Printed and bound by CPI Group (UK) Ltd, Croydon, CR0 4YY
01/10/2026
02225892-0005